# HEMISPHERIC IMAGINATIONS

## RE-MAPPING THE TRANSNATIONAL

A Dartmouth Series in American Studies

---

SERIES EDITOR
Donald E. Pease
Avalon Foundation Chair of Humanities
Founding Director of the Futures of American Studies Institute
Dartmouth College

The emergence of Transnational American Studies in the wake of the Cold War marks the most significant reconfiguration of American Studies since its inception. The shock waves generated by a newly globalized world order demanded an understanding of America's embeddedness within global and local processes rather than scholarly reaffirmations of its splendid isolation. The series Re-Mapping the Transnational seeks to foster the cross-national dialogues needed to sustain the vitality of this emergent field. To advance a truly comparativist understanding of this scholarly endeavor, Dartmouth College Press welcomes monographs from scholars both inside and outside the United States.

For a complete list of books available in this series, see www.upne.com.

Helmbrecht Breinig, *Hemispheric Imaginations: North American Fictions of Latin America*
Jimmy Fazzino, *World Beats: Beat Generation Writing and the Worlding of U.S. Literature*
Zachary McCleod Hutchins, editor, *Community without Consent: New Perspectives on the Stamp Act*
Kate A. Baldwin, *The Racial Imaginary of the Cold War Kitchen: From Sokol'niki Park to Chicago's South Side*
Yuan Shu and Donald E. Pease, *American Studies as Transnational Practice: Turning toward the Transpacific*
Melissa M. Adams-Campbell, *New World Courtships: Transatlantic Alternatives to Companionate Marriage*
David LaRocca and Ricardo Miguel-Alfonso, editors, *A Power to Translate the World: New Essays on Emerson and International Culture*
Elèna Mortara, *Writing for Justice: Victor Séjour, the Mortara Case, and the Age of Transatlantic Emancipations*
Rob Kroes, *Prison Area, Independence Valley: American Paradoxes in Political Life and Popular Culture*
Etsuko Taketani, *The Black Pacific Narrative: Geographic Imaginings of Race and Empire between the World Wars*
William V. Spanos, *Shock and Awe: American Exceptionalism and the Imperatives of the Spectacle in Mark Twain's* A Connecticut Yankee in King Arthur's Court

HELMBRECHT BREINIG

# HEMISPHERIC IMAGINATIONS

## North American Fictions of Latin America

DARTMOUTH COLLEGE PRESS
HANOVER, NEW HAMPSHIRE

Dartmouth College Press
An imprint of University Press of New England
www.upne.com

Manufactured in the United States of America
Typeset in Sabon and Scala Sans by Integrated Publishing Solutions



Library of Congress Cataloging-in-Publication Data
Names: Breinig, Helmbrecht, author.
Title: Hemispheric imaginations : North American fictions of Latin America / Helmbrecht Breinig.
Description: Hanover, New Hampshire : Dartmouth College Press, [2016] | Series: Re-mapping the transnational: a Dartmouth series in American studies | Includes bibliographical references and index.
Identifiers: LCCN 2016027168 (print) | LCCN 2016056397 (ebook) | ISBN 9781611689723 (cloth : alk. paper) | ISBN 9781611689907 (pbk. : alk. paper) | ISBN 9781611689914 (epub, mobi & pdf)
Subjects: LCSH: Latin America—In literature. | American fiction—History and criticism. | Canadian fiction—History and criticism. | Latin America—Relations—America. | America—Relations—Latin America.
Classification: LCC PS374.L33 B74 2016 (print) | LCC PS374.L33 (ebook) | DDC 810.9/3588—dc23
LC record available at https://lccn.loc.gov/2016027168

*For those who*
*first introduced me*
*to Latin America:*
Marta Salomé Cosenza
Helga Breinig de Müller
Horst Müller

# CONTENTS

# PREFACE

WHEN I VISITED MACHU PICCHU in the 1980s, I encountered a scene that thousands of tourists in Peru must also have witnessed. While the bus slowly labored down the serpentine road from the ruins to the valley of the Río Urubamba, a small group of barefoot Indio boys raced downhill on the most direct route, through shrubbery and scree. Whenever they met those on the bus, they gleefully, perhaps insultingly, shouted "¡gringo!" or else "¡gringa!" according to whoever the primary butt of their taunts might be. The same thing happened when we walked down on foot, which we preferred to do, because we could experience the stunning landscape more directly, including the torrential downpours. The boys' race with the strangers, the grown-ups, and technology, underlined as it was by shouts, a race they always won, can easily be interpreted as a demonstration of their own strength, their own competences, and a ridiculing of those of the foreigners. And yet the young mockers, when they had reached the bottom, demanded money from those they had mocked, as a reward for their physical prowess. A contradictory behavior, I felt, illogical and decidedly strange. Did it reflect the conflicting attitude many Latin Americans had and have vis-à-vis the visitors, particularly if they come from the United States, a mixture of admiration, envy, contempt, and hatred that is easily understandable from the history of inter-American relations?

However, their shouts might also have reflected something else, something of the—presumably—universal uncertainty we experience when we encounter the alien, the Other. I felt such uncertainty myself during my travels through numerous Latin American countries, as a tourist or a visitor of family or close friends, and always as an ignoramus. I also felt such uncertainty, although to a lesser, and lessening, degree, during my long sojourns in the United States and Canada. All this, while I was fully aware of the enormous differences between the countries, regions, and populations of both South and North. The whole Western Hemisphere was and is part of "the West" and thereby shares not only major developments of its modern history but many attitudes, institutions, and, depending on the social class and the ethnicity you are in contact with, many so-called civilizational advantages. I got more and more interested in this interplay of familiarities and strangenesses that characterized not only my own experiences but the relations between those peoples, cultures, and socioeconomic systems. As a European Americanist, I was particularly interested in the traces the complicated hemispheric history had left in the minds of people I met, both south and north of the Rio Grande/Río Bravo del Norte. In particular, I was interested in the literary constructions of self and Other on either side, the northern side of which was to turn into a major research project—to include the southern one would have overextended my competency, although I love to look at critical studies on such issues from the pen, nay, PC of Latin American colleagues.

I team-taught several classes on the literatures of North and South together with colleagues from the romance departments of the universities I happened to be affiliated with, the first in 1984 with Walter Bruno Berg. Walter and I tried to make the students comprehend some basic structural elements of the literary history of the countries that formed our respective fields of scholarship, Peru in his case, the United States in mine, and the first thing we learned was how little we knew of each other's textual and cultural worlds. I am grateful for the things I learned then, as I am grateful to my colleagues of later seminars, Wolfgang Matzat and the late Titus Heydenreich, with whom I shared insights at a much later stage of what was to become a central area of research for me: what is now called hemispheric studies. The interdisciplinary research project on inter-American studies that I initiated at Erlangen University, involving Wolfgang Binder, Ute Guthunz, Friedrich W. Horlacher, Titus Heydenreich, Hans-Joachim König, Friedrich von Krosigk, Wolfgang Matzat, Dieter Meindl, Anton P. Müller, Michael Richter, Roland Spiller, Rolf Walter, and Rüdiger Zoller, scholars from the fields of Latin American, US American and Canadian literature, history, political science, geography, economics, and linguistics, bore testimony to the fact that hemispheric studies requires more than the data from just two fields.

I owe much of my knowledge to our discussions then; with the political scientist Friedrich von Krosigk, I team-taught a seminar that combined literary with empire studies, a conjunction that made our students aware of the widely differing approaches of scholars focusing on social and political "facts" and others like myself, who tend to see reality more as a discursive construction and to direct our attention to the symbolic levels of texts. I should also mention that the interdisciplinary discussion groups at Erlangen under the mentorship of a much-esteemed social scientist, the late Joachim Matthes, and particularly the advanced doctoral and research program "Cultural Hermeneutics: Perspectives on Difference and Transdifference" provided me with a wide range of theoretical models transcending those I had started out with. I am immensely grateful to my colleagues and my doctoral students in this program but also to the students in the classes mentioned earlier and in those I taught alone for their readiness to confront theoretical problems and literary texts not to be found in our ordinary reading lists.

The Deutsche Forschungsgemeinschaft/German Research Foundation generously supported my work and that of others in our study group. It financed a sabbatical year I used for extended research in the United States and a number of shorter research stays. A Canadian government grant made my first extended stay at the University of British Columbia–Vancouver possible. I am thankful for such financial support, as I am for the help provided to me at the Library of Congress, where two of my research assistants and I stayed for several months; at Harvard's Widener Library and, by the generous intercession of Werner Sollors, the Charles Warren Center there, whose hospitality included office space; and finally, at the Library of the University of California–Berkeley.

What I encountered during the first research stays at these university libraries were awe-inspiring, long, and sometimes dark and dusty aisles of books, most of which were not used very often. Hemispheric studies was alive in the fields of history, political science, economics, and anthropology. It was only at its beginning in the fields of American literature, Hispanic literature, and cultural studies in general. When I first tried to find North American literary works dealing with Latin America, thumbing my way through the old card catalog of the Library of Congress, I found very little, for an excruciatingly long period of time. Stanley T. Williams's *The Spanish Background of American Literature* was helpful as a start, and then Drewey Wayne Gunn's *Mexico in American and British Letters*, Cony Sturgis's *The Spanish World in English Fiction*, and A. Curtis Wilgus's *Latin America in Fiction* and his other bibliographies provided a great number of titles. My first impression that there existed hardly any literary material vanished, and over time I had to realize that there were not just a few dozen or even a few hundred, but thousands upon thousands of books.

This insight influenced my decision of what to study for the fairly long series of articles and lectures I was to publish or present during the years to follow, and it does so for this book. To include drama and poetry proved to be unfeasible, and thus Tennessee Williams's *The Night of the Iguana* was left out, as was practically all of Elizabeth Bishop's Brazilian poetry; only some early American Columbus poems are included, a poem by Jeannette Armstrong, and one by William H. New, which concludes the book. Needless to say, matters of scope also forbade the inclusion of nonliterary production such as film or painting that reflect discursive approaches to the Other just as well as novels or short stories. As far as fiction was concerned, I excluded juvenile texts and spy and mystery novels as well as most, but not all, of the myriad novels of adventure dealing with, preferentially, Mexico or the Caribbean. True, such texts reveal stereotypical notions more clearly than more complex works do, and this is why they sometimes furnish me with examples for typical features of the discourse. Yet most texts I deal with are more ambitious—it is especially rewarding to see dominant discourses both presented and deconstructed in works that have at least a modicum of literary complexity. Thus, the degree of sophistication varies enormously among the texts I have selected, between, say, Richard Harding Davis's popular *Soldiers of Fortune* and Malcolm Lowry's *Under the Volcano*, one of the chef-d'oeuvres of literary modernism. As will be seen, and as was unavoidable in a book dealing with texts that thematize power relations, among other things, aesthetic and ethical aspects intertwine. My preferences for certain literary techniques often converge with those concerning ways of behavior on the individual and on the national or cultural level. However, in modern literature the coming together of ethics and aesthetics does not lead to trivial didacticism but to openness and complexity.

Because my object was to study literary symbolizations of attitudes, discourses, and the cultural imaginary, the decision what to exclude was more difficult with respect to travel literature, of which there exists an at least equally large body as that of fiction. However, as my study—due to the bulk of available material—had to remain selective rather than comprehensive, I decided to analyze only few examples from this corpus of texts. The same applies to historiographic representations, of which there remain only Washington Irving's biography of Columbus and a few glances at William H. Prescott. Although their discursive construction of the Latin American Other is often quite similar to that in US or Canadian texts, I also excluded European works, with two exceptions that were highly influential in North America: Alexander von Humboldt and D. H. Lawrence. With very few exceptions, I resisted the temptation to present Latin American versions of a reciprocal discursive representation of the United States because such a comparative approach would have threatened the format of my book and would often have been beyond my competency. This exclusion should therefore not be regarded as further evidence of hegemonic thinking. Finally, I have to say that my focus is on twentieth-century literature and that, therefore, the number of nineteenth- or even eighteenth-century texts is rather limited. The reason is simply that I was fascinated by the way century-old approaches have survived into my own lifetime.[1] Initially I wanted to use the end of the Cold War as a *terminus ad quem* but finally felt that a few more recent novels might shed light on the discursive world of our present time. Except for Daniel Curley's *Mummy*, though, none of the texts I have selected focuses on the drug war as an essential facet of contemporary inter-American relations.

One decision I made early in my work was to see the whole hemisphere as my object of study rather than to restrict myself to the United States on the northern and, as is often done, Mexico on the southern side (because of the dominance of that country as the theme of inter-American fiction). Using the whole of Latin America (including the Caribbean) can help to indicate the way US or Canadian texts homogenize (or do not homogenize) the fantastic variety of the world south of the US-Mexican border. Nonetheless, this study bears witness to the overpowering number of books published on Mexico. To include Canadian literature followed from my impression that this huge country was often neglected in hemispheric studies, although some Canadian texts belong among the best works dealing with Latin America. I was also interested in the question to what extent these texts followed the same discursive patterns as "American" fiction did. Nonetheless, my topic is literature about Latin America, and thus Canadian fiction about the United States or US texts on Canada are excluded even though they belong to the totality of inter-American literature.

Finally, I have to admit that, all these decisions notwithstanding, this study cannot claim to be truly representative. There is an element of haphazardness in my selection of texts, often resulting from the chances of thorough firsthand knowledge but also from those of sheer availability. I had Erlangen University Library acquire a large number of primary and secondary texts as well as background material, which must have made its collection of inter-Americana one of the best in Europe. However, when we set out on this journey, there was no Google and no Amazon to find out-of-print books, and our search through the catalogs of secondhand booksellers often ended in frustration. The major reason for my selectiveness, though, is that the size of my study had to remain manageable. Thus, for instance, Ernest Hemingway's *Islands in the Stream* and the relevant works of both Jane and Paul Bowles are absent, just like those of Peter Matthiessen and Cormac McCarthy, although they provide excellent examples.

I mention background material—histories, political analyses, geographic descriptions—very sparingly in order not to clutter this study with innumerable notes. I give (and refer to) background information where I find it particularly pertinent. On the whole, however, I rely on the readers' capacity and willingness to check the readily available and electronically traceable sources of information if they are so minded.

Beyond the persons and institutions already mentioned, over the years this book has profited from the help of numerous people. Ralph Bauer and David F. Krell read the entire manuscript and made numerous cogent suggestions, the former from the point of view of the hemispheric studies specialist, the latter from that of the philosopher and cultural critic. Pertinent and very helpful comments on the entire book came from the readers of University Press of New England. Susanne Opfermann loyally tolerated my long absorption by this project; she read major portions of the book and made valuable contributions. Klaus Lösch saved the chapter on theory from a number of problems that my eclectic approach had produced. Hans-Herbert Räkel graciously used the library facilities in Montréal to ferret out obscure and, for me, inaccessible texts concerning Lowry, Atwood, and Gibson. Christina Strobel, Klaus Lösch, Hanne Breinig, and Susanne Opfermann helped me find relevant titles at the Library of Congress and at Harvard's Widener Library, the former two at that time in their capacity as research assistants. They and their colleagues at the University of Erlangen-Nürnberg, Tomás Christ, Karin Höpker, Susanne Mayer, Christian Schmidt, and Silvia Weinrich greatly contributed to the influx of relevant primary and secondary material, its bibliographic organization and classification for the large bibliography that turned out to be a side product of my project and is waiting for separate publication. Hannelore Horlacher tirelessly took care of the acquisition and handling for Erlangen University Library of those titles we thought important enough to have in our local holdings. All of them are entitled to my profound gratitude.

I wish to thank Jeannette Armstrong for permission to use her poem "History Lesson" in Chapter 10 and William H. New for permitting a portion of his book-length poem *Touching Ecuador* to be used as the conclusion of Chapter 12.

My thanks to Richard Pult, Sara Evangelos, Mary Garrett, and the entire staff of University Press of New England for help at every stage.

Earlier versions of parts of this book were published in the following publications:

A passage on Asturias's "¡Americanos Todos!" (Chapter 1) in Gerald Vizenor, ed., *Survivance: Narratives of Native Presence*, University of Nebraska Press, 2008.

A German version of parts of Chapter 3 in Titus Heydenreich, ed., *Columbus zwischen zwei Welten: Historische und literarische Wertungen aus fünf Jahrhunderten*, Vervuert Verlag, 1992.

A shorter version of Chapter 4 in *Americastudien/American Studies* 53.1 (2008).

An early version of Chapter 5 in *ZAA: Zeitschrift für Anglistik und Amerikanistik* 40.4 (1992).

A shorter German version of Chapter 6 in Konrad Groß et al., eds., *Das*

*Natur/Kultur-Paradigma in der englischsprachigen Erzählliteratur des 19. und 20. Jahrhunderts*, Gunter Narr Verlag, 1994.

Portions of Chapter 7 in Josef Raab and Martin Butler, eds., *Hybrid Americas: Contacts, Contrasts, and Confluences in New World Literatures and Cultures*, LIT Verlag, 2008.

Parts of Chapter 9 in Roland Hagenbüchle and Josef Raab, eds., *Negotiations of America's National Identity*, Stauffenburg Verlag, 2000; and in Armin Paul Frank and Helga Eßmann, eds., *The Internationality of National Literatures in Either America: Transfer and Transformation*, Wallstein Verlag, 1999.

Parts of Chapter 10 in Bernd Engler and Kurt Müller, eds., *Historiographic Metafiction in Modern American and Canadian Literature*, Schöningh Verlag, 1994; and in Simone Pellerin, ed., *Gerald Vizenor*, Presses Universitaires de la Méditerranée, 2007.

I thank editors and publishers for their permission to use this material.

# PART ONE

# [1]

## INTRODUCTION

Is it lack of imagination that makes us come
to imagined places, not just stay at home?
—Elizabeth Bishop, "Questions of Travel" (*The Complete Poems*, 94)

THE CONCLUDING STANZAS of the title poem of Bishop's volume *Questions of Travel* (1965), quoting a "traveller['s] notebook," indicate the uncertainty of perception, the imaginary nature of both home and the away from home. *Questions of Travel*, her book about her impressions during her long stay in Brazil, one of the most impressive collections of poetry on a Latin American country by a US author,[1] holds a central position in Bishop's work and in the development of her thought about intercultural awareness and communication. And yet her most frequently anthologized poems deal with North American or universal topics, as if the Brazilian themes were less interesting or less accessible for the average US reader. One of the poet's major achievements, the questioning of the traveler's point of view,[2] appears to present uncomfortable reading material.

The vast body of North American fiction on Latin America, which is the subject of this book, bespeaks such feelings of discomfort but also of fascination in view of the exotic Other.[3] A complicating factor, also noted by Bishop, is the discursive nature of both self and Other. The "*Continent, city, country, society*" mentioned in her poem are not only objects of her personal imagination but "*imagined places*" in the public discourse; "*the choice is never wide and never free*" (94) because it is pre-shaped by those anonymous societal structures organizing speech and thought that we have come to call (in a vaguely Foucauldian sense of the term) discourses.[4] It is also shaped by what has been called the cultural imaginary: the range of feelings and imaginings concerning a given subject that is available to a sociocultural group of people. And of course such discursive and imaginary construction of the Other occurs in either direction. Sometimes, as in Ariel Dorfman's memoir *Heading South, Looking North*, a single person is capable of representing both major perspectives. Whether articulated, felt, or thought, such constructions are efforts to make sense of the world, that is to reduce its complexity, as the early Niklas Luhmann has put it. They simplify whatever may be considered as reality, and they tend to structure the world by binary approaches: self and Other, south and north, new and old, and so forth. But cultural constructions, be they literary, filmic, graphic, or belonging to other symbolic subsystems, have a double tendency. Man's "[b]lessed rage for order," as Wallace Stevens put it, "[t]he maker's rage to order words of the sea," finds its creative complement in "man's rage for chaos," the role of the arts to prepare humans for the contingency of the world.[5] Hence, the imaginative constructions of the Western Hemisphere are caught between order and chaos.[6]

Let me insert here a few remarks about the nomenclature used in this book, which has to be taken with a good degree of leniency. I speak of "North America" as excluding both Mexico and all of the Caribbean—a term that is therefore obviously inadequate but common practice. "North American" is the direct translation of the Spanish *norteamericano* that is used throughout Latin America, including Mexico.[7] Occasionally, reluctantly, and mostly for stylistic reasons, I speak of "America" where I refer specifically to the United States; mostly I use "US American" rather than "American." I speak of "Latin America" as including the Anglophone nations of the Caribbean and formerly British Guyana, formerly Dutch Suriname, and French Guiana, as well as the other French *départements d'outre mer*, but excluding the United States in spite of its growing Latino population and Canada in spite of Québec. All this is on the basis of today's boundaries, but we have to bear in mind that these have proved to be highly flexible. One has only to look at Wikipedia's map video of the "History of Central America from 1700 to the Present" to experience the shifting colonial and postcolonial affiliations within a few seconds and to thus realize the instability of order over time.

We ought to remember, too, that until the Mexican-American War (1846–48) and Mexico's loss of half of its territory to the United States in 1848, the longest border separating what was claimed to belong to Latin America (*avant la lettre*) and the United States was the latter's *western* frontier. And we should finally remember that the very terminological construct *Latin America* was first used (by Francisco Bilbao, in 1856) in the context of French plans to establish a special sphere of influence in the Americas as a counterweight to (British and US American) Anglo-America, although it was later used to invoke a coherence and uniformity that did and does not exist (cf. Mignolo, *Idea*).[8] I use the terms *Old World* and *New World* in a metaphorical, common-language sense, Edmundo O'Gorman's impressive refutation of the acceptability of such usage notwithstanding. It should be remembered, though, that this terminology also has its history: "From the Old World came a conception of the New, from the New a conception of the Old by means of which Americans could announce what they were not and thereby proclaim their superiority" (Martin 18). The same procedure informed the mutual conceptions of Anglo-America and Latin America.

MANY NORTH AMERICAN WORKS of fiction on Latin America follow rather simple discursive patterns in making sense of the Other. In Michael Rumaker's short story "Gringos" (1966), a young American man crosses the bridge into a Mexican border town. What he experiences there is heat, dirt, poverty, inefficiency, primitiveness, brown-skinned people with "flat black eyes" (*Gringos*, 57). He drives off a small boy who tries to sell him chewing gum, but relents when the boy's little sister joins them because, to all appearances, she has a crippled leg. After the American has given her some pesos, she runs off—her lameness was just a trick. The boy runs after her and forces her to give up the money. Things get worse after that. Virtually all adult women the American sees are prostitutes. Older women attending church service and piously kneeling on the paving stones seem to be the only exception. The young *gringo* is befriended by an American sailor with whom he has some drinks, and tours the town. Finally the two Americans have sex with a prostitute in one of the cabins on the outskirts of the town. When they walk back through the night, they are attacked from behind by three Mexican men armed with knives, who try to rob them, but the Americans easily win the fight and return to their hotel.

On the surface, what we have here is one of the most stereotypically clear specimens of a discourse-governed perception of the Latin American Other based on examples from the sphere of gender relations. Mexican society is presented as consisting of pimps, prostitutes, and desexualized older people. From childhood on, there is an asymmetrical power relation between exploitative, primitive machos who are sexually aggressive, brutal, and treacherous on the one hand, and, on the other, exploited but equally treacherous women, whose sole power lies in their physical properties. Both are victimized by the Catholic church; the golden cupola of the church building symbolizes a pseudo-maternal bosom whose true function is not nourishment but self-enrichment at the expense of a poor but brainwashed population. Between this society and that of the United States, there is no Anzaldúan "borderland," no zone of transitions and hybrid fluctuations, of psychological, spiritual, and sexual third spaces, but only the border, period.[9]

While this perception of Mexico epitomizes crucial, but also superficial, cliché aspects of the US American discourse on Mexico and on Latin America in general, it also reveals more fundamental discursive structures. For the basic pattern alluded to in this story is the dominant one of an invasion, an intrusion, a taking possession. That it is Latin America's manifest destiny to be controlled and exploited by US power is supported by specifically racist assumptions: Mexicans, Guatemalans, and so forth are collectively regarded as brown-skinned people, as racially inferior, as "Indians." In Rumaker's story, brown skin is one of the leitmotif observations made by the American protagonist. As we shall see later in this book, the story has complexities concerning the interaction of the discourses of ethnicity and gender that deserve closer scrutiny.[10] In any case, it is a good example of the discursive complex of cognition and power I shall call *Latinamericanism* and which forms a central topic of this book. The term was first used by Enrico M. Santí in "Latinamericanism and Restitution." I employed it the same year and independently in its German version, *Lateinamerikanismus*, in "Alteritätsdiskurs und Literatur." Alberto Moreiras uses the term more strictly as denoting a scholarly or intellectual approach, "the sum total of engaged representations providing a viable knowledge of the Latin American object of enunciation," and makes an argument for a new, subversive Latinamericanism that will counteract the homogenization of the traditional discourse in the process of globalization that entails the tendency toward "some totality of allegedly neutral, universal knowledge of the world in all its differences and identities" ("Global Fragments," 86).[11] For my present purpose, I shall use Latinamericanism in its initial sense as demarcating the construction of Latin American otherness and its circulation in the public mind. The term and its theoretical and practical implications will be defined in detail in Chapter 2.

When we look at the other side, that of the invaded, the pattern can be equally simple. Take a text by Nobel prize winner Miguel Ángel Asturias, a Guatemalan with, possibly, some Maya ancestors. In his story "¡Americanos Todos!" ("We Are All Americans!"), the Guatemalan tourist guide Emilio Croner Jaramillo, called Milocho, is immensely popular among American tourists. He has acquired US citizenship, and after a stormy affair with the blonde Californian beauty Alarica Powell, he is dreaming of a future life with her in the United States, when the CIA-sponsored invasion of Guatemala by foreign mercenaries in the 1954 coup that was to topple the democratically elected Arbenz government prevents his return from the coast to Guatemala City.[12] He witnesses the bombing of the *indio* and *mestizo* villages near the coast by American airplanes whose national identification symbols had been removed, and the massacre of the Indian population of whole villages suspected of sympathizing with "the Communists." Although no Maya himself but a light-skinned *mestizo*, he identifies with the poor population of his native country and particularly the *indios*, who are once again being robbed of life or property and cultural identity. Sometime later, Milocho is again guiding American tourists through the Guatemalan highland. Alarica has joined him, and their plans for a touring business connecting the American East and West Coasts have matured. But when she teases him about the passivity of his country, of even the majestic volcanoes, which, in the colonial past, destroyed the cities of the conquistadors, his memories of the massacred Indians and his guilt feelings for having done nothing to defend his country, nay, for being "an American" himself, rise up again, and he drives the bus full of *gringos* into a deep gorge, killing all aboard. In his death plunge, he shouts the ironic leitmotif phrase of the story, "We are all Americans!" a slogan that before had been uttered even by the Guatemalan military officers, who, in the service of the United Fruit Company and the CIA, had led the coup against their own government.[13]

Again, at first glance, the discursive construction of the North American invaders looks simple enough. Yet Milocho is more than an anti-American suicide killer. His increasing awareness of the ironies of his own situation, his growing engagement with the political and social conditions of his country, past and present, make him part of a resistance that is not limited to acts of physical revenge but entails a mental and emotional identification with those who have been victimized for centuries and, what is more, an imaginary transcending of the state of helplessness. He turns into a representative of what Gerald Vizenor has called *survivance*.[14] The series of surreal images rushing through Milocho's mind reveals him as capable of transforming reality in line with traditional Maya beliefs concerning the creative power of the word without literally following Maya symbology. He thus becomes a representative of the author who, in his rage and frustration, fictionalized the events of the coup in his collection of eight stories, *Week-end en Guatemala* (1956), a series containing "¡Americanos Todos!" and culminating in an imaginary overthrow of the new rulers by the masked masses during the native feast of Torotumbo. That this event was never to take place in reality, that, indeed, it took decades of guerilla resistance against a brutal military dictatorship until some kind of political compromise could be reached, a first level of national reconciliation including elements of a recognition of indigenous rights, does not diminish the function of these texts to demonstrate how the imagination can overcome victimization. At the same time, the story questions the discourse on nationality and national culture, the very nature of the term *American*.[15]

Because the topic of this study is North American fiction dealing with Latin America, there will not be space for a discussion of Latin American counter-discursive approaches to the United States or, sometimes, Canada. I want to point out, however, that the relevant texts are highly diverse.[16] One of the dominant themes is the idea of "America" as a point of desire, a refuge from political oppression or economic misery, a theme also touched upon in "¡Americanos Todos!" This idealization of the United States is nicely presented, for instance, in Peruvian-born Daniel Alarcón's *New Yorker* story "Second Lives."[17] The narrator tells of the vain hope of his parents, who live in a poor South American country (modeled after Peru), that their eldest son could be used as a forerunner to establish himself in the States and to enable the rest of the family to follow him. Another central topic of Latin American fictions dealing with the North is the question of national or cultural identity, which is often discussed in the context of the contrasting and influential North American or, for that matter, European self-definitions. One such text is the novel *Ciudades Desiertas* (1982) by the Mexican author José Agustín, which takes its Mexican protagonists on an extended visit to the United States and ironically plays with the identity and alterity discourses of both sides (Matzat 185–99). It might be read as counter-narrative to the postmodern novels discussed here in Chapter 9.

The stereotypical reduction of complexity that occurs on the surface level of both Rumaker's and Asturias's stories is an essential feature of literary texts dealing with the Other in terms of foreign countries, societies, cultures; that is, a binary approach to social reality, no matter how much such binarism will be undermined in the course of the text. That is, we have to come to terms with the fact that not only popular literature—for instance, the thousands of North American crime and spy mysteries dealing with Latin America or the numerous works of juvenile fiction with a setting south of the border—use such patterns (often together with a hierarchization of customs and value systems), but also narratives by landmark authors. The epistemological power of binary, comparative perspectives is considerable. However, the age of globalization has pointed our gaze also in the direction of what humans around the globe have in common or may soon have in common.[18]

LITERARY IMAGININGS ARE ALWAYS linked to extratextual "reality," to space and time, albeit always in the shape of mental constructions. A holistic view of texts and contexts, an approach often called Humboldtian, is beyond the needs and the scope of this study. Moreover, if taken seriously, it is a utopian goal, and often the accumulation of so-called facts would result in positivism. However, space and time remain essential factors. I have therefore included a chapter on perceptions of nature, that is, space as natural landscape, because these perceptions form an inevitable element of Latinamericanism. Much more often I refer to historical events and developments that resulted from then current views or in turn had an impact on them. This is necessary because discourse and power are inseparable. The mutual discursive construction of the Latin American or else the North American Other has been part and parcel of the hemispheric power games having taken place for 200 years.

One historical factor that has left its traces in all inter-American contacts is the dominance the United States developed over all other countries of the Western Hemisphere. Whether this unique asymmetry of power may be challenged in the future by the rise of Brazil to the status of global player is of no concern in the context of this study. However, even before the Monroe Doctrine, US politicians had claimed a privileged role for their country, not only as a protector of the hemisphere against European aggression but also as an arbiter of affairs elsewhere in the Americas in order to further the Unites States' own economic or political interests, if needs be by military intervention, a fact that has resulted in a deep-seated distrust of the "Giant of the North" (or South, for that matter). The US American conquests and other acquisitions of territories beyond its initial boundaries, and Washington's imperial ambitions of the late nineteenth and early twentieth centuries have left their traces in the public attitude throughout the Americas. None of the many wars between Latin American countries, traumatic and map-changing though they may have been, has had such hemispheric effects as did the series of US invasions and interventions. US American patronizing attitudes concerning Latin America, even with regard to social institutions and cultural production, have evoked envy, feelings of inferiority, but also a counter-discourse of cultural and moral separateness and superiority that have created feelings of a pan–Latin American identity and coherence hardly warranted by sociopolitical, economic, or even cultural facts. Whether in the shape of José Martí's ethnically hybrid "nuestra América" in contrast to the more purely white, European United States, of José Enrique Rodó's notion of an idealized Ariel-like cultural tradition in contrast to US utilitarianism, or of Roberto Fernández Retamar's placing of a Latin American "Calibán" against the US American domineering Prospero, to name only the most prominent spokespersons, there exists a Latin American tradition of cultural and intellectual resistance that until recently has found remarkably little echo in US American perceptions of the neighbors to the south. This is not the place to discuss the many changes of US policy toward Latin America, including its role in the Pan-American movement, the Good Neighbor Policy under Franklin Delano Roosevelt, or the current efforts of President Obama to introduce a new era in American relations with Mexico. Nor can I deal with the changing political situation in Latin American countries that directly influenced their policy vis-à-vis the United States, for instance the recent changes in (post-)Castro Cuba. Such aspects will be addressed only when my analysis of a given text demands it.[19]

ALTHOUGH I CANNOT HERE do justice to the work by historians and political scientists concerning inter-American relations, some comments are necessary concerning the place of my project in the context of cultural and literary hemispheric studies scholarship. For a long time, inter-American studies consisted mainly of works concerning the history, particularly the political and economic relations, of the United States and Latin America. In keeping with the dependency model describing and thereby also perpetuating the asymmetrical power relations, much of this scholarship was produced in the United States, and the nonetheless considerable body of books and articles published in other American countries was largely ignored by monolingual US scholars. The rapid development of inter- or multidisciplinary hemispheric American studies, including literary and cultural studies, has been masterfully summarized by Ralph Bauer in his survey *PMLA* article "Hemispheric Studies" of 2009.[20] Inter-American studies appears as a treasure trove, a mine, but also as a minefield. "The potential pitfalls of hemispheric American studies lurk [. . .] in any attempt to transpose the age-old epistemological binaries that have burdened American studies (culture/nature, ideology/experience, Europe/America, Self/Other, *otra/nuestra*) to a hemispheric scale" (242).[21]

What an interactional, comprehensive, transnational, and certainly nonbinary approach might be like has been delineated in Sandhya Shukla and Heidi Tinsman's introduction to their interdisciplinary volume *Imagining Our Americas: Towards a Transnational Frame*.

> We are interested not so much in "comparative history"—the side-by-side examination of different "countries"—but in the experiences, imaginaries, and histories of interaction. These spaces of dialogue, linkage, conflict, domination, and resistance take shape across, or sometimes outside, the confines of national and regional borders and sensibilities and therefore allow for new epistemologies. Shared problematics, then, rather than a common geography, colonizing power, or language, might define an "Americas" inquiry that radically de-privileges the never fully inclusive Anglo-Iberian axis around which area studies currently constructs American "regions."
>
> In challenging the analytical primacy of the nation, thinking across the Americas illuminates how many of the most significant social formations that mark the Americas' various regions and states were profoundly nonnational in character: diverse and complex indigenous societies, European conquest and colonization, African slavery, Enlightenment-based independence movements

> and republic-building projects, mass (im)migrations, populist welfare states, Cold War political cultures, neoliberal economies, to name but a few. (6)

This neatly sums up the historical and geographical conditions that have to be taken into account in any hemispheric project but also the very relativity of this so-called factual background. It is encouraging that the idea of imagined rather than of factographically described nations, cultures, and geographies has taken root even outside of literary and cultural studies, although the degree to which a scholar can accept her or his subject as imaginatively constructed differs considerably among the contributors to this volume as it does between the various disciplines engaging with hemispheric topics in general. In this respect, the volume *Hemispheric American Studies*, edited by Caroline F. Levander and Robert S. Levine, appears to be more consistent. In their introduction, Levander and Levine also discard the nation (notably the United States) as the conceptual frame of the investigations they have assembled in their book, but they also reject its replacement by other forms of regional identity that we find in recent area studies. "Rather, we approach the hemisphere and the shifting, evolving nations and regions within it from a spatio-temporal vantage point where comparative approaches bring out the contingency of both the nation and region" (6). My own analyses, while focusing on a national and transnational (US, Canadian, and sometimes European) discourse concerning the Latin American Other, share Levander and Levine's premise that the nation is "a relational identity that emerges through constant collaboration, dialogue, and dissension" (5), although this approach cannot be constantly foregrounded.

However, with few exceptions my readings do not aim at the comparative perspective that is applied in much of the work done in literary and cultural studies on hemispheric American matters. Obviously it is possible to find intellectual or territorial vantage points from which one can study cultural productions from various parts of the Americas, particularly if the focus is on certain areas, periods, or genres. What has come under consideration in recent years is the respective imaginative construction of reality as it occurs in texts from all parts of the two continents, with Bell Gale Chevigny and Gari Laguardia's edited volume *Reinventing the Americas* of 1986 functioning as a pioneer venture. But the search for pan-American aspects can lead to quite misleading hopes in the emancipatory potential of an all-American literature supposedly characterized by common features such as "magical realism."[22] The question raised in the title of editor Gustavo Pérez Firmat's *Do the Americas Have a Common Literature?* can be answered only in the negative where it refers to a specifically New World literature based on the topical material shared by both Americas. The predilection of Latin American writers for Hawthorne, Poe, Whitman, and Faulkner, or that of US writers for García Márquez may yield some influence studies, but this also has to be seen in the light of cultural misunderstanding.

What is more promising are studies such as Anna Brickhouse's *Transamerican Literary Relations and the Nineteenth-Century Public Sphere*. Her book on (mainly) nineteenth-century literary contacts between Anglophone US and Spanish or French Caribbean and Mexican writers and intellectuals reveals

> a kind of *trans*american literary imaginary within the US public sphere. [. . .] The writers emerging from this cultural milieu sought alternately to solidify and to signify across the unstable boundaries of nation and race within a New World arena characterized precisely by its transnationality: by the overlap and simultaneity of different national claims upon territories as well as upon literary texts and traditions. (6–7)

Brickhouse's study has the additional advantage of engaging with Spanish and French texts in the original, multilingualism still being rare even in the age of transnational American studies. The close interaction she describes between writers and texts from various parts of the Americas north of South America has not remained a standard feature of inter-American literature of later periods and is therefore not an object of study in this book, although such an approach could be applied in the case of some writers I will discuss. It would not change the centrality of the discourse of Latinamericanism I try to describe as functioning as well as being questioned.

Quite a few of the authors to be studied in this book might be called "ambassadors of culture," the subject of Kirsten Silva Gruesz's *Ambassadors of Culture: The Transamerican Origins of Latino Writing*. Her study uncovers a rich network of nineteenth-century Latin American (often exile) and borderlands poets and essayists visiting or working in the United States as well as corresponding US writers, such as Longfellow or Whitman, who were interested in Latin America, imagined the Americas as a field of cultural interaction, translated Spanish texts, or even visited some of the countries to the south. Her book shows that inter-American cultural contacts were much more common than is often imagined and therefore makes a major contribution to hemispheric literary studies. There is little overlap with my study because the period Gruesz studies is more limited, and her textual material consists of poetry and essays rather than prose narratives. Also, I discuss Latin American material only very rarely and only rarely analyze US Latino writing. However, I will refer to Gruesz's book in the context of some of the most "ambassadorial" writers or characters under discussion.

Many of the North American characters entering Latin America in the texts I study could also play the role of cultural ambassadors, if they were so minded and intellectually or psychologically equipped. Most of them are white, whatever whiteness may have meant at a specific time in history. In her *Shadowing the White Man's Burden*, Gretchen Murphy has shown not only that the racial category *white* was modified and adapted to accommodate more or less recent waves of immigrants into the United States, but also that it is an oversimplification to assume that even during the heyday of imperialism, the domestic notions of racial groupings and the color line could be and were completely transferred to new areas coming under US domination. Instead, she argues "that U.S. racial categories were adapted to fit shifting transnational and international relationships in a process that was multidirectional and informed by new kinds of comparative thought" (*Shadowing*, 11). Murphy analyzes texts by nonwhite authors who visited and/or wrote about such territories and contributed to complicating the debate about racial formations at home and abroad. Still, John Carlos Rowe's statement (which Murphy quotes and questions) that the tendency to analogize constructions of racial otherness produced "an adaptable and yet surprisingly stable racist, sexist, and classist rhetoric that could be deployed for new foreign ventures even as it was required to maintain old systems of controlling familiar groups within the United States" (Rowe, *Literary Culture*, 8; qtd. in Murphy, *Shadowing*, 11) retains its validity. The tension between discursive stability on the one hand and the questioning and modification of the discursive order on the other has been a feature of culture and literature through the ages.

In my book, which covers a much longer time span than studies dealing with US imperialism in the strict sense, both tendencies are always present and under scrutiny. Although it is in tune with Murphy's observation that the nonwhite protagonists of the novels by Taylor, Castillo, and Wylie I analyze in Chapters 7 and 8 do not share the racist preconceptions of so many other visitors of Latin America discussed in this book, the counter-discursive complications of race vary widely, and in many, but not all cases, their presence is a mark of the literary complexity of the text in general. I have not thematized race separately, but the issue is part and parcel of my discussion of Latinamericanism. In particular, the forms and extent of *mestizaje* since the eighteenth century are a striking example of difference in sameness throughout the hemisphere. It is no coincidence that important theories of racial, social, or cultural hybridization and diversification have come from countries and scholarly communities as widely apart as Canada and Argentina, and that they are just as diverse as the phenomena they refer to.[23]

Discourses of identity and alterity are formed not so much among the cultural elite but in a dialogue between the population at large and the nation's or group's spokespeople, not only its political leaders but journalists and producers of popular culture. For this reason, Shelley Streeby's *Ameri-*

*can Sensations: Class, Empire, and the Production of Popular Culture* is an essential study. Streeby analyzes popular novels, story-papers, dime novels, and journalistic texts reacting to (and also lending impulse to) the Mexican-American War, therefore taking the year 1848 as its focal point. She demonstrates how what I would call the US American identity discourse develops in the face of class struggle, mass immigration, the race and slavery issue, and the question of contiguous territorial expansion and/or colonization and, eventually, empire building. Both in domestic and transnational contexts, various discourses of alterity exist and undergo modification, for instance when in the work of George Lippard, immigrants from northern Europe are de-alienized and widen the dominant group beyond people of Anglo-Saxon extraction but stand in ever more rigorous distinction from Native Americans, Mexicans, and southern European Catholics.

The extension of the textual field to include popular literature is a fruitful endeavor. Other critics have gone beyond that by studying political texts as part of the cultural production. In *Hemispheric Imaginings: The Monroe Doctrine and Narratives of U.S. Empire*, Gretchen Murphy endeavors "[t]hrough a cultural analysis of the Monroe Doctrine [. . .] to better understand how the United States came politically to dominate and culturally express 'America,' and how 'the hemisphere' became a meaningful cultural and geopolitical frame for American nationalism" (*Hemispheric Imaginings*, 4). Murphy traces the doctrine's changing interpretations and applications from 1823 through the early twentieth century and beyond—a development, that is, from a statement concerning the responsibility of the United States to protect the Western Hemisphere to its claim to being hemispheric arbiter, controlling power, and authority. She goes beyond political historians by seeing the Monroe Doctrine "as a cultural ideology rather than strictly as a foreign policy" (17), and therefore studies its expression in popular fiction and pictorial representations. Murphy's "theory of discourse" (18) approach makes it possible to "look to literature not only as a medium that registers dominant national narratives or expresses anxiety and uncertainty about them but also as a causal force that constructed and negotiated bonds of affiliation and national belonging" (18).

I sympathize with Murphy's approach, though I do not start from a political idea but from a more general cultural discourse informing elite and popular cultural production just as much as political and social thinking. The same applies to what distinguishes the present study from another book dealing with a political concept, Stephen M. Park's monograph *The Pan American Imagination*. Park focuses mainly on the period that can be considered the heyday of Pan-American thinking, from 1910 through 1940. He describes that section of Latinamericanism that refers to Latin America as a field of North American knowledge under the auspices of the Pan-American idea. For this purpose he studies literary and nonliterary texts as well as pictorial representations of this idea but also of its pitfalls. His analyses often reveal patterns of dividedness, ambiguity, and contradictoriness among authors, photographers, painters, and those archaeologists who tried to unveil the pre-Columbian past of Latin America; such patterns resemble the conflict between discursive and counter-discursive writing that I have found in the temporally wider and thematically less restricted context of many of the fictions under scrutiny in this book.

The studies just mentioned share a temporal orientation, being concerned with specific historical periods, generally more limited than the period covered in my book. Their spatial focus on Latin America is also restricted, Mexico and the Caribbean figuring most prominently in the political and cultural discourses they analyze. Where hemispheric studies is part of empire studies, the spatial range will necessarily be global, as in Murphy's *Shadowing the White Man's Burden* mentioned earlier, and in José David Saldívar's *Trans-Americanity* referred to later. Naturally, a compound of spatial and temporal orientations, what Mikhail Bakhtin has called a *chronotopos*, will inform any given literary text. In *Our South: Geographic Fantasy and the Rise of National Literature*, Jennifer Rae Greeson quotes Bakhtin when she describes the Plantation South "as a key *chronotope* for U.S. nationalization" (62). This South has been and still is being linked to a greater geographical area formed by the Caribbean, including the surrounding coastal countries or at least areas. Such notions existed in the eighteenth and were still propagated in the twentieth century (for instance, on several occasions by Gabriel García Márquez). Thus, the south is also an inter-American topic. Greeson traces the idea and the role of the Plantation South through the end of the nineteenth century and shows how it served as a model for several concepts, for instance an American expansion into the greater Caribbean in the service of the system of slavery or as part of empire building in the Reconstruction period, that is, as a continuation of the "liberation" and "civilization" of the South.[24]

Clearly, this shifting idea of the south involves several versions of a discourse of alterity that resemble those discussed in my book. Thus in 1776, Timothy Dwight, conflating "the internal other of the nation (the southern states) with its immediate external surround (the Spanish North American dominions)" speaks of the "'southern and western parts of North-America'" as being

> peopled with as vicious, luxurious, mean-spirited and contemptible a race of beings, as any that ever blackened the pages of infamy. Generally descended from the refuse of mankind, situated in a hot, wealthy, and plentiful country,

> and educated from their infancy under the most shocking of all governments, . . . can we wonder that they . . . are tainted with all the vices and blots of their parent nation, increased and deepened by a multitude of their own? (qtd. in Greeson 67)

Here, as Greeson points out, we have a version of the anti-Catholic, anti-Spanish *leyenda negra* opening the door to northern colonial desires. We will find verbal echoes of Dwight's statement in, say, John L. Stephens's remarks about "so beautiful a country in such miserable hands" discussed in Chapter 6 of this volume. However, the temporal scope of my study extends from Dwight's period to the present, and the spatial extension includes all of Latin America as defined earlier. That is, although I acknowledge the insights of Greeson and other scholars into the imaginations concerning specific or even extended *chronotopoi*, my aim is to show the transhistoric persistence of Latinamericanism and its directedness at virtually the whole hemisphere outside the United States and Canada. This is not to deny that there are overlaps with discourses of domestic alterity, from African slaves and Native Americans to the Other in the shape of the other gender, other social class, or other ethnicity. Let me repeat here that the other focus of this study is the counter-discursive, antireductionist questioning that characterizes at least the more substantial of the texts under scrutiny.

The imaginary constructedness of chronotopic subjects applies whether a given spatial and temporal entity is seen from within or from without. In this sense, studies such as Ana Patricia Rodríguez's *Dividing the Isthmus: Central American Transnational Histories, Literatures, and Cultures* form an important complement to what is being undertaken in this book. Rodríguez discusses twentieth-century fictional narratives from various transnationally perceived Central American countries, fictions that "transect and transcend national political boundaries and traverse the entire region, destabilizing not only insular and isolationist notions of national literatures but also integrative and holistic readings of the Central American region and its cultures and peoples" (3). The spectrum of texts she analyzes, a spectrum of imaginative constructions of that area and those periods, provides a good example of both the discursive and the counter-discursive construction of, in this case, the Latin American self, with corresponding glances at the US Other. However, as I have already mentioned, such a reversal of perspectives can be offered here only very rarely, in an exemplary function. To apply it generally would swell the book out of its proportions. Besides, much good comparativist work has been done by others.

Widening the scope of American studies to hemispheric American studies required a major shift of perspective and was strongly supported and in many cases initiated by the development of Chicano/a and Latina/o studies in the context of the various ethnic movements and the ethnicity studies beginning to blossom from the 1960s onward. Subsequently, border and borderland studies, the idea of Greater Mexico, the reemergence of notions of pan-America, the rediscovery of the texts by José Martí and others, or the idea of a Circum-Caribbean played formative roles. That even these contexts can be fruitfully extended by seeing the Americas as part of a global world has been argued and demonstrated by José David Saldívar in his recent *Trans-Americanity: Subaltern Modernities, Global Coloniality, and the Cultures of Greater Mexico*. Saldívar takes his clue from Aníbal Quijano and Immanuel Wallerstein's seminal essay "Americanity as a Concept," with its pontifical beginning:

> The modern world-system was born in the long sixteenth century. The Americas as a geosocial construct were born in the long sixteenth century. The creation of this geosocial entity, the Americas, was the constitutive act of the modern world-system. The Americas were not incorporated into an already existing capitalist world-economy. There could not have been a capitalist world-economy without the Americas. (Quijano and Wallerstein 549)

For Saldívar, this world-system approach makes it possible and stimulating to link ethnicity studies and subaltern studies globally because ethnicity and coloniality, according to Quijano and Wallerstein, are part of the emergence of a hierarchical system of states. In his own book, in a series of exciting readings, Saldívar therefore feels free to compare Latina writings with those of Arundhati Roy and to follow Américo Paredes to Japan, or to study (this is the title of Saldívar's Chapter 2) "Subaltern Modernity and José Martí's Trans-American Cultural Criticism."

Clearly, the discourse of Latinamericanism I investigate here has to be linked to current and historic power structures and would not exist without "coloniality" as "the creation of a set of states linked together within an interstate system in hierarchical layers," all of them "new creations" (Quijano and Wallerstein 550). Also, global events like the Africa of slavery days, the Pacific expansion, the Philippine War, the Cold War, and Vietnam are background factors for many of the texts I will discuss. However, I will not address texts set in other parts of the world because this would take the focus away from my main subject. And because I write about North American authors, most of them not belonging to any minority group, the questions of the subaltern's language authority and the international network of non-metropolitan writers and intellectuals play only a minor role in what I have to say. My aim is not to inscribe myself into subaltern, minority, diaspora, or postcolonial studies, but to show the literary manifestations of a—clearly hierarchical—alterity discourse but also the workings of counter-discursive creativity among elite as well as popular writers from the dominant North of the American hemisphere. That such a project is related and indeed indebted to the current discussion of dealing with the Other in the context of empire, postcoloniality, race and ethnicity, migration, and other critical considerations of asymmetric power relations goes without saying. Most of the scholarly books just referred to share a critical political perspective, and such an approach informs my own work as well. But beyond that I am interested in the epistemological and hermeneutic problem of dealing with the Other, with the ethical questions it has laid open, and with the aesthetics required for dealing with it.

This book shares the constructivist and sometimes deconstructionist approach in the wake of the New Historicism and postcolonial studies with many of the texts cited here. However, where they exemplify the discourses (under whichever name) they study by a broad spectrum of cultural production, including popular literature, travelogues, journalism, political speeches, works of fine art, or movies, I venture only rarely into the field of nonliterary texts and use popular fiction primarily to demonstrate the force of Latinamericanism in certain historical contexts. More often, I study what might be called elite or mainstream literature because my intention is to show not only the power of discursive thinking but also the capacity of literary art to disrupt and subvert it, to show self and Other with more complexity, uncertainty, ambiguity, openness.

I am concerned with the discursive and imaginary constructions of that Other, and of the encounter of self and Other, because there can be no novel, no poem, no painting dealing with the other part of the Americas that is not informed by what Fredrick B. Pike in the title of his imagological study has called "myths and stereotypes of civilization and nature," by the respective discourses of identity and alterity, and by the concomitant power relations. In this context it is necessary to step away from the concept of dependency as the exclusive model of Latin American–US American interaction. Though the existence of hegemonic power cannot be ignored, it is helpful to study such power under the aspect of the counter-power necessarily arising under apparently asymmetrical conditions. Where power is defined not in Weberian terms as the capacity to achieve intended effects but according to Anthony Giddens's more flexible definition as *transformative capacity*,[25] the whole range of ways by which Latin Americans have reacted to US political, economic, and cultural pressure comes into view and, in turn, helps to define the qualities of northern supremacy. Obviously, this aspect can only rarely be addressed in this volume, but it forms a backdrop against which unilateral imaginations need to be seen and evaluated.

Power and counter-power cannot be seen separately from the collective images, structures of knowledge, and textual manifestations we have come to call discourses in a somewhat loose and imprecise application of Michel Foucault's term. Discourses contribute to and in turn depend on social institutions or, more generally, systems of power. They stabilize such systems where they occur as discourses of national, ethnic, or cultural identity or alterity, but where interdiscursive overlapping and interference occurs, they may also acquire a destabilizing function. Literature, like other fields of explicit culture, is part of the discursive system of its society. Although it often supports the dominant structure of power, the interdiscursive overlappings characteristic of many texts, the imaginative freedom at work, and the non-pragmatic use of language and speech-act conventions will frequently endow it with a subversive, counter-discursive potential. Literature can therefore function as an element of counter-power: both with respect to the dominant elements of its own society and with respect to power exerted from outside.

It is here that inter-American studies as the study of political-discursive interaction ties in with questions related to the various ideas of culture. First, the hierarchy of cultural expression comes into play: so-called popular texts will usually function as part of an affirmative discursive order of self and Other, power and submission, while texts belonging to the level of elite culture tend to have a stronger subversive potential, although this need not always be so. To study only mainstream highbrow literature, therefore, will lead to a distorted view of the discursive substratum of intercultural and international relations. Second, and even more important, is the insight into the fluidity and hybridity we have come to discover in cultural entities. Any essentialist position is clearly obsolete, but if "self-other relations are matters of power and rhetoric rather than of essence" (Clifford 14), power and (discursive) rhetoric in turn are dynamic and contested areas. To speak of a US American versus a Latin American culture is inadequate not only because of the diversity of Latin American societies and cultural traditions, but also because it presupposes a homogeneity, comprehensiveness, and monolithic stability of national cultures convincingly rejected in the writings of, for instance, Homi K. Bhabha and Gayatri Spivak. We must endure the tension between binary, bipolar models as they have been employed in empire studies and the explosive decentering, the multiplicity of forms of power and interaction, the diffusion of the local and the foreign or, indeed, the many locals and many foreigns, in order to speak about inter-American relations and perceptions with a complexity that appears at least momentarily adequate.[26]

Let it be said, finally, that for all the wealth of material covered here, this book is not a history of Latinamericanism in North American literature.

Certain developments are laid open, to be sure, and historical perspectives are applied, but there are also temporal gaps and, on the other hand, strong emphases on specific periods that I found particularly interesting. Thus, the period from the mid-1970s through the mid-1990s is heavily represented. It is my strong impression, although I cannot corroborate it by statistical surveys, that more inter-American fiction was published in the United States during that period than at other times, and that this was a consequence of the Vietnam War and the political, moral, and psychological problems connected with it.[27] Clearly, this fiction responds to a renewed US government interest in Latin America (including the new covert wars in Central America) but also to the traumata left behind by that disastrous dealing with a tropical Other. This wave of inter-American writing continues through the end of the Cold War and into the 1990s, with Cuba and some left-leaning governments in other Latin American countries serving as almost nostalgically seen reminders of old certainties and the new problem of redefining hegemony and its Other. To write a serious literary history, though, would have required more comprehensiveness and more continuity than I found possible to present.

THIS BOOK IS ORGANIZED in the following way: Part I (Chapters 1 and 2) contains this introductory chapter and an introduction into my theoretical and terminological premises. Part II (Chapters 3–5) is devoted to US American literary versions of historical material: Columbus, US interventions in Latin America, and the Mexican Revolution. Part III (Chapters 6 and 7), while also analyzing texts dealing with certain historical developments, discusses specific components of the discourse of Latinamericanism: the nature-culture dichotomy and gender. Part IV (Chapters 8–10) deals with novels of the late 1970s through the early 1990s, that is, the post-Vietnam and covert Central American war period, which is also an era of considerable social changes in the United States. It refers to both realist and nonrealistic, metafictional texts, including postmodern versions of Columbus. While the first four parts deal with US literature, Part V (Chapters 11 and 12) is devoted to Canadian fiction. It takes us from World War II to the early twenty-first century. Because Canadian literature presents many similarities to the textual material from the United States but also notable differences, and because it in a way sums up but also transcends problems and approaches of US American fiction, I have decided to not include the Canadian texts in the previous parts, but to use them as a concluding and in part crowning corpus of inter-American literature.

All parts are historical inasmuch as the texts under discussion refer to historical events, persons, and developments, from the voyages of Columbus through the contemporary situation in Argentina. Although I try to follow the chronological sequence of such historical material, I often have to jump back and forth because there is the second branch of history to consider: literary history. Here, I also tendentially follow the chronology, but considering the sociohistorical or other thematic material handled by the author in question, I often have to combine texts from different periods in one chapter. This is so because all chapters are also thematic, be the topic a specific historical event, an aspect such as the treatment of gender questions, or the mode of representation.

Obviously, thematic aspects, historical time, and literary historical time overlap. The themes of nature and gender play important roles in many works discussed in other chapters, but gender can also be relevant for the description of authorial positions. The aesthetics of representation is of importance in many other analytic contexts. One further aspect that might be noted is ethnicity: texts by Chicana (Chapter 7), African American (Chapter 8), or Native American (Chapter 10) authors display variations of the mainstream picture, but issues of ethnicity, "race," culture, and ethnic mix also form an element of narrative content and are thematized in many of the texts discussed in this study.

I have not attempted to use the aspect of political or cultural geography as a structural element. Without having been consciously planned that way, my selection of fiction and the few travel books and historical studies I discuss reflect the distribution of countries or areas that form the setting of inter-American literature in general, at least according to my impression when studying bibliographical lists. That is, half of the texts use Mexico as their field of action. Central America (represented repeatedly by fictional or fictionalized countries) and Cuba are the runners-up, with Brazil and the rest of the Caribbean following. The remainder is made up of Chile, Argentina, Venezuela, and Peru. The specifics of each country or area, especially their geo- and biotopographical features are often represented, and to varying degrees their respective history. Nonetheless, the discursive construction of these countries and their people homogenizes them more or less strongly and made me reluctant to use geographical distribution as a structuring element for this book.

I conclude this introduction with a short summary of the individual chapters. Before I come to the analytical parts of the book, Chapter 2 discusses the theoretical and terminological substratum of this study. In particular, some basic aspects of the theories of identity versus alterity and the respective range of cultural hermeneutics and discourse analysis have to be addressed before I come to the specific discourse governing North American perceptions and representations of Latin America, that is, what I and others have called Latinamericanism. I also discuss theoretical aspects of culture, and notably the interference of cultural allegiances, under the topic of transdifference. Finally, I try to indicate in which way literature can serve as an epistemological tool for exploring the Other or failing to do so, and in this context I address the problem of literary adequacy to the thematic material, that is, the question of realism. Literary examples are discussed to show the potential of textual art to reveal aspects of interculturality beyond what sheer description can do.

In Part II, Chapter 3 is devoted not so much to inter-American topics, but a hemispheric one: Columbus, whose achievements, deeds, and misdeeds form a common, pan-American theme. Although Columbus, as Wey Gómez has shown, was informed by the idea of a Global South as an area of untold riches and exploitable natives, his image diverged early in two directions. The colonial American and especially the early US discourse of "American" identity required and used foundation stories and foundational figures, and it is here that Columbus could fulfill an important function. As early as in Joel Barlow's long poems, he is made a tool of historical progress whose highest previous step was made in Barlow's eyes by Manco Capac when he founded the Inca empire, so that pan- and inter-American aspects of the topic come into view. But from the start, there was also the possibility of seeing Columbus (and not only his followers) in terms of the anti-Spanish, anti-Catholic Black Legend as a destroyer of the Native civilizations, a view that linked him directly to the negative stereotypes of Latinamericanism. Such skepticism would later prevail around the time of the Columbus quincentennial, as will be shown in Chapter 10.

Chapter 4 studies early manifestations of the discourse of Latinamericanism in conjunction with the rise of US hegemonic politics vis-à-vis Latin America, that is, with the history of interventionism in the nineteenth century. It is therefore more directly connected with empire studies than the later chapters. The literary texts inscribing into the discourse are primarily popular novels by Frank Stockton, Richard Harding Davis, and others, voicing the authors' assent, but there were dissenting opinions both among the political elites and among the writers who found or at least tried to find literary strategies to avoid falling into the mainstream patterns, writers such as Herman Melville, James Fenimore Cooper, Stephen Crane, and, after the turn of the century, Joseph Hergesheimer.

Chapter 5 addresses the problem of how to represent the foundational stories of the Other, how to take its respective identity discourse seriously. The Mexican Revolution, a central event for the national identity formation, has received only scant interest in US literature on Mexico. Though contemporary reports by leftist US writers and journalists remained disappointingly superficial, the post–World War I, modernist period brought interesting fictional treatments of the topic by Carleton Beals, John Dos Passos, and Katherine Anne Porter, the latter two applying a nonteleological view of history to the event, and, in Porter's case, seeing it in the context of primitivism and the psychological barriers of comprehension. Of the two novels of the 1980s discussed here, Rosalind Wright's *Veracruz* is an attempt to overcome these barriers by adopting elements of magical realism, whereas Laurence Gonzales's *El Vago*, whose frame narrative is set in 1945, at the first atomic explosion, presents a powerful picture of the revolution from the perspective of a participant who realizes that he cannot make his young companion understand its essence just as neither of them can comprehend the dawning of the Atomic Age. Gonzales succeeds in undermining not only the US American but also the Mexican discursive construction of national identity.

In Part III, Chapter 6 discusses concepts of nature and culture or civilization as components of the discourses of alterity and identity. Taking its cue from Carlos Fuentes's *Gringo viejo* and using Freud's *Civilization and Its Discontents* and other theoretical models, the chapter compares nineteenth-century travelogues by Alexander von Humboldt and John L. Stephens and then analyzes Mary Peabody Mann's antislavery novel *Juanita*, set in Cuba, for its significant use of nature symbolism. After a brief glance at two popular novels of the early twentieth century, a critical reading of those escapist parts of Jack Kerouac's Beat novel *On the Road* that are set in Mexico takes us to mid-twentieth-century versions of a discourse-ridden perspective on the Other even among those opposing the official US policy toward Latin America. The chapter concludes with an analysis of another oppositional text in the context of the then current discourse of Third World development, Paul Theroux's *The Mosquito Coast*. This major text not only deconstructs the North American protagonist as a self-styled bearer of nondestructive progress, but by showing his built-in contradictions also reveals US materialism as threatening to annihilate both nature and culture in Latin America and around the globe.

Gender perceptions form the topic of Chapter 7. The discourses of ethnic alterity and of gender often overlap, either mutually supporting each other or, as is the case in the texts under discussion, undermining the discursive structure. Again, either discourse is part of contemporary political, social, and intellectual developments. Interdiscursivity questions binary constructions of reality, revealing hidden ambivalences and conditions of transdifference. My model text is Melville's *Typee*, not an inter-American novel but exemplary in the representation of the disconcerting loss of a clear boundary between the male-dominated symbolic order and the maternal semiotic (in

Julia Kristeva's terms) that the American protagonist encounters among the Typee tribe. Interdiscursivity figures prominently in D. H. Lawrence's *The Plumed Serpent*, which served as an important model for much North American inter-American literature. Fascinating examples of twentieth-century interdiscursive US texts are Rex E. Beach's popular novel *Jungle Gold*, but also Katherine Anne Porter's "Flowering Judas" and Michael Rumaker's "Gringos," which are therefore studied a second time. The interaction of the discourses of gender, sexual orientation, and ethnicity in the context of late-twentieth-century Third Wave feminism is particularly interesting in texts by Mexican American authors. Sheila Ortiz Taylor's *Faultline* and Ana Castillo's experimental *The Mixquiahuala Letters* present a humorously debunking and a grimly disillusioning version of the confrontation of Chicana women and the gendered world of Mexico.

Part IV discusses novels of the period between the late 1970s and early 1990s, the period of post-Vietnam disillusionment but also of continuing surrogate warfare in Central America, and a period of many social and cultural disruptions in the United States. Chapter 8 is devoted to texts that have been classified as (neo)realistic or at least use descriptive and other details realistically. Paul Theroux's *Mosquito Coast* and Margaret Atwood's *Bodily Harm*, which are analyzed extensively in other chapters, belong to this group and are briefly mentioned, but the main texts under consideration are Robert Stone's *A Flag for Sunrise*, Joan Didion's *A Book of Common Prayer*, and James Wylie's *The Sign of Dawn*, the last one a politically utopian adventure novel that nonetheless has some realistic aspects. All of them are political novels, almost all dealing with the post-Vietnam condition of US–Latin American relations during the period of the covert wars in Central America. The chapter therefore addresses questions of realism in the representation of the Other, notably as far as sociopolitical aspects are concerned.

The limitations of a realistic approach have led some authors of the same period to varieties of nonrealist writing, the topic of Chapter 9. One such approach is to use techniques generally associated with "typical" Latin American modes of literary writing that are assumed to be appropriate for the representation of the Latin American Other, notably the so-called magical realism. John Updike's *Brazil* is discussed as an attempt—to my mind, a failed one—to combine the myth of Tristan and Iseult with magical realism in order to represent the multiethnic essence of Brazil. Texts belonging to postmodern metafiction are more successful. One example is Daniel Curley's *Mummy*, a novel that parodies just about any aspect of a discourse-following way of writing about Mexico. Walter Abish's *Eclipse Fever* goes one step further in metafictionally and, indeed, metadiscursively questioning truth claims about the Other per se by representing attempts at making sense of whatever appears as reality both by the US American and by the Mexican characters. In this, they contribute to the author's own efforts at shattering illusion on the textual and the metatextual level and thereby liberate the imagination of characters and readers alike.

Chapter 10 continues the topic of postmodern approaches to alterity and identity. The romantic idealization of Columbus by writers of the nineteenth century finds its skeptical counterpart in the late twentieth that is here represented by Stephen Marlowe's metafictional, debunking, and deconstructive *The Memoirs of Christopher Columbus*. Not surprisingly, Native American authors used the occasion of the Columbus quincentennial of 1992 to present their dissenting view of the matter. The novels by Louise Erdrich and Michael Dorris, *The Crown of Columbus*, and by Gerald Vizenor, *The Heirs of Columbus*, are metahistoriographic fictions just like Marlowe's, but their agenda has to do with historical rights and wrongs as well and thus belongs into the context of postcolonialism. They use a wide range of narrative techniques and genres and not only deconstruct the traditional Euro-American foundation stories, but also point to the difficulty of assuming a vantage point from which a narrative not only or even primarily of victimization but of cultural exchange and of transdifferent identities can be told. By taking ethnicity into account more seriously than most other texts under discussion, they also question the discursive construction of the Other that dominates so many other texts.

Part V is devoted to Canadian literature. In Chapter 11 I discuss specific aspects of Canadian views of Latin America and then focus on one text that may arguably be called the most important inter-American novel, Malcom Lowry's *Under the Volcano*, which belongs in the historical context of World War II. This masterwork of modernist literature cannot be profitably approached primarily in terms of an analysis of the discursive treatment of Mexico, but such elements are to be found here, too. *Under the Volcano* uses Mexico as a multilayered symbolic field in which central aspects of the main characters' psychological situation, their communicational failures, and their longing for deeper or, as it were, higher truths are revealed. Some passages from the beginning of the book are read closely in order to demonstrate the way Lowry transforms physical landscape into bewildering symbolic space.

Chapter 12 shifts the discussion of Canadian texts to those more directly associated with Latinamericanism, both from the post-Vietnam era and the beginning of the twenty-first century, thus bringing the period of literary history covered in this book to the present time. In Margaret Atwood's *Bodily Harm*, gender issues form an important topic, but the Other encountered by the protagonist appears in other important varieties as well. The elements of alterity the protagonist Rennie notices—nature, language, food, and, most important, touch—appear to her as dangerous or abject, disgusting. Only when she overcomes her disgust is she able to proceed beyond the symbolic to what Kristeva has called the semiotic, the motherly *chora*, and here to encounter the Levinasian absolute Other. The physical is even more pervasive in Graeme Gibson's brilliant short story "Pancho Villa's Head." The last part of Chapter 12 turns to recent Canadian fictions on Latin America: Jessica Morrison's chick lit *The Buenos Aires Broken Hearts Club* that does away with alterity altogether; Amanda Hale's *The Reddening Path* that follows the consequences of the Guatemalan civil war into the present time and represents the situation of the victims of ethnic and sexual marginalization; and Anthony Hyde's *A Private House* that deals with the overwhelming and confusing experience of Cuban alterity and of a variety of shifting identity positions: white and black, gay and straight, Native and non-Native, European, Canadian, US American, and Cuban. The chapter concludes with a look at William H. New's lyrical encounter with Ecuador as epitomizing the experience of the Other.

The analytical chapters do not follow any regular pattern but, essay-like, present individual interpretations, often taking appropriate theoretical aspects into account. Therefore, theories of space, history, narrative, nature, genre, gender, the abject, and so on are not discussed in Chapter 2, whose function is to introduce theoretical approaches and terminologies that are relevant for the book as a whole.

# [2]

## ALTERITY AND IDENTITY: REFLECTIONS ON APPROACHING THE OTHER

What is a thing?
What is the other?
What is the other when it comes to making of me . . . what?
Some thing. What is the other when he or she employs him or herself in making a thing of me? Such and such a thing, for example a thing that, like a corpse, is both a thing and something other than a thing?
What is a thing?
What is the other?
—Jacques Derrida, *The Beast and the Sovereign* (Vol. II, 179; French pagination)

JACQUES DERRIDA'S QUESTIONS opening the fifth session of his last seminar, *The Beast and the Sovereign*, epitomize the problem of self and Other as a relational constellation in a manner that is both unsurpassable and frustrating: I and other, human and thing, living and dead appear in their existential interdependence, their sameness in difference. In the original, Derrida uses *l'autre*, which for him "includes other people but also refers to other animals, to the unconscious, to death, etc."[1] Are matters easier when we move from the most profound philosophical questions to the field of intercultural differences and similarities, to collective identity and mutual alterity, or else, mutual alienity?

Or else: Are the various parts, regions, cultures of the Americas each other's Other or mutually alien? There is a terminological crux that has to be addressed right from the beginning. European philosophy has devoted much attention to the question of the alien, and it is immediately obvious that while French thinkers prefer *l'autre*, the other, German philosophy has focused on *das Fremde*, the alien. The German phenomenologist Bernhard Waldenfels, who has published numerous books on the alien/the Other, insists on the logical difference of the oppositions of *same/other* and *own/alien*. Referring to traditional dialectics, Waldenfels states,

> Something is only the *same* if it distinguishes itself as *other* from others [. . .]. The contrast of the same and the other, on which every order of things is

> based, arises from a *division* that distinguishes one from the other. The result is a pervasive reversibility of positions: Asians are not Europeans, just like Europeans are not Asians. Moreover, this differentiation occurs in a common medium that mediates between the opposites. No matter how different Europeans and Asians are, they are undoubtedly human [. . .].
>
> However, the difference between the own and the alien [. . .] has as such nothing in common with the distinction between the same and the other [. . .]. The own is grouped around the *self*, as a bodily, ethnically, or culturally marked self [. . .]. The opposition between the own and the alien does not emerge from a mere separation, but from a process of *in-* and *ex-clusion* [. . .]. We do not do justice to cultural differences if we compare them to different species of a plant- or animal-world where differences are sublated in a universal genus. There is a threshold between the cultures, which is similar to those thresholds which separate one gender from the other, old age from youth, awakeness from sleep, and life from death. (*Phenomenology*, 72–73)

The phenomenological approach appears to mark clearer and more stable oppositions than are warranted when we remember Derrida and deconstruction.[2]

Horst Turk made a similar attempt to distinguish the terms *alterity* and *alienity.* For him, the Other is not really alien as long as it remains within the same system. It is the *alter* of the *ego*. Thus, members of Western societies may appear different, *other*, to each other, but not alien, whereas for the ancient Greeks the barbarian stood outside the system of language, literature, culture, and hence was *alien* (Turk 173). However, as Turk is aware, the order of things classifying the respective systems is liable to change in terms of historic development or individual experience-based insight. Thus, in European cultures there has been a constant process of acceptance and hence "alterization" of the alien, but the reverse is also true: the constant redefinition of inside and outside often entails an "alienization" of what was hitherto considered as simply "other" (175–76). What lies at the basis of such processes is the fact that self and other, own and alien are not simply contrastive but relational categories.[3] The borders between identity and alterity or alienity are constantly renegotiated. The resulting processes of alterization (or, for that matter, familiarization) and alienization apply to all interpersonal relations (and even to intrapersonal ones). Although Waldenfels's differentiation may be true in terms of a phenomenology of ego-constitution, common scholarly usage tends to handle the terms *other* and *alien* much more loosely and often as synonyms, *Other* with a capital O covering both. At least this seems to apply to English and French.[4] Therefore, it seems acceptable to stick to the common term *Other* that has acquired a semantic—albeit logically imprecise—range from alterity to alienity, and to restrict the use of *alien* to contexts where strangeness, distance, and radical difference are emphasized.

One of the best-known examples of exactly this, the alien, the more than just other, occurs in Michel Foucault's discussion of the classification system "quoted" by the Argentine Jorge Luis Borges in his essay "El idioma analítico de John Wilkins" ("The Analytical Language of John Wilkins"), reputedly found in a Chinese encyclopedia and again supposedly unearthed by the famous sinologist Franz Kuhn. In the wake of Foucault's discussion, Borges's text has become a cause célèbre among anthropologists, literary scholars, and social philosophers. In the preface to his *The Order of Things* (*Les mots et les choses*), Foucault describes his astonishment and fascination when reading a text by Borges that threatened "with collapse our age-old distinction between the Same and the Other":

> This passage quotes a "certain Chinese encyclopaedia" in which it is written that "animals are divided into: (a) belonging to the Emperor, (b) embalmed, (c) tame, (d) sucking pigs, (e) sirens, (f) fabulous, (g) stray dogs, (h) included in the present classification, (i) frenzied, (j) innumerable, (k) drawn with a very fine camelhair brush, (l) *et cetera*, (m) having just broken the water pitcher, (n) that from a long way off look like flies." In the wonderment of this taxonomy, the thing we apprehend in one great leap, the thing that, by means of the fable, is demonstrated as the exotic charm of another system of thought, is the limitation of our own, the stark impossibility of thinking *that*. (Foucault, *Order*, xv)

It is not the fabulous animals that are beyond our imagination but their closeness to stray dogs in the same context. "[W]here could they ever meet, except in the immaterial sound of the voice pronouncing their enumeration, or on the page transcribing it? Where else could they be juxtaposed except in the non-place of language? Yet, though language can spread them before us, it can do so only in an unthinkable space" (xvi–xvii). Foucault is not concerned here with the knowledge of the Other as an object, but with the question whether the radical Other can be known at all, if it is epistemologically accessible at all, if it is not simply indescribable, ineffable. It is on the basis of this textual heterotopia that Foucault builds his theory of epistemes, of systems of knowledge underlying the codes of a culture and their reflective superstructure (cf. Topinka). Thus, first of all, the Other in its radical, alien form is an *epistemological problem* that is insoluble.

The fact that such alienity appears in a text refers, one might conclude, to the special capacity of literature to confound us by familiarizing what lies beyond our ken, thereby defamiliarizing our stock of knowledge, that is, to question familiar, culturally given, even encoded patterns of thinking and imagining—notably those concerning alterity—of which more will be said shortly. More often than not, however, literature, even in its representations of the Other, conforms to established patterns of ideation, in particular to the historical frames of consciousness they are based on, that is, discourses of alterity. Discourses, again as Foucault used the term, are anonymous, socially specific forms of organizing knowledge, notably in connection with certain fields of reference. They have immediate relevance for the exertion of power.[5] Discourses regulate what will be thought and said in a given society and about a given object. They differentiate sense from nonsense, relative truth from relative falsehood, and this entails what is socially included and excluded. Rather than being verbal, mimetic representations of reality, discourses *construct* reality and thereby set the limits of representation. The Other, secondly, is *a discursive construct.*

But there is third aspect of the Other that has to be mentioned right at the start, an aspect that takes us away from Foucault. The Other has always also been considered a phenomenological object, an *object of cognition and scientific description.* A tamale is an item in the traditional Mexican cuisine and can be dealt with quite pragmatically, namely eaten, without regard to its discursive constructedness. But for an image of Mexico, for the discourse of Mexican identity or alterity, its ontological givenness is made into a sign. Any discussion of the "realistic" adequacy of a literary representation of the Other will depend on the way the tension between the "factually" given and the discursively constructed is handled—phenomenology and constructivism do not go well together. The discipline dealing with the symbolic order at home and away from home is cultural hermeneutics.

THE LITERARY TEXTS ANALYZED in this study form part of a collective endeavor at understanding the Other, and in this sense belong to the overarching field of cultural hermeneutics. Understanding these texts, then, is a hermeneutic undertaking of the second order. Classic hermeneutics focused on the understanding of texts. According to Hans-Georg Gadamer's *Truth and Method*, this means moving in the direction of a *Horizontverschmelzung*, a fusion of horizons, as he has termed the coming together of the contexts of meaning one brings into the process of understanding and those of what is to be understood, a process that remains necessarily incomplete, open, suggestive of further steps of an ongoing dialogue. For Gadamer, art, notably literature, in the hermeneutic process reveals not only further horizons but glimpses of a totality that encompasses truth and beauty.

*Cultural* hermeneutics aims at a process of understanding not only of texts, but of cultures in the sense of communities of meaning production involving not only a symbolic order but also praxeological aspects (Reckwitz) and material culture as they are related back to the cultural system of meaning.[6] The difficulties of understanding, the openness of the horizons acknowledged or even celebrated in traditional, intracultural hermeneutics virtually explode when hermeutics turns intercultural, when one takes the multitudes of relevant texts and contexts into consideration. "Where even one's 'own' culture represents a complex, dynamic and heterogeneous processuality, one has to accept that in cultural hermeneutics, while it mediates the understanding of self and Other, nonetheless self-understanding and alterity-understanding remain asymmetrical" (Sparn 19).[7] Beyond tradition, the historical contexts of meaning seen as an essential element in Gadamerian hermeneutics, (inter)cultural hermeneutics has to take into account the anonymous patterns of knowledge that shape our thinking and speaking about self and Other and that we have become accustomed to call *discourses*. Thus, we have a paradoxical situation when trying to understand cultural alterity. While discourses, and particularly alterity discourses, reduce and delimit meaning, cultural hermeneutic processes open meaning exactly when they explore the Other. Hermeneutics and discourse analysis need to be seen as complementary.

The intercultural understanding aimed at in literary texts about the Other is delimited by the discursive prestructuring of the perception of self and Other. It is culture-specific, but so is the discipline of hermeneutics that is usually seen in contrast to discourse analysis. Hermeneutics is a contingent cultural phenomenon although it is and needs to be intended as a universally valid method of understanding.[8] In the Heideggerian and Gadamerian tradition, it points to the essential openness of meaning. Intercultural literature may, thus, foreshorten our understanding of the Other or else open our eyes and minds to the complexity, vastness, and incomprehensibility of the Other. Neither side can be completely excluded, but the works analyzed in this study can follow quite divergent tendencies.

IDEALLY, INTERCULTURAL UNDERSTANDING is a mutual, dialogic process, but few people are capable of representing several cultures and their interplay at the same time. The finest demonstration of such interplay occurs in Ariel Dorfman's autobiography *Heading South, Looking North*, where the writer—Jewish Argentine, American, and Chilean—draws a map of languages that define his plural identities in the course of his forced and unforced migrations: English is North, Spanish is South (*Heading South*, 13). Language means territory for him but also history, culture, family connections, that is, identity in a complex sense. His immigrant grandparents and parents had brought a wealth of languages from Europe—Russian, German, French, (British) English, Yiddish—only to exchange it in Argentina for Spanish, which for Ariel meant home. Being transplanted to the North as a child, he adopts the English of his new US American environment and renounces Spanish and his native South, the beginning of a series of moves, migrations, and exiles between North and South. These migrations between the United States and Latin America, that is, Chile and Argentina, are mostly motivated by political repression directed against the leftist author and before him, his parents, a series of victimizations by grim power structures both North and South, from McCarthy to Pinochet. Not surprisingly, Dorfman later proceeds "to renounce English along with the America of the North and its empire and its culture, renounce and denounce and try to suppress henceforth the man inside me who had spent his life identifying through that language" (101). Consecutively, the author experiences both South and North as lifesaving, home giving, and as threatening, oppressive. That is, the cliché notion of the North's oppression of the South is made to appear more complicated on the personal level, although Dorfman chimes in with the usual complaint by Latin Americans against US dominance and its offshoots in the shape of southern dictatorial regimes. The initial psychological and territorial feeling of the small child is one of comfort in Spanish as an all-embracing "mother country" and life principle, but complexities are foreshadowed:

> Nor did Spanish report that on its boundaries other languages roamed, waiting for me, greedy languages, eager to penetrate my territory and establish a foothold, ready to take over at the slightest hint of weakness. It did not whisper a word to me of its own imperial history, how it had subjugated and absorbed so many people born into other linguistic systems [. . .]. It did not hint that English was to the North, smiling to itself, certain that it would father the mind that is writing these words even now, that I would have to surrender to its charms eventually, it did not suggest that English was ready to do to me what Spanish itself had done to others so many times during its evolution, what it had done, in fact, to my own parents: wrenched them from the arms of their original language. (13)

Thus, while North and South enact their historical struggle in the contested spaces of the author's body and mind, their respective ambivalences reveal that a realignment of the geopolitical compass is not enough. Unidirectionality is subverted by the fact that during the author's formative years, English is just about to become the global language: "I was there at the outset, at that time and place in history when English became the first truly international language of humanity, the beginning of that language's conquest of the transnational spaces of the planet" (67). The map of the Western Hemisphere that Dorfman will eventually sketch, and which is also a map of his personal identity, is finally characterized by what the author calls a "hybrid condition": "I would someday become [. . .] this man who is shared by two equal languages and who has come to believe that to tolerate differences and indeed embody them personally and collectively might be our only salvation as a species" (42).

Instead of "hybrid," which always entails the notion of some kind of mixture, I would call Dorfman's inter- and bi- or pluri-cultural identity construction transdifferent. I have introduced the term *transdifference* in order to name and define phenomena occurring between the poles of binary differentiation such as those operative in the distinctions of the self and the Other in the discourses of gender and of ethnicity, as will be seen in a later chapter. While the reductionism inherent in binary thinking has evoked a number or concepts of transculturality, hybridity, or other ways of transcending the rigid bipolarity, transdifference implies a shift of emphasis away from notions of difference and also from notions of a mélange in the direction of a simultaneity of—often conflicting—positions, loyalties, affiliations, and participations. To quote from a paper in which Klaus Lösch and I have tried to establish the term and delineate its range,

> The term *transdifference* refers to phenomena of a co-presence of different or even oppositional properties, affiliations or elements of semantic and epistemological meaning construction, where this co-presence is regarded or experienced as cognitively or affectively dissonant, full of tension, and undissolvable. Phenomena of transdifference, for instance socio-cultural affiliations, personality components or linguistic and other symbolic predications, are encountered by individuals and groups and negotiated in their respective symbolic order. As a descriptive term transdifference allows the presentation and analysis of such phenomena in the context of the production of meaning that transcend the range of models of binary difference. It is not to be confused with de-differentiation. (Breinig and Lösch, "Transdifference," 105)

Obviously, there is no fusion of horizons here, not even as an ongoing process. Intercultural hermeneutics has to deal not only with problems of understanding self and Other, even radical Other, but also with phenomena of an irreconcilable co-presence of identity positions and contexts of meaning.

TO RETURN TO THE discursive construction of otherness: the alien or, more generally, the Other causes uncertainty and frequently weird reactions.[9] While it produces unstructured situations and hence anxiety and fear, it occasions the creation of stereotypes or stimulates the use of previously existing ones, that is, noncognitive prejudices that offer orientation by facilitating the *appropriation of the Other* by its subjugation under one's own discourse. The way such appropriation may eventually lead to the destruction of the Other has never been presented more clearly than in Tzvetan Todorov's *The Conquest of America: The Question of the Other*. The conquest of the New World is there studied under the aspect of the different semiotic systems and hermeneutic procedures employed by Spaniards and Natives, respectively. According to Todorov, the process of discovering and conquering America was unique in world history not only because of the scope of its consequences but also because of the mutual alienity of the cultures involved. But the opportunity of a coming together with the radical Other was wasted when Sepúlveda and other sixteenth-century Spanish representatives of church and state insisted on the inferiority of the strangers. Their method of deduction was analogizing binary oppositions: in comparison to the Spanish, the *indios* were like children versus grown-ups, like women versus men, animals versus humans, savagism versus gentleness, immoderacy versus moderation, matter versus form, body versus soul, desire versus reason, evil versus goodness (Todorov 146–67).

The historical process analyzed by Todorov is of particular relevance because similar oppositions have found their way into the mutual stereotypes of Latin Americans and North Americans. In addition to the old European sets of opposites brought along by the white conquerors—British versus Spanish, fair versus dark, Protestant versus Catholic—the assumption of an admixture of inferior Indian blood allowed North Americans a further level of negatively discriminating disassociation.[10] However, this need to disassociate oneself has older roots. Considering that America had been imagined in the minds of the Europeans long before its actual "discovery" makes it easy to see that identity construction was (and still is) a complex process for Americans in all parts of the two continents. It was and is a process in the course of which the triangle of Europe, Anglo-America, and Latin America (with Africa in the background) provided a framework for the production of stereotypical elements in changing combination for a definition of the self and the Other. It should not be overlooked that the desire to reduce mutual alienity stemmed not only from epistemological insecurity, but also from concrete political and economic self-interest.

Thus, Todorov's study describes not only the European discourse of alterity and its disastrous consequences but also the beginnings of a regional variant, the discourse of Latinamericanism. The term is used here in analogy to Edward Said's *Orientalism*. In Said's hotly debated study, the term denotes the scholarly occupation with the Orient, but also, more generally, "a style of thought based upon an ontological and epistemological distinction made between 'the Orient' and [. . .] 'the Occident'" (Said, *Orientalism*, 2). As a third area of reference, Said mentions that of a "corporate institution for dealing with the Orient—dealing with it by making statements about it, authorizing views of it, describing it, by teaching it, settling it, ruling over it: in short, Orientalism as a Western style for dominating, restructuring, and having authority over the Orient" (3), an institution manifesting itself since the late eighteenth century.

Orientalism as a complex of ideas and forms of description legitimizing the exertion of political but also intellectual and cultural power—a complex of ideas and forms of description, however, that is often concomitantly produced by the very exertion of such power—hence can be called a discourse in the Foucauldian sense. It takes only a little nuancing to transfer this definition of an Orientalist alterity discourse and its claim of mediating knowledge, its unacknowledged function to establish the identity of the self and its role as an instrument in the striving for hegemony, to the discourse on Latin America as it was developed in Anglo-America and particularly in the United States. The model is especially useful because it documents the direct connection between the epistemic and the politico-economic appropriation of the Other. It must not be forgotten that alterity discourses form part of such appropriation, even where the Other is not demonized but idealized, for instance in images conforming to the model of the noble savage.

Said's inclusion of scholarship in the complex structure he calls Orientalism has made many social scientists, ethnographers, and historians quite uneasy. Many scholars do not want to admit and accept being part and parcel of alterity discourses, that is, the appropriation of the Other, notably in contexts explicitly marked by power politics. They subscribe to a second form of dealing with the Other, the ideal of a *mediation of the Other* that is free of any power interest, nonreductionist, objective in the sense of adequate to the object studied. Their aim is a gain of insight that neither distorts nor destroys the object. Thus, in 1981 Justin Stagl, in a frequently quoted paper, defended the scholarly description of the Other as an adequate form of approaching the culturally alien. He asks for an intercultural hermeneutics operating between the poles of extreme subjectivism and the scientific claim of exactness and exclusiveness. Such description renders "a highly complex model of a section of reality, integrating objective, subjective, and socio-cultural components"[11] (Stagl, "Beschreibung," 287). However, it is doubtful whether this ideal can be realized, and if such realization would be desirable, notably in the field of intercultural auto- and heterodescription, because Stagl's assumptions of a "fundamental comprehensibility of all human utterances on the basis of a shared humanity"[12] (281) and of the probability that scholarly descriptions are adequate and objective appear to be a relapse into a period when the humanities still believed in an access to reality that was direct and unvarnished by discourse.[13] After all, the observer always changes the observed and can never be neutral. Comprehension that might be possible in the case of otherness in the sense of alterity cannot be reached in the case of alienity. Stagl's hermeneutics remains one of appropriation.

Thus, even studies that claim to guarantee objectivity by assuming a presumably neutral position have to be regarded with skepticism. Take the example of Heinz Göhring's undertaking to "apply a contrastive analysis to certain characteristic value judgments of Latin America and the USA"[14] (84). His richly documented synopsis of earlier sociopsychological studies and of diverse other sources shows, for instance, that in the United States the view still dominates that "human nature is inherently evil but capable of perfection"[15] (87). This notion entails the principle of the moral responsibility of the individual, an optimistic concept, but a heavy burden for those who have failed to live up to it. Latin Americans, on the other hand, regard humans as a mixture of good and evil, whose weaknesses can be contained only partially and whose individual responsibility consequently does not amount to much. Another such pair is the North American concept of work as closely related to virtue versus the Latin American notion of work as an unpleasant, preferably minimized, and in the case of physical labor, even contemptible part of one's lifestyle.[16] Although Göhring relativizes his findings by numerous qualifications and caveats, his closeness to well-known national stereotypes has brought him harsh critiques, notably from the Latin American side, all the more so because most of the sources and terminological patterns he uses come from the United States.[17] Nor does Geert Hofstede's current undertaking to define "national cultural dimensions" by a comprehensive and worldwide statistical study of employee values score sheets—according to which, say, Mexicans tend to feel farther removed from power, less individually independent, more masculine, but also more threatened by and desirous to avoid uncertainty than US Americans[18]—provide an objective picture of what defines a society because it does not consider the respective national or cultural semantics. What it does, though, is to contribute to the description of national identity discourses.

It would be a big mistake to assume that Latin American scholars and intellectuals are immune to reciprocal prejudices—just read, for instance, the Brazilian Darcy Ribeiro's depiction of US American society as an apocalyptic machinery of oppression, as a destructive semi-civilization (*Americas*, 382–88).[19] Nonetheless, and in spite of its susceptibility to the current discourses, mediation remains an indispensable procedure if we try to transcend a view of the Other as either an epistemological wall or an irritating obstacle on the way to a nostrification of reality. Mediation is particularly relevant where it is undertaken with an awareness of its provisionality, and where complementary representations from the point of view of the Other are taken into account in order to initiate a dialogic process. In other words, mediation can be the ideal result of truly intercultural hermeneutics. In its ideal form, however, it remains a utopian goal.

The philosopher Emmanuel Levinas has warned us most insistently of the pitfalls of the stereotyping approach to the Other not only in the context of social contact but also and particularly in scholarly discourse. At the same time, he has pointed out that in experiencing the Other, we experience the diversity of all-that-is. He has thus shown us a third approach to alterity. According to Levinas, Western philosophy in its focus on ontology has reduced the Other to the same and has robbed it of its alterity. However, the Other, notably the other human being, cannot be grasped by the structure of thinking that we use in order to come to grips with reality: "The strangeness of the Other, his irreducibility to the I, to my thoughts and my possessions, is precisely accomplished as [. . .] the calling into question of the same by the other" (*Totality*, 43). He thus indicates a third way of approaching the Other, namely, the *experience of the Other* in his, her, or its alienity. This approach entails regarding the epistemological problem as an enrichment and accepting uncertainty in a positive sense. It provides openness of cognition and may stimulate the development of an ethics that is not oriented toward self-benefit.[20] Foucault's critique of Western discourses and their respective claims of cognitive and social superiority, too, is informed by the hope for the possibility of an opening toward the radical Other.[21] As his quotation from Borges has shown, in his opinion this opening, this transcending of dominant discourses, is to be experienced most likely in (literary) texts.

CULTURAL ALTERITY DISCOURSES (including the discursive approach to alienity) are here regarded as central aspects of intercultural encounters or comparisons. We should not forget, however, that they are closely intertwined with discourses of national identity and alterity. Following Benedict Anderson's well-known definition of nations as "imagined communities," discussing US or Canadian inter-American literature under the aspect of the discourse of Latinamericanism also means that we have to deal with nations as discursive constructs and with the discursive quality of national literatures. If one of the roots of nationalism was the rise of vernacular languages, it is the development of former colonies *not* differentiated by a language of their own into nation states that, according to Anderson, reveals most clearly the discursive nature of nation building. Although in both Americas, the breaking away from the respective mother countries was expedited by the fears and hopes of the property-owning classes, the formation of a plurality of independent nation states stemmed from the original and often quite fortuitous shaping of colonial administrative units, which, "over time, [. . .] developed a firmer reality under the influence of geographic, political and economic factors" (Anderson 54). Among the reasons adduced by Anderson to explain the rapid progress of the imaginative construction of distinctly separate nations (and not just politico-administrative states) in the New World are the difficulties of communication over vast distances; colonial policies favoring the forming of separate economic areas; the fact that promotional chances of the administrative elite were much higher in these self-contained units than in a centrally controlled system; the emergence of Creole populations; the eighteenth-century notions of the influence of climate and "nature" on the character and culture of a given population; and the rise of a regional print culture.[22]

This may explain why the nations of the Western Hemisphere regard themselves as unique entities in spite of the striking similarities of their origins and, in many cases, of the cultural elements they have in common. Nationness as a discourse of cultural identification expresses itself primarily in shared narratives of historical and even mythic (or, rather pervasively, mythified historical) beginnings and definable progress: not only in the United States has the notion of modernity been indispensable for the self-conception of the nation state since the nineteenth century. Thus, nation and narration are interconnected, as the essays in Homi K. Bhabha's essential collection by this title prove over and over again.[23]

Such national narratives predetermine the structure of perception and ensuing behavior by reducing the complexity of the world along certain axes of selection. In terms of systems theory, however, the contingent but excluded other aspects remain a constant reminder of what cannot be systematized. In the case of the discourse of nationness, Bhabha himself has pointed out the inadequacies of any totalizing "pedagogical" national narrative in the face of the complex actuality of the living population:

> We then have a contested conceptual territory where the nation's people must be thought in double-time; the people are the historical "objects" of a nationalist pedagogy, giving the discourse an authority that is based on the pre-given or constituted historical origin *in the past*; the people are also the "subjects" of a process of signification that must erase any prior or originary presence of the nation-people to demonstrate the prodigious, living principles of the people as contemporaneity: as that sign of the *present* through which national life is redeemed and iterated as a reproductive process.[24]

As we have seen, identity is always relational to alterity. Thus, national identity discourses cannot be separated from alterity discourses with intra-

and extranational areas of reference. Thus, when we shift the focus from nationness to trans- and international perception, another aspect comes into view. The doubleness of the "nation-space" (Bhabha, *Location*, 146), the presence of the Other, the heterogeneous, within and not only outside, will necessarily create complexity in the national identity discourses in spite of their linear and unifying thrust. Extranational alterity discourses, on the other hand, tend to be much more reductive. In the case of US narratives on Latin America, there is a characteristic absence of historical development as a subject matter, yet this denial of past change does not lead to an emphasis on the other side of Bhabha's two-sided image of nationness, the complex and contradictory present, but to a reduction of temporality altogether.[25] Since even before the Monroe Doctrine of 1823, Latin America has been both the object of a discourse of North American superiority as well as an object of hegemonic politics for the same length of time. This discourse and the corresponding, discourse-governed politics vis-à-vis the southern neighbors are closely linked to American expansionism, Manifest Destiny thinking, and the winning of the West. But although these events and ideas are integral parts of the historical referentiality of the US American national discourse, they have become dehistoricized or even removed from history when it comes to those whose destinies were so "manifestly" shaped by their US American neighbors. Concomitantly, the discourse on the Latin American Other, even where it contains historical references that are also constitutive of the discourse on the Self,[26] has remained much more constant than even the latter. In part, these stereotypes go back beyond the colonization of America and were formed by European notions of primitivism, of elements of the *leyenda negra*,[27] and of social Darwinist racism. The thinking of superiority results in concepts of the Other as evolutionarily backward and less (historically) dynamic.

Thus, although the shared hemisphere and the sizable number of parallels of colonial and revolutionary history seem to suggest a North American perspective on the Latin American Other in terms of alterity rather than alienity, many US and Canadian texts on the southern neighbors have tended to emphasize elements of strangeness. At the same time, these texts make the Other available for purposes of cultural comparison and thus practice what might be called "nostrification." In this body of literature, typical and stereotypical notions referring to Latin America, that is, important areas of thematic reference comprised by the national and cultural alterity discourse are Indianicity, primitivism, race relations, and *mestizaje*; a dominant femininity of people and landscapes, strangely at odds with glaringly *machistic* tendencies to be noted in gender relations in general; the body and sexuality; external nature; orality; social heterogeneity, class stratification, political chaos, and/or authoritarianism; atemporality and the absence of historical progress; religion, magic, and myth; violence and death. The contrasting North American and European autostereotypes involve homogeneity, linearity, and representability; logocentric order and a culture based on written communication; masculinity and instinctual control; historicity and progress. In particular, these notions inform the US American discourses of national identity and alterity. It is remarkable how many of the points mentioned still echo those articulated in texts by conquistadors and early explorers, but also correspond to those elements of difference constitutive of modern patriarchal discourse. This observation holds true of texts using Latin America as both a negative and a positive foil of the home nation and culture. The basic and common feature of such alterity representation is the reduction of the complexity and dynamics of an alien culture and a concentration on some chosen characteristics from the reservoir of cultural patterns (cf. Welz). What changes, though, is the value attached to these elements.

The discourse of national identity of the United States has undergone a number of changes as the role the country plays in the world and its socioeconomic order at home have developed over the decades. The winning of the West and South; the perfection of a capitalist, competitive consumer economy and its defense against Fascism and Communism; the integration of large numbers of ethnically diverse people and the survival or even reemergence of multicultural diversity in the face of the homogenizing factors of modernity; and finally, the self-positioning in a globalized world are some such general elements that have shaped US America's identity discourse. (The Canadian counterpart shows a number of parallels, although the idea and role of world power and its consequences are missing.) But while we now speak of multiple and overlapping, intersectional *cultural* identities created by race, ethnicity, gender, class, age, religion, and while the discourse of cultural identity has had to accommodate difference to an unheard-of degree, the discourse of *national* identity has remained much more stable.[28] It entails what Sacvan Bercovitch has called the American "consensus" of ideas and values, and a number of cultural elements, such as the dominance of one language (which, of course, is now being challenged). If stereotypes are instruments for the reduction of world complexity, of cognitive dissonance and affective anxiety, they go back a long way. The following passages from a review of a work by a South American historian by Edward Everett, in the *North American Review* of 1821, demonstrate how auto- and hetero-stereotypes (for example, "mild Americans" versus "bloodthirsty Latin Americans") are part of a binary construction of social reality that ignores aspects such as the cruelties of the then quite recent American Revolution.

> The state of society and of life among them [the Latin Americans] forbids our feeling a sympathy with them. How can our thrifty regular merchants sympathize with a people, who send the letter post down the river, on the back of a swimmer? how can our industrious frugal yeomen sympathise [*sic*] with a people that sit on horseback to fish? how can our mild and merciful people, who went through their revolution without shedding a drop of civil blood, sympathize with a people, that are hanging and shooting each other in their streets, with every fluctuation of their ill organized and exasperated factions? It does not yet appear that there exist in any of those provinces the materials and elements of a good national character; of a character to justify our putting our own interests at hazard, by interfering in their present contests. (434)

Unmistakably, Everett denies Latin Americans the qualities necessary for the formation of a nation (or several nations), which, he insists, characterize his American countrymen down to the level of the individual: neither money nor advice "would transform their Pueyrredons and their Artigases, into Adamses or Franklins or their Bolivars into Washingtons" (433–34). Everett sees nations in almost positivistic terms as real structures made up of "elements" and "materials." In the case of the Latin Americans, these are the descendance from Spain or Portugal whose "degeneracy" they have inherited; the shaping influence of the European colonial "tyrannies, political, feudal, and ecclesiastical"; in many parts, the "seductions of [. . .] tropical climates"; the possession of precious metals contributing to a system of exploitation and oppression; and, especially, the racial consistency—"none but the [. . .] climates which produce and retain the European complexity of skin in its various shades, admit of the highest degrees of national character" (434). In particular, it is the mixture of races that leads to degeneracy because it activates the most negative features of each "race": "Spanish bigotry and indolence, [. . .] savage [Indian] barbarity and African stupidity" (438). In sum, Latin America is related to the United States as Asia is to Europe: the land connection, that is, the relative proximity and accessibility, does not prevent the rise of fundamental "national" differences. Although Everett admits that to generalize about people living in a variety of climates, landscapes, and other circumstances will be presumptuous, he does so nonetheless. His generalizing approach permits him to praise Argentine literature and fine arts while sticking to his overall opinion.[29]

Comparatively speaking, the stereotypical components of the national identity discourse, though simpler than of those of the discourse of cultural identity, can yet incorporate much more complexity than those of the corresponding alterity discourse. The winning of the West and not the Mexican-American War has become a central reservoir of US national images. While the idea of "America" has undergone significant changes, that of Latin America has remained remarkably enduring albeit modified by the developments in the political, economic, and military dealings of the United States with the other Americas during more than two centuries or the influx of Latinos/as in recent decades, however much this may have changed and certainly is changing the internal picture in major areas of the country.[30]

To repeat: Identity and alterity are relational terms. The discourse of American national identity developed primarily through comparison with Europe. In that context it was a *postcolonial* discourse, heavily shaped by real or attributed notions of inferiority. Facing a plurality of cultural continuities and a shared part in the project of modernization, it had to emphasize difference in a few chosen areas. Political institutions ranked first among these, with size, nature, and natural resources second. Next, ethnic and religious diversity played a role in the emphasis on difference, although the components of Anglo-Saxonism and Protestantism had to remain dominant for a long time; and finally, cultural achievements growing out of the new conditions, and with these, nativeness, Americanness. With respect to Latin America, a *neocolonial* discourse of superiority had originated and continued to be effective: here, the "Americans" were seen as virtually exclusively Anglo-Saxons (Africans, Native Americans, and other, initially even European, ethnic groups were cut out, although in some cases, like the works of George Lippard, the boundaries became more flexible[31]), Protestants, ingrained democrats, industrious farmers (North American landownership was played down), industrial workers, technological inventors, and prudent merchants. This discourse of identity and the corresponding alterity discourse tended to reduce pan-American similarities to a weak bond of (1) common independence from Europe and (2) common residence in the New World, a bond allowing for a certain measure of paternal feelings of responsibility but primarily meaning the fact of common property, the exploitation of which could naturally only be left to the older and more advanced member of the pan-American "family."

Otherwise, sameness was redefined as difference. American landscape compared favorably to that of Europe because of its sublime features, but the same or similar features turned into something hostile and an obstacle to progress south of the border. In the construction of Latin America, there was either too little or too much vegetation, the mountains were too high, the climate too hot, and so forth. Liberty appeared as license, a series of endless revolutions and a penchant for renewed tyranny. Multiethnicity was not an enriching factor, but a cause of degeneration into primitivism, in particular because the Iberian populations were still seen in accordance with the Northern European and especially the English versions of the *leyenda negra*. The stereotypes used by Everett have to be supplemented by sexual amorality, *machismo* as the dominant principle in gender relations, immaturity and hence irrationality as a general feature. In other words, difference and diversity—which were increasingly seen as a potential for growth and progress in the United States, as long as African Americans and Native Americans or, on another level, women were kept in their respective places—appeared as the hotbed of chaos and anomie in Latin America. Such chaos was described as a pervasive and hence, paradoxically, homogenizing factor: all of Latin America was basically the same and could be dealt with in the same manner. Similarly, movement through time did not bring any radical change; Latin American societies often appeared to be in turmoil, but seemed to remain static, frozen in time, nonetheless. Atemporality, in particular, was an aspect linking the southern continent with the world of the so-called primitives. Thus, if the discourse of national identity grew from a corresponding discourse of alterity when Europe was at issue, the Latin American complement was more a discourse of *alienity*. Frederick B. Pike's comprehensive study *The United States and Latin America: Myths and Stereotypes of Civilization and Nature* (1992) confirms the stability of stereotypical images of self and Other and in turn exemplifies a widespread belief in stereotypes.

Beyond what has been said thus far, a few structural features of the discourse of Latinamericanism can be pointed out (they show great similarities and share a long tradition with the European discourse on Latin America):

1. Like all discourses of alterity, Latinamericanism is based on a strict division of subject and object. As Jacques Derrida has reminded us, such binary thinking always implies a hierarchy. Latinamericanism is a discourse of superiority based particularly on assumptions of racial or, more generally, ethnic difference. Though the object position was first forced upon the Native population of the Americas, soon enough imported Africans, immigrants of "color" (a term that, in the nineteenth century, included many Europeans) and, eventually, people of mixed descent were included in the group of people considered inferior because of supposed racially inherited properties.

2. Again in line with other discourses of alterity, Latinamericanism tends to manifest itself not as what it is, namely a social construction of reality created by "communities of interpretation" (Said, *Covering*, 45), but as describing the natural order and hierarchy of things. For this purpose, it em-

ploys chains of binary analogies like those employed by Sepúlveda, quoted earlier. Although each of these binarisms may open up a semantic field of its own, on the paradigmatic level they are frequently used as mutual substitutes. The alterity pole is therefore generally associated with a set of differences based on evolutionary or God-given backwardness, meaning closeness to nature, the animal kingdom, the irrational, even the material.

3. The discourse of Latin American alterity is remarkably comprehensive in that it applies to all of Latin America, notwithstanding its enormous size and variety. That is, Latin America is first seen as an amorphous mass, not as one continent and part of another organized in nation states with distinct sociocultural structures. In its essence it has also remained remarkably stable (albeit modified to accommodate current developments) in spite of the political and intellectual changes from the period of so-called discovery through Enlightenment humanitarianism and egalitarianism, romantic exoticism, nineteenth-century evolutionism, and the intellectual phases of the twentieth century, from the primitivism of the modernist period to the decentering of subject positions in the age of postmodernism and postcolonialism. The transformation of US society by the massive influx of Latin American immigrants has initially done hardly more than extend the geographical and social range of where Latinamericanism is applied. Change is underway, particularly in urban areas, and the pressure to acquire Spanish as a second language is growing. In many circles, however, the traditional discourse is still strong.

4. Latinamericanism focuses not only on cultural differences, cultural distance, as it were, but also on the spatially remote, and in this sense alien, distance playing a role in perception and interpretation. The geographical properties of certain areas come into play. But it also comprises what is temporally distant, both in the sense of historical narratives of, say, the time of the conquest and, more important, in the sense of a supposed or imagined "backwardness" of the cultural group under inspection. Here, the blending of pro- or, more often, anti-Mediterranean and pro- or anti-indigenous notions and emotions in the popular mind plays a major role, but similar verdicts can be found in much traditional ethnology adhering to an evolutionary model of cultural classification.

5. Latinamericanism manifests itself most clearly in narrative patterns involving the conquest, exploration, penetration, exploitation, and so on, of the Latin American Other by some North American protagonist. In an essay on Latinamericanism as a scholarly occupation, Alberto Moreiras calls Latin America an "epistemic object of desire" ("Restitution and Appropriation," 14), but it has been an object of North American desire in more pragmatic ways since at least the eighteenth century. As an object of desire, Latin

America means a continent plus part of another to be dominated by US political and military power and to be economically exploited—in a word, an object of imperialism and neocolonialism. Although this is too crude a picture to describe the actual interaction of power and counter-power, as Anthony Giddens has shown, it serves to explain the genderized or, more specifically, feminized notion of Latin America one finds in many literary and other US texts dealing with the neighbors to the south.

6. Because many of the texts I am going to discuss refer directly to the construction of gender and are representations of that other dominant discourse defining identity and alterity, I want to point out that both discourses interact and frequently seem to support each other. Traditional gender constructions, such as the supposed physical, rational, technical, and dynamic superiority of men and the corresponding supposed inferiority, irrationality, naturalness, and passivity of women, are often superimposed on the constructions of the ethnic Other.[32] Feminizing descriptions have been applied, for instance, to local business or political collaborators of North American companies in those parts of the world. On the other hand, although Latin American, notably Mexican, *machismo* was long seen as merely operatic, the rise of the drug kings and their extremely brutal wars has given the *macho* a different role in the North American mind and thus modified the gender stereotypes at least with respect to some parts of the south. In any case, the *macho* has always been considered as governed by his passions and thereby still inferior to his US or Canadian male counterparts.[33]

7. The interaction of the discourses on gender and alterity has made for a stabilization of both. The changes in the intellectual perception of gender that inform the public debate in postindustrial societies are only partially or occasionally reflected in representations of ethnic alterity, and vice versa. Because the gendered construction of reality seems to be more fundamental, anthropologically speaking, than even the ethnic binarism, the latter remains tied to the former. In the crudest version of such thinking, Latin Americans, like other exotic people, are regarded as belonging to the sphere of the feminine to be conquered and controlled. Nonetheless, it is important to remember that the two identity-alterity discourses are not identical, and that both may inform a given literary text in a sometimes parallel, but often also an ambiguous, complexity-generating fashion.

8. Finally, both alterity discourses can be linked to Freud's notion of the uncanny, the Other in ourselves, often associated with the feminine, psychoanalytically described—notably by Julia Kristeva—as that which we separate off, reject, repress, or project (Kristeva, *Strangers*; cf. Chapter 7 in this volume). Our defense mechanisms protect our ego against anything alien threatening its integrity and biopsychological continuity. In this sense,

the exotic Other, here Latin America, can be seen as the dark underside of the Eurocentric cultural imaginary; it is the realm of fears and desires. This means that a description of the Latin American Other is always also a description of the North American self.

As the last observations have made clear, the concept of alterity discourses has to be supplemented by that of the *cultural imaginary*. This term, which is enjoying great popularity, is often situated at the border of social discourses and the world of public fantasies. Thus, in Graham Dawson's definition, the cultural imaginary is seen as "those vast networks of interlinking discursive themes, images, motifs and narrative forms that are publicly available within a culture at any one time, and articulate its psychic and social dimensions." Cultural imaginaries "furnish public forms which both organize knowledge of the social world and give shape to fantasies within the apparently 'internal' domain of psychic life" (Dawson 48). If the term is to supplement and not to replace that of the cultural discourse, however, because the latter largely ignores the affective side of intercultural contact, its field of reference should be restricted to the world of "imagined meanings striving to find articulation [. . .] and at the same time the fund of images, affects, and longings stimulating [. . .] the individual imaginary."[34] If a cultural discourse regulates what can be thought and said, the cultural imaginary circumscribes what can be felt and imagined. This division is heuristic, of course.

LITERATURE, LIKE OTHER KINDS of artistic representation, can be informed by an assortment of irreconcilable wishes that govern our dealings with the Other: first, to be better able to delineate the self by way of contrasting it with the Other and by having one's identity thus hold its own; second, to bring that Other close to oneself, that is, to appropriate or "nostrify" it; and third, to maintain it in its specificity and alienity, to experience it as such. Exoticism can be seen at play in every variant. Literary art will usually reflect current discourses; it can inscribe itself into them. But it may also question such discourses and make us aware of their role in cognition in the first place.[35] This holds true for the discourse of alterity as well. Art can be particularly useful where, on the one hand, it exposes the discursive nexus between insight, interest, and the exertion of power and where it explores potential new ways of dealing with alterity, on the other. In particular, art is the best and perhaps only method of allowing us to experience the Other as Other in the sense of the third wish.[36] It is literary art, in particular, that has the potential of creating open models of reality by the convention of fictionality, by the use of images and analogies, by its rule-breaking use of language, and by joining what is irreconcilable according to binary logic. Its representation of reality need not aim at coming to grips, at controlling its field of reference, but may evoke the latter's strangeness without erasing it.[37] If, as Niklas Luhmann has phrased it, "[m]eaning serves the conception and reduction of world complexity and only in this manner serves to orientate experience and action,"[38] this must be true of literature and other art forms, too. But art may be superior to other ways of producing meaning in also doing justice to another assertion by Luhmann: "Meaning is a selection *from* other possibilities and hence at the same time a reference *to* other possibilities."[39] Art has the power to keep the nonselected elements of reality present besides those that are foregrounded. By its suggestiveness and ambiguity, it makes them accessible to experience to a degree that is unmatched by other forms of representation. In addition, the use of paradox, the contiguity of what is seemingly mutually exclusive, may expose in the nonsensical the dependence of meaning on consensus and system and thus question it. If the artist is willing and able, art can make the Other come closer and yet make its incommensurable alienity visible.

Indeed, art may create a degree of alienity not commonly found in empirical intercultural encounters. Borges's Chinese encyclopedia is a case in point. After Foucault referred to it, scores of scholars invaded the *sanctum sanctorum* of Asian studies, for instance the library of the Fairbank Center for Chinese Studies at Harvard, in order to find Borges's source as well as information on Chinese encyclopedias in general.[40] To no avail, but much to the chagrin of the colleagues from sinology who found themselves called upon to defend the sanity of Chinese systems of knowledge. For all we know, Borges's list is a fiction (and presumably Foucault recognized it as such). Literature may not only create images of the Other ranging from the almost familiar to the fundamentally alien, but also demonstrate ways of dealing with alterity.

Let us look at an example in nineteenth-century American literature. In 1855, Herman Melville published his famous story "Benito Cereno." It reports the encounter of the American ship captain Amasa Delano with a Spanish slave ship under the command of a Captain Benito Cereno off the coast of Chile in the year 1799. Cereno's ship is in a deplorable condition, the crew appears decimated, and some of the African slaves are enjoying remarkable liberties. Cereno solicits the American's assistance, but only when he follows the latter by jumping after him into his boat does it dawn upon Delano that there has been a slave mutiny, that the Spanish ship is in the hands of the blacks who have forced Cereno and the surviving white sailors to act in a masquerade. Captain Delano and his crew recapture the other ship for the white owners and take all to Lima, where the black leader Babo is executed and where Cereno, a broken man, soon dies in a monastery.

"Benito Cereno" is an adventure story based on a historical incident, but transformed by Melville into a formidable text about the uncertain moral foundations of power exertion (shouldn't Delano have helped the slaves rather than the slave owners?), about the encounter with the Other and the problem of understanding it, and about the limits of epistemological endeavor. Against the background of the conflict between the American North and South over the issue of slavery, the complex developments in the Caribbean, and the expansionist tendencies of at least part of the American political elite concerning Mexico and Central America as well as Canada, Melville draws a picture of the political and socioethical confusions existing among his compatriots and of their participation in a racist and a regional alterity discourse. The story is exemplary in persistently but indirectly referring to what is going on in the author's own country and to its position vis-à-vis the rest of the world, notably Latin America.[41] In the situation of crisis with which he is suddenly confronted, Captain Delano, from whose naive perspective the action is mainly told, decides in favor of what to him is less alien, that is, the Spanish, although he will often react to them, too, with consternation and a lack of understanding. The blacks, in their turn, elicit a reaction of at first positive, later on rather negative stereotypes, but Delano's idea of the Spanish American whites is also riddled with discursive clichés notably concerning Catholicism and monarchy. Delano himself stays within the range of the US American autostereotype: he behaves righteously (in his opinion), pragmatically, and efficiently.[42]

At the same time, Melville succeeds in presenting the insufficiency of such ways of looking at reality: the alien remains incomprehensible; neither Cereno nor Babo can ever be fully understood, and reality reveals itself as epistemologically open and far too complex for any reductionist approach. Again and again the symbolic colors black and white blend into indefinable gray,[43] and Delano is incapable of deciphering the story's central symbol, that is, of undoing the enigmatic knot that is thrown to him by a Spanish sailor. Neither can the readers of this much-interpreted story that is a demonstration of the way we are forced by our epistemological and ethical inadequacies either to come to foregone conclusions or to bear and accept the inscrutablity of the Other's reality as it is suggested by the text.

Melville's story achieves what may be desired of a literary work in this context. The author depicts the stereotyping appropriation of the Other and, in the shape of historical and geographical details, suggests which aspects might be—prematurely—taken as neutral, scientific information about the Other. But he also makes clear that each of these possible approaches, including their critically self-questioning metalevels, is prestructured by the reality concept, the discursive order of knowledge of one's own period and culture. And he makes us experience the ineradicable alienity of the Other, which cannot be done away with even by a plurality of approaches (as suggested by the multiple points of view used in the story), by making the disturbing openness of his text symbolize the Other in its "factual reality."

BY SYMBOLICALLY HIGHLIGHTING THE epistemological problems raised by the encounter with the Other, Melville's story questions the then current discourses on Latin America, slavery, colonialism, and so forth to an unheard-of degree, even while it also and inevitably belongs to the discursive field of its time. The experience of the Other conveyed by this text is powerful, almost overwhelming. Most fictional texts on Latin America are much less self-questioning and many fit squarely in the discursive mainstream. In this sense, they follow the appropriatory approach to the Other. But often this is done with a sense of what Stagl has called mediation, that is, with the aim to provide a "realistic" picture of the world they represent. It may not be immediately plausible that such appropriation of the Other by subjecting it to one's own culture's simplifying discourse on Latin America is reprehensible. Aren't poverty or a series of revolutions in Latin America facts—and what else should be textualized if we leave out such phenomena? When we reflect upon the way the Other can be made visible, upon the informative side of dealing with subjects from alien cultures, we find it easier to show our unease than to articulate our desiderata. Literature about the Other, in particular, raises the question of the adequacy of the representation of physical and social reality in fiction, of the kind and degree of adequate referentiality. The bothersome problem of the relation of art and life that has occupied thinkers from Aristotle to Bakhtin, and of which we have grown weary in the debates on realism of the last centuries, turns out to be impossible to avoid when we are concerned with alien cultures.

When we do this, we have to admit that we are not concerned with reality per se, but with models of reality—cultural, scientific, everyday pragmatic, ethical, religious, aesthetic, and so on—models that we may well be aware of, in contrast to the often unconsciously used discourses they are based on or connected with. We should also remember that literature primarily refers to other models of reality, that it negotiates prestructured rather than raw reality.[44] Such admission seems easier for literary scholars than for representatives of other disciplines. The questions that are often asked in the context of modern art—namely if art itself also creates reality, and if it can thus construct primary models of reality—are not of primary importance in dealing with texts like those under consideration here. What is immediately relevant is the relationship of literary reality models to the Other they are based on, because this aspect informs our criteria of evaluation. These refer to not only the adequacy of, by some definition, realist or symbolist (or in other ways defamiliarizing) strategies of representation in general, but quite specifically the adequacy with regard to the "reality" of a particular cultural area.

Wherever a mediating, descriptive approach to the Other is desired, we find ourselves on the hotly debated ground of realism. There is realism as a period in literary history whose chief tenets were best formulated in American literature by William Dean Howells. In his *Criticism and Fiction* (1891), Howells assumes that reality is simply given and similar in its essential features at least as far as human motivation is concerned. It can be adequately perceived, and it can also be adequately represented if the writer remains true to experience, if he or she employs precision and richness of descriptive details, a proper proportion of the characters, plot elements, and things represented. But what looks like a simple set of criteria in the context of an epoch much interested in a social reality no longer buffered by a transcendental authority may well look questionable when we focus on inner, psychological reality as the modernists did, or on the textual constructedness of any view of reality as poststructuralist theory and postmodern practice have taught us over and over again. When such changes of the concept of reality and its representation are brought to bear on representations of the cultural Other, the question of adequacy often gains an ethical dimension: to misrepresent the Other may be not only an aesthetic weakness but an injustice done to people who have here taken the place of the underprivileged as the focus of so much nineteenth-century realist and naturalist fiction. But, as I will show in a later chapter, deliberately nonrealist writing may sometimes be the very way of mediating the Other, particularly where it is to retain some of its strangeness.

The questions of realism in theory and practice, the philosophical concepts informing notions of reality and of adequate literary approaches notably by means of fiction as a semantic or pragmatic category, have been briefly and comprehensively presented by Darío Villanueva in his *Theories of Literary Realism*, a study that stands out inasmuch as it uses a vast array of international scholarly sources.[45] Villanueva concludes by arguing in favor of a pragmatic approach, that is, by focusing on the readers' response to certain textual stimuli as realistic. Clearly, such response depends not only on individual notions of the real but on communities of consensus about what constitutes reality and its adequate representation. Once again we are in some version of the hermeneutic circle.

In the case of literary texts dealing with Latin America, we will have to decide whether adequacy can be approached by familiarizing us with the Other, or the reverse. But even where a Howellsian fidelity to experience is aimed at, there will be competing subjects of experience—the author, narrator, focalizer, or some other character(s)—and competing emphases as far as the represented objects are concerned: representative members of the population, current social conditions, material conditions, or else background details like landscapes, biology, material culture, and so forth. After all, that the social sphere should take precedence over other themes may be considered adequate only according to one, namely the Western, model of reality (Matthes 1988), a model that may be only partially applicable to Latin America. Thus, we would have to take into consideration not only this model, but also the possibility of others that may be dominating in the other culture referred to. Other aspects to be considered concern the mutual influence of cultures, but in particular the role played by North American cultural models in Latin America, the differences between the nations of Latin America, and finally the cultural and ethnic diversity of all of its countries and societies. And there exists a hierarchy of realism markers, it seems. That the wealth of anthropological and nature-descriptive details in a novel such as James Wylie's *The Sign of Dawn* (whatever their measure of verifiable correctness may be), in combination with the improbabilities of (political utopian) plot and characterization, creates the very opposite of an impression of adequate reality representation is revealing with respect to the importance we—we?—may attribute to such textual elements and the selection of which they are composed (cf. Chapter 8 in this volume). Due to the lack of intercultural studies on reader response, we have no way of deciding if such evaluation applies only to specific groups of readers.

We are left then with a confusing and exciting realization. Literature, and the fictional and other texts discussed in this study bear witness to this, is the most fertile way of approaching the cultural Other. It is beset by the discourses it is part of and which it also continues. Its "realist" adequacy depends on often only partly compatible models and expectations applied by authors and readers alike. It greatest achievement, however, I think, is its capacity to rupture discursive constraints, to transcend the limits of realism by exposing those areas of meaning escaping the hermeneutic fusion, and to make us experience albeit not really understand the Other in its epistemological, ethical, and aesthetic openness. Literature is capable of providing deeper insights into our situation in the world without lessening our wonder that such wealth of thingness, symbolic orders, cultural imaginaries, difference and transdifference, inter- and intrapersonal strangeness exists.

# PART TWO

# [3]

## FOUNDATIONAL NARRATIVES: SOME VERSIONS OF COLUMBUS

I said, Shall we begin at the beginning?
Yes, he said, I've always loved beginnings.
Men do, I replied. No one knows if they will ever get over this.
—Grace Paley, "The Story Hearer" (*Later the Same Day*, 133)

THE DISCOURSE OF LATINAMERICANISM developed in the early nineteenth century, after the United States had won its independence, and after many parts of Latin America had also shed the colonial yoke and begun to form a number of republics, albeit with shifting boundaries and not at all following Bolívar's concept of a great Spanish American union. But the roots of this discourse lie in the colonial past. Some of its principal components had been connected with the idea of the tropical south for centuries: the abundance of nature in a temperate climate, the luxuriant plant life that promised to be a source for food production, the idea of richer occurrences of gold and gemstones than anywhere else, and for some, the notion that people there had been shaped by the place they inhabited and that had made them lazy, passive, docile, and intellectually underequipped, like animals of burden and hence ideal slaves or workers. In his monumental study *The Tropics of Empire: Why Columbus Sailed South*, Nicolás Wey Gómez has explored the impact these views had on Columbus's project and its realization during his four voyages to the Caribbean and northern South America, that is, why he intentionally sailed not only west but south. And Wey Gómez points out that Columbus was also influenced by the opponents of this idea who held the view that the south was intolerably hot and threatening, home only of monstrous and barbarous occupants. The southern Other as a complex of what Terry Goldie has called "fear and temptation" has left its traces in geopolitics from Columbus to the present day. For Columbus, these contradictions were welcome because they allowed him to pursue the enslavement of the indigenous population. Others, like Bartolomé de Las Casas, argued that

> if experience had shown that nature was even more "perfect" in the American tropics than anywhere else on the globe—not excepting Mediterranean Europe—why should Indians be treated as Europe's "natural" subordinates? Indeed, it is largely Las Casas's attack on the contradiction attendant to Columbian geopolitics that lends significance to his monumental *Historia de las Indias*, undoubtedly the most conscientious and fearless treatment ever written of early modern Europe's devastation of the tropics. (Wey Gómez 56)

Although such ideas of the south and its people "were conceptually significant to emerging local elites who began to imagine themselves politically autonomous from the Old World" (56), their very contradictoriness helped shape a northern discourse that saw the south as inferior and desirable.

> To the extent that five hundred years after Columbus's death we continue to wrestle with the divide between the "developed" nations of the north and the "developing" nations of the south, we too are heirs to an intellectual tradition whose ancient notions of place paved the way for recent colonialism. (57)

Columbus and the Age of Discovery, then, can be seen as the beginning of a discursive construction of the south that will develop into Latinamericanism. However, Columbus is also the mythic figure standing at the beginning of the respective discourses of identity in both North and Latin America. The textual formation of this figure over the centuries varied widely in both parts of the Americas, as it did elsewhere. I cannot deal with Latin American texts using the Columbus material. Suffice it to say that they reflect the ambivalence connected with the explorer just as much as the North American texts. He, and he alone, embodies the imaginative potential of both Americas: the south as a romantic, soon to be corrupted exotic Other, and the north as a world of success soon to be de-romanticized. Although US culture was instrumental in idealizing Columbus and thus made it possible to appropriate him as a founding figure of what was to become the United States, there were opposing voices in the tradition of the Black Legend linking him with everything that was or went wrong in the south: Catholicism, the exploitation or genocide of the Native population, and the destruction of nature. It is useful, therefore, to take Columbus as the starting point of a diverging discursive development. His gradual idealization and heroization turned him into an important element of the US American identity discourse. This made it necessary to heap all the blame for what was seen as negative in the south on his companions and the conquistadors following him, on the racial mixture soon taking place, and on the religion forced upon the indigenous population. Sometimes, as in Joel Barlow, Native civilizations appear as a positive counter-model, while for others like

William H. Prescott, they have their share in the negative side of Latin American history.

For most people, at least for those parts of mankind strongly affected by the Western tradition, the (re)discovery of the New World by Christopher Columbus counts among the most important historical events.[1] This holds true whether we define *event* in narratological terms as the process of change between two contrasting states along a temporal axis or, according to information theory, as that change which is considered significant or informationally rich by a given person or group of persons (participants, descendants, readers, and so on). The event of the discovery or the individual events connected with it are part of any number of possible narratives with varying degrees of significance (again depending on the persons concerned) and temporal or configurational extension. The Spanish historian Francisco López de Gómara, secretary and private chaplain of Hernán Cortés, called it "[t]he greatest event in world history, excepting the birth and death of Christ" (qtd. in Block 101), but others, notably around the time of the quincentennial in 1992, pointed out its disastrous consequences. It forms the subject of a central and foundational inter-American story because the way the different countries and cultures of the Americas have dealt with it reflects on their notion of the New World. Thus, although in many versions of this story, Central and South America do not even get much attention and North America remains beyond the horizon, it has to be addressed in the context of this study.

Obviously, the so-called discovery forms the climax of Columbus's own life story. In the (hi)story of Spain in the fifteenth and sixteenth centuries, it is part of a whole complex of changes that established the country as the Catholic superpower for a long time afterwards. The conquest of the Muslim kingdom of Granada, the expulsion of the Jews, and the rise of the Inquisition are other notable components of this process. According to what Alfred W. Crosby has called the "bardic version of the Columbian voyages and their consequences" (1), the event (including the Columbian voyages as a whole) is a decisive step in the providentially ordained rise of the West, particularly of North America and its political, economic, and cultural system, as it was envisioned in the Rising Glory poetry of the American Revolutionary period and outlined in the historiographic writings of William H. Prescott, George Bancroft, Francis Parkman, or other American historians of the nineteenth century, and, for that matter, in many literary works, once again especially those by North American authors—of which more will be said in this and a later chapter. The bardic version persists in the twentieth century in a work such as Samuel Eliot Morison's biography *Admiral of the Ocean Sea: A Life of Christopher Columbus.*

According to Crosby, historians such as Prescott, Parkman, or Morison

> all liked to approach history through biography; they chose sides and were transparently loyal to their heroes. For all three men, the stuff of history was almost always documents, preferably letters, diaries, and memoirs, and not statistics. Seldom did they turn for help to economics, archaeology, biology or any of the sciences. (3)

But by examining such sources of information—and Crosby's study neatly sums up the results—one arrives at another series of narratives putting the central event in a different light. The political narrative tells us the story not only of the growth of democratic institutions but also of the ascendancy of Europe and, later, of North America over the rest of the world. The economic story is one of the rise of capitalism, which reduced most parts of the globe to providers of raw materials and human labor (this includes more than 10 million black slaves brought to the Americas). This story then leads up to the Industrial Revolution, which was at least prepared for by the discoveries and their aftermath. The nutritional narrative sees Columbus as "the greatest benefactor of all time because by bringing the agricultures of the Old and New Worlds into contact, he added many useful plants to each" (Crosby 17; see also Mann, *1493*) and made the transformation of vast portions of North and South America into meat-producing areas possible. The complementary ecological narrative, though, would come up with an entirely different evaluation. But it is the demographic story that contains the most controversial information. Due largely to the economic, territorial, nutritional, and other opportunities offered by the various regions of the New World, "the number of Caucasians on earth increased 5.4 times between 1750 and 1930, Asians only 2.3 times, and black Africans and Afro-Americans less than two times" (Crosby 23). The American Indian population dropped from a high at the Age of Discovery of (according to different models of estimation) anywhere between 30 and 100 million to a nadir of 4.5 million.[2] One has to assume a very Eurocentric position in order to avoid realizing that the demographic story presents what was "surely the greatest tragedy in the history of the human species" (25).

Columbus's voyages are facts verifiable by documentary and, to a limited extent, by material or archaeological evidence.[3] Many of their consequences have been proven by a variety of scientific methods. To achieve the status of (macro- or micro-) events, though, the facts of the voyages have to be placed into narrative contexts.[4] By now, the narrative quality of historiography (as opposed to history-writing as the accumulation of annals or the establishment of structural patterns) has once again come to be so widely accepted that the claims made for narrative history by scholars such as R. G. Collingwood or Arthur C. Danto look modest enough.[5] That historians follow aesthetic patterns of representation resembling those of literature, and, indeed, fictionalize history, has been demonstrated most impressively by Hayden White, who has discovered the fictional element of history-writing in the ideologically motivated establishment of order and coherence according to preestablished patterns.[6] But later narratological theorists have moved even beyond this position and see narrative as a universal procedure of truth finding, sense making, and the processing, storage, and retrieval of knowledge. The philosopher David Carr has taken up Kenneth Burke's argument that human experience and reality perception are narratively structured. He goes beyond Burke by claiming that this is true not only of the temporal experience of individuals but also of groups, whose history is therefore an essential part of the formation of the community. Thus, narrative not only enters at the level of the textual processing of reality data, but is an integral part of the individual's and the group's way of living and acting. Obviously, Carr cannot say what reality per se is like, but his view of culturally experienced reality as "configured and reflexively structured, as if by a storyteller unfolding a tale,"[7] makes the boundaries between historical reality and narrative text as permeable as those between historiography and fiction.

The inflated use of the concept of narrativity creates a number of theoretical and methodological problems that cannot be dealt with here.[8] One cannot help noticing, for instance, that the nonliterary concepts imply a much heavier emphasis on goal orientation and the causal linking of events than do contemporary notions of good fiction. Indeed, one may wonder if the narrative elements in everyday experience of reality do not evince a remarkable similarity to the patterns of popular literature, and one may wonder, too, about the possibility of a mutual reinforcement of such patterns. In any case, it should be noticed that the formation of narratives in any context is determined by the value systems applied in each case. As can be seen in the case of the Columbian voyages, it is not the higher or lower degree of scientifically verifiable factuality that turns facts into events and makes events part of a certain story, but the systems of sense making and evaluation informing this process. The social construction of reality, the discourses (in the Foucauldian sense) of institutions, nations, or periods, and the aesthetics of a given culture govern the selection and hierarchization of the story and its elements; the temporal, causal, emotional, or other organization of events and existents; the communicational and hierarchical arrangements between teller, subject, and audience, including the narrative point of view; the question of closure versus open ending; and so forth. Changes in the ideological (in the most general sense) and cultural system, such as the feminists' questioning of male predilection for linearity and for always going back to the beginning or the postmodern doubts in goal-oriented *grands récits*,[9] affect the types of narrative used in certain fields. And, certainly, the contemporary awareness of the provisional nature of any narrative or other effort at finding or positing meaning and order makes for a tendency toward ironic metanarratives or satiric, closure-denying forms of emplotment even outside of fiction in the ordinary sense.[10] This is true of the story of the Columbian voyages as well.

As we have already seen, this story can be shown to form a part of a variety of macro-stories depending on the line of argument. Consequently, the story can also be classified as belonging to several basic plot patterns: that of tragedy, when we think primarily of Columbus's personal disasters; that of romance, when we focus on the successful overcoming of formidable obstacles; that of the epic, when we leave the level of the individual and place the story in the context of the rise of the West or the opening of new nutritional sources; and, once again, that of tragedy, when we see the event as a decisive factor in the destruction of peoples, cultures, and ecological systems. But the very inconclusiveness of any attempt at definitive evaluation will provoke ironic, self-reflexive versions as well.

The fact that we know much more about Columbus and what followed from his activities than earlier historians did, and that we have gathered such information not only from textual sources but also from scientific investigation does not diminish this inconclusiveness, not only because of remaining gaps or because informational increase cannot do away with the evaluative problems indicated earlier, but also because scientific referentiality per se has come to be seen as determined by language.[11] Here, again, the problem of the truth value of a given statement will take us in the direction of self-reflexive narration. This applies both to historiography and to historical fiction. But given the former's usual claim of deriving its authority from the revelation of the true order of reality, the imaginative freedom of the historical novelist may enable him or her to expose the ideological premises and hence the fictional components of scholarly history-writing.[12] The postmodern historical novel will tend to be not only metafictional but also metahistoriographic. It will subvert the claim made with respect to the traditional historical novel of the school of Walter Scott, as Georg Lukács defines it, that it uncovers the true essence of historical change and the teleological inevitability of the process. Examples of this will be discussed in Chapter 10. But early Columbus narratives also deserve our interest because they contributed significantly to the discourse of national identity (and hence also of alterity) in the early decades of the United States. In all the textual analyses to follow, I am not concerned with the question whether any details of the image of Columbus developed by the author are true according to our level of knowledge, if they conform to Columbus's own testimonies or those of others, but with the emerging, discursively organized image as such.[13]

IN THE INTRODUCTION TO his *Lectures on the Philosophy of History*, Hegel comments on the New World.[14] He contrasts a prosperous, dynamic, individualistic, Protestant North America (meaning the United States) with a South America characterized by violence, autocratic rule, and a backward Catholicism. But he restricts his historical comments to noting that South America was conquered—which resulted in quelling all life energy in the surviving Native population, a passivity later adopted by the Creoles; this is Hegel's version of Buffon's theory of the inferiority of American life forms—while the North was settled, and as a settlers' community it provided ample incentives for enterprise and development. However, for Hegel, America (meaning the North) was the country of the future and thus not yet interesting for a philosophy of history. He therefore proceeds to focus his attention exclusively on the Old World, meaning Eurasia from China to Western Europe.

Though many US citizens of Hegel's period would have shared his views of the respective character of the Americas, many intellectuals of the Early Republic objected to the idea of their country as lacking history: Where else, if not in a common past, could one find a national identity? This, at least, was the concept they had learned from the existing and the emerging European nation states. Many authors of the late eighteenth and early nineteenth centuries tried to refute European notions of an American a-historicity by writing narratives of the American past as well as by envisioning versions of an American future. Because the indigenous peoples were considered either as not being part of history or as doomed to vanish, most writers looked for beginnings in the post-contact past. Nothing could better serve the purpose of providing historical depth and identity-founding narratives than Columbus and the history of discovery and conquest.

The Hegelian triangle of Europe, South America, and North America opened three immediate approaches to and appropriations of Columbus, the history of contact and of conquest. They could be supplemented by a pan-American one (barely touched upon by Hegel), a future-oriented view and a global perspective that was as yet hardly discernible but would have found a place in any teleological philosophy of history, the most prominent version of which Hegel's thinking remains to this day. The North American authors who functionalized the explorer for literary and historiographic purposes selected from among these approaches and provide instructive examples of their country's struggle for national self-definition. Columbus was made the principal agent or at least main witness of precisely the *North*

American part of hemispheric history. He who, after all, primarily belongs in the context of European and, after that, Latin American history, was removed from those contexts with the argument that it was only in North America (meaning the Anglophone parts of the continent and, later, specifically the United States) where his achievement had come to its full fruition, that it was only there where the course of world history would reach its climax and fulfillment, a course that had taken a decisive turn by his deed. Over and over again, and in contrast to his Spanish and Latin American contemporaries and successors, Columbus is regarded as responsible for the key aspects of North American development adumbrated by Hegel: freedom, individualism, (agrarian) colonization, and industrialization.

This separation of North America and Latin America has come under attack. In *Puritan Conquistadors: Iberianizing the Atlantic, 1550–1700*, Jorge Cañizares-Esguerra shows that the identification of the United States and Canada as central nations of the West and the countries of Latin America as part of the Third World ignores similarities in development from the colonial period through modernity. Concerning the topic of the present chapter, the beginnings, Cañizares-Esguerra demonstrates "that British Protestants and Spanish Catholics deployed similar religious discourses to explain and justify conquest and colonization: a biblically sanctioned interpretation of expansion, part of a long-standing Christian tradition of holy violence aimed at demonic enemies within and without" (9). The Amerindians were portrayed as followers of Satan who had taken over the Americas a long time ago (12). But these attributions changed over time:

> Curiously, once the friars embraced the natives as the ideal pliable clay with which to build the Church of the millennium, and once the friars began to vie with the settlers for control of the bodies (not the souls) of the natives, the Franciscans became more prone to see the wiles of Satan in the New World manifested in the actions of [. . .] the lay settlers. [. . .] Bartolomé de las Casas [. . .] tirelessly argued that the conquistadors were demons and the colonial regime was hell. [. . . T]he main satanic enemy of both the Iberians and the English in the New World was a moving target, constantly shifting according to the party involved and the circumstances. (20)

For the Spanish, the satanic enemy now appeared in the shape of religious apostates, witches, and other offenders, and of English pirates, while English Protestants first saw Satan in the Spanish and only later in the Natives. "The narrative of the Spanish conquest as a demonic butchery was paradoxically kept firmly in mind as Puritans struggled to justify in writing their own barbarous acts against their newfound demonic enemies" (28), the Amerindians. However, this misconception was the root of later and increasingly crass distinctions made in North America between the progressive self and the backward, violent, church-governed and racially mixed southern Other.

Thus, it comes as no surprise that the narrative image construction did not start out too well for Columbus in British America.[15] When Cotton Mather was at work on his religious history of New England, *Magnalia Christi Americana* (1702), two centuries after Columbus's first voyage, he saw the European opening of the Americas in the context of two other world-shaking developments at the turn of the sixteenth century, namely the "*Resurrection of Literature*" (118), probably primarily a reference to the invention of book printing, and the Reformation. Because his history is *Heilsgeschichte* from a Puritan and (New) English point of view, Mather has only a few lines for Columbus before he focuses his gaze on North America, on the Cabots' explorative voyages in the service of the British, and on the founding of colonies. Where the prevailing opinion is that "the over-ruling *Providence* of *the great God* is to be acknowledged, as well in the *Concealing* of *America* for so long a time, as in the *Discovering* of it, when the fulness of Time was come for the Discovery" (117), the person of the discoverer merits little interest. Moreover, "If this *New World* were not found out first by the *English*; yet in those regards that are of all the *greatest*, it seems to be found out more *for* them than any other" (119). Columbus is honored with the feat of the discovery, but as a representative of the Catholic European and, in its initial stages, Latin American world, he is not credited with any discernible insight into the fact that he has contributed to the coming foundation of God's kingdom on earth. In spite of his detachment from England because of the religious suppression, Mather's view is not Anglo–North American, but British-American, notably Puritan, and this leaves no room for Columbus. A pan-American perspective was not unthinkable for Mather, but only if this meant a Puritan Pan-America. For efforts in achieving this, he was even ready to learn Spanish (S. T. Williams I: 16–19).

Mather is therefore part of an intellectual movement toward bedeviling the Catholic south, and it would take major efforts to save the figure of Columbus as well as his personal, tragic story from a transferal of the European, anti-Spanish Black Legend to the Americas, where it would merge into the discourse of Latinamericanism as it developed in the nineteenth century. As Eric Wertheimer, rephrasing David Shields, put it,

> The legend presents a heroic Columbus discovering a New World reminiscent of the Protestant Eden or Arcadia, a luxurious yet ordered natural domain subject to the care and wisdom of original civilizations like the Incas and Aztecs. Spaniards proceed to destroy this romantic world in the name of greed, thereby betraying the virtuous discovery—and betraying Columbus in particular, who

> had only meant to bring Christianity to the benighted. Hence, Columbus, the Incas, and the Aztecs all stand as New World martyrs of corrupt empire. (Wertheimer 20)

However, as we shall see, Columbus is not immune to being implicated in the evils of the conquest. Three-quarters of a century after Mather, at the time of the "American" Revolution, there was a demand of not only religious but secular heroes and leaders. Secular history, too, had to be given a teleological direction. Bhabha's double-time nexus of nation and narration quoted in the previous chapter can be fully applied here. What was needed was the formation of nationalist narratives with the people as "the historical 'objects' of a nationalist pedagogy, giving the discourse an authority that is based on the pre-given or constituted historical origin *in the past*" and of such narratives where "the people are also the 'subjects' of a process of signification that must erase any prior or originary presence of the nation-people to demonstrate the prodigious, living principles of the people as contemporaneity: as that sign of the *present* through which national life is redeemed and iterated as a reproductive process" (Bhaba, *Location*, 145). We may be used to regarding the nineteenth century as the period of the greatest belief in progress, but an impressive number of optimistic poetic visions of the future had been produced during the formative years of the American nation since the 1770s, texts that focused on "America's" mission for the rest of the world.

The important narratives of the event of discovery and conquest of that period were presented in verse. The so-called Rising Glory poems of the late eighteenth century gave Columbus a variety of functions. In Philip Freneau's juvenile dramatic monologue "Columbus to Ferdinand," supposedly written as early as 1770, Columbus demands the king's support with the argument that it was reasonable to think that the creator would not have left the Western Hemisphere unused, that is, covered by water—Columbus is the proto-rationalist. In the Princeton commencement poem "The Rising Glory of America," written together with Hugh Henry Brackenridge one year later, British North America is seen as the place of liberty, of prosperity based on agriculture and trade, and of a moderately humane policy vis-à-vis the Native peoples, all this, as with Hegel fifty years later, in marked contrast to the Spanish policy of conquest, exploitation, and extermination. This boded ill for the image of Columbus, and indeed, in the poem "Discovery" (probably written in 1772), Freneau paints a disastrous picture of the European expansion, the acquisition of a new Eden, and historical progress: "Howe'er the groves, howe'er the gardens bloom,/ A Monarch and a priest is still their doom!" (*Poems* I: 88). The most noteworthy of such reflective and narrative poetic texts by Freneau is the long sequence of poems "The Pictures of Columbus, the Genuese" (supposedly of 1774). Not only is it one of the first longer texts in North American literature devoted to Columbus, it also one of the most remarkable. Twenty-two year old Freneau displays considerable skill in handling diverse meters and stanza forms, and he writes a version of the material that is far from flattering for the protagonist.[16] The sequence tells about significant situations and scenes in the life of the explorer, beginning with Columbus as a cartographer who is induced by the large empty space on the globe manufactured by him (a case of poetic license) to think that nature would not have left this space unused—the same argument as in "Columbus to Ferdinand," but now the creating power is no longer the divinity but nature. The poet has made a step forward in the direction of rationalism.

Columbus, however, is not only a rationalist but a superstitious person who seeks the advice of a witch (a gothic element replaced by an inner voice in later editions). What that woman has to tell him ought to suffice to keep him back: she prophesies Spain's ingratitude and the misery of the Natives. However, neither this nor her insinuation that he is acting out of greed and cruelty will deter him. Even more remarkably and in contrast to most of the fictional and historiographic literature, Freneau draws a negative image of Columbus's sponsor Queen Isabella as a vain woman craving splendor and glory. Columbus wins her not by appealing to her piety, that is, by the prospect of spreading the Gospel, but by quasi-seducing her with the promise of gold and jewelry and the chance to undo Eve's sin by opening a new paradise. Columbus is calculating, a Machiavellian when he praises the crew he secretly despises as "'my equals, / Men of true worth and native dignity'" (I: 114). When one of the sailors kills a Native in order to get his gold, Columbus is upset and regrets his discovery but immediately finds solace in the hope that they might get at the gold elsewhere "without murder" (I: 118). Freneau's Columbus displays the craving for power, the scheming and arrogance of a Shakespearian stage king, but also his greatness. Yet it is only in the penultimate stanza of the last "Picture" that he acquires the role of the founding father of a new and free civilization, the role most American contemporaries liked to see him in best:

> Yet, in this joyless gloom while I repose,
> Some comfort will attend my pensive shade,
> When memory paints, and golden fancy shows
> My toils rewarded, and my woes repaid;
> When empires rise where lonely forests grew,
> Where Freedom shall her generous plans pursue. (I: 122)

Joel Barlow was soon to transform the message of the last two lines into the program for an epic poem of book length.

Freneau's Columbus is a liminal man on the border between medieval piety and superstition on the one hand and modern rationalism and scientific thinking on the other, between the old tyrannical order of Europe and the chance of an American new beginning. His character is equally divided between vision and obsession, between the amorality of the greedy conqueror and the morality of a person capable of recognizing and honoring in the New World and its inhabitants some kind of innocence and a natural sense of freedom. He is simultaneously agent, tool, and victim of a historical process whose prospective, American utopian aspects the poet was reluctant to recognize as realizable even later in his life. The split Freneau saw both in the character and the event was soon to be rephrased into diverging images of the backward, superstition-ridden and violent Latin America of Latinamericanism and a progressive, free and enlightened North that governed the US American identity discourse from the early nineteenth century through much of the twentieth.

THE REPRESENTATIONS OF COLUMBUS by the early Freneau contain elements from highly diverse schools and tendencies: classicism, progressive rationalism, Jeffersonian democratic thought, Common Sense philosophy's skeptical pragmatism, a vague Rousseauism, and the pre-romantic penchant for the nightsides of life. This medley was quite typical for this formative, identity-seeking period in the history of the emerging new nation. None of it was derived from thinking in hemispheric, inter-American terms. On the contrary, much of it is based on British and Continental thought and gains its discursive potential by the double impulse to belong within the European intellectual tradition and yet to reformulate it for the purpose of defining a new, democratic community at least partly informed by Enlightenment ideas. The figure of Columbus continued to be the incarnation of a variety of competing positions in the process of (US) American identity formation. It was Joel Barlow, a member of the Connecticut Wits group, who defined this figure most clearly and in a manner that seemed to run counter to the general cultural-discursive tendency. That he enlarged his vision poem in heroic couplets of 1786, *The Vision of Columbus*, to a quasi-epic poem in even more clearly classicist manner, *The Columbiad* (1807), brought mocking reviews from both sides of the Atlantic, where Romanticism was now firmly entrenched. But Barlow's formal conservatism is balanced out by one of the most radical concepts of progress in the literature of the Early Republic. Barlow's Columbus is allowed to take the step from a retrospective to a prospective view in a manner that goes far beyond the "fancy" of Freneau's protagonist and thereby is made to encompass not only Anglo-American, but hemispheric issues.

The rise of history-writing during the eighteenth century had also produced an English-language, revisionary study of the voyages of discovery, the *History of America* (1777) by the Scottish scholar William Robertson. Like his colleagues Edward Gibbon and David Hume, Robertson was interested in the rise and fall of empires and in their forms of government.[17] Like other historians of the period, he believed in the didactic function of historiography. What was decisive for any evaluation of Columbus and the consequences, however, was the question whether one saw mankind as essentially the same everywhere and at all times, and hence subscribed to a cyclic model of history, as did Hume in *An Inquiry Concerning Human Understanding*, or else considered the exemplary material provided by history as proof of the progress of enlightenment and emancipation. Robertson's Columbus was given the latter function.

Barlow had read Robertson's *History* in 1779 and thus not only had much better historical information at his disposal than his predecessors, but also a linear model of history that met his intention to write a national epic poem. Many thinkers of the period saw the proximity of historiography and literature, notably the epic, as a given, just like the usefulness of writing history in the shape of biographies, because it was considered to be especially instructive and entertaining to reveal general developments by using the example of particular events and characters.[18] It is remarkable, however, how little Barlow was interested in an epic primarily about Columbus, and this may have had to do with the character of the Genuese.

In both versions Barlow shoves Columbus's biography into the introduction. There, he writes rather briefly about the most essential components of life and character. By and large, he follows the material he had at hand and copies it also in its crass idealization:

> This extraordinary man [. . .] appears to have united in his character every trait, and to have possessed every talant [*sic*], requisite to form and execute the greatest enterprizes. He was early educated in all the useful sciences that were taught in that day [. . .]. He had now been a number of years in the service of the Portuguese, and had acquired all the experience that their voyages and discoveries could afford. His courage and perseverance had been put to the severest test, and the exercise of every amiable and heroic virtue rendered him universally known and respected [. . .].
>
> Such was the situation of Columbus, when he formed [. . .] a plan, which, in its operation and consequences, unfolded to the view of mankind one half of the globe, diffused wealth and dignity over the other, and extended commerce and civilization through the whole. (*Works* II: 109)

This idealization of person and achievement is later only supplemented by the commentary that Columbus's treatment of the Native population was impeccable—the fault lies entirely with his companions and successors. What else could be expected of a writer who identifies "the view of mankind" with that of the Europeans? Subsequently, Barlow also points out Columbus's greatness in suffering.

However, neither Columbus's chivalrous ideality nor his acts, nor his misfortune are sufficient to give him the status of an epic hero. Not his deeds are sung, but the poet has an angel visit the explorer when he is dying in a Spanish prison[19] in order to give him the solace of a vision of future developments. The whole text is thus a monumental piece of poetic justice. In addition, Barlow has Columbus realize what he was reluctant to do in real life, namely that he had found not a part of Asia, but a new continent. Like the introductory biographical sketch, consolation and insight serve the purpose of engaging the reader's sympathy, but only superficially in favor of the explorer. Barlow employs the biographical elements to confirm the myth of Columbus as it had been created by Columbus's son Fernando, Peter Martyr, Las Casas, and others. The role of the victim that these writers had emphasized so insistently is used here to win the reader as an ally against those who, in the tradition of the Black Legend, persecuted Columbus and exploited his discoveries: king and nobility, church and backward institutions. In his preface to *The Columbiad*, where the angel is replaced by the Genius of the Western World, Barlow grows explicit:

> [T]he fictitious object of the action [. . .] is to sooth and satisfy the desponding mind of Columbus [. . .]. But the real object of the poem [. . .] is to inculcate the love of rational liberty, and to discountenance the deleterious passion for violence and war; to show that on the basis of the republican principle all good morals, as well as good government and hopes of permanent peace, must be founded. (II: 381–82)

As a victim of oppression, Columbus can be made to serve the idea of liberty, as a scientific rationalist the march of the Enlightenment, as an opponent of violence Barlow's pacifism that permitted only the praise of defensive fighting.

In his introduction to *The Vision of Columbus*, Barlow justifies his use of the vision poem instead of the epic proper by pointing out that he had found the consequences of the discovery and especially the patriotic history of North America more interesting than the voyage of discovery in itself. Thus, the vision part of the epic where the hero is given the solace of positive future consequences of his achievements and that is a feature of, for instance, Virgil's *Aeneid* and Milton's *Paradise Lost*, becomes an extensive text in its own right. This decision brings Barlow in line with a whole school of contemporary poets of prophetic poems on America (McWilliams 160–61).

And he was not alone in introducing the prehistory of the central event, that is, the American Revolution, in order to show the all but inevitable course of world history in the direction of its fulfillment on American soil. What was unusual is that he gave the role of the visionary not to a contemporary, and that by placing the visionary scene in the year 1506, he extended the vision to monumental proportions. To repeat, the reason was not that Barlow wanted to enhance the character of Columbus, but to give more weight to the vision itself by associating its content with the well-known, simultaneously historical and mythic figure of the voyager. When he strengthened the epic element in *The Columbiad*, this, too, served the historical-political theme rather than the protagonist. One is tempted to ask if the typically epic title refers primarily to Columbus or rather to "Columbia," a poetic name that was given to the United States in many texts of the period.[20] The epic opening of this version—

I sing the Mariner who first unfurl'd
An eastern banner o'er the western world,
And taught mankind where future empires lay
In these fair confines of descending day (II: 413)

—only pretends a central role of Columbus, while the invocation of the Muse names the true subjects: freedom and nation.

Almighty Freedom! give my venturous song
The force, the charm that to thy voice belong;
Tis thine to shape my course, to light my way,
To nerve my country with the patriot lay,
To teach all men where all their interest lies,
How rulers may be just and nations wise:
Strong in thy strength I bend no suppliant knee,
Invoke no miracle, no Muse but thee. (II: 414)

Surely, this is closer to Ishmael's "great democratic God" in *Moby-Dick* than to Virgil.

The nine books of the *Vision* degrade Columbus to the role of passive observer who only has the privilege, as a precursor of Enlightenment thinking, to ask those questions about the meaning of the history of mankind that provoke the angel to explain how, in the final analysis, everything is optimally ordered or at least on the way to perfection, whatever there may come by way of setbacks. This makes Columbus ponder occasionally if he is not himself one of the setbacks. However—and here the affirmative image of Columbus presented in the introduction proves its value—he is not made responsible for the negative consequences of his doings, notably the extermination or enslavement of the Natives, but only for his contribution to overall progress. Seen from the US American angle applied by Barlow, Columbus is only a domino on the road to the millennium. He may be enthusiastic about the spirit of freedom shaping the "new man" in Book IV (II: 550), but he is no more singularly responsible for the democratic turn of history than other cultural heroes making their appearance in *Vision* or *Columbiad*: Manco Capac and Copernicus, Luther and Raleigh, Penn and Washington. African slavery is deplored in Books IV and VIII but not described as a consequence of Columbus's discovery nor put into the context of his own fateful enslavement of Amerindians. On the other hand, he has no role in the emancipation of slaves, either. This textual tendency might be seen as a whitewashing of the title character, but it serves primarily to reduce his power of shaping historical developments in favor of a Spirit of History that could well be linked to the Hegelian version. Barlow's Columbus is split into three clearly separated figures: the idealized quasi-mythic Columbus of the biographical introduction, the sympathetic recipient of the liberty-and-progress message of the angel/Genius, and the historical Columbus of the major metric parts of the text who turns out to be a rather modest instrument of inevitable historical progress. Nowhere does he gain the stature we might expect of the protagonist of a poem of epic format.

What Columbus is lacking as a founder of civilizations can be deduced from the two books (II and III) devoted to Manco Capac. In Barlow's view, the founder of the Inca empire reached the highest civilizatory achievement in human history when he made the wild tribes of Peru accept a beneficent religion and form of government, in obvious typological foreshadowing of the forms of religion and state organization in the United States: the cult of the Sun is replaced by the Enlightenment,[21] the place of a benevolent monarchy is taken by democracy. Not accidentally, it is the Manco Capac books that most closely resemble a heroic epic.

The other books of *The Vision of Columbus* deal with history as, primarily, the history of America, with the focus gradually narrowing upon the North American East. The Reformation is presented as a precondition for the Anglo-American development and as a contrast to Catholicism that is regarded as bearing much of the guilt of the annihilation of the great Native empires, then the British colonization, the colonial wars, and the War of Independence. In the final three books, Barlow turns his (that is, Columbus's) attention to the present and future progress of the United States and humanity in general. Trade and business, educational institutions, the arts, technology, and science are the bearers of this development. For the future, the angel prophesies the most important canal constructions of the coming 150 years, explicitly mentioning the Suez Canal and the Panama Canal.

The symbolic refunctionalization of the figure of Columbus is never more drastic than here, where the great mariner is called upon to imagine himself as a bargeman. Even more impressive than the long list of technical and scientific inventions, discoveries in medicine (*The Columbiad* will add chemistry), machines for weather control, the use of geothermic energy, submarines, and aircraft, agricultural improvements, and so on, is the prospect of a new order of international relations culminating in a global confederation with common language, political institutions, and the guarantee of eternal peace. Barlow's progressivist euphoria is more convincing in *The Columbiad* because he has in the meantime adopted a remarkably radical rationalism (faintly camouflaged by some slight bows to religion that have led some to call him a deist). This rationalism caused him to replace the angel by Hesper, Genius of the Western World, to eliminate all allusions to the role of God in the plan of the world, and to insert references to human faculties, notably reason. Equally radicalized is his rejection of all monarchist or feudal models.[22]

Critics of the nineteenth and twentieth centuries found Barlow's poetic gifts deficient, but it is deplorable that they ignored him as a remarkably advanced philosopher of history.[23] They also missed his emphasis on the need for a pan-American perspective.[24] His hemispheric approach allowed Barlow to reject the Buffon-de Pauw thesis of the general inferiority of American soils, climate, plants, animals, and, consequently, humans that had been made known all over Europe by Robertson's *History of America*, Barlow's source (cf. Gerbi; Lang, "Joel Barlows," 234). For Barlow, the Western Hemisphere has produced exemplary early civilizations like that of the Incas, and in the shape of the United States, the most advanced positive sociopolitical model to date from which the whole world will benefit.

In Barlow's view, then, it is not Columbus but Manco Capac who should play the role of founding father for the Americas. Hans-Joachim Lang argues that the Inca story, notably in the prose "Dissertation on the Genius and Institutions of Manco Capac," which the poet placed between Books II and III of *The Vision* and which became an extended note in *The Columbiad*, should be seen as presenting a contribution to the discussions about the American constitution ("Joel Barlows," 231). By the time of *The Columbiad*, George Washington had replaced Manco Capac as the superlative cultural and political hero, and the latter's story could therefore be relegated to the sphere of myth proper (Lang, "Joel Barlows," 241). Indeed, as Joseph Tusiani has observed, in the postrevolutionary fervor "an American epic was no longer conceivable without Washington as its protagonist" (35). But the fact that Barlow did not eliminate the Peruvian parts of the text indicates that the question of a not only North American but hemispheric founding story had remained important for him.[25] Indeed, it could be argued that here we have a North American text arguing for a second *translatio imperii*, that from South to North America, an idea that turned up in various shapes among Latin American intellectuals of the nineteenth and early twentieth centuries, but ran counter to the US American self-image of representing the last and crowning act in the drama of human progress and in the movement of knowledge and power from the ancient Orient, the classical world, Catholic Southern Europe, the Protestant North to Anglo-Saxon America. "Westward the course of empire takes its way," was the most famous line in George Berkeley's poem "On the Prospect of Planting Arts and Learning in America" (*Works* III: 232). In celebrating Columbus, Barlow subscribes to this topos, but in relativizing his stature he shows Columbus as standing at the crossroad of two competing lines of historical development, that is, two competing narratives of the rise of the new nation: the customary transatlantic one and an inter-American one. Sadly, the latter was to be forgotten all too soon.[26]

BARLOW'S *COLUMBIAD* WAS A literary fossil when it was published in 1807, a leftover of eighteenth-century formalism, but in its progressivist message that went beyond patriotism, in its propagation of universal aims and values, it differed considerably from the nationalist proclamations of the period of the War of 1812, from the openly expansionist slogans and the beginning of Manifest Destiny thinking, although many of its passages could be used for the bolstering of such arguments. The nineteenth century had no taste for the cultural criticism of Freneau and the didacticism of Barlow. The American version of European Romanticism broke with the functionalization of literature for public morals and practical life that was still being preached by the successors of the Scottish Common Sense philosophy. It brought higher aesthetic standards, but also a different view of history that saw the specific features and ideas of past periods, but also of the individuals embodying them. It was Washington Irving who was to shape the picture of Columbus as a solitary romantic figure. At the same time, he radicalized the split between the explorer and his followers in the manner of the Black Legend, definitively claiming Columbus as a cornerstone of the US identity discourse while relegating the others to the roles of founders of the alien big South as seen by Latinamericanism.

Mostly, and during the first half of the nineteenth century as a rule, Columbus and a number of other discoverers were seen in a positive light because their colonizing and "civilizing" enterprises were regarded as foreshadowing the foundation of the United States. They counted as trailblazers of the establishment of the one and only country fully realizing the ideal of a New—and better—World. American poems on Columbus are melodramatic and glorifying, like J. W. Miller's "Columbus. His Last Embarkment from the New World, a Captive," or sentimental, like Lydia H. Sigourney's "Columbus Before the University of Salamanca." Such simplifications were upheld by people knowledgeable in the field, like Caleb Cushing, who together with his wife Carolyn was one of the leading experts on the Iberian world. In a review essay of 1825, Cushing states,

> We, in common with the whole human race, are under infinite obligations to him for giving an extension to the efforts of commercial enterprise, of which no past ages could have formed any conception; for opening to mankind a boundless field for the exertion of industry, skill, intelligence, the cultivation of science, literature, and the arts, and the acquisition of riches and all its consequent advantages; for giving that impulse to colonisation, by reason whereof so many enlightened millions have sprung up to inhabit the soil he discovered; in fine, for enlarging the bounds of civilisation and improvement, by adding another world to their empire. (398)

This remarkably openly capitalist and expansionist view of the explorer that pays no attention to the Native and African victims of the European opening of the Americas is intended to be the standard one for US citizens who, according to Cushing, owe their republic and their individual liberty to Columbus and "that we enter into the great family of civilised nations, who inhabit this continent" (398)—the only reference to the pan-American dimension of the subject. But this economic-historical interpretation is combined with a character portrait whose idealization conforms to those of gift book poetry:

> He was remarkably abstemious, uniform and regular in his habits, singularly devout, and distinguished for his scrupulous observance of all the rights of the Catholic faith. His character is visible in his achievements. The dignity and independence of his feelings, his ardent enthusiasm, his invincible resolution, the enterprising cast of his temper, his perseverance amid the frowns of fortune, his fortitude under suffering, and his modest yet manly carriage in prosperity, his courage in withstanding, and spirit of conciliation in forgiving his enemies, and his faithful devotion to the interests of his sovereign,—these are leading traits of his character, not loosely inferred from partial observation, but gathered from the crowded incidents of a life passed in the world's eye. For he was not one, concerning whom posterity can err. On the contrary, he was of the number of those men [. . .] whose acts stand forth in high relief on the page of history, and who seem, as it were, singled out by destiny to impart a new direction, and communicate an extraordinary impulse to the age in which they arise upon earth. (420)

This ideal image goes beyond Barlow's and is presented with the claim of infallibility. Where Barlow humanized his mythic Manco Capac by mentioning his and his sister's quasi-divine first appearance as a fraud played upon the wild Natives in order to win them for the new model of society, Cushing turns Columbus into a saintly, superhuman figure, into a cultural hero whose features cannot be doubted or changed. He does so although his subject was an Italian edition of newly found material on the biography and genealogy of Columbus, material that should have made the awareness of the mutability of history-writing in its dependence on the sources inevitable. Instead, Cushing presses his readers to accept a preestablished reading that conforms to the discourse of national identity by presenting it as if it were supported also by the latest scholarship. It would take US American studies of Columbus decades before it recovered from such apodictic argumentation.

WHEN WASHINGTON IRVING decided in 1826 to write a biography of Columbus on the basis of the source material that had been made available to him in Madrid, rather than translate it as he had planned initially, he did not do so with the intention of questioning the monument erected by Cushing and others. He used the material collected by Martín Teodoro Fernández de Navarrete and other sources not in order to devalue the whole previous literature on Columbus, but to surpass it. Irving's *The Life and Voyages of Christopher Columbus* (1828) was to remain the standard biography until the end of the century. It was better than previous studies because of its literary quality, its wealth of details, its historical accuracy (within the limits of then available knowledge), and its well-balanced argument. Occasionally Irving comments explicitly on the affirmative, defensive function of the biography:

> There is a certain meddlesome spirit which, in the garb of learned research, goes prying about the traces of history, casting down its monuments, and marring and mutilating its fairest trophies. Care should be taken to vindicate great names from such pernicious erudition. It defeats one of the most salutary purposes of history, that of furnishing examples of what human genius and laudable enterprize may accomplish. (Irving, *Columbus,* 31)

We need not take the neoclassical reference to the didactic function of history-writing too seriously. Irving's motives for undertaking this task were manifold, but his concept of writing was that of a member of his own generation, that is, of Romanticism. He tried to promote the development of a national American literature by enhancing American topics with historical or legendary depth as he had done in his famous tales, notably "Rip Van

Winkle," by widening the range of historical associations connected with a given area in order to make them suitable for art, thus following contemporary beliefs formulated by Associationist philosophy. He also wanted to mute the voices criticizing him for his overlong stay in Europe. And he hoped to gain a higher reputation by writing a major historical-biographical work than he could hope to achieve by his short fiction and essays, thus making part of Columbus's monumentality his own. As he puts it in one of his journal entries, "The literary success of the Hist[ory] of Columb[us] [. . .] gives me hopes that I have executed something which may have greater duration than [I] anticipate for my works of mere imagination" (*Journals and Notebooks, Vol. IV*, 245).[27]

What becomes evident here is that Irving saw his success primarily as that of a literary writer, not a historian.[28] The figure of Columbus made it possible to unite factography and imaginative literature without being at risk of getting lost in a realm of the imagination, a risk he saw for his tales and that he had thematized in "The Legend of Sleepy Hollow" (Breinig, *Irvings Kurzprosa*). The figure of Columbus provided him with a romantic hero who was nonetheless attractive for the pragmatic, common-sense-oriented Americans of the Young Republic. That this is a literary character is not left in doubt right from the beginning.

> It is the object of the following work, to relate the deeds and fortunes of the mariner who first had the judgment to divine, and the intrepidity to brave the mysteries of this perilous deep; and who, by his hardy genius, his inflexible constancy, and his heroic courage, brought the ends of the earth into communication with each other. The narrative of his troubled life is the link which connects the history of the old world with that of the new. (*Columbus*, 10)

The rhetorically heightened style and the intertextual echo of Barlow's "I sing the Mariner who first unfurl'd" make it obvious that Irving here claims the epic tradition for his own purposes. His literary aim is made even more explicit in a later passage:

> [T]o feel these voyages properly, we must in a manner, divest ourselves occasionally of the information we possess relative to the countries visited; we must transport ourselves to the time, and identify ourselves with Columbus, thus fearlessly launching into the seas, where as yet a civilized sail had never been unfurled. We must accompany him, step by step, in his cautious, but bold advances along the bays and channels of an unknown coast, ignorant of the dangers which might lurk around or which might await him in the interminable region of mystery that still kept breaking upon his view. We must, as it were, consult with him as to each new reach of land, and line of promontory,

> faintly emerging from the ocean, and stretching along the distant horizon. [. . .] In this way we may enjoy in imagination the delight of exploring unknown lands, where new wonders and beauties break upon us at every step; and we may ultimately be able, as it were from our own familiar acquaintance, to form an opinion of the character of this extraordinary man, and of the nature of his enterprizes. (239)

By asking empathy and imagination of his readers as their contribution to understanding history, Irving establishes an analogy between the process of the voyage of discovery and that of its historical-biographical representation. Although he does not tire of emphasizing Columbus's practical and theoretical competences in preparing and executing the voyages, he also, in addition and often in the foreground, draws the picture of a man with great poetic fancy. Columbus's well-known enjoyment of nature and of what he saw as the paradisiacal life of the Amerindian population documented in his own texts provides Irving with the material for impressive descriptions of tropical landscapes, plants, and animals, as well as the idyllic and ideal communities of the Natives, descriptions that often echo Columbus's own words. This is about the admiral's first impressions of Cuba:

> There is a wonderful splendour, variety, and luxuriance in the vegetation of these quick and ardent climates. The verdure of the groves, and the colours of the flowers and blossoms, derive a vividness from the transparent purity of the air, and the deep serenity of the azure heavens. The forests too, are full of life, swarming with birds of brilliant plumage. Painted varieties of parrots, and woodpeckers, create a glitter amidst the verdure of the grove, and humming-birds rove from flower to flower, resembling, as has well been said, animated particles of a rainbow. [. . .] Nor is the least beautiful part of animated nature the various tribes of insects peopling every plant, and displaying brilliant coats of mail, which sparkle like precious gems. (103–4)

In a note attached here, Irving comments that the "ladies of Havannah, on gala occasions, wear in their hair numbers of those insects, which have a brilliancy equal to rubies, sapphires, or diamonds" (104). The later and the contemporary Latin America are relegated to a footnote. The Caribbean appears in such descriptive passages, and only here. Irving is quite clear about what he wants to leave out: "The present work does not profess to enter into detailed accounts of the countries and people discovered by Columbus, otherwise than as they may be useful for the illustration of his history" (229). Occasionally we are told that Columbus, the romantic traveler, is misled by his imagination into undue euphoria, but on the whole the author's detachment from his protagonist remains so minimal that the readers will associate the *ubi sunt* complaints about the destruction of an earthly paradise in the later parts of the book less with the discovery and colonization according to the notions of Columbus than with the colonial policy of his subordinates and opponents in the newfound regions as well as at the Spanish court. Columbus's views of the wonders of tropical nature are such that a nineteenth-century traveler can identify with them. In this sense, these passages are an imaginative appropriation of the south. The destruction of paradise, on the other hand, is perpetrated by the Other in its most negative variety, that of the Black Legend, even though Irving admired the supposedly chivalrous, late medieval side of the Spanish conquest.

For the modern reader, the imaginative side of the admiral becomes quixotic when he insists upon investing the fruits of his discoveries in a new crusade, but this idea is true to Columbus's own writings. Irving heightens such features of the religious visionary and of the believer in the literal truth of books that gave him the certainty of having rediscovered Marco Polo's East Asia. But for a literary author who was soon to emphasize the romantic and legendary motives in the wars between Christians and Muslims in his many writings on the Spanish-Moorish past—courage and self-sacrifice of individual heroes, love and loss, the intervention of supernatural powers—these features of his protagonist must have been attractive because they put him in a line with those figures from the medieval legendary tradition that were still embedded in a closed, stable, quasi-mythical view of the world. For Irving, Columbus's quixotism need therefore not be regarded as "a flaw of potentially tragic proportions," as William L. Hedges has seen it (245), but as part of his romantic attractiveness. The ambivalence that John D. Hazlett discovers in Irving's portrait of Columbus boils down to the unusual combination of pragmatic efficiency and poetic imagination, because the problem of how to evaluate an event that combined discovery and genocide in global historical terms is taken off Columbus's shoulders by the "double standard" (Hazlett 567) applied by the author. As Hazlett points out, the reader is aware of the sinister sides of the event, but they are made to appear the fault of the other discoverers and conquerors. Thus, we are made to see Columbus's hope for a crusade as part of his religiosity and proof of the unselfishness of his undertaking. Irving's critique of the crusader's doctrine according to which the Christian princes "had the right to invade, ravage and seize upon the territories of all infidel nations, under the plea of defeating the enemies of Christ" (*Columbus*, 167), a doctrine that in its extrapolation legitimized the conquest of the Americas (a misconception of his time), refers not to Columbus but to his opponents.

There is a futile debate whether Irving failed as a historian because he could not really make use of the wealth of source material at his disposal in

Spain (S. T. Williams, II: 39) or rather, by conscientious and diligent work, created a work of lasting value (McElroy). What Irving aimed at was not history-writing but the biography of an exceptional person who, due to his unique faculties, changed the course of world history. True, Irving hints at the context of the Age of Discovery and also at the temporal coincidence of Columbus's first voyage with the conquest of Granada and the expulsion of the Jews from Spain, events that documented the new Spanish power politics and the Eurocentric, imperialist claims made upon the Other. But in no case does he follow these leads. He does not intend to lay bare global historical structures. Rather, and on a limited scale, he presents us with aesthetically interesting scenes from the Spain of that period and from the exotic Caribbean. The individual figures he parades in front of our eyes make up, in sum, the Spanish national character of the *conquista* period from the North American point of view. They are proud, chivalrous, adventurous, bigoted, caballing, rapacious, economically ignorant. The major players also fit into aesthetic, literary patterns: the noble, benevolent queen; the king lusting for power and money; Pinzón, who by a single mistake, his ambitious wish to be himself the principal discoverer, turns into a tragic character; villains such as Fonseca and Bobadilla; the noble and the savage Natives.

All of these positions had been developed by the Columbus tradition, but Irving was able to draw them more vividly than his predecessors. The decisive element, however, was Irving's central character, who was not to be assigned to any of these roles and categories and was unique precisely because of the combination of his qualities: a figure from "real" history who nonetheless by his somewhat doubtful family background and unclear young years resembled the hero of the epic-mythic tradition, and who through later biographical texts had acquired additional legendary features; a poetic dreamer and pragmatic realist (not a rationalist as with Freneau, the man of the Enlightenment); a man from the common people with an elitist claim who wanted wealth and power not as ends in themselves, but as a just reward for a great deed (and in this was not really a model for the American common man, but very much so for the commercial bourgeoisie that was about to create the first business empires[29]); a man of medieval religious fervor and modern civilizatory ideas; an embodiment of the highest success and the bitterest humiliation, irritable and patient, power-conscious and generous. For Irving, the character's only unpardonable sin is the enslavement of the Amerindians, which Irving explains by the Old World spirit of the times but does not excuse. This, too, contributes to the aesthetic richness of the portrait that gains effective shadows without making it necessary to reevaluate the character in its entirety.

From here, we get an idea of what Irving means when he claims a balanced judgment. It is precisely this union of the opposite in a complex, but on the whole and in several aspects positive figure which creates a balance that should not be jeopardized. Irving therefore never tires of explaining the all-too negative away, to blame it on false records. Even the late letters by the admiral, which for twentieth-century scholars have become testimonies of a growing psychic disorder, are seen by Irving as expressing heightened imaginative faculties:

> He is not to be measured by the same standard with ordinary men in ordinary circumstances. It is difficult for the mind to realize his situation, and to conceive the exaltations of spirit to which he must have been subject. The artless manner in which, in his letters to the sovereigns, he mingles up the rhapsodies and dreams of his imagination, with simple facts, and sound practical observations, pouring them forth with a kind of scriptural solemnity and poetry of language, is one of the most striking illustrations of a character richly compounded of extraordinary and apparently contradictory elements. (493)

For Irving, Columbus is a singular man, an original character as Melville would later describe it:

> [T]he original character [. . .] is like a revolving Drummond light, raying away from itself all round it—everything is lit by it, everything starts up to it (mark how it is with Hamlet), so that, in certain minds, there follows upon the adequate conception of such a character, an effect, in its way, akin to that which in Genesis attends upon the beginning of things. (Melville, *Confidence-Man*, 239)

Columbus is not only a literary original character but also a historical original genius in the romantic and the pragmatic sense. He is the man with a world-shattering idea and the faculty to make it come real. In spite of his later suffering, he is to an unusual degree the agent and not the object of history. The life of Columbus and his personality are presented as the unity of idea and action, and thus there is hardly any room for a presentation of his inner development and his private life, notably his marriage and love affairs. If we accept Hedges's dictum that Irving has dehistoricized Columbus (Hedges 250), it is also true that he makes us experience history in the shape of this character as an aesthetic realm. Columbus is the outstanding example of a unity of art and life, an example that would encourage the American inventive genius just as much as the American literary production.

Using elements of the *leyenda negra* and barely touching upon topics (for instance the economic gain that might be expected in the big south, cf. Wey Gómez), areas (the Caribbean including the northern coast of South America), and people (conquistadors, settlers, Natives) that would become prominent in the development of the North American discourse on Latin America, Irving hinted at the potential of this discourse but on the whole firmly planted the figure of Columbus in the evolving identity story of the United States. As such, the explorer has remained a mythic figure. But we have to be aware of the fuzzy edges of this picture. Irving's Columbus occupies the place from where the discourses of identity and alterity seem to follow radically divergent paths. But do they? Isn't it a flip of coin whether chivalry is seen as barbarous or as a complex of lost and nostalgically mourned-for ideals? Wasn't this nostalgia for the past also part of the imaginative repertoire of the United States, notably the American South, during the nineteenth century and beyond, alive in certain branches of popular culture to this day? Self and Other are oscillating constructions, and their formative discourses share this quality. That Irving's successors focused on only the ideal and identity-affirming side doesn't mean that the Other, with its menacing or disgusting, but also its alluring properties wasn't lurking around the corner.

I CANNOT AND NEED not follow the development of the myth of Columbus beyond the early nineteenth century; its function as the point where alterity and identity discourses take different directions should have become clear enough. I will therefore only give a few hints concerning the further tendencies of representation. While the glorification of Columbus continued into the second half of the century, skeptical notes concerning the consequences of his discoveries appeared in Cooper's *Mercedes of Castile* (1840), in Melville's and Mark Twain's works, and in Albion W. Tourgée's novel *Out of the Sunset Sea* (1893), whose hero is an Englishman in Spanish services (cf. Lang, "Kolumbus," 559–62). But on the whole, Columbus remained a positive founding father not only of Spanish America but also of the United States, whereas the conquistadors were seen more discriminatingly. Basically, most writers followed the model established by William H. Prescott and the other major American historians of the nineteenth century who regarded world history as the advance of civilization that had finally reached its most developed form in the United States. In Prescott's *A History of the Conquest of Mexico* (1843) and *A History of the Conquest of Peru* (1847), the focus is on the clash of cultures.[30] Prescott tries to do justice to the great achievements of the Native empires, but in the final analysis finds them doomed to fall because they are in the way of the march of history toward a higher and better humanity. The atrocities of the conquistadors are mentioned and criticized, but they, too, are but the tools of progress. Such progress, however, has not really taken place in Latin America:

> Those familiar with the modern Mexicans will find it difficult to conceive that the nation should ever have been capable of devising the enlightened

> polity which we have been considering. But they should remember that in the Mexicans of our day they see only a conquered race; as different from their ancestors as are the modern Egyptians from those who built [. . .] the temples and palaces [. . .] at Luxor and Karnac. (33)

Instead, progress has been transferred to North America and can be fully realized only in the capable hands of people of Anglo-Saxon descent; Prescott is less tolerant than Barlow as far as the Latin part of the formation of the Americas is concerned. He uses the high drama of the exploration and conquest for more than just historiographic purposes, and so do the novelists: William Gilmore Simms in *The Damsel of Darien* (1839), whose material is Balboa's expedition, and *Vasconcelos* (1853), which deals with de Soto's explorations;[31] Robert Montgomery Bird in *Calavar; or, The Knight of the Conquest* (1834) and its sequel, *The Infidel; or The Fall of Mexico* (1835); Lew Wallace, a high-ranking officer in the Mexican-American War, who transferred his interest in Mexico into the past in *The Fair God; or, The Last of the Tzins: a Tale of the Conquest of Mexico* (1873); and a number of lesser-known writers (cf. Sturgis; Wilgus). The common denominator of these works is the transmission of the moral guilt of genocide, ethnocide, and enslavement to a past stage of civilization, to blame the Spanish and Portuguese for not being able to carry on with the work of progress and to see the manifest destiny of the United States in the dynamic continuation of modernization.

Columbus the rationalist and scientist, Columbus the tool of Manifest Destiny, Columbus the romantic hero—the eighteenth and nineteenth centuries provided sufficient patterns of history-plus-biography to answer the needs of a nation seeking its self-definition and changing it over time. This development reached its climax with the Chicago World's Columbian Exposition in 1893 that turned Columbus into "a representation of 'the official national deity, Progress.' During the first century of independence [. . .], Columbus had become what the United States wanted to be" (Martin 31, quoting Sale 350). The discursive appropriation of the explorer for the US American self-image as a hegemonic, business-oriented nation, and his glorification in this role, has been traced by Claudia L. Bushman and others. There were competing narratives, notably that of the Vikings who were not only, correctly, believed to have reached North America centuries before the Spanish exploration but also, probably erroneously, to have settled in various parts of what is today the United States. Annette Kolodny's *In Search of First Contact* traces this story and its cultural and literary consequences in the later nineteenth century in great detail. Her admirable study also makes a point of including the Native American echoes of this early encounter. The Viking heritage, as Kolodny shows, was seen as belonging to North America alone. It was regarded as that of a warlike, energetic, expansion-oriented Nordic people somehow related to the English ancestors of the Americans during the Age of Imperialism. As Scandinavians, the Vikings were also associated, however anachronistically, with the Protestant, anti-Catholic, anti-Mediterranean tradition celebrated in the work of the great American historians of the nineteenth century (cf. Levin). The idea of other identity-providing discoverers helped those who would have liked to relegate Columbus to the Black Legend view of things. Eventually, however, the positive Columbus tradition won out. It was appropriated by ethnic minorities, first the Italian Americans, later the Latinos, but the latters' view of the explorer showed cracks in the image, dividing those who saw themselves as descendants of the Spanish *conquistadors* and those who were aware of their indigenous ancestry.

I cannot trace here the growing ambivalence of opinions regarding Columbus as it developed from the predominantly affirmative discourse at the quatercentenary to the increasingly drastic rejections of the official celebrations at the quincentenary in 1992. In the wake of decolonization, the Civil Rights movement, the American Indian movement, and the growing diversification of the US (and Canadian) population, the foundational narratives of the discourse of national identity had come to be questioned, and that included the Columbus material. What surfaced was "not the epic story of feats beyond compare but the tragic tale of invasion and loss; not a sublimely romantic fable of discovery and creation but a sadly ironic narrative of misunderstanding and error" (Summerhill and Williams 116–17).[32] Among the host of publications making their appearance in the years around the Columbus quincentenary, there were quite a few new literary works, some, true enough, celebratory in the epic or tragic tradition like Foster Provost's long poem *Columbus: Dream and Act. A Tragic Suite* (1986), but others more skeptical, self-reflexive, and metahistorical. Three of these I will analyze in Chapter 10 because they demonstrate the changes that the concepts of identity and alterity have undergone in the age of postmodernism and postcolonialism.

[4]

# INVASIVE METHODS: THE OPENING OF LATIN AMERICA IN NINETEENTH- AND EARLY TWENTIETH-CENTURY US LITERATURE

What I invaded has
invaded me.
—Denise Levertov, "Ways of Conquest"
(*The Freeing of the Dust*, 19)

AMY KAPLAN AND DONALD E. PEASE'S groundbreaking volume *Cultures of United States Imperialism* (1993) has done much to remedy the "three salient absences" Kaplan deplores in her introductory essay "'Left Alone with America'": "the absence of culture from the history of U.S. imperialism; the absence of empire from the study of American culture; and the absence of the United States from the postcolonial study of imperialism" (11). What has been said there and in numerous publications since need not be repeated here. Suffice it to say that I consider the term *imperialism* appropriate for US policies, economic activities, and sociocultural practices in other parts of the world, but specifically in Latin America since the early nineteenth century, whatever its usefulness in the age of globalization and the shift of power to transnational companies and agencies may be. The discursive construction of the Other under the auspices of imperialism has been accompanied and, indeed, is part and parcel of the domestic cultural production. Imperialism is intricately connected with US discourses of national and cultural identity. As Kaplan reminds us, "To reconsider the meaning of imperialism in American studies is to make statehood unavoidable as precisely the site of the monopoly of power and the production of ideology" (16). The "internal" expansion of the United States across the continent and its eventual consolidation cannot be seen separately from the external expansion by the war with Mexico, by the acquisition of colonies, or by various other forms of intervention abroad during the nineteenth and early twentieth century.

Donald Pease, in his part of the introduction to the same volume, "New Perspectives on U.S. Culture and Imperialism," emphasizes the bicontinental aspect of the culture-imperialism nexus:

> The anthropological concept of culture depended upon the Americas as the theater for colonial encounters wherein it discovered its objects as well as its mode of knowledge. When resituated within the inexorable logics of imperialism, modernization, and world capitalism, these imperial encounters resulted in cultural technologies that in facilitating colonization and colonial rule had also spawned the utterly new sociopolitical categories of nationality, race, geography, history, ethnicity, and gender; prefigured political organizations that would later guarantee the authority of the modern U.S. security state (and legitimate resistance to its repressive apparatus) and later still would consolidate for the United States an international cultural hegemony. (22–23)

Yet inter-American issues form only one among many thematic focuses of Kaplan and Pease's book. Therefore it is important to remember a second hefty volume of collected essays, *Close Encounters of Empire: Writing the Cultural History of U.S.-Latin American Relations* (1998), edited by Gilbert M. Joseph, Catherine C. Legrand, and Ricardo D. Salvatore. As Joseph writes in his introductory "Close Encounters: Toward a New Cultural History of U.S.-Latin American Relations," the essays demonstrate that

> U.S. power has been brought to bear unevenly in the region by diverse agents, in a variety of sites and conjunctures, and through diverse transnational arrangements. Forms of power have thus been multiple and complex: simultaneously arranged through nation-states and more informal regional relationships; via business and communications networks and culture industries; through scientific foundations and philanthropic agencies; via imported technologies; and through constructions of nationality, race, ethnicity, gender, and sexuality. (5)

The contributors to this book turn their attention more to economic and material culture aspects than Kaplan and Pease's, who are more concerned with the literary and cultural effects the encounters had in the United States. *Close Encounters* also devotes more space to these effects in Latin America. However, both volumes emphasize the fluidity of cultures and societies and the bidirectional nature of any "encounter."

The discourse of Latinamericanism developed in the period of expansion to the west and south and was formed in conjunction with the supposed need to stabilize US identity perceptions in the age of the conquest of indigenous territories; chattel slavery (until the end of the Civil War) and continuing racism; mass immigration from Europe, but to a certain extent, also from East Asia; industrialization and class struggle; a growing gender debate; technological and rationalistic-scientific modernization; as well as, on the other hand, diverse forms of irrationalism, for instance in the shape of numerous competing religious movements.[1] Latinamericanism therefore had the function not only of legitimizing foreign interventionism but also of consolidating the nation by presenting not a past (as in the Columbus myth) but a contemporary external Other that allowed for more projections and rejections. Where as early as in colonial and revolutionary times, the figure of Columbus had to be salvaged from the Black Legend with its schizophrenic distinction between the Spanish destruction of great pre-Columbian indigenous empires and the ongoing extermination or displacement of North American Indian peoples, the discursive bolstering of interventionism could do without such differentiating constructions. This does not mean that there were no dissenting voices. This chapter, then, deals with literary texts referring to US interventions in Latin America through the nineteenth and, by way of an echo, into the early twentieth century. Inevitably, it will present more historical information than is offered in the other chapters.

The rise of the United States to the status of empire from the early nineteenth through the late twentieth century was felt most immediately in its dealings with the other countries and territories of the Western Hemisphere. The increasing (and presently, finally, lessening) exertion of economic and political power, the interventions to stabilize or overthrow existing elites in order to further American interests and to ward off those from overseas, the conquests, occupations, and sometimes retreats have to be seen in the context of a dominant notion of availability and openness of at least the southern neighbors, and for a short period even the northern one. This is the story of many penetrations, one is tempted to quibble, penetrations by the pennant, the penny, the penis, and the pen. Military conquest as in the case of Mexico, dollar-imperialism and colonialism, considerations to overflow one or the other of these countries by American settlers, thereby genetically assimilating the Other, and the dominant, sometimes modified but remarkably constant discourse of dominance over the weak brethren to the south are to be seen as one complex. US literature has responded to this development virtually from its beginning, sometimes supportive, sometimes critical, as the case might be. Not surprisingly, the conjunction of power politics and discourse formation is particularly obvious in these early stages of US American and Latin American relations. Therefore, popular literary texts fully inscribed into the discourse of Latinamericanism will have to receive more attention than they would get otherwise.

A CHRONOLOGY OF INTERVENTIONS by US armed forces in Latin America on presidential order compiled from a report of the Committee on Foreign Affairs lists eighty-four such interventions between 1806 and 1933 alone (Ronning 26–32). Geographically, the target areas of these interventions range from Florida (while under Spanish rule) to Argentina and include Mexico,

Cuba, Honduras, the Dominican Republic, and Nicaragua as the countries or overseas possessions most frequently invaded, but also other Caribbean islands, Peru, Uruguay, Paraguay, Colombia, Chile, and Brazil. Included are two major wars: the Mexican-American War of 1846–48 and the Spanish-American War of 1898. Many interventions, however, were "minor" incidents, such as the naval shelling and destruction of the town San Juan del Norte (British name: Greytown) in Nicaragua to avenge a supposed insult to the US minister to that country, but in reality an attempt to oust the British from Nicaragua's east coast (Schoultz 59–61). Other examples were the many marine landings "to protect American interests during an insurrection," the current formula. This list does not contain invasions by private armies—the many filibustering expeditions against Mexico and Central America—or, simply, by little bands of adventurers or robbers.[2] Not listed are the countless cases of political pressure, the often not very light-handed opening of Latin America by US companies with the purpose of exploiting natural resources like minerals, tropical fruit plants, wood, and so forth.

There were and are other forms of intervention, notably pressure to adopt elements of US culture and social order. Among the major purposes behind these measures were territorial expansion following the Manifest Destiny idea—sometimes blatantly racist in favor of replacing "inferior" people incapable of modernization and democracy by "the Anglo-Saxon Race" (Langley 70); the extension of territory that could be used for plantation slavery; the opening of land where future freed slaves might be relocated; the repulsion of European economic or political competitors in tune with the Monroe Doctrine; the establishment of road, rail or shipping connections through Nicaragua or Panama in order to shorten travel and transportation time between the American East and West Coasts; the protection of American business interests in mining, agriculture, railroad construction, and the selling of American products; and the (re)establishment of an acceptable level of order and stability in one's "backyard."

With the exception of Pancho Villa's raid of Columbus, New Mexico, in 1916, and the activities of some Mexican bandits north of the border, interventionism has been a one-sided affair, although, as Anthony Giddens has told us, power will always encounter counter-power of some sort, and Idaho county commissioner Robert Vasquez was not the only one to compare illegal immigration into the United States to an invasion (cf. T. Egan). And, of course, there is a way of using one's own notion of desired ownership to turn defensive action into an invasive aggression. This is what happened when, just before the outbreak of the Mexican-American War, President Polk ordered General Zachary Taylor to occupy the territory between the Nueces River and the Rio Grande claimed by the American government.

When Mexican troops attacked what they considered an invading force, Polk delivered his war message, saying that "after reiterated menaces, Mexico has passed the boundary of the United States, has invaded our territory and shed American blood upon the American soil" (qtd. in Schoultz 28). When one ignores such pseudo-justifications, there remains the idea that the neighboring territories and even nation states to the south or at least their riches are up for grabs for those strong enough to take them, meaning primarily the United States and its citizens and companies. This is indeed a remarkable feature of the social and political discourses prevalent even before, and even after, what historians have called the "Age of Imperialism" in a narrower sense than the one applied here, that is in the second half of the nineteenth century and the beginning of the twentieth. It can be linked to religious or Enlightenment ideas about the spreading of civilization and the true belief, and later to social Darwinism. Posterity simply forgot the moral and legal problems of aggressive expansionism, as in the particularly problematic case of the Mexican-American War: "With the passage of several more generations most Americans forgot they had added roughly a third of the national domain at the expense of almost 50 percent of Mexican territory" (Langley 67).[3]

Of course, this is not the complete picture. The first aspect that has to be added is that the United States was not alone in opening Latin America to its economic and political interests in the period of industrialization, especially after independence from Spain had been achieved and the centuries-old semi-isolation from the rest of the world had ended.[4] Britain, in particular, did not hesitate to use armed intervention, for instance in the occupation of Buenos Aires and Montevideo in 1806–7. One remembers the French attempt to install an emperor in Mexico, or the 1902–3 German-British-Italian naval intervention in Venezuela intended to collect the debts that country owed but eventually resulting in the Roosevelt Corollary to the Monroe Doctrine that made European interventions more difficult. European efforts to gain control of parts of Latin America—the chief reason for the Monroe Doctrine in its original form—entailed exploration and the production of a host of travel reports, scholarly studies, and literary texts on this part of the world that often show great similarities to the pertinent US literature (cf. Pratt 109–97). Second, the impact zones created by US intervention and expansion immediately became or continued to be what Mary L. Pratt has called "contact zones" (6 and passim), and what has been named the *reconquista* by Latin Americans started right then.[5]

A third point to be mentioned in order to avoid one-sidedness is that particularly in the second half of the nineteenth century, many among the Latin American elites considered the United States a model of modernization, of capitalist utilization of natural and human resources, of a liberal transformation of society (Langley 82–103). The Argentine Domingo Faustino Sarmiento called upon his compatriots to emulate the North Americans, and not a few interventions took place at the request of Latin American leaders themselves. President Abraham Lincoln's and Secretary of State William H. Seward's support of Benito Juárez against the French invasion and the puppet emperor Maximilian is a notable example of hemispheric solidarity in the effort to ward off European and local conservative attempts to reinstall monarchy and to expand or reconsolidate European colonial empires. The Mexican dictator Porfirio Díaz called in American capital and know-how, entrepreneurs and engineers, and there are other examples of benign (or seemingly benign) forms of intervention. But the fact remains that US Americans did little to pressure the reluctant Latin American political elites to give up their privileges and share the new wealth with the (often *indio*) masses, and as the nineteenth century progressed, and later in the twentieth century, interventionism again and again took the form of outright expansionism as in the case of the attempted annexation of the Dominican Republic or in the role the United States played in Cuba's struggle for independence. Where the United States acted as arbitrator, as in the conflict between Chile and the Peru-Bolivia alliance, it was clearly done with an eye on American economic and political interests.

SUCH INTERVENTIONISM HAS A history going back to the period shortly after the founding of the Republic. In 1801, Thomas Jefferson formulated an early version of Manifest Destiny thinking on a hemispheric scale:

> However our present interests may restrain us within our own limits, it is impossible not to look forward to distant times when our rapid multiplication will expand itself beyond those limits, and cover the whole northern, if not the whole southern continent, with a people speaking the same language, governed in similar forms, and by similar laws. (qtd. in Merk 9)

In 1820, he speaks of "the advantages of a cordial fraternization among all the American nations, and the importance of their coalescing in an American system of policy, totally independent of, and unconnected with that of Europe" (*Writings* 1439). In 1823, when it was feared that the Holy Alliance would restore Spanish rule in Latin America, and Monroe sought his advice, Jefferson advocated an alliance with Britain against the rest of Europe and supported the policy shortly to be proclaimed by the president in his annual address and later to become known as the Monroe Doctrine:

> Our first and fundamental maxim should be, never to entangle ourselves in the broils of Europe. Our second, never to suffer Europe to intermeddle with

> cis-Atlantic affairs. America, North and South, has a set of interests distinct from those of Europe, and peculiarly her own. She should therefore have a system of her own, separate and apart from that of Europe. While the last is laboring to become the domicile of despotism, our endeavor should surely be, to make our hemisphere that of freedom. (qtd. in Karnes 30)

Yet in the same letter, Jefferson toys with the idea of acquiring "to our own confederacy any one or more of the Spanish provinces" and confesses that for strategic reasons, "I have ever looked on Cuba as the most interesting addition which could ever be made to our system of States," preferably "with her own consent," although the consideration of British interests required that America rely on "future chances" rather than on immediate action (qtd. in Karnes 31).

Jefferson's statements appear simple, albeit not entirely consistent. There are two basic oppositions: On the level of a global struggle for hegemonic power, it is America versus Europe. On the level of ideology—if one sees ideologies as "schematic images of social order" (Geertz 218)—it is "freedom" versus "despotism." Apparently, freedom is conceived of *ex negativo* as freedom from European colonial dominance and as freedom from monarchical government. But complications arise. Jefferson hopes that the United States might be able to separate Britain from the rest of Europe and draw it—a monarchy, after all—to the side of freedom. Although he does not mention it, one surmises that aspects of a common ethnocultural heritage and the comparatively numerous liberties enjoyed by British subjects play a role.

Another complication is the fact that Jefferson's notion of freedom does not exclude but rather invites *US American* dominance and the imposition of democratic institutions. Here, the level of cultural systems in a more comprehensive sense ("language," "laws") is addressed. If around 1813 Jefferson developed some kind of hemispheric view with romantic notions of a pan-American brotherhood of democracies, he was yet afraid that cultural differences might prevent this: "The different castes of their [the Latin American countries'] inhabitants, their mutual hatreds and jealousies, their profound ignorance and bigotry, will be played off by cunning leaders, and each be made the instrument of enslaving the others" (letter to Alexander von Humboldt, qtd. in Karnes 52). He hoped that the growing numbers of people in "the other parts of the American hemisphere" would "catch [. . .] the principles of our portion of it" (53), but shortly thereafter he returned to his earlier idea of a unity achieved by American political, military, and economic hegemony or even by acculturation achieved either through the submission of Latin Americans to US ideas and values or through absorption by the expanding US American population. In other words, although

Jefferson avoids the opposition of Anglo versus Latin American cultures by invoking the bipolarity of Europe and America, he can do so only by positing a homogenization under US American auspices. Cultural harmony is achieved by eliminating the alien aspects of the Other, which then appears as an *alter ego*, sharing essential properties such as occupying (after having conquered) parts of the same hemisphere and having shed the linked yokes of transatlantic colonial and monarchic or aristocratic government. As we saw in Chapter 2, such "naturalization" or even "identification" is helped by a further discursive aspect: all of Latin (or Spanish) America is seen as basically the same; only the comparative proximity to the United States might work as an accelerating factor in the process Jefferson envisions (see also Bauer, "Jefferson").

Such considerations took place during the first decades of the nineteenth century, when the various revolutions against colonial power in most parts of Spanish America invoked feelings of solidarity and even of a pan-American identity among US citizens who had rid themselves of *their* colonial rule just a few years earlier. At the same time, however, it was a decisive period in the discursive construction of a US American *national* identity, and this required contrasts rather than similarities. Where this national identity was seen as defined by the totality of discursive and nondiscursive elements interacting in the cultural system, the United States had more in common with Britain or even other parts of Europe than with Latin America. What Jefferson had admitted in his letter to Humboldt, others pronounced publicly. Edward Everett's statement in the *North American Review* has already been quoted (see Chapter 2). Everett denies Latin Americans the qualities necessary for the formation of a nation (or several nations) and, indeed, of ever becoming like US citizens.

Both approaches to the Latin American Other, on the one hand Jefferson's reduction of difference by pressure from the North and on the other Everett's insistence on the permanence of difference, have been at work in US policies with respect to its southern neighbors to the present day. As it turned out, the acquisition of Spanish or Mexican territories (Florida, Texas, the Southwest) could be seen as an extension of partial sameness (as would have been the incorporation of Canada) because the areas concerned bordered the United States and, by and large, belonged to the same climate zones. The southward expansion envisioned by Jefferson, on the other hand, would have entailed the incorporation of vast areas characterized by comprehensive otherness.

One last point to be made here is that the political and popular opinion in the United States concerning expansionism and interventionism was by no means unanimously supportive. One would expect writers and other intellectuals to deal in more sophisticated ways with borders, alterity, and the claims of the Other than the dominant political discourse demanded. In the following pages, I will study a number of nineteenth- and early twentieth-century fictional and factographic texts for their treatment of US intervention in the south. As will be seen, writers more often than one would hope did not try to transcend intercultural borders in the sense of both understanding and respect, and therefore, paradoxically, joined those whose border crossing took the form of transgression. These texts foreshadow those of the later twentieth century, which are often very similar in their use of Latin American subject matter but, at least in part, more sophisticated in manner and message.

THE SPACES TO BE invaded or avoided were, of course, discursively textualized even outside the range of literature proper. The imagery used on both sides of the border(s) is both telling and to be expected. Latin Americans often saw US American interventions as bodily invasions, as a cutting-up of their land or as a destruction of their cultural tradition (which many considered to be superior to that of the "barbarians to the North") by an infection through unwanted alien ideas and practices. The title of one of the best-known books on the subject, Eduardo Galeano's *Las venas abiertas de America Latina* (1971), makes use of this imagery. But US dissenters used the same metaphors of physical violence or at least surgical penetration. Thus, in the question of the aims of the Mexican-American War, Senator John Berrien suggested an amendment to the Wilmot Proviso: "the war with Mexico ought not to be prosecuted by this Government with any view to the dismemberment of that republic, or to the acquisition, by conquest, of any portion of her territory" (qtd. in Schoultz 32). The negative aspects to be expected from an addition of millions of Mexicans to the American population were also described in medical terms. Thus, South Carolina senator Andrew Butler remarked, "Why infuse the lifeless blood of a ruined Republic into the healthy veins of this Confederacy?" (qtd. in Schoultz 37). And, of course, there was the customary feminization of the spaces to be opened up, although the genderizing of geographical imaginations was not total.

What was invaded was a space by no means easy to define. Both the United States and Latin America are geographical areas demarcated not only by physical features such as coastlines and rivers or mountain ranges, and also by political borders that have changed over the course of time, but also by the "geographical imaginations" (Gregory) their populations as well as outside observers have associated with them. In recent years, the social construction of space has become one of the dominant fields of scholarly attention in the humanities and has brought about many mutual incursions of the disciplines devoted to geographical, social, and cultural studies. It is a fruitful approach to be used in inter-American studies, too. I find it useful to apply here a modified version of Michel de Certeau's distinction between place and space: "A place (*lieu*) is the order (of whatever kind) in accord with which elements are distributed in a relationship of coexistence. It thus excludes the possibility of two things being in the same location (*place*)." Space, on the other hand, "is composed of intersections of mobile elements [. . .]. Space occurs as the effect produced by the operations that orient it, situate it, temporalize it, and make it function in a polyvalent unity of conflictual programs or contractual proximities" (117). One needs to extend the concept of ordered, material place to whole geographical areas in order to become aware of the complex interplay of ordered (though not necessarily stable) physical but also political and cultural entities, on the one hand, and the dynamic conceptualizations that imbue geographies with a host of shifting properties, on the other, in order to describe the cultural practices and discursive orders that have created such unities as "America" or "Latin America." That is, it is necessary to complement the dichotomy of stable order versus dynamic force field by the distinction between material and mental, imagined space as well as their dynamic interplay.[6] The penetration of geographical areas takes place in a network of forces, fears, desires, and projections.

The problem of how our geographies influence our scholarly approaches has been addressed only fairly recently (cf. Hones and Leyda). Common discussions of US–Latin American relations assume a United States in today's borders, while Latin America begins at "America's" southern border and ends at Cape Horn, with language being a dominant criterion. Not only is such a description open to many questions: How about the French-, English-, or Dutch-speaking Guyanas and Caribbean islands? Why not include such portions of the United States where Spanish is becoming the dominant language? It also ignores the historical genesis of both terms as descriptors of physical or political areas as well as of mental mappings. Before the Adams-de Onis Treaty of 1819, "Spain asserted ownership over all the territory west of the Mississippi, including today's Louisiana, Arkansas, and at least part of Missouri" (Schoultz 16), leaving the acquisitions of the Louisiana Purchase a doubtful affair. Until the treaty of Guadalupe-Hidalgo, huge portions of today's United States were claimed by Spain's postcolonial successor Mexico, so that until 1848 major portions of "Latin America" lay west, not south of the US borders, as I have said earlier. For many US Americans, however, following the logic of Manifest Destiny, these western areas had long been seen as a natural part of their country, so that Latin America was clearly a southern if otherwise ill-defined territory. Sometimes it included the Caribbean, sometimes not, but in any case it was characterized by a stereotypical homogeneity of wild nature, either with luxuriant tropical vegetation or vast deserts, of a backward society, and of constant political upheaval. It contained incredible wealth but was poorly administered because the population was of mixed Spanish and Indian descent and hence, following the belief of that period, degenerate. There was a vast difference between the notions conveyed by the equally homogenizing epithet of "our sister republics to the South," which sketched a pan-American brotherhood of democratic peoples distinct from those of Europe, and the condescending notion of a Latin American population radically inferior to the people of North America and, in its basic structure, similar throughout Latin America.

The United States, on the other hand, was imagined by Americans as shaped by a great variety of landscapes, people, urban and rural regions, institutions, economic enterprises, and social structures. It was seen as both ordered and stable as well as dynamic and growing. And yet by no means did everybody see its contours as including the West (which would then have to be "filled in" by the complexity the country had arrived at east of the Mississippi). There were anti-expansionist dissenters and semi-dissenters, and there was a long debate as to whether the acquisitions to be made by means of the Mexican-American War should include only the western territories or also portions or the whole of Mexico south of the Rio Grande. James Fenimore Cooper is a case in point, and I will use him as my first literary example.

Contrary to common opinion, Cooper was a writer of the East rather than the West, a defender of old landed property interests dating back to the colonial or Early Republican periods who saw the further advance of the frontier with skeptical eyes (cf. Breinig, "Turn"). Even in *Notions of the Americans* (1828), one of his most optimistic works as far as the future potential of the United States is concerned, Cooper approves of the settling of the West only within the boundaries of what is taking place at this historical moment:

> Until now the Americans have been tracing the outline of their great national picture. The work of filling up has just seriously commenced. The Gulf of Mexico, the Lakes of Canada, the Prairies, and the Atlantic, form the setting. They are now, in substance, a vast island, and the tide of emigration, which has so long been flowing westward, must have its reflux. Adventurers in the arts, in manufactures, in commerce, and in short, in every thing else, are already beginning to return from the western to the eastern borders. (*Notions* 2: 83–84)

That is, the experience of Western settlement will influence national discourses and institutions, as the Jacksonian version of America was making clear at this very point. But this was to be a process of solidification, not of expansion. As the island metaphor indicates, Cooper sees the territorial expanse of the United States as having reached its ultimate western extension at what he calls the Western Prairies just west of the Mississippi. The ocean of the prairies—a widely used metaphor—forms the western shore of what he, endorsing the position of those who saw the USA as a maritime rather than a continental power, called the American island. Cooper's imagined geography of America was therefore radically opposed to those who even at that point envisioned the country as spanning the continent.

THUS, AT THE TIME just previous to the Mexican-American War, Cooper sees the conflict with Mexico as defensive concerning ownership or quasi-ownership already held by the United States, notably in the case of Texas, particularly against European powers like Britain, as he indicates in a letter to the editor of *The Tompkins Democrat* (*Letters and Journals* 4: 477). Even during the war, consolidation rather than further expansion appears to be his primary objective. In a letter of 1847, he writes, "There seems to be no expectation here that California will ever be given up, nor ought it ever to be yielded. Mexico can never keep it, and we must occupy it to prevent the French, or English from attempting to do so" (*Letters and Journals* 5: 207). His ambivalent attitude—anti-expansionist but defending any expansion that has already taken place—finds its clearest expression in his fiction, for instance in the only novel he wrote about the Mexican-American War, *Jack Tier* (1848). Given the imagined space he ascribes to the United States, a corresponding geographical imagination of Mexico should have been developed. However, *Jack Tier* represents a group of texts that, instead, leave Latin America largely unimagined.

In fact and surprisingly, *Jack Tier* does not take us to Mexico at all. If one leaves aside the fact that General Winfield Scott's invading troops were transported by ship to Veracruz, where they set out on their march toward the Mexican capital, the Mexican-American War was a land war, but Cooper's novel is a return to his earlier sea fiction. Most of its action takes place in the maze of islands off the Florida Reef, a fitting locale for a plot that is over rich in duplicities, conspiracies, in uncertainty about appearance and reality, right and wrong. The romantic freebooter of Cooper's earlier novels has been replaced by a villainous *American* sea captain, Stephen Spike, who is smuggling a cargo of gunpowder to the Mexicans and is thus a traitor to the US cause. Jack Tier himself, the titular character, is not what he pretends to be, either. The sailor turns out to be Spike's wife, whom he had left for another woman twenty years earlier and who has adopted a man's role in order to find him again—an explanation for the ambivalence toward Spike shown by "Tier," who is otherwise a positive figure.[7] Even the young protagonist, mate Henry Mulford, takes a long time to find out what is going on and is not above suspicion about his own role before all complications are cleared up and he and the woman he is in love with are saved and united. Just about the most positive character is a Mexican gentleman, Don Juan Montefalderon, who is to receive Spike's cargo in the service of his country, for which he speaks repeatedly and obviously with the author's approval. Montefalderon represents a class of gentlemen Cooper seems to miss in his own country. His unhappiness about the situation of Mexico is presented with great sympathy, as is the country in general, for instance in the following authorial comment:

> It is too much the habit of the American people to receive their impressions from newspapers, which throw off their articles unreflectingly, and often ignorantly [. . .]. In this manner, we apprehend, very false notions of our neighbors of Mexico have become circulated among us. That nation is a mixed race, and has necessarily the various characteristics of such an origin; and it is, unfortunately, little influenced by the diffusion of intelligence which certainly exists here. Although an enemy, it ought to be acknowledged, however, that even Mexico has her redeeming points. (*Jack Tier,* 167)

In the introduction, Cooper finds the war justified but hopes that by divine providence it will rid Mexicans of ignorance, bigotry, and political corruption and prepare them for a better future, which decidedly does not lie in annexation. Like his spokesman Montefalderon, he sees Mexico as a sister republic rather than an object of conquest but regards the social and cultural assimilation of the Mexican population as impossible. However, Mexico remains an abstraction, an unimagined space. The invasion of the country is transferred to that of a sea wilderness, a neutral space between US and non-US territory, where, besides Spike's ship, a Mexican schooner and the US Navy as well as two ferocious tropical storms are involved in the action, which in the end sees many of the characters, including Montefalderon, dead because of Spike's brutality. The maritime space is a symbolic projection of the author's ambivalence, and indeed of his fears concerning the course of events. Though the novel shares the stylistic and structural defects of most of Cooper's fiction, some structural devices have to be taken not as flaws of credibility, but as symbolic signposts. The fact that there are two storms and that the Mexican schooner coming to receive the contraband capsizes and sinks twice, the second time under US American control and now for good, appears to me as a clear hint concerning the nature of second chances. The United States as mankind's second chance cannot be recovered once it gets sunk in the shallows of an expansionist policy resulting from internal factionalism.

Cooper is not the only author writing about the entering of Latin America who has his characters hardly touch Latin American terra firma. The most famous example is Herman Melville in "Benito Cereno," whose relevance for a nonappropriating representation of an encounter with the Other I have discussed in Chapter 2. At the opening of this classic text, the American Captain Delano's ship "lay at anchor, with a valuable cargo, in the harbor of St. Maria—a small, desert, uninhabited island toward the southern extremity of the long coast of Chili. There he had touched for water" (46). Except for the final part with the trial, which takes place in Lima, the whole action unfolds in the waters of that island bay. Melville follows his source in placing the action not in the present, which it undoubtedly refers to, but in the year 1799, when Latin America was still largely under colonial rule and Benito Cereno could still be called a Spaniard although he was a native of Chile. Thus, the role of the Castilian elite in Spanish America and colonialism in general are further issues. Latin America thereby emerges as an alien, fog-covered, sinister coastline, a space whose conditions remain just as much in doubt as the role the American commercial and armed intruder might or should play there.

Just as for Cooper, the coastal waters are a fitting locale for the symbolic investigation of political, moral, and, beyond Cooper, profound philosophical problems. By keeping the material space limited and hazy, the mental space looms large but remains empty in many respects. Just as the slaves' view is missing in the court testimonies because their leader Babo remains silent, so is the *indio* and *mestizo* population missing in this narrative that pits Spanish, North Americans, and Africans against one another and thereby skirts the central social groups of major parts of Latin America just as it skirts the territory. At a point in history when entering Latin America turns into a major US American pastime, Melville even more than Cooper evokes the risks and uncertainties associated with such a venture. Because the action is situated on board ships, the tension between the strict order of things in a narrow *place*, on the one hand, and the heterotopic openness of the *space* of conflicting energies, interests, and needs, on the other, becomes oppressive and reveals the explosive potential of de Certeau's formula. Where so little is known, the totalizing approach used in the very generalization of "Latin America" turns out to be absurd and dangerous.

Yet to remain on the outskirts can also be used as an evasion of such and other issues. Frank R. Stockton's *The Adventures of Captain Horn* (1895) is a pure novel of adventure. Its action is set in 1884. Captain Philip Horn is on his way to Valparaiso when his ship is "struck by a tornado off the coast of Peru" (3). The laconically told shipwreck leaves him, his crew, and three passengers—an elderly lady, Mrs. Cliff, and a young woman, Edna

Markham, with her fifteen-year-old brother—on an isolated beach where the Peruvian desert reaches to the shore. Those of the crew who are sent off in a boat to get help do not come back, nor do other men who set out on their own. It turns out that the cave system the party discovers contains an artificial lake that covers a large dome containing the gold of the last Incas (conveniently in the shape of ingots). Horn finds out about this when he accidentally drains the lake and, by sheer luck or divine providence, floods a camp of desperados in their vicinity who were about to rob and kill them and who get drowned just in time. The rest of the book deals with the problems of how to salvage the incredible treasure, how to hide it from a group of friendly blacks who had been kept captive by the criminals, but even more from others who might try to take it. For legal purposes, Horn and Edna are married by a medicine man from among the blacks so that she should be legally entitled to claim the treasure if Horn should die. At the end of the novel, she waits for him in Paris, and they are finally happily united. However, before that, Horn has to survive another shipwreck, this time at the equally desolate coast of Patagonia, but again he manages to survive with his loyal helpers, saves the gold, and defeats the crew of another ship who are trying to rob him. The final, legally sanctioned settlement is that Horn keeps 50 percent of the treasure for himself and those close to him, the other half going to the government of Peru with the stipulation that a major portion "be devoted to the advantage of the native inhabitants of the country, to the establishment of schools, hospitals, libraries" (446).

With the exception of a short mention of Mexico City and Acapulco in one of Horn's letters to Edna and a tavern scene in Valparaiso involving one of the minor characters, Latin America in this novel is an empty cipher. For the protagonists, it consists of a few square miles on the coasts of Peru and Patagonia, where all the Latin American events take place. In other words, the main characters do not have to get involved with the countries, landscapes, social systems, and peoples of the "other" America in order to get what they want. Latin Americans figuring as minor characters are either involved in criminal action or at least unreliable like that Chilean captain who is supposed to assist Horn. Horn's reliable business partners remain vague. The blacks are African ex-slaves and therefore do not count as Latin Americans. They are depicted in friendly but extremely racist terms. Suspense is created mainly concerning the question whether Horn will succeed in salvaging the treasure, save it and himself from his criminal foes, and convert it into money. A secondary question is whether he has married Edna only for business reasons or if he really cares for her, as she hopes and is finally reassured about. The minor question attached to this plotline, whether the Peruvian marriage is legally valid, parallels the third major question of who is the legal owner of the treasure and what responsible use should be made of it. Of these, the third is the most interesting in our context.

From the start, there is no doubt that the blacks, whatever their role as loyal helpers might be, are not entitled to any part of the gold. Mrs. Cliff puts the problem of ownership in her own New England businesswoman way:

> "In the first place, it does not belong to the people who govern Peru now. They are descendants of the very Spaniards that the Incas hid their treasure from, and it would be a shame and a wickedness to let them have it. [. . .] Then, again, it would not be right to give it to the Indians, or whatever they call themselves, though they are descendants of the ancient inhabitants, for the people of Spanish blood would not let them keep it one minute, and they would get it, after all. And, besides, how could such treasures be properly divided among a race of wretched savages? [. . .] They would drink themselves to death, and it would bring nothing but misery upon them. The Incas, in their way, were good, civilized people, and it stands to reason that the treasure they hid away should go to other good, civilized people when the Incas had departed from the face of the earth. Think of the good that could be done with such wealth, should it fall into the proper hands! Think of the good to the poor people of Peru, with the right kind of mission work done among them!" (101–2)

Horn claims exclusive ownership by right of discovery in order to avoid quarrels among the party and possibly with other people but does not want to keep it all for himself. Because he is troubled by the issue, he seeks legal counsel and thereby arrives at the arrangement just quoted. He shares his wealth with Mrs. Cliff, his American crew members, and some other helpers but leaves no doubt that, while there is some obligation toward the Peruvian government and particularly toward the *indio* part of the population that should receive the benefit of modern (US) civilization, the other half should belong to himself and those US American "discoverers" who had the courage, intelligence, and hardihood to win the treasure in the first place. Applied to the public discourse concerning Latin America, this gives US interventionists and entrepreneurs a free hand in dealing with the wealth of the countries south of the Rio Grande with no need beyond a civilizatory responsibility to get involved in local affairs. It should not go unmentioned that in the sequel volume, *Mrs. Cliff's Yacht* (1896), the Peruvian government in its haste to get hold of its share of the treasure does not send a warship to take it home, but uses an ordinary merchant ship, which happens to be available. The predictable result is that as a consequence of fights with pursuing pirates, both ship and treasure sink and are irretrievably lost. While the Peruvians thus confirm their incapacity to handle the money,

Mrs. Cliff decides to use part of her share to start a mission for the benefit of the *indio* population of Peru. Thus, the US Americans prove to be the only ones capable of finding, salvaging, and keeping a Latin American treasure, but also the only ones sufficiently ethically minded to put some of it to charitable use for those deserving it. The heritage of the Black Legend with its distinction between noble Incas and cruel, treacherous Spaniards makes Latinamericanism a rational basis for self-serving interventions. In spite of the presence of courageous Edna and the pragmatic Mrs. Cliff, everything taking place abroad depends on masculine initiative, courage, competency, and self-confidence. Thus, the novel also conforms to the gender discourse of the times.

WHEN IT COMES TO the literature about massive military intervention, the popular romances on the Mexican-American War follow predictable patterns. As described by Wolfgang Binder, they represent the expansionist discourse of the day.[8] George Lippard's *Legends of Mexico* unabashedly proposes that the North Americans as the stronger "race" should simply absorb the Mexicans: "As the Aztec people, crumbled before the Spaniard, so will the mongrel race moulded of Indian and Spanish blood, melt into, and be ruled by, the Iron Race of the North" (15, qtd. in Binder, "Romances," 251). Thus the treacherous, cruel, animal-like part of the population, which is frequently represented by Mexican guerillas, will simply be wiped out. The paradisiac tropical landscapes will be put to good agricultural use, sinister Mexican Catholicism will be overcome by American Protestantism, and the US American war heroes assume the rank of saviors of a fallen and backward humanity.[9]

It is interesting to look at the way this discourse is handled at the end of the century, when the complexities of US involvement abroad had become more apparent. A good example is Richard Harding Davis, the leading American journalist of his day, war correspondent, writer of travel reports but also of short stories and some novels. In his travel book *Three Gringos in Venezuela and Central America* (1896), he writes about his and two companions' trip to Honduras in order to report on an American lottery that had run into trouble at home and emigrated to Central America, where it is but a shadow of the former brilliant—and semi-fraudulent—enterprise, a commentary on the way some US Americans use Latin America as a haven from the law. But his verdict about the host country and the neighboring republics is disastrous:

> The Central-American citizen is no more fit for a republican form of government than he is for an arctic expedition, and what he needs is to have a

> protectorate established over him, either by the United States or by another power; it does not matter which, so long as it leaves the Nicaragua Canal in our hands. [. . .]
>
> There is no more interesting question of the present day than that of what is to be done with the world's land which is lying unimproved; whether it shall go to the great power that is willing to turn it to account, or remain with its original owner, who fails to understand its value. The Central-Americans are like a gang of semi-barbarians in a beautifully furnished house, of which they can understand neither its possibilities of comfort nor its use. (*Three Gringos*, 146–47)

How such American imperialism is to work where a direct, colonial appropriation of territory is not to be desired is shown in Davis's novel *Soldiers of Fortune* (1897). The protagonist, Robert Clay, a youngish engineer, has fought in some colonial wars, built railroads in Mexico, and worked as a mining engineer. His father was a filibuster who joined one of the ill-fated attempts to free Cuba from the Spanish and was executed there. Thus, Clay's life as a "soldier of fortune" runs in the family, and one has to see the boundaries between working abroad as a soldier and an engineer as fluid. Clay has served English, German, French, and American companies, and, after his discovery of some coastal hills rich in iron ore in the fictitious South American country Olancho, he is sent there by the big industrialist Mr. Langham in order to establish a mine. At the beginning, there is the possibility of a romance between Langham's daughter Alice and Clay, but she turns out to be shaped too much by her notions of class, and her place is taken by her more socially and intellectually open, adventurous, self-sacrificing younger sister with the fitting name of Hope, whom he marries in the end,[10] while Alice sees her future with Reginald King, a society and travel author (like Davis himself), an art collector, mundane and wealthy. Besides Clay, there are three other soldiers of fortune, but only one, Captain Burke, is without high moral principles. He makes his fortune by selling arms to whoever pays well enough and will always be on the winning side.

Olancho, "'one of those little republics down there'" (*Soldiers*, 26), is a thinly fictionalized version of Venezuela as Davis had experienced it during his travels.[11] The plot concerns Robert Clay's establishment of the mine "'to open up the largest iron deposits in South America'" (26), a task in which he shows his authority both as the technical expert and a leader of men. When the novel's villain, opposition leader General Mendoza, shows up to demand better conditions for his country than the 10 percent that had been agreed upon by acting president Alvarez, Clay insists that the conditions are fair because neither the Olancho governments nor the Spanish colonial administration had been capable of making use of the ore. It has taken American capital and "'a certain energy to begin the attack,'" as Clay puts it, both obviously lacking in the native population, which gets "'ten per cent on nothing, for the mines really didn't exist, as far as you were concerned, until we came, did they?'" (52). He then humiliates Mendoza by demonstrating that the latter is just as corruptible as Latin American politicians are expected to be, and finally meets Mendoza's menace of an armed rebellion by threatening him with a US military intervention.

Clay is arrogant beyond the point many readers would find acceptable for a positive character, but his behavior is obviously endorsed by the author because he regards big-stick policy as the proper way of dealing with "those countries" and their old elites. Clay hosts the presidential family, an occasion that reveals Alvarez's dictatorial ambitions, when the whole Langham family arrives, as does King with his yacht, and all are endangered by the armed conflict when Mendoza's revolt starts in earnest. Alvarez tries to escape with his money but is caught and shot, Hope acts heroically, and Clay finally leads his own troops to victory and shoots Mendoza in the last showdown. At this point, the marines from a US American man-of-war march into the city and are enthusiastically greeted by the Americans there. The US troops give Clay a military salute and recognize his role as "'a sort of a commander-in-chief'" (346) until the vice president can assume the presidency. Clay's role in Olancho now conforms to the stereotypical fantasy of omnipotence that occurs in many fictions showing the representatives of empire among the "savages."

It is the writer, Reginald King, who in a conversation with Alice Langham characterizes the American civil engineer as the new soldier:

> "There are no men to-day, Miss Langham [. . .] who lead as picturesque lives as do civil engineers. [. . .] Now those men I met [. . .] were all young fellows of thirty or thereabouts, but they were leading the lives of pioneers and martyrs [. . .]. They were marching through an almost unknown part of Mexico, fighting Nature at every step and carrying civilization with them. They were doing better work than soldiers, because soldiers destroy things, and these chaps were creating, and making the way straight. [. . .] And they knew all the time that whatever they decided to do out there in the wilderness meant thousands of dollars to the stockholders somewhere up in God's country [. . .]. They are the bravest soldiers of the present day, and they are the least recognized. [. . .] But it seems to me the civil engineer [. . .] is the chief civilizer of our century." (12–13)

In the figure of his protagonist, Davis shows that the metaphorical soldier ideally is also a real soldier when need be. With reference to the stockholders, the term *soldier of fortune* gains a new significance, but the plot rewards Clay with a fortune of his own, both financially and in the shape of his wife-to-be. However, the important difference from the Captain Burke type of adventurer is that Clay follows moral principles rather than selfish greed. As for Stockton's Captain Horn, the spoils are for those who are clever and brave enough to win them and who will therefore physically invade the body of Latin America (the sexual connotations are hard to miss): "Clay felt a boyish, foolish pride rise in his breast as he looked toward the great mines he had discovered and opened, at the iron mountains that were crumbling away before his touch" (100). He sees it as his task to take up these iron mountains "'and transport them from South America to North America, where they will be turned into railroads and ironclads'" (150). Ironically, it is one of these ironclad warships that guarantees the reestablishment of order in Olancho. The iron returns as a force of invasion. Place (cf. de Certeau) is here physically transformed and "replaced" in order to conform to the mental space that had been associated with it.

The picture drawn of Latin America is the stereotypical one of beautiful or dangerous nature to be overcome by technological progress, even if this should happen at the expense of natural attractiveness. It is a picture of ignorant, easily inflamed people, of a corrupt oligarchy of landowners and military, of countless revolutions and assassinations, of picturesque city streets with Latin music and equally picturesque men and women: "It was an old story to Clay and King, but none of the others [the Langhams] had seen a Spanish-American city before; [. . .] and so their eyes were wide open, and they kept calling continually to one another to notice some new place or figure" (105–6). The tourist version of the invasion, the acquisitive gaze, is another form of inroad whose future potential is indicated here. Once again, Latin America is a stable, even static place, and all the dynamics of a space of multiple interactions are contributed by the foreigners whose geographical imagination is in turn dominated by a stable asymmetry of power and exploitative chances.

In her excellent analysis of the novel, Gretchen Murphy has argued that Venezuela's border conflict with Great Britain and the question of the applicability of the Monroe Doctrine to this case is "at the thematic center of Davis's novel. *Soldiers of Fortune* is significant not only for generating enthusiasm for U.S. intervention in Cuba, but also for narratively resolving larger conflicts over imperialism and the global role of the United States inside and outside the Western Hemisphere" (*Hemispheric*, 122). Other than in 1823, and as in Claude Wetmore's *In a Brazilian Jungle* (1903), which I will briefly discuss in Chapter 6, American self-interest demands solidarity and cooperation with the British or, possibly, other European nations as being much closer to US Americans than the Latin Americans. Nonetheless, Clay manages to defend Olanchan democracy while giving it a chance to flourish if the country should open itself to North American money and expertise. "Davis's novel contributes to this process of re-interpretation. *Soldiers of Fortune* reconstructs a coherent national narrative by linking the supposedly exceptional past with a mobile, progressive future, and reconciling the tradition of New World unity with racial and economic inequality in the Americas" (Murphy, *Hemispheric*, 130–31). Seen from the angle of Latinamericanism, however, this reinterpretation is less radical than might appear in the context of political ideas. The national narrative with respect to the Americas has never undergone any complete disruption but has maintained a perception of racial, cultural, and even political inequality among the nations of the Western Hemisphere from the start.

FREDRIC JAMESON HAS MADE the pertinent observation that, in the Age of Imperialism, the colonized are all but invisible in the dominant modernist literature but find their place in popular adventure stories (49). This is true of nineteenth-century US fiction on Latin America as well. With the exception of Melville, whose primary thematic focus lies elsewhere, the writers show a conspicuous inability to give the subject the complexity it deserves, and thus corroborate what I have said about Latinamericanism in its most stereotype-ridden variety. The raids against Mexico, Cuba, and Central America in the middle of the nineteenth century by bands or small armies of American filibusters, who invaded foreign countries for a variety of reasons—from personal gain to promoting freedom from colonial oppression, but also in order to spread American control according to the Manifest Destiny discourse—did not find adequate literary treatment before the twentieth century. Even William Walker, who first invaded Baja California and then, in 1855, Nicaragua, where he arranged to be made president, and who was finally executed by a Honduran firing squad, was properly fictionalized only in Robert Houston's *The Nation Thief* (1984). Houston uses a multi-perspectival narrative in order to convey not only the events and the motivation of friend and foe, but also what the eyewitnesses might have made of Walker's far-out personality and to place him in the contemporary discourse of a US American empire. Amy Kaplan's complaint quoted at the beginning of this chapter, "If the importance of culture has gone unrecognized in historical studies of American imperialism, the role of empire has been equally ignored in the study of American culture" ("Left Alone," 14), might be extended to the field of literary production of a certain caliber, although the twentieth century makes up for some of what remained to be desired in the nineteenth.

Then, it was virtually only Stephen Crane who, at the end of the century, at least represented the shortcomings of the American invaders' (of any variety) conceptions of the southern neighbors with sufficient perspicuity. In his journalistic sketches of Mexico and in some of his short stories, Crane keeps insisting on the incomprehensibility of the Other, on the ignorance of travelers, on the stereotypical nature of their expectations and observations. Thus, in "Stephen Crane in Mexico: I" (1895), the two men riding the train from San Antonio to Mexico City, "the capitalist from Chicago" and "the archaeologist from Boston" (*Crane in the West,* 41), utter one cliché remark after the other, from the initial "'Well, here we go'" (41) to the final "'A-a-ah'" (51) when they arrive at the station and "the city of the Aztecs was in their power" (51). Economic and cultural imperialism show their marks in the travelers' ignorance of the language and the place:

> "Don't you understand the conversational part at all?" demanded the capitalist.
> "No," replied the archaeologist.
> "Got friends in the City of Mexico?"
> "No!"
> "Well, by jiminy, you're going going [*sic*] to have a daisy time!"
> "Why, do you speak the language?"
> "No!"
> "Got any friends in the city?"
> "No!"
> "Thunder!"
>
> These mutual acknowledgements riveted the two men together. In this invasion, in which they were both facing the unknown, an acquaintance was a prize. (42–43)

In "The Five White Mice" (1898), one of the drunken young US Americans who get into a confrontation with some Mexicans expects to die in the inevitable fight with superior opponents, but another manages to draw his revolver, whereupon the Mexicans step back and reveal that they are also afraid. The "New York Kid" then starts swearing: "He was bursting with rage because these men had not previously confided to him that they were vulnerable. The whole thing had been an absurd imposition. [. . .] And after all there had been an equality of emotion—an equality!" (*Complete Short Stories,* 418), an equality where nothing but difference is expected. The situation dissolves in mutual good night wishes.

Similarly, in the short story "One Dash—Horses" (1896), which is based on an incident Crane had experienced himself, the American Richardson finds himself riding at nightfall with his servant José through a stereotypically perceived Mexican landscape—mesquite shrubs and the colors of sky and mountains are sufficient to characterize it. Stereotypically, the servant cannot be trusted and later on proves to be, equally stereotypically, a coward. Further stereotypes are provided by the Indian woman who serves Richardson his tortillas in a village tavern, or by his status symbols saddle, sombrero, and revolver, all of them richly decorated. Stereotypically, Richardson suspects that his situation is dangerous. His suspicion seems to be confirmed when at night a group of drunken Mexicans enter his room, seemingly threatening to rob and kill. They are held back by their stereotypical fear of his revolver and his (pretended) Yankee calm and superiority. They vent their aggression on Richardson's Mexican servant before they retire. After a sleepless night, Richardson and José escape in the morning on their fast horses and are promptly pursued by the drunken Mexican horsemen. They are, one assumes, saved by a detachment of *rurales* cavalry whose officer will not punish the pursuers but simply sends them off with a curse—all of these events form a series of bewildering situations about whose meaning Richardson can never be quite certain, the more so because his rudimentary Spanish and his own drunkenness during the night limit his perception and comprehension. What remains as certain and reliable are the horses mentioned in the title. They at least can justly be praised for their performance.

The sequence of experiences resembles a nightmare and still has something ludicrous because it follows stereotypical expectations that nonetheless seem to be true, although we can never be quite sure about this. The situation thus creates epistemological anxiety. Confronted with the Other, the North American loses his superiority and is made speechless, so that patting his horse's shoulders indicates the only reliable form of communication, whereas his attempt at intercultural understanding remains fragmentary, as is indicated by his very first observation in the text: "'Man, [. . .] I want eat! I want sleep! Understand—no? Quickly! Understand?'" (*Complete Short Stories*, 239). Crane's story is a representation of his own limits of perception and understanding, and hence part of a US American self-portrait.

THE MEXICAN-AMERICAN WAR had been a war of conquest, of territorial and economic expansion. The Spanish-American War of 1898, fifty years after the Peace of Guadalupe-Hidalgo, marked the beginning of a new era. It was, indeed, the beginning of what Henry R. Luce in a *Life* magazine editorial called "the American Century." With the acquisition of the Philippines, Guam, and Puerto Rico, and the status of quasi-sovereign over Cuba, the United States established itself as one of the imperialist world powers.

President McKinley went to war not so much to help the Cuban insurgents against the Spanish colonial power, but to save and expand US American economic investments on the island and to use its strategic potential (O'Brien 67–69). The discourse of Latinamericanism soon changed the image of the rebels from heroic freedom fighters to a pitiful rabble that could not be left in charge of the island's political system, its economic riches, and its cultural future. Intervention out of self-interest was thus reinterpreted as a civilizing mission that was to shape American policy with regard to Latin America for decades to come (O'Brien 70–95). The glaring discrepancy between the real issues at stake and the romanticized view of their country's role among the US public was epitomized in the image of future president Theodore Roosevelt's cavalry charge up San Juan Hill at the head of the First United States Volunteer Cavalry, popularly called the Rough Riders.

In 1927, the New York writer Hermann Hagedorn, a friend of Roosevelt's, published his novel *The Rough Riders*, significantly labeled as "A Romance." The novel describes the war mainly from the point of view of a number of soldiers whose private lives form the background of their immediate war experience.[12] The author can thus introduce several, sometimes widely diverging approaches to the issue of the intervention in Cuba, but with a clear hierarchy of positions, the top of which is obviously reserved for Teddy Roosevelt, who is the supreme leader but also a hero in physical action:

> The men were firing by volleys now. Roosevelt strode among them. He wore no coat; his blue shirt was torn, his nondescript old riding-breeches were coated with mud. [. . .] His arms were bare to the elbow and black with dirt and sweat and blood from a dozen gashes cut by the cactus and the brush. A kind of fierce enthusiasm seemed to possess him; every muscle of his body seemed to be in action; his mobile face seemed to radiate with a ferocious joy. (*Rough Riders*, 310–11)

Here is one who knows the good cause he is fighting for,[13] while others are more after individual self-realization, for which the Latin American issue provides the good and stereotypical opportunity:

> This new life! [. . .] There was something in it which he had not known since his football days, something which gave the hardships meaning and, somehow, dignity; something which gave him, Stephen Van Brunt, somehow meaning and dignity. A cause. The glory of his country? No. He didn't seem to care greatly about that. Cuba? No. It was too bad about the Cubans; they ought to be fed and clothed and the Spaniards ought to be hung for treating them as they had; but *Cuba libre* was not the cause which was thrilling him. It was just

> the sense that he was working with others whom he respected and liked for something wholly apart from the narrow personal interest of any of them. He was a member of a team again! (293)

Yet individualism and collective values are united in the greater good, which is to establish American order but at least also includes the salvation of a country in dire need to be saved:

> A company of Cubans came trooping in [. . .]. They were more ragged if possible than the aged and decrepit who had preceded them; some wore only a few wisps of what might once have been clothing; a cartridge belt, generally empty; a rag about the loins; some scarcely that. [. . .]
>
> "I reckon we know now why we're here," said Metropolitan Charlie. (278–79)

A people in ruins, as is the country:

> The Rough Riders were in a region mournful with the desolation of cultivated fields reconquered by the wilderness. Beyond a barbed wire fence, dimly among trunks hung with webs of interwoven vines, on one side, they discerned what had once been a hacienda; a palm-tree had grown up in the middle of it, lifting its roof. Beyond a similar fence, on the other side, dipped a narrow, treeless slope on which tall guinea grass waved lazily. [. . .] The place was oppressive with something else than damp and breathless heat. (305)

*The Rough Riders* was made into a silent movie directed by Victor Fleming in the same year, 1927, an indication of its popularity.

Five years earlier Joseph Hergesheimer had published *The Bright Shawl*, a novel that deals with the end of such romantic idealism. The protagonist, Charles Abbott, an elderly American, comments upon the disillusioned state of mind of the young soldiers having come back from World War I, their realism and skepticism. He remembers—and his remembrances make up the bulk of the novel—his own, completely idealistic participation in the Cuban revolutionary movement as a young man around 1880. Sent to the island for health reasons, he becomes the close friend of young Andrés Escobar, who is actively involved in the struggle. For the sake of the fight for freedom, Charles rejects the amatory advances both of Andrés's sister and of La Clavel, a fabulous Spanish dancer who takes the side of the revolutionaries and whose bright shawl becomes the symbol of the passionate nature of the issue. He witnesses the death of Andrés's brother, the arrest of La Clavel, who has brought about the death of a Spanish officer courting her, and finally the murder of Andrés by a female agent before Charles is deported, lucky to get away alive. In his juvenile heroics, Charles has made a veritable fool of himself, but still seems to possess much of his older, reminiscing self's sympathies, and presumably those of the author as well. The book is alive with atmospheric descriptions, the magic of the country and the people, chivalric honor and self-sacrifice:

> [H]is first actual breath of the tropics, of Cuba, was [. . .] charged and surcharged with magical peace: the steamer was enveloped in an evening of ineffable lovely blueness. The sun faded from the world of water and left an ultramarine undulating flood with depth of clear black, the sky was a tender gauze of color which, as night approached, was sewn with a glimmer that became curiously apparent, seemingly nearby, stars. (*Bright Shawl*, 27)

However, even less than in Hagedorn do we find references to the economic side of the struggle and to the US American interest at stake, and the hints of the possibility of a US intervention to save the revolution given by Charles's friends, culminating in the idea that his martyrdom might be the immediate cause of such intervention, only "slightly cooled his ardor; he was willing to accept it, in his exalted state he would make any sacrifice for the ideal that had possessed him; but there was an acceptance of brutal unsentimental fact in the Latin fibre of the Escobars foreign to his own more romantic conceptions" (79). It is the white Creole Cuban elite Charles sympathizes with; blacks appear to him as "tainted by Africa" (112). Charles remains the unredeemed idealist even in the late stage of his life sketched in the frame narrative. At the end of the novel, he muses: "If liberty, justice, were to come, one life, two, could make no difference; a hundred years, a hundred hundred, were small measures of time" (220). The idea of freedom, in Henry Luce's essay the key errand for the "American Century," is here separated from the nation that Charles may no longer be able to believe in. In this, and in this alone, he foreshadows later, more skeptical fictions about the interventionist role that the United States continued to play throughout the twentieth century. In his exoticism, Charles may not be too far removed from the author whose choice of a colorful shawl rather than the explosion of USS *Maine* as central symbol can be seen as symptomatic for one version of invasive engagement. While the destruction of the warship, erroneously ascribed to a Spanish mine, served the American yellow press and hence the nation as a *casus belli*, the highly individualistic campaign of Charles, just like the aesthetic penetration of Cuba attempted by Hergesheimer, bears witness to a version of Latinamericanism characterized by keeping one's eyes half shut.

In other words, the nineteenth century as the age of interventionism in its most drastic and belligerent forms produced and was in turn shaped by the discourse on the Latin American Other in its complete range of aspects, reflecting the period's obsessions about race, gender, social equality, the definition of freedom, Manifest Destiny, ownership and land use, and the overarching question of empire. As my examples have shown and as those in the chapters on nature and gender will confirm, the literary versions of the discourse from this period are mostly conformist, with popular fiction leading the way, as it were. Slight complications occur where issues such as slavery and, especially, gender roles are addressed, as we will see in Mary Peabody Mann's *Juanita*. Quite a few texts from the early twentieth century will continue this tendency. Nineteenth-century racism in its unmitigated form shapes the view of the Latin American Other in a manner that makes the priority of economic desire and the means to fulfil it seem legitimate. The sympathetic enthusiasm for the anticolonial revolutions in the various parts of Latin America that was displayed by some gives way to condescension that informs even the discourse-modifying novels by Cooper or Hergesheimer. While the texts that were published in the context of the Mexican-American War reflect the debate about the expediency of acquiring not only much land, but also an unwanted population that could not so easily be made to disappear or be contained as the indigenous peoples further north, later fictions represent imperialism proper.

That is, throughout the century there is less change in the components of Latinamericanism than in the discursive construction of one's own nation and culture against which the Other will be seen in an increasingly negative light. The increasingly asymmetrical relationship between the United States and Latin America finds its perfect expression in the feminization of the spaces to be conquered or exploited. What is there to admire, luxurious nature or beautiful dark damsels, can easily be regarded as part of this feminine quality of the land. While imperialism in the narrow historical sense and notably the Philippine War elicited much opposition among the intellectuals of the late nineteenth century, for instance by Mark Twain and William Dean Howells, the penetration of Latin America found much less critical attention. Those who opposed the material and discursive appropriation of the southern parts of the hemisphere, for instance Herman Melville and, self-ironically, Stephen Crane, did so not by trying to write more respectful, complex, suggestive representations, but by pointing out the epistemological problem presented by the Other, a cautioning that went largely unheeded by the general public.

[5]

# REPRESENTATIONS OF THE MEXICAN REVOLUTION IN US LITERATURE

The Revolution has hardly any ideas. It is an explosion of reality: a return and a communion, an upsetting of old institutions, a releasing of many ferocious, tender and noble feelings that had been hidden by our fear of being. And with whom does Mexico commune in this bloody fiesta? With herself, with her own being. Mexico dares to exist, to be. —Octavio Paz, *The Labyrinth of Solitude* (149)

AT THE BEGINNING of the novel *El Vago* (1983) by the Mexican American author Laurence Gonzales, old Agustín, formerly a fighter in the Mexican Revolutionary War but now living in the United States, wonders how he might make young Paco comprehend the nature of that war. The following is part of their conversation:

> [Paco:] "In this Mexican conflict of yours—[. . .]. How come we never hear about it if it was such a big war?"
>
> "The European war," Agustín said. "That was much. Much, much, much. That involved the most powerful countries, the ones with the most money and the most newspapers and people who talked to one another of their own importance. And it was a bigger war. They killed ten million. We only killed two million."
>
> "Two million!" Paco said. "You exaggerate."
>
> "We killed one out of every eight Mexicans—one out of every eight people in the entire Republic of Mexico—in ten years' time. And we did not have tanks and airplanes to do it."
>
> "*Me cago*," Paco whispered. "How is this possible?"
>
> Agustín thought, How is it possible? How, indeed? It takes a great deal of work to kill two million people, as Hitler had found out. And if one out of eight in Mexico were killed, how many wounded, maimed, blinded, crippled, and how many related to one who was killed or maimed or crippled? It had been no conflict, as this boy called it. It had been something else entirely. Agustín had been there, yet he still had no idea what it had been. In the century between independence and the time Agustín had left his country to live in the

> United States, there had been seventy-three presidents of Mexico, and one of them had ruled for thirty years. (*El Vago*, 10–11)

When Paco asks, "On whose side did you fight?" Agustín answers, "On my side." And when the boy says "*No comprendo*" (11), the old man has to admit to himself that he doesn't understand it either. He can only try to make Paco get an idea of that war by telling him his life story—the resulting narrative takes up most of the novel. But only when it turns out that Agustín's stepbrother, with whom he lived as a bandit for some years, was none other than the man who later, as a revolutionary, called himself Pancho Villa, can Paco connect the report to his own range of knowledge. He says, "Villa was a hero," and is immediately corrected by Agustín: "No. He just liked to have people shot. And he was in the right place for doing this" (84–85).

Comprehension takes place within the epistemic and informational range open to the individual. It is thus necessarily hindered by stereotypical notions and, on a more comprehensive scale, by the discursive system one belongs to. On the other hand, it can be furthered by narrative. As we have seen, stories are the most relevant repositories of information or tools for the retrieval of information. Historical narratives are the most essential form of storytelling in the discursive establishment of group identity because they structure and give meaning to the communal experience of time through the demarcation of beginnings, middles, and (at least implicitly) ends. This process of selection and structuring in turn highlights the supposed existence and continuity of certain group values and characteristics and thus provides orientation for practical behavior now and in the future. As we have seen with regard to the narratives concerning Columbus and the Age of Discovery, these identity elements will change over time, but there is sufficient continuity for the society's consensus that this world historical event has in some way shaped the role of the nation. However, while narrative is a dominant mode of defining the identity of one's own group, it is less common in the discursive conception of alterity. The exclusionist nature of discourse as sense making manifests itself in the reduction of the complex reality of the Other by the denial of historical development and change. The Other is seen as far more static than the Self, and the stories concerning the former are much simpler. This may account for some of the deficiencies of American narrative literature on Mexico, and the Mexican Revolution is a case in point.

IN THE UNITED STATES, there has been a specific Mexico-oriented discourse as a special variety of Latinamericanism since the early nineteenth century, with significant discriminatory additions during the Mexican-American War of 1846–48. Apart from the war period itself, the principal textual manifestations of this discourse occurred around and especially after the turn of the twentieth century, during the decline of the Díaz regime and the subsequent revolutionary period, when the Hearst press clamored for drastic measures in order to protect American citizens, property, and interests. Obviously, this has to do not only with developments in Mexico but also with the prominence of nationalism and imperialism as the then dominant macro-discourses concerning the we-group and the rest of the world.

Mexico has always been a favorite alterity pole for the United States in the dialogic process of identity formation. For a long time it was considered to be a territorial competitor. Its population combined the heritage of two cultural groups particularly alien to and mistrusted by the Anglo-Saxons. One was the Southern European tradition stereotypically defined by Catholicism, that is, church dominance and hence the suppression of knowledge and enlightenment; by the lack of political liberty; by moral and political corruption; and by an overall resistance to progress. The other was the cultural tradition of the American Indian associated with savagism or, at best, with great cultural achievements accomplished at the expense of barbarous suppression and cruel heathen rituals, a tradition incapable of surviving in the modern world. The mixture of both made Mexicans a hybrid people—very different from the American notion of a WASP-dominated melting pot and hence necessarily victims of American civilizing imperialism. Backwardness, moral laxness, and a lack of trustworthiness were among the principal charges leveled against the Mexicans, enough to justify the proposed annexation of what was left of their territory after the Mexican-American War, if we are to believe the jingoist papers at the turn of the century. The other side of the coin was a certain exotic attractiveness or even seductiveness, which manifested itself in the beauty of landscape, nature, and women, and one of whose components was the allegedly harmonious Mexican way of dealing with death. The American discourse concerning Mexico thus comprised interdiscursive elements of nationalism, racism, sexism, and cultural-ideological superiority.[1] It was a concomitant of American expansionist power and justified the use of force against the southern neighbor, whose negative qualities were summarized in the largely imaginary concept of a destructive or at least unproductive, uncooperative, and chaotic counter-power that one might use, at best, for temporary escape from the more rigid American way of life.

Nothing fits this discourse better than the Mexican Revolution. The last invasion of the mainland United States before September 11, 2001, took place on March 9, 1916, when revolutionary general Pancho Villa raided the city of Columbus, New Mexico, and killed seventeen of its citizens. But this event and the subsequent (unsuccessful) punitive expedition under General

Pershing soon slipped from the public memory: Mexican counter-power—in case Villa's raid should have been intended as revenge for American interventionism—was and still is considered negligible. The motives behind the slaughter of millions have not received much attention. Where the revolutionary wars have left their traces is in the stereotype of the Mexican infatuation with death. The most notorious response of an American writer to this cliché notion was that of Ambrose Bierce, who crossed the border in 1913, at the age of seventy-one, to join Villa's troops and who presumably met the violent end he had envisioned for himself in one of his last letters: "Good-bye—if you hear of my being stood up against a Mexican stone wall and shot to rags please know that I think that a pretty good way to depart this life. It beats old age, disease, or falling down the cellar stairs. To be a Gringo in Mexico—ah, that is euthanasia!" (Bierce 196–97). The Bierce myth quickly became part of the general myth of the revolution and has survived even the deconstructive aspects of its last major literary rendering in Carlos Fuentes's *Gringo Viejo*, of which more will be said in the next chapter.

Not much can be said here about the revolution, which, after all, was one of the most significant social upheavals of the twentieth century. It followed upon thirty-five years of comparative political stability under the dictatorship of Porfirio Díaz, a period of economic and technological modernization with an enormous influx of foreign investments, a development that took place under the benevolent eyes of the United States and the major European powers. However, progress and profit were made at the expense of brutal repression, the expropriation of the rural Indian or *mestizo* population, and the mutual enrichment of landowners, foreign investors, the administration and the church by widespread corruption, and the exploitation of virtually anybody else. That the colonial victimization of the majority of the people had been followed by a capitalist variety that was often even worse explains the inevitability and the violence of the revolution as well as its strong anti-*gringo* component. But the centuries of oppression also explain the informational deficits among the population and the lack of concepts defining remedies for a host of problems, and thus account for some of the more chaotic aspects of the coming events.

The revolution, a series of rebellions and civil wars lasting roughly from 1910 to 1920 (with political instability for many years to come), cost about 2 million lives. It was fought by a series of leaders and their armies (often including women and children) for personal gain and/or for the benefit of certain parts of the population. Among the principal groups were the *indio* farmers of the south under the anarchist agrarian Emiliano Zapata Salazar, the Northerners under the populist ex-bandit Francisco ("Pancho") Villa, and the urban middle class under Venustiano Carranza, but allegiances and the respective status of "rebel" or "government soldier" changed often and rapidly. Most of the leaders died violent deaths; there was heroism as well as treachery, idealism as well as inhuman brutality. The constitution of 1917 as one of the results of the revolution demanded social reforms, among other things a redistribution of landed property, a nationalization of natural resources, the right to adequate education and a reduction in the power of the church—some of these aims have hardly been achieved even now.

Finally, the revolution brought the United States to the brink of out-and-out intervention. In 1914 American troops occupied the important seaport Veracruz, and in 1916 some northern regions. Although the attack on Veracruz was also intended to destabilize the new dictatorial regime of Victoriano Huerta, both military measures served to underline the fact that the United States saw vital interests at stake, especially as far as the property rights of American investors were concerned. More than once the US government found it hard to decide whose side to take in what often appeared to be a chaotic struggle. Yet apart from the period of 1913–15, when President Woodrow Wilson tried to stabilize Mexico by supporting the more democratic forces, US policy was shaped by the view that "authoritarianism was the unavoidable destiny of backward peoples, especially those of color" (Meyer 98), and this was the category into which Mexicans were placed. The tension between the two countries after 1920 was not a consequence of the fact that "the victorious revolution [. . .] created a dominant party system that resulted in a new authoritarianism, which was very careful to preserve the democratic forms while emptying them of content" (Meyer 102). It resulted primarily from the Mexican nationalization policy, which was at odds with American economic interests.[2]

With all its drawbacks and disappointing sequels, the revolution has remained for Mexico one of the major events of its history, indeed the one event that eventually created a national identity because it involved all social groups and served to confirm the central role of the *mestizo* part of the population, thus also linking the Indian past and the postcolonial present. *Mestizaje*, the mixture of Indian and European population and culture, has appeared as a blemish in the US discourse of identity until quite recently, and for some until today, but it was seen as an aspect of Mexican superiority by Mexican intellectuals such as José Vasconcelos or Octavio Paz.[3] The revolution has been mythicized, to be sure, but it has also been made a central topic for serious historiographic as well as fictional narratives.

For US Americans, on the other hand, the Mexican Revolution is hardly more than a footnote to history and has become an element of the alterity discourse on Mexico mainly in a trivialized version. This is in keeping with the American Mexico discourse in general, which, as I have pointed out, emphasizes the exotic and the adventurous. And this impression is confirmed by the fact that of the 546 titles in the belles-lettres section of Gunn's indispensable bibliography *Mexico in American and British Letters*, 118 are for young readers. What is even more significant: of 275 novels concerning Mexico published since 1910 and listed by Gunn, only 17 appear to deal with the Mexican Revolution—the others belong to the genres of the Western or the thriller, or they focus on topics such as the Mexican-American War, the situation of US exiles in Mexico, or the *conquista* and early colonial history. If one excludes the (German) novels of the mysterious B. Traven, whose place in American literature is doubtful, to say the least, the revolution has largely remained an "unwritten war" in serious US American fiction. After all that has been said, this neglect amounts to a denial of Mexican identity as a dynamic concept. Mexicans are denied the role of a people shaping its own destiny, the role of subjects of history, whereas this is unhesitatingly attributed to one's own group.

Mexico has remained a topic for mainly popular adventure literature, yet one has to add that in certain other areas of Western high culture during the early part of the twentieth century, notably in the fine arts, the cultural achievements of Mexico were highly esteemed. However, this revaluation occurred under the heading of primitivism and thus did not influence the view of the Other as a-historical and nondynamic. All of this holds true for much of the US American literature on the Mexican Revolution as well. The topic is either ignored or reduced to the element of colorful background for an adventure story involving at least one American character, a pattern that is even more obvious in the movies.

In the following I will focus on three groups of the comparatively few US texts dealing with the revolution more seriously: those by contemporary witnesses, those written in the postrevolutionary period, and those of the late twentieth century.

THE CONTEMPORARY REACTIONS included those of a number of journalists and travel writers, such as J. P. Alexander, Charles M. Flandrau, Frederick Palmer, and John Kenneth Turner, who wrote critically about the Díaz era or sympathetically about the revolution. Indeed, journalism forms the bulk of US early textual representations of the revolution. The most serious attempts to engage with the topic could be expected from those authors who were the most outspoken advocates of social reforms at home.[4]

The first was John Reed, later an eyewitness of the Russian Revolution, whose account of that event, *Ten Days That Shook the World* (1919), was to make him famous. Before he went to Europe, Reed had been sent to Mexico in 1913 by some American papers. He joined Pancho Villa's troops and wrote glowing reports that were collected together with other material in the volume *Insurgent Mexico* in 1914. These sketches and narrative accounts are fascinating, not only because of the events and characters they depict, but also because the author is quite aware of the limitations of his own point of view. Sometimes he simply leaves it open whether what he observes are the strange customs of an alien people or the dissolution of such customs, and this very openness destabilizes the rigidity of the dominant view of the southern neighbors. Still, Reed's major tendency is to romanticize the war and the fighting population. Above all, he paints a romantic picture of Pancho Villa, whom he sees as a "Mexican Robin Hood" (Reed, *Insurgent*, 118). Contrary to his own Marxist notions of the workings of anonymous socioeconomic forces, Reed thus makes Villa into an individual shaper of Mexican history, and thereby returns to the romantic notion of individualism and hence to a central tenet of the American discourse of identity. Villa remains the self-made Western hero even as a politician because Reed minimizes the role of his supporters and exaggerates his political intelligence: "It has often been said that Villa succeeded because he had educated advisers. As a matter of fact, he was almost alone. What advisers he had spent most of their time answering his eager questions and doing what he told them" (122). Thus Villa's vague populism is never clearly shown in the context of his tensions with other revolutionary leaders and their political positions. Reed's counter-discursive narrative report hardly ever leaves the structural confines of the discourse he is trying to oppose.[5]

Reed is more successful in his semi-fictional story "Mac—American" (1914), where he exposes as sheer cant the ideological system of beliefs governing the minds of the uneducated lower classes, the ideology of the superiority of one's own nation, and the inferiority of the other.

> "Mexican women," said one [American], "are the rottenest on earth. Why, they never wash more than twice a year. And as for Virtue—it simply doesn't exist! They don't get married even. They just take anybody they happen to like. Mexican women are all whores, that's all there is to it!"
>
> "I got a nice little Indian girl down in Torreon," began the other man. "Say, it's a crime. Why, she don't even care if I marry her or not!" (*Daughter*, 44)

The protagonist, the proto-American Mac—ex-cowboy, ex-overseer of a Southern plantation, and ex-deputy sheriff—who is made to utter all the current stereotypes concerning the "greasers," turns out to have earned a reputation as an unfair fighter, a never-do-well, and a bloodthirsty member of a lynch mob. Needless to say, though, such simplistic satire can at best be a first step in the establishment of a counter-discourse. The binary structure of identity versus alterity remains intact because Reed simply reverses national clichés and unmasks the US Americans involved as a group of uneducated, racist, sexist, immoral, and violent people.

Reed's friend and mentor Lincoln Steffens, the famous muckraking journalist, went beyond Reed by trying to open his readers' eyes to the historical dimensions of the revolution. Steffens traveled to Mexico after having returned from Europe, where World War I had just started. He made the provocative claim that the Mexican events were more comprehensible than those in Europe, which he also saw as more barbarous. The Mexican Revolution, on the other hand, was in a line with the social upheavals starting with the French Revolution and a forerunner of the revolutions to be expected in Germany, Russia, and even England. Steffens managed to convey an idea of how US policy itself was responsible for the development. Although his equation of American bossism with the Díaz regime and his celebration of Carranza as a representative of the worldwide march of social liberation reveal that he was in constant danger of replacing the US hegemonic discourse by that of the World Revolution, his reports are among the best to reach the American papers at that point.[6] Moreover, Steffens's advice was instrumental in keeping President Wilson from a more massive military intervention. But he was no fiction writer, and thus did not write the stories that might have conveyed a deeper feeling for what was going on.

Such stories were expected of Jack London when he went to Veracruz in the wake of the US occupation forces. In 1911 London had published "The Mexican," a melodramatic short story about a young Mexican in the United States who wins a boxing fight against an American champion but also against his own promoter, who has prearranged his defeat because of a betting swindle, and against the racist *gringo* spectators—all of this so that he can use the prize money to buy arms and thereby save the revolution. The story has been praised as "moving" (Perry 254) and a "masterpiece" (Sinclair 165), but it is stylistically weak and thematically trite and cliché-ridden: it follows the pattern of the lone underdog who wins against all odds because he is fighting for a noble cause. London sacrifices all historical probability by placing the fate of the revolution in this individual's fists, but the contemporary events south of the border only form the backdrop for what is primarily a narrative of a single fight. Apart from some brief passages where the protagonist remembers the exploitation of the Mexican workers and the massacre of his family by the soldiers of Díaz, we get little information about the conditions in Mexico, and what we get is misleading because, contrary to London's socialist convictions, the revolution was not primarily one of the industrial proletariat but of the rural population. Like Steffens, London applies the discourse of class struggle; like Reed, he cannot overcome his belief that the world is to be saved by heroic individuals.

Still, London could be expected to write more discerningly after he had acquired firsthand knowledge in Mexico itself. But when he went there to write for *Collier's Magazine* in 1914, his socialist and antimilitarist opinions soon gave way to his Darwinist racism. In his reports he admires the blond US soldiers, their discipline, their cleanliness, their sense of order, justice, and honor, and he looks down upon the Mexicans, especially the Indians, with a mixture of commiseration and contempt:

> What chance could such lowly, oxlike creatures, untrained themselves and without properly trained officers, have against our highly equipped, capably led young men? These soldiers of the peon type are merely descendants of the millions of stupid ones who could not withstand the several hundred ragamuffins of Cortés and who passed stupidly from the harsh slavery of the Montezumas to the no less harsh slavery of the Spaniards and of the later Mexicans. (*Jack London Reports*, 145)

London regards the peons as essentially savages with a slave mentality, the victims of "a cruel and ruthless selection" (154) by their rulers, the worst variety of whom are those of mixed blood. Therefore he favors US military and economic intervention in order to help those who are incapable of ever helping themselves, and he develops sympathies even for the US American profiteers in the Mexican oilfields. For all his efforts to work up some pity and understanding for the Mexican masses, his war dispatches are impressive testimonies of the power of the discursive order over the perceptions of even the cultural opposition. Needless to say that in the two years remaining of his life, London never wrote the novels and short stories on the revolution his readers had expected of him.

Journalistic writing was decidedly superior to the fictional versions of the events while the war was still going on. While oppositional writers like Reed, Steffens, and London managed to develop an awareness of the importance of the Mexican Revolution as a historical event, it may not come as a surprise that even they, as contemporary eyewitnesses, could not find a stance for the creation of narratives that might have formed a contrast to the dominant pattern. Romantic hero worship and exoticism on the one hand and, in the case of London's later writings, racist stereotyping on the other made them confirm notions they would have rejected on an abstract ideological level. In other portions of their texts, they applied the ideological discourse that had shaped their thinking to events only partially comprehensible on such grounds.

THE SITUATION WAS ENTIRELY different for the next group of authors, those writing about Mexico after 1920. If they had any firsthand experience of the country during the revolutionary period, it was only of the last stages of the struggle. But all of those to be discussed here witnessed the conditions in postrevolutionary Mexico, the institutionalization of the revolutionary movement, and the creation of new, cooptative hierarchies of power including bureaucrats, union members, members of peasants' organizations, as well as property owners and entrepreneurs. They witnessed the armed resistance of radical Catholics to the anti-church policy of the government, and other instances of violent unrest, but also the redistributive policies, the cultural renaissance, and the educational programs for the rural population.

The period from 1910 through 1934 forms the historical skeleton for Carleton Beals's novel *The Stones Awake* (1936). Beals had taught and done newspaper work in Mexico and through extensive travel become one of the best-informed US American writers as far as Latin America was concerned. *Mexican Maze* (1931), a volume of travel reports and political analyses, is one of the most interesting books on postrevolutionary Mexico. But Beals's forte, his ability to handle a great amount of factual material, turned into a drawback when he wrote his novel on the revolution and its aftermath. Basically he follows the realistic model: reality can be known even if it should be that of an alien society, and it can also be shown if only a sufficient number of historical and local color details are presented. Sometimes, Beals uses such material both for descriptive and symbolic purposes in order to represent the specific world order of the rural Indian population:

> She wove and wove. She began thinking of straw mats—a trick the mind has of avoiding sadness and recovering tranquility.
>
> The reeds, from out of the mire of a distant river, nearly a day's foot-journey away, were cut, dried, then re-moistened during the weaving. A mat brought eight centavos on the hacienda, thirty in the city, but the reeds cost four, unless you cut them yourself.
>
> She loved the rich straw odor. A freshly made mat seemed to make the body that rested on it clean and spry again. In time a mat gathered the smell of the earth on which it was laid and the smell of the body, and of the love acts performed on it. It gathered the blood-stains of childbirth. Straw mats were bed and nuptial couch, hospital and shroud.
>
> Old mats had their death-knell uses. They were tied at the corners with maguy fiber to carry bundles. Old fragments covered crannies to keep out the chill upland air and rain. Though timber was plentiful, the hacienda owner, Joaquín de la Selva, wouldn't let the peons fell a single tree, not even for coffins; so the corpses of loved ones were wrapped in the mats that had been their beds when they were quick; they were rolled up, just like meat in a corn tortilla, and lowered into the fresh earth. (*Stones*, 22)

This is suggestive both of an archaic lifestyle and of social repression, but it is also in danger of turning into sheer blood-and-soil mystique. Already at the beginning of the novel, we wonder about the reflective level attributed to such uneducated peasants, and the problem will continue particularly with respect to the protagonist. The characters are often mere representatives of certain social groups or political factions, and the central character, an Indian woman symbolically named Esperanza, is to experience and embody the changes the country undergoes and will, it is hoped, continue to undergo. She is introduced as the naive and ignorant orphan daughter of peons who were murdered by bandits. The plot opens with her rape by the owner of the hacienda where she lives. Later on, she marries a revolutionist and, after the latter's death, lives with a painter and unionist in the capital before she returns to her hacienda as a schoolteacher taking part in the educational movement on behalf of the rural population. Her growing awareness of political, social, and cultural issues makes her the heroine of some kind of *bildungsroman*, but many of her adventures follow upon each other in the contingent sequel of a picaresque novel. This structural looseness, which is meant to mirror the open process of history, is offset by the often coincidental reappearance of other characters, notably an archetypal opportunist and a dwarf who is mysteriously linked with the ancient Aztec gods and who appears to be influencing the course of events. Indeed, some of the characters, for instance Luis, Esparanza's lover, still seem to half-believe in the ancient divinities, in a strange mixture of social progressivism and a return to the roots, irrespective of the actual inequality of Aztec society:

> "Yesterday one of the Indian woodmen down from Huetantzinco told me that when the God of the Smoking Mountain grows angered at his people, he will hurl down poisonous smoke and burning stones and boiling lava—he has done it before—and wipe them out in a single night . . . It's coming I guess . . . When the lava cools, Xochiquetzal, Goddess of Flowers, and Flaloc, the Rain-God,[7] will come strewing bronze violets and white lilies, and the lilies will be women breasted like the sun, and the violets will become men with tireless loins—a race more splendid than any. The peons will be free—no more serfs. There will be plump corn and fat deer and magic music. Then the great Smoke Mountain will waken his sleeping companion, and they will vanish from the eyes of mankind—like all things enchanted." (29–30)

Many romantic relationships and conflicts make for suspense and turn parts of the book into a popular romance. An incident like Esperanza's quasi-affair with a fraudulent faith healer, for instance, may contribute a little to our understanding of the deep religiosity and the gullibility of the Indian population, but its main function is to heighten the sensational aspects of the novel. Beals unabashedly uses the point of view of Esperanza or, occasionally, other main characters. It comes as no surprise, then, that the depiction of the *gringos* follows the counter-stereotype of the Mexican discourse on the northern Other: "The white 'Meester,' George Howell Caldwell, was the manager of the big foreign-owned sugar estate [. . . He] had a ruddy if tanned complexion that made him look like a perambulating sun, an impression of youth and square grimness. His cold blue boring eyes were those of a man accustomed to command" (49). Caldwell will later give the authoritative *gringo* comment on the current event: "'Tell him to watch his step. Madero can't last. No government that doesn't enjoy the full support of the United States can endure in Mexico'" (164). However, the US invasion at Veracruz plays no role in this novel.

The clichés are less associated with the point of view of a given character than an authorial element, as can be seen from comments like the following, which borrows from the language of primitivism:

> The Indian is ever rooted in an introspection sufficient unto itself, not like white introspection which feeds on the subtle nuances with another person, which leads to tortured emotional conflicts and adjustments. Her [Esperanza's] introspection rather fed on life's own roots, so that the sap flowed up through the body and mind within the inner crust. It was tree-like. (399)

It is hard to believe that this is the same woman who some time earlier was a member of the avant-garde Mexican art scene[8] and defended antimimetic modernism:

> "The painter, since the invention of the kodak, has been liberated from childish realism and recording. There is no significance in copying a milk jug exactly when a kodak can do a better job—a silly conception to demand faithful unimaginative reproduction. One doesn't demand such boredom from a writer. The artist has to go beyond photography—not reality but the illusion of super-reality." (373)

Beals himself is obviously not ready or capable of sacrificing the popular appeal of his sympathetic portrait of (post)revolutionary Mexico for a more modernist way of writing. Instead he presents a mixture of literary modes and genres that only partially succeeds in escaping the control of the discourse he appears to oppose. His feeling of superiority manifests itself in his presumption to be totally informed about the way the Mexicans characters from various spheres of life experience their reality. In a chapter on Mexican literature and painting after the revolution, published in *Mexican Maze*, Beals admits his fascination with the more experimental avant-garde of the *Estridentistas* and their revolutionary techniques of dealing with topics related to the revolution (*Maze*, 259–83), but his own text remains fairly conventional albeit combining too many models. If anything, he presumes to be following the dominant Mexican discourse of revolutionary identity—down to the set of characters and the optimistic ending of the plot, which gives the events more meaningful coherence than many of the incidents seem to warrant.

The literary approaches of Beals's contemporaries Katherine Anne Porter and John Dos Passos were entirely different, more aesthetically refined and complex in a modernist way. Among other things, both contributed to the basic insight that the Other cannot be known, that is, subjected to our system of knowledge, without making it lose part of its alterity. True, Porter insisted on her excellent familiarity with Mexico, and her early story "María Concepción" still pays obeisance to the primitivist part of the alterity discourse so fashionable among modernist artists. However, she as well as Dos Passos managed in several works to demonstrate the basic condition of the experience of the Other, that is, the alienity of the writing self and hence its limited perspective.

The importance of Mexico for Porter's œuvre is well known; in the case of Dos Passos, it needs to be elaborated. In 1926, shortly after the publication of his novel *Manhattan Transfer* had established his position as one of the leading writers of literary modernism, Dos Passos made a trip to Mexico. His volume *In All Countries* (1934), which contains travel reports from several parts of the world, presents the following striking image of Mexico's relation to the United States: "On the map you can see Mexico being pushed into the small end of the funnel of North America with the full weight of Yanquilandia crushing it down" (*Countries*, 80). Considering Dos Passos's critical view of capitalism and of the American role in the world, it may appear disappointing that so very little of Mexico is to be seen in his novel *The 42nd Parallel* (1930), the first part of his trilogy *U.S.A.*, although Mexico City is the locale for one of the narrative plot segments.[9] However, Dos Passos's purpose in writing his trilogy was not primarily a reconstruction of history, but its deconstruction. The three novels cover the first three decades of the twentieth century. For the author, these decades represent the period during which the United States has lost once and for all its role of a model home of liberty, social justice, and the unfolding of the human spirit. Instead, it has turned out to be just another imperialist superpower run by industrialists, compliant politicians, and expansionist military. For this nation, the southern neighbor could hardly have any significance beyond that of a more or less useful appendix. And this is its symbolic role in the novel, as well.

In view of this degeneration of historical progress, traditional holistic storytelling that aims at the creation of consistency and of endings suggestive of an overall meaning has lost its place. Dos Passos therefore alternates between four textual modes that mutually and often ironically reflect upon each other without ever achieving anything like narrative totality. Instead, they mirror the fragmentariness, disjunction, and contingency of experienced reality.[10]

The first textual mode is that of the "lives"[11] of a number of fictional characters. These (incomplete) biographies are cut up into several segments distributed over the novel(s). The characters act and make decisions, but placed against a backdrop of the major historical processes, they are revealed as impotent, outer-directed, and without insight into what is really going on. Significantly, only one of them, the businessman J. Ward Moorehouse, gains a modicum of history-shaping power. Equally significantly, the contrasting character, the proletarian Mac, tries to solve the perpetual conflict between his marriage and his engagement in the cause of the union movement by evading both in going to Mexico City during the revolution. Instead of joining Zapata as he had intended to or, at least, of cooperating with his political friends in the capital in order to strengthen the international Left, he drifts about, winds up in a love relationship with a young Mexican woman, by sheer luck becomes the co-owner of a bookstore, and, using the local connections of another American, turns into a bourgeois exactly at the time and place of the most violent social struggle. When Zapata and Villa threaten to take the city, Mac escapes with his household to Veracruz. He even considers returning to the States and leaving his girl behind because there isn't enough money for both of them. But when the danger is over, his next impulse drives him back into his affair and his life as a bookseller, and fittingly it is at this point that he disappears from the pages of the novel. Needless to add, Mac never makes a serious effort to comprehend the nature of the struggle in Mexico but remains the outsider. Yet Dos Passos seems to imply that not only is this a typical approach for US Americans in the country, but that both the feeling of superiority of those sharing the discourse of power and the alienated state of the working population make it impossible to overcome the barrier of separating the visitor from what and whom he encounters. Mac is thus doubly alienated without being aware of it.

That business is indeed as usual in spite of the revolution is confirmed when Moorehouse and a corrupt American labor leader show up in Mexico City some time after Mac's arrival there. The revolution, which Beals describes as "a drama being fought out [. . .] all over the land—a great tragedy, shaking the country from end to end" (*Stones*, 96), is rendered undramatic and reduced to a mere piece of decoration for Mac's and Concha's living room, where two white Persian cats with the names Porfirio [Díaz] and Venustiano [Carranza] symbolize the insignificance of political positions.

What looks like a confirmation of the dominant American alterity discourse on Mexico is put into perspective by the second textual mode, the "headliners," short portraits of real people Dos Passos considered as positive or negative representatives of the period. At the beginning of *1919*, the next novel of the trilogy (1932), we find this headliner passage about John Reed:

> The Metropolitan Magazine sent him to Mexico
> to write up Pancho Villa.
> Pancho Villa taught him to write and the skeleton mountains and the tall organ cactus and the armored trains and the bands playing in little plazas full of dark girls in blue scarfs
> and the bloody dust and the ping of rifleshots
> in the enormous night of the desert, and the brown quietvoiced peons dying starving killing for liberty
> for land for water for schools.
> Mexico taught him to write. (Dos Passos, *1919*, 14–15)

The passage reveals what Mexico also meant for Dos Passos: poetry and the potential for historical greatness seeping out through the lower end of the funnel under the pressure of the "inconceivably powerful financial bloody juggernaut Colossus of the North" (*Countries,* 82). Reed, who is intended to contrast favorably with Mac, is one of very few to resist this colossus.

The two remaining textual modes are also used for complementary allusions to conditions in Mexico. In the stream-of-consciousness fragments from the author's memory called "Camera Eye," there is a passage alluding to a railroad trip his parents took through Mexico when it was still possible to hunt antelopes from the train, and when "one night Mother was so frightened on account of all the rifleshots but it was allright turned out to be nothing but a little shooting they'd been only shooting a greaser that was all" (*42nd Parallel*, 25)—an American recollection, indeed. And in the collages of newspaper clippings called "Newsreels," the fragment "troops guard oilfields America tends to become empire like in the days of the Caesars" (57) yields sufficient if unintentional information about the way history develops in the Western hemisphere.

Taken together, the different presentational modes and the fragmentation of the texts achieve an impression of history as anti-history, as a series of sheer happenings in whose sequence the Mexican Revolution appears as only a digression. The American hegemonic discourse manifests itself directly in just a few passages and quotations, but the reduction of any historical counter-discourse to an apparently random collection of language material reveals Dos Passos's disillusionment with regard to the possibility of any serious opposition. His disillusionment also extends to the power of language or literature to change or even recapture events because, as the case of Mexico will show, the discourse of power has robbed them of their very status of event.[12]

Katherine Anne Porter spent major portions of the postrevolutionary decade in Mexico and became a sympathetic observer of the political, social, and cultural developments. It is interesting to compare her earlier short story "María Concepción" (1922) with her later, more famous story, "Flowering Judas" (1930), which will be discussed again in the context of gender issues in Chapter 7.

"María Concepción" is set at some time during the revolutionary wars, but the fighting forms only the remote background and is described only from below, as it were:

> Juan did not come home that night, but went away to war and María Rosa went with him. Juan had a rifle at his shoulder and two pistols at his belt. María Rosa wore a rifle also, slung on her back along with the blankets and the cooking pots. They joined the nearest detachment of troops in the field, and María Rosa marched ahead with the battalion of experienced women of war, which went over the crops like locusts, gathering provisions for the army. She cooked with them, and ate with them what was left after the men had eaten. After battles she went out on the field with the others to salvage clothing and ammunition and guns from the slain before they should begin to swell in the heat. Sometimes they would encounter the women from the other army, and a second battle as grim as the first would take place. (*Collected Stories*, 8)

Fighting a war here seems to follow the premodern pattern that, say, the armies and their hangers-on followed during the Thirty Years' War in the seventeenth century. For the rural *indios* who form the subject of the story, there exists no moral or political cause one might wish to fight for, not even the improvement of one's own situation in life. They go to war as a temporary way of spending one's life, and they walk away from it just as casually:

> Juan and María Rosa, disgusted with military life, came home one day without asking permission of anyone. The field of war had unrolled itself, a long scroll of vexations, until the end had frayed out within twenty miles of Juan's village. So he and María Rosa, now lean as a wolf, burdened with a child daily expected, set out with no farewells to the regiment and walked home. (10)

The revolution here is not an identity-shaping event in Mexican history, but at best an event in the lives of the two characters. The war is an unstructured fabric eventually coming apart. Sure enough, the military police threatens to execute Juan for desertion, but he is saved because of the friendship between the captain and the American archaeologist Givens for whom Juan had worked. All of this is of marginal importance and confirms the notions most US Americans had of the Mexican Revolution as a remote, exotic, and chaotic event acted out by rather immature people.

What is highlighted, instead, is a private struggle no less passionate and no less immature. The story's local setting is some Indian village; few details as to the region are given, underscoring the exemplary nature of the plot, although we learn that the eponymous protagonist comes from the Guadalajara region.[13] Thus, maguey agaves and organ cacti represent sufficient local color. María Concepción, eighteen years old, is happily married to Juan, who is the same age. Accidentally she observes him with María Rosa, three years her junior. Her world falls apart, her whole hatred is directed against her rival, but because Juan and María Rosa leave the same day before any confrontation could have occurred, she withdraws within herself and her world of feelings. She loses her newborn child but shows no emotion, having grown, to all appearances, "'mere stone'" (9). When Juan and María Rosa return after one year, she kills the other woman. Juan and the village community shield María Concepción from the police investigations, and when she has recovered her calm, she takes María Rosa's newborn baby as her own and experiences the happiness of a recovered harmony of life, whereas Juan is somewhat sobered when he looks ahead to the coming routines of marriage and work.

The story is well told, with precise but economically used descriptions of significant forms of behavior, including gestures and facial expressions. Porter sheds ironic light on the condescending primitivism of Givens, the only US American character in this text, but she rests her representation on her own, positive concept of primitivism. Thus, she introduces her heroine in the following way:

> Her straight back outlined itself strongly under her clean bright blue cotton rebozo. Instinctive serenity softened her black eyes, shaped like almonds, set far apart, and tilted a bit endwise. She walked with the free, natural, guarded ease of the primitive woman carrying an unborn child. The shape of her body was easy, the swelling life was not a distortion, but the right inevitable proportions of a woman. She was entirely contented. Her husband was at work and she was on her way to market to sell her fowls. (3)

Primitive life and culture—from today's perspective an outrageous notion—are seen as harmonious, involving physical and emotional well-being. When this harmony is shattered by Juan's carefree, equally primitive *machismo*,

María Concepción finds a way of restoring it by the simple means of stabbing her rival to death. After the police are gone and the baby is fed, she can return to her natural rhythms:

> The night, the earth under her, seemed to swell and recede together with a limitless, unhurried, benign breathing. She drooped and closed her eyes, feeling the slow rise and fall within her own body. She did not know what it was, but it eased her all through. Even as she was falling asleep, head bowed over the child, she was still aware of a strange, wakeful happiness. (21)

Such harmony, including the blending of waking and sleeping, signifies a totality that proved to be appealing to Porter's readers. The unity of the story is made possible by the unity of the world it represents, and this, in turn, rests on the simplicity of life, death, thinking, and feeling that US Americans like their European contemporaries associated with primitive peoples. Other than in the short stories by Porter's contemporaries Sherwood Anderson or Ernest Hemingway, the simplicity of what is being told and the laconic way of telling it do not serve as stimuli for the readers to fill in the lacunae by thematic depth and figural complexity. True, even Porter does not assume that it is easy to reconcile Mariá Concepción's murderous lust for revenge with her calm and easygoing character, but if anything should be considered strange in these sudden reversals, we do not ascribe it to the protagonist's emotional complexity but to the fact that she belongs to another race. And that race can be comprehended well enough, as can be seen from the author's ease in presenting the protagonist's thoughts and feelings, alterity notwithstanding. What we get on the whole is a picture of simple people with simple passions that they act out in a straightforward manner, a Gauguin tableau of Tahiti with strong colors and clear-cut figures but little depth.

Porter's representation of Indian village life in Mexico thus results from a projection of a Western concept, that of primitivism, on a certain region and culture. What gets lost in the process is most regional and cultural specifics, because the underlying assumption is one of a universally shared set of archaic forms of behavior as well as the existence of a more or less homogenous, poor Indian population in rural Mexico. If this story embodies the spirit of Mexico at that time (Gunn 107), the impression of distance from concrete reality is even heightened.[14] And that reality was the Mexican Revolution, which in and through this story is removed into the exotic distance. The narrating voice enters not only the individual imaginary of the main characters but also the cultural imaginary of the nation, that is, the Other, thereby shedding light on a historic event that in this narration loses all its monumentality.[15]

Porter's approach was to change drastically in the years to come. The still turbulent situation under President Alvaro Obregón (1920–24) forms the background for one of her most famous short stories, "Flowering Judas" (1930). Contrary to Dos Passos's handling of the theme, the failure of Laura, Porter's US protagonist in Mexico City, is seen not so much as representative of the decline of the West and its loss of anything like a meaningful history, but as a personal defeat in view of the discrepancy between high pretensions and insufficient fulfillment, applying to Laura's personal role as well as to the fate of the revolution. Laura, an American teacher of Indian children at Xochimilco, lives in the capital, supports her syndicalist friends, and serves as their secret messenger. The story has often been analyzed, usually as a tale of betrayal—betrayal of the revolution, betrayal of the young revolutionist Eugenio who commits suicide in prison, betrayal of Laura's own womanhood.[16] The aspect most relevant here, however, is Laura's inability to overcome her own detachment from the Other. Although she has achieved a level of participation in the political events usually denied to foreigners, she does not find what she considers the true life. She is disappointed in the all-too-human revolutionaries; she is particularly put off by the courting of a boastful and cynical revolutionary general with the telling name Braggioni, whom she finds intolerable but tolerates nonetheless.

> The gluttonous bulk of Braggioni has become a symbol of her many disillusions, for a revolutionist should be lean, animated by heroic faith, a vessel of abstract virtues. This is nonsense, she knows it now and is ashamed of it. Revolution must have leaders, and leadership is a career for energetic men. She is, her comrades tell her, full of romantic error, for what she defines as cynicism in them is merely "a developed sense of reality." (*Collected Stories*, 91)

On the other hand, Laura even rejects more positive contacts and finds herself incapable of any deeper emotional commitment. At the end of the story, she dreams of the dead Eugenio who forces her to eat the flowers of a judas tree. Laura, who feels betrayed by her life as an idealist, is thereby made to realize her own betrayal of life. In fact, Eugenio forces her into a kind of communion with his living and dying, but it remains doubtful whether this experience will get her anywhere. Her detachment, in spite of her ideological closeness to the revolutionists, as well as the distance separating a hedonist and corrupted former hero like Braggioni from a young escapist from a non-ideal life like Eugenio, have become elements of her own psyche. She has internalized the contradictions, the failures and incomprehensibilities of the revolution and can therefore control her rebellious unconscious only by repression:

> She is not at home in the world. Every day she teaches children who remain strangers to her, though she loves their tender round hands and their charming

> opportunist savagery. She knocks at unfamiliar doors not knowing whether a friend or a stranger shall answer, and even if a known face emerges from the sour gloom of that unknown interior, still it is the face of a stranger. No matter what this stranger says to her, nor what her message to him, the very cells of her flesh reject knowledge and kinship in one monotonous word. No. No. No. She draws her strength from this one holy talismanic word which does not suffer her to be led into evil. Denying everything, she may walk anywhere in safety, she looks at everything without amazement. (97)

This fine psychological study is also a kind of psychogram of postrevolutionary Mexico where the disillusionment of the participants of the revolution contrasted curiously with the initial enthusiasm of the newly arrived foreign visitors—and this is where the text meets Dos Passos's overall critique: "Not for nothing has Braggioni taken pains to be a good revolutionist and a professional lover of humanity. He will never die of it. He has the malice, the cleverness, the wickedness, the sharpness of wit, the hardness of heart, stipulated for loving the world profitably" (*Collected Stories*, 98).[17] Even if Laura's emotional defenses somehow match the growing political repression, we may not deduce anything like her entering the communal Mexican experience. Porter's approach is totally different from that in "María Concepción." The US American visitor is put into the center, not like the invaders discussed in the previous chapter, but as a witness to the alienity of what is going on. The story confirms the gulf between the two worlds, the impossibility of sharing the emerging historical identity discourse of the Other. But it also suggests that the discrepancy between the respective ideals and the respective achievements could be a structural feature of humanity in general.

DOS PASSOS ANTICIPATED POSTMODERN notions of eliminating the privileged status of historical narration and, indeed, of any dominant narrative, and Porter pointed out in some of her works how illusory any claim must be to share the (historical) experience of an alien people and impose a narrative order on it. Nonetheless, writers of the 1980s have tried to reintroduce the Mexican Revolution into the group of narratable events. Rosalind Wright did so rather highhandedly by returning to the nineteenth-century "loose baggy monster" type of society fiction. Her novel *Veracruz* (1986) traces the fates of an American coffee planter, his family, and a number of other characters, US American and Mexican, before and then during the US occupation of Veracruz. Time and place are well chosen: the years 1911–14 (with some flashbacks to previous events) saw the rebellion of Francisco Madero against Porfirio Díaz; Madero's short presidency aiming at social reforms looked on askance by the United States and those European powers having invested in Mexico; the coup d'état of Victoriano Huerta and the murder of Madero in February, 1913; and finally, the US invasion and occupation of Veracruz in April, 1914.

The port city and the province of Veracruz was a suitable locale because Mexican, US, and European economic and political interests came together and sometimes clashed there, and because a sizable number of Americans lived there because of business engagements. Wright introduces a wealth of historical information in lengthy passages that might have been taken from a history book or an encyclopedia. She quotes from diplomatic documents and other historical sources. Like Beals's *The Stones Awake*, the book is informative—in a positivist way—about a great variety of aspects of Mexican life from political developments, social manners, and habits of speech down to cooking recipes, and it often avoids traditional stereotypes. US arrogance is exposed over and over again, as when the American journalist Dorothee Thompson is quoted as saying, "'Somehow these people must be brought to their senses. The more intelligent among them quite naturally—the wealthier class, the ones with education—they understand that Madero must go. But there are so few of them'" (*Veracruz*, 315). And yet, even while the following is the view of one of the US American fictional characters, it appears like a bow to a US readership: "[A]s much as her physical features, her manner marked her as American. She had that open, friendly quality that stood out in sharp contrast when Americans were in the company of other more sophisticated or wary nationalities" (89).

The book, with its sympathetic portrayal of Mexico and the social issues that were at stake during the first years of the revolution, could have also become a text reappraising the imperialist past and hence been part of the postcolonial literary movement. Yet although there are scenes that make the revolutionary turmoil real enough, on the whole the material is not sufficiently dramatized because the focus is on the private affairs of the characters, and what an assortment they are! In many ways a successor of Beals, Wright, too, mixes authorial and figural narration without qualms about entering the minds of any of her characters, Mexican or other. The sheer mass of plotlines, themes, and ordinary or eccentric characters (among them an American spiritualist-plus-feminist), the conversations about philosophy or cultural differences, forms of racism and ethic values, and the portrayals of Mexican politicians overwhelm the book. When, at the end of the novel, the characters simply scatter in all directions, this may look like a postmodern variant of historical openness. However, many of the subplots follow the romantic pattern of popular fiction, thus clashing with the demands of literary realism that Wright evokes by the many details minutely described.

*Veracruz* exemplifies the quandaries that the writer of historical fiction about identity-shaping events in another culture and society will run into when he or she tries to avoid giving the impression of arranging the plot according to discursive models while at the same time claiming total insight. By an unintentional self-parody, Wright explodes her own method when she has Limbano Cox, a mysterious relative of one of the Mexican characters, a man of mixed Mexican and American descent and uncannily resembling Francisco Madero, telepathically enter not only the mind of the president, but also the world of the ancient Aztecs. After the murder of Madero, Limbano falls into a six-week coma, that is, a descent "near death" (339), during which he travels to the ancient Tenochtitlan before the Spanish conquest. This gothic excursion into the world of Latin American magical realism only helps to reconfirm cultural barriers even with respect to literary modes, even where the novel, due to the easy contacts between US Americans and Mexicans depicted, might apply a double perspective to the confusions of the revolutionary years. The line between counter-discursive subversion by means of a blending of discursive conventions and a relapse into a discourse of dominance is very thin, indeed.

Thus old Agustín's question referred to initially has to be posed in a more specific way: What kind of narrative will make a historical event like the Mexican Revolution comprehensible? Among texts of the last decades, Agustín's own story, that is, Laurence Gonzales's novel *El Vago*, is perhaps the most successful. Gonzales introduces two time levels, namely that of a frame narrative taking place in 1945 on the day of the explosion of the first atomic bomb in the New Mexican desert and featuring the old Mexican and the young boy Paco, and, on the other hand, the events of the revolution in which Agustín took part on Pancho Villa's side. Agustín and Paco are on a hunting trip, get lost in the lava fields, and, at the end of the book, witness the incredible event of the explosion from close enough to be blown over, but they cannot explain it and Agostín only knows that the radio announcement of an explosion of an ammunition depot must be a lie. Thus, the frame story holds the nucleus of another historical narrative and raises the problem of how and from which temporal and conceptual vantage point the principal story of the revolution can be told. The dawn of the Atomic Age is an event just as much beyond Agustín's comprehension as the Mexican revolutionary wars are beyond Paco's. Again and again the present situation shaping the conversation of the two men interrupts the narration of the past, indicating that all narrative is speaker- and context-bound. Much of the conversation is supposed to be in Spanish, although both speak English as well. Spanish phrases, usually with rough translations, serve to remind us of the dependence of narrative historical truth also on the potential of language.

This is from the beginning, after Agustín's sweetheart Consuelo has been raped by the son of the hacienda owner and after Agustín's foster brother Doroteo, who will later change his name to Pancho Villa, has shot but not killed the attacker:

> "I was too afraid to go back to Consuelo. I was a coward in many ways."
>
> "No," the boy scolded. "You were twelve. Come on, *Tío*, there are no twelve-year-old cowards."
>
> "I was terrified."
>
> "Did you shit your britches?"
>
> "This mouth of yours. Your mother didn't teach you that. Were you raised in a barroom?"
>
> "*Tío*," Paco said, then switched to English. "I was raised in rural New Mexico, for Christ's sake, where every other word I hear is 'shit.' It's hard to avoid."
>
> "*Qué va*," Agustín said. "Then don't say it in Spanish. Dirty up your English if you please. Obscenities in Spanish are more poetic, less direct." (*El Vago*, 25)

Later in the book, Agustín's narrative memories sometimes slip into a style vaguely echoing the Spanish the speaker is supposed to use, as Hemingway did in *For Whom the Bell Tolls*: "'I know. Equally do I love you. But never have I said it because of Consuelo'" (*El Vago*, 229). And the question of language and communication is intensified when we learn that Agustín, coming from an uneducated peon family and going to learn how to read only fairly late in his life, again meets Consuelo, who has mastered this art. She has also in the meantime become a revolutionary fighter like himself, and after they have made love for the first time, she leaves him, but scratches a message into the sand that he cannot read. "I stared at the unfathomable markings with a growing sense of helplessness. Such a stupid thing, I thought, as the skill of reading—that such a small omission could mean the difference between finding Consuelo and not finding her" (108). Here, we have the condensed version of all inequality but also of the limits of communication.

Yet Consuelo will not remain a fixed star in Agustín's life because she, like everybody else, changes roles, allegiances, life purposes. She turns into a cold-blooded sniper begging to be allowed to kill another enemy soldier, and finally winds up serving as minister of propaganda for the government that Agustín is fighting. In the meantime she has vainly tried to get Agustín to escape with her to the United States, to "'freedom'" (204). He asks, "'Are we not bound to stay here?' [. . .] It had never occurred to me to escape from this world [. . .]. I was Mexican. Mexico was at war. Therefore I was at war. For my purposes I had been at war for nearly two decades. I knew nothing else." But she answers, "'Bound how? What have we done but make the people of Mexico more miserable that they were before?'" (205). Before she turns completely cynical, Consuelo has become disillusioned about the revolution and above all about the revolutionary leaders in this *machista* country. "'I have sought a true leader of men, but I have found only barbarians, bandits, murderers, rapists, and many, many of those who have made the ultimate act of faith and cannot be faulted'" (105), that is, who have died in this war. Shortly before, Agustín tried to rape a woman:

> "It was only for a moment, and only just a glance from her, but it hit me like a bullet [. . .]. In that moment I saw her entire life and the lives of all the peasant women in Mexico, who are born, who grow up in tumbledown shacks wearing rags, who have one or two brief years of beauty—a flowering in which there is a surge, like sap rising in the stalk—and then they enter the long state this woman was just entering, of widening face and widening hips from bearing children, of exhaustion and disappointment and depriving themselves of even the little they have so that their children can go through the same thing all over again.
>
> "And like this process was the process of banditry and of revolution. They go around and around and around and can do anything at all except stop." (102)

If this makes the gender aspect of the pervasive social injustice and the failure of the revolution to overcome it abundantly clear, Consuelo later on founds a "Circus of the Revolution," which for Agustín means that

> "[s]he has solved the riddle of how to embrace the horror [. . .]. Always, through all my years of running and fighting and suffering, through all my years of loving her, through everything I always thought that one day there would be meaning or understanding. I once thought Madero would bring it, but he did not. And I thought Doroteo might, and Zapata, and even when I found Consuelo, I thought she might. And now she has [. . .]. It brings people joy." (255)

She, like himself, has also accepted the meaninglessness of the war, but it will take him until after the final defeat of the Zapata army to which he feels most attached, in 1919, to finally flee to the United States and begin a new life. Before that, the revolution had reached its final stage and the anomie of Mexico as a failing state was pervasive:

> Now began the final sacking and looting of the Mexican nation. [. . .] The shattered remnants of the revolutionary forces raided all across the country, taking whatever could be taken, burning buildings, villages, cities. Priests and nuns, because they had always represented the worst oppression of the Mexican people—the Catholic Inquisition—were hauled out of their churches and convents and rectories and shot or hung or tortured to death. Nuns were raped. The churches, which had been ablaze with precious gems and golden

> ornaments, were stripped to the stones. The revolutionists wandered, stunned, broken, venting outrage and attempting to fill the unfillable void. (277)

Before his flight, wounded Agustín is healed by an old Indian medicine man who tricks him into eating the heart of a dead enemy soldier:

> [I]t took me a moment to realize what I was seeing. The soldier's chest had been wrenched open and his heart cut out.
>
> I was unable to control my panic as I ran from the scene and hid in the hut, shivering and weeping, certain that I had finally lost my senses once and for all. I could not stop myself from weeping. My God, I thought, there are my people, this is what I am, I have made the final leap into the abyss and have eaten my enemy to save myself. (289)

This is not an attempt at magical realism, but a gothic incident on the edge of believability. The gruesome scene literally boils all of Mexico's history since the human sacrifices of the Aztecs into one dish of horror, but this has its inner logic, and that extends beyond the war-ravaged country still vainly hoping for salvation to encompass all of mankind. If there is a meaning to the revolution, if there is a meaning to atomic warfare, it is beyond the protagonist to figure out.

Thus, all we get is a life story containing fragmentary insights into the past and its causes. Agustín's very limitations, however, his drifting between the armies and, later, between the two countries, his unreliability, his alternating between self-sacrificing devotion and egotistical betrayal, but also his lack of sufficient information about causes and aims of the fighting make him an adequate symbolic representative of many Mexicans at the time of the revolution but also of the human species as such. His subjective stylizations and private mythmaking turn his narrative, insufficient as it may be, into a convincing combination of history-telling and storytelling. In the Atomic Age, even Mexican Americans will find it hard to demonstrate the historical importance of the revolution to non-Mexicans, and their lack of a historical discourse is shown to correspond to a lack of power. But the construction of a new identity by narrative reinvention calls into question the survival of even the dominant discourse and is thus an articulation of cultural counter-power. In its rejection of the national discourses of both Mexico and the United States, the narrative may be part of a new dialogical identity formation. The fact that this is the text of a bicultural writer may have helped to overcome the impasses of the historical narrative discourses, but the challenge to write historical identity stories across the boundary of self and Other remains.

# PART THREE

# [6]

## NATURE AND CIVILIZATION: NINETEENTH-CENTURY TRAVELERS AND TWENTIETH-CENTURY ESCAPISTS

Ascending, we [. . .] saw behind us a beautiful valley extending toward Hocotan, but all waste, and suggesting a feeling of regret that so beautiful a country should be in such miserable hands.
—John L. Stephens, *Incidents of Travel in Central America, Chiapas and Yucatan* (1: 86)

ONE OF THE RECURRENT elements of many representations of the Latin American Other is nature—nature as sublime mountainscapes, forbidding deserts, or luxurious tropical vegetation and wildlife. Often, exotic nature is linked to the local population; for better or worse, *indios* and *mestizos* are seen as closer to nature, that is, in beautiful harmony with their natural environment or else as equally savage. In a hemispheric perspective, this tied in with fear and temptation as parts of the cultural imaginary concerning the south. It was closely linked to fantasies or politico-economic programs of exploration, penetration, appropriation, and exploitation. In her article "Landscape and the Imperial Subject: U.S. Images of the Andes, 1859–1930," Deborah Poole has shown how the scopic regimes governing pictorial representations of the mountain ranges—a painting by Frederic Edwin Church, an engraving by Ephraim George Squier, and photographs by Hiram Bingham—can be regarded as deriving from differing and competing intellectual approaches, but also "as part of a single discursive and political formation premised on the unquestioned right of North Americans to appropriate the South American landscape to their own, sometimes fanciful ends." But in her conclusion she also states, "I would not want to argue that these—or any—images are bound by any single ideology or discourse. The images [. . .] also carried within them [. . .] a sensuous undercurrent of historical memory, myth, and desire" (Poole 132). Art, cultural productions in general, we may say, carry their share of subjectivity, openness, possibly even antidiscursive messages. As far as Latinamericanism is concerned, it is necessary to consider to what extent the nature-culture complex is part of the appropriative approach or else a redeeming feature. This chapter focuses on travel narratives and fictions from the nineteenth and the middle-to-later twentieth century. But whose nature? Whose culture? Isn't the imperial gaze part of a reciprocal process? An example from Mexican literature may shed some light on the questions to be asked.

Shortly before his violent death in revolutionary Mexico of 1913, the male American protagonist of Carlos Fuentes's novel *Gringo Viejo* (1985) comments that for US Americans, there is no frontier left except the one toward the south. The old *gringo*, that remarkable fictional version of the American writer Ambrose Bierce, and the female protagonist, Harriet Winslow, have traveled to Mexico,

> he consciously, she unintentionally, to confront the next frontier of American consciousness, the most difficult of all, [. . .] the strangest, because it was the closest and therefore the one most often forgotten, most often ignored, and most feared when it stirred from its long lethargy. (Fuentes, *Gringo*, 186)

The experience of crossing the border makes Harriet wish that she might learn not to have the urge "'to save Mexico for democracy and progress'" but to "live with Mexico in spite of progress and democracy, that each of us carries his Mexico and his United States within him, a dark and bloody frontier we dare to cross only at night: that's what the old gringo had said" (187).

The equation of national and individual identity in this passage reveals that the novel depicts the experience of collective identity formation as a process of intercultural reciprocal mirroring. This process is presented in the shape of interpersonal encounters that, in turn, influence as well as symbolize the *intra*personal discovery of selfhood. Alterity thus appears as the alien self. In keeping with Freud's *Civilization and Its Discontents*, Fuentes points out the parallelism of the processes of individual and social development and emphasizes that instinctual repression is the decisive albeit irksome achievement of culture/civilization.[1]

The three main characters all have difficulties in their confrontation with Eros and their death instinct, and in their efforts to mediate between egotistical, chaotic-instinctual desire and altruistic, culturally promotive self-restriction.[2] Individually and in their interaction, they demonstrate, however, that the borderline between nature and culture is an artificial one, the effect of force, an abstraction, and as such part of a model scientifically described in psychoanalysis and cultural semiotics. It would be fatal to equate the two poles with certain national properties. The pole of nature, for instance, is as present in the United States as beyond, because the Mexican desert is but a continuation of the American one: "He was deep in the Mexican desert [. . .], continuation of the Arizona and Yuma deserts, mirror of the belt of sterile splendors girdling the globe as if to remind it that cold sands, burning skies, and barren beauty wait patiently and alertly to again overcome the earth from its very womb: the desert" (*Gringo*, 15).

Their profession and, indeed, calling may make both American protagonists representatives of the party of culture: Ambrose Bierce as a writer and cultural critic, Harriet Winslow as a teacher who initially claims the position of the superego vis-à-vis the Mexicans. Yet both also follow nature, that is, their instinctual nature. The old *gringo* satisfies his death instinct, he fulfils his desire for dissolution. Harriet, on the other hand, is made aware of her problematic ego structure by the sexual experience that the revolutionary general Tomás Arroyo provides for her. Arroyo, in his turn, is associated with nature both by his sensuality and by his ambiguously symbolic name: *arroyo* meaning both "creek" and "dry wash" or "gully." To regard him exclusively as associated with nature, however, is a typically American misunderstanding. His ethnic and social status as a *mestizo* and as the son of a hacienda owner and a servant woman, born out of wedlock and deprived of his material as well as his cultural inheritance, make him the representative of that racial and sociocultural *mestizaje* seen by the author (but also, for instance, by Octavio Paz) as a characteristic feature of the Mexican people.

By linking individual and national varieties of identity formation and the construction of alterity, Fuentes is primarily concerned with the Mexican self-image, namely a coming to terms with the assumed US American perspective, but he is also an astute observer of stereotypical problems US Americans have in dealing with their southern neighbors, and by no means only those near the border. This includes the discursive occupation of the opposition of culture and nature. The border on the Río Bravo/Rio Grande marks a historical trauma for the Mexicans who, after having lost the war with the United States, had to cede more than half of their territory. For them, nature on both sides of the river is not pristine but has been changed by their civilization, a mixed culture of Spanish and Native origin. Seen from the US side, on the other hand, the border rather has the appearance of an extension of the frontier, the historical border connecting and separating wilderness and civilization. This view entails the claim that US civilization has to be spread in the south in order to make those territories usable after the West has lost its potential for perfecting American society.

Hence the old *gringo* still rides into Mexico on horseback, in the tracks and, as it were, in expiation of what his father had done when he rode with the American army of conquest. Harriet, however, travels by railroad. On the one hand, she thereby represents a view of civilization that is more one-sided and more dominantly technological than that of her older and wiser compatriot. On the other hand, this difference corresponds to that of their respective age groups, a generation gap making the historical development manifest. The United States, like its colonial predecessors, had seen itself as to a large extent defined by the uniqueness of "American" nature, as "Nature's Nation" (cf. Perry Miller). At the beginning of the twentieth century, its self-understanding was derived from the complete subjugation of this very nature. At the end of this process, the wilderness was to be permitted to survive only in shape of the nature preserve, the national or regional park, and that is, as a part of culture, in refuges for the collective imagination, which according to Freud can be defined "as the place of compensational pleasure, the fulfillment of impossible desires, the affirmation of the greatness of one's ego, but at the same time as a medium for the establishment of cultural identity."[3]

NATURE, CULTURE, AND CIVILIZATION are highly contested terms.[4] To make them useful for my present argument, each has to be briefly discussed.

1. The age-old distinction between *nature* as all that is given in the universe that is not the result of human activity and, on the other hand, *culture* as the sum total of human ideas, belief systems, forms of social organization, pragmatic activities, and products is highly problematic. Philosophers have posited and evolutionary biologists have proved that humans form a separate species of animals, nothing more. All of human culture is therefore also part and product of human nature (and may be distinguished from the cultures that other animals have developed). To see nature and culture as a totality and to speak of "naturecultures" as Donna Haraway has done appears therefore as much more adequate.[5] Nonetheless, the distinction is still in use and heuristically valuable to describe forms of interaction of humans with their environment. It turns up, in particular, in contexts where a developmental model is used: the closer a group of people are to nature, the more primitive, the less civilized they are, and vice versa. In the inter-American context, this distinction forms part of the discursive construction of the Other.

2. The second use of culture, that of an identity-defining category, also goes back a long way and was brought into discussion most forcefully by the eighteenth-century German philosopher Johann Gottfried Herder. The idea that different groups have different sets of cultural values, ideas, and praxes, and thus form different *cultures* in the plural, is the basis of modern anthropology and cultural studies. In this sense, it is a relational category. In Fredric Jameson's well-known, succinct formulation,

> culture [. . .] is not a "substance" or a phenomenon in its own right, it is an objective mirage that arises out of the relationship between at least two groups.

> This is to say that no group "has" a culture all by itself: culture is the nimbus perceived by one group when it comes into contact with and observes another one. ("Cultural Studies," 33)

In the holistic notion of culture as introduced in the late nineteenth century by the British founder of social anthropology, Edward B. Tylor, "Culture or Civilization, taken in its wide ethnographic sense, is that complex whole which includes knowledge, belief, art, morals, law, custom, and any other capabilities and habits acquired by man as a member of a society" (*Primitive Culture*, 1). Tylor assumes that culture in this sense comprises every aspect of the collective life of a given human population that is not the result of biological inheritance, and that for the individual members of a group, culture is a complex of knowledge and behavior to be acquired by socialization, that is, enculturation. This holistic concept has since come under severe attack and has to be supplemented by a series of additional aspects: all cultures are subject to historical change from within or from contact with other cultures; there is a wide range of intracultural variation depending on factors such as gender, upbringing, and individual choice; there are cultural group formations even within a given society so that an individual will belong to more than one cultural group and her or his identity will be formed by several affiliations and thus often represent some kind of hybridity or else transdifference.[6] This is particularly relevant for multicultural societies like those of both Americas.

3. *Civilization* is often used purely synonymously with *culture* but is always associated with a comparatively high complexity of social organization, technology, systems of exchange of products, and communication systems (particularly writing), but also art, religion, as well as institutionalized and enforced value systems, that is, predominantly, *urban* culture. In this sense of the term, the contrast with an assumed natural state becomes particularly obvious. Hence, civilization is often seen as a process, either in the sense of progressive affectional control, in which the term *civilisation* was used during the French Enlightenment,[7] or, following Condorcet, as the historical process of gaining more and more knowledge and skills as well as developing increasingly complex social structures and institutions, growing emphasis being put on technological innovation. Civilizations can thus be stages in the process of historical cultural refinement as in Norbert Elias's concept of a "civilizing process."

The claims to the highest kind of civilization have been part of the US American self-image since the nineteenth century, but this civilization is primarily associated with material wealth and technological advancement.[8] Latin Americans, on the other hand, have claimed a higher form of culture, epitomized, for instance, in the figure of Ariel versus Caliban mentioned in Chapter 1.

THE CONFLICT OF NATURE and culture in US American history and its literary echoes have been described in Leo Marx's classic study as that of "machine" and "garden," but this conflict has been inherent in the idea of pastoralism, that is nature directed toward the human sphere, from its very beginning. No matter whether America was seen as a paradisiac garden or a threatening wilderness, as a protective, maternal or a dangerous, seductive woman, whether the amount of human work necessary for its full use was considered as small or gigantic—an improvement mentality became dominant in US American history almost from the beginning. This made it possible to view the transitions from the state of nature to an agrarian country and then into an urban, industrial society as continuous, however dramatically and full of tension they might have been experienced and appeared in the cultural imaginary, including its artistic forms of expression.[9] However strongly the ideal of a reentry into paradise, that is, a nonconflictual merging of nature and culture, may have been hoped for initially (cf. Achilles), the practice of settling the country and its discursive foundation was soon more shaped by the idea of an appropriation of the natural, if needs be, by force. The discussion about the nature of the frontier here offers material galore (cf. Fussell; Slotkin). Vestiges of the idea of paradise have survived, for instance in tourism advertisements, but by and large it has dwindled to the function of a rhetorical figure.

It is not possible here to dwell exhaustively on the changes of the ideas of nature in the United States and its colonial predecessors, nor on those of the terms *nature* and *culture* in general. There is an enormous semantic range from the religiously informed concept of nature employed by the Puritans to the notion of a nonteleological nature forming the precondition of a scientific-technological control of it. The most interesting forms of dissent have been elicited by the question as to what extent the human is part of nature. What is essential in the present context is only the basic assumption of an opposition, that is, of a sphere contrasted with nature, a sphere than can be minimally defined as that of free, and thus not nature-directed human action. In the United States, the term *culture* has been closely linked with the notion of a process of civilization.

When the United States saw its Manifest Destiny in its original sense as fulfilled, that is, when it had occupied and to a large extent put to use its part of the continent from east to west, but even before, when the end of this process was in sight, more attention was devoted to those other areas of the Americas that had been included in the American sphere of interest at least since the Monroe Doctrine. Primarily this meant the south, Latin America. The paradigm of nature versus culture that had served as a discursive figure of thought during the development of social, political, and certainly also literary models of one's own country now served as an important instrument of perceiving Latin American reality, too. However, it could not be applied to the new terrain without much difficulty.

As far as external nature (topography, flora, and fauna) was concerned, utilitarian as well as aesthetic ideas in the United States through the late nineteenth century were governed by the given or potential usefulness of the area. For a long time, only (originally) wooded regions were considered acceptable in this sense, whereas the treeless prairies were thought of as "barren" in every respect (Stilgoe 23). After it had been shown that the prairies could be developed after all, these experiences were projected onto Latin America. It was assumed that those areas most similar in climate and landscape, that is the moderate zones of Argentina and Chile, could be opened up for progress in the same manner. American investors and potential emigrants were disappointed when these countries were not ready to create or were incapable of creating the necessary conditions with respect to military security as well as political and social stability (cf. Fifer).

In his important book *Facundo, o civilización y barbarie* (1845), the Argentine writer and later president Domingo Faustino Sarmiento contrasted "barbarism," that is the Catholic, colonial Spanish tradition and the wild nature of his country, including the *indios* and gauchos, with "civilization," that is the modern, Europe-oriented, urban culture. This version of the nature-culture paradigm remained very influential in nineteenth-century Latin America, whereas North Americans regarded it as rather disconcerting because of its sweeping disparagement of nature. If such differences existed even regarding areas that were topographically and demographically the most similar to those of parts of the United States just mentioned, the dissimilarity of the regions covered with tropical forests or the Andean mountains was regarded as much more striking. The excess of the familiar regarding the dimensions of space, the variety of flora and fauna, the formations of landscape, and the phenomena of weather and climate, which European immigrants registered when traveling in North America, was once again surpassed by what one found in the southern continent. US Americans also noticed a backwardness in the process of utilization of nature that was partly attributed to these geographical conditions, but partly also to a different attitude among Latin Americans, one more passive than shaping and changing.[10]

To place the peoples south of the Rio Grande into any pattern of nature and culture proved even more difficult if they happened to be the descendants of the pre-Columbian great civilizations.[11] Most US citizens regarded the majority of Latin Americans as comparatively primitive, but it was a primitiveness that differed considerably from that attributed to the "savages" of one's own country by appearing less based on a proximity to wild nature. This observation was easily explained by the concept of degeneration. Anglo-Saxons had applied this concept to Mediterranean Europeans when their captivity in outdated political and religious institutions, their civilizational backwardness, and their reputed moral deficiency were compared to what one imagined classical antiquity to have been like.[12] According to race theories popular even in the twentieth century, it was primarily the mixture of races that produced such degeneration. In many US American texts, mixed-bloods of Spanish or Portuguese colonists and the Indian aboriginal population fare particularly poorly.

THE DIFFICULTIES RESULTING FROM a modeling of reality based on the dichotomy of nature and culture or civilization are visible already in early US American fictions and travel literature. Indeed, not only those North Americans coming as invaders, but also those entering Latin America as visitors, travelers, tourists, engineers, entrepreneurs, or even immigrants, found the spaces they encountered prestructured by their discursive order of things and by their geographical imaginations (as explained in Chapter 4). This becomes most obvious in what we call travel literature because this genre will usually adhere to patterns of experience or of mental configuration rather than to the demands of plot and character development. One influential book about Latin America that was known to many US writers and that escapes the invasive model at least to a certain extent is Alexander von Humboldt's *Vues des Cordillères et monumens des peuples indigènes de l'Amérique* (1810).

As Laura Dassow Walls has shown in her impressive study *Passage to Cosmos: Alexander von Humboldt and the Shaping of America*, the influence of the German explorer and polymath on the scholarly world, the arts and letters not only of Europe and Latin America, but particularly the United States during the nineteenth century, can hardly be overestimated. And of course he served as a model, inspiration, or source of information for numerous later explorers, naturalists, travelers, and, yes, invaders. Obviously, Humboldt's enormous venture of first exploring and then textually constructing Latin America, his decisive role in the "reinvention of América" (Pratt 112) cannot be separated from the European efforts of that period to arrive at an understanding of the globe from a Eurocentric perspective and to thereby also open it to economic exploitation and political control, a process that has much to do with industrialization beginning in the eighteenth century. Humboldt's and Aimé Bonpland's travels through the Americas from 1799 through 1804 therefore figure prominently in Mary Louise Pratt's *Imperial Eyes*. Yet, as Walls's study makes clear, Humboldt as the politically, intellectually, and materially independent liberal, opponent of slavery and defender of the indigenous peoples, was not guided by the acquisitive, assimilating gaze of others.[13] His explorations of the physical, cultural, anthropological, economic, and political structure of the parts of the globe he visited, and his achievement to form his insights into a cosmos (to use his own word) of coherences and correspondences remain unique. Although he cannot be separated from his age, as, indeed, he would have emphasized himself, and although quite a few of his findings served others well—for instance, the maps he had drawn when it came to the US expansion into Mexican territory—his aim was to enlarge the human mind, not the property of his or other countries. His combination of what we are used to call science and humanities may look idealistic and, indeed, is influenced by the ideas of German and international Romanticism. But, as Walls's book shows again and again, his major works opened many vistas, for instance in the direction of modern ecology and environmental science. His influence on Charles Lyell and Charles Darwin is well documented. His descriptions of Latin American countries and regions were an eye-opener by breaking through the wall of colonial Spanish secretiveness. And his insistence that natural and cultural phenomena, space, and (historical) time had to be seen together carried rich fruit, for instance among American literati such as Irving, Prescott, Poe, Emerson, Thoreau, and Whitman.

Bridging fields, impressions, and opinions is also the basic structural principle of *Vues des Cordillères*. As Oliver Lubrich and Otmar Ette have demonstrated in their postscript to the marvelous German edition of 2004, Humboldt transgresses the conventions of the travelogue by replacing the chronological itinerary with discontinuity and a nonchronological moving backward and forward, organized by a relational, retinal order of observations, learned treatises, travel narrative, and illustrations. Humboldt begins his *Views and Monuments*[14] with the discussion of an Aztec statue, that is, with his stay in Mexico from 1803 to 1804, and ends with an observation from his visit of Tenerife in 1799. This dissociation from the travelers' spatiotemporal itinerary continues throughout the book, so that the temporal references are the history of mankind and geological history rather than the autobiographical chronology. Humboldt avoids the narrative approach prevalent in the travel writing of his time because it focuses on the merely personal (Pratt 120–21).

In addition, Humboldt gives a more complex impression of the social diversity of the countries and regions of many parts of Latin America than either the metropolis-centered Spanish perspective or the homogenizing Northern superiority discourse would allow. And he finds a generic blend of personal travelogue and scholarly treatise that fits this avoidance of an ingression turning into transgression (cf. Lubrich and Ette 415–18). Central to his work is a view of the New World as characterized by an overwhelming nature, and the archaeological objects included are those of peoples in tune with the wild nature of the Andes, the llanos, or the volcanoes of central Mexico. Culture is seen as in dialogue with nature and, in a sense, as its offshoot. Human figures usually form only illustrative supplements to the views of natural wonders depicted on the plates, and where, rarely, contemporary civilization comes into play, as in the picture of the Peruvian letter carrier swimming down the river with the mail securely carried in a head scarf, Humboldt points out the efficiency of this method in the absence of roads—quite a far cry from his admirer Edward Everett's derisive comments on the same method quoted in Chapter 2. Humboldt sees, and by the book's arrangement presents, primal nature and human culture and civilization as "harmony and connection" (Pratt 133), even though his aesthetic standard concerning cultural productions remains that of the Mediterranean world.

John L. Stephens's *Incidents of Travel in Central America, Chiapas and Yucatan* (1841) presents a completely different model of travel literature. As Humboldt was accompanied by the French botanist Aimé Bonpland, so was Stephens by the Englishman Frederick Catherwood, who created the engravings for the book (of which those of Mayan antiquities have gained great reputation in archaeological and art historical research). Stephens and Catherwood had planned to travel in Central America in order to study the archaeological sites when Stephens was made United States Minister to the Central American Federation that had been formed in 1825 after independence from Spain had been achieved. The country had newly been united under Francisco Morazán (1831–39), but his and the Liberals' purge of the Conservatives and the clergy had met with strong opposition in several of the states that formed the federation, and Stephens arrived at the very time when the *indio* Rafael Carrera, leading the troops of the Conservatives and particularly his religiously fanaticized Native regiments, defeated the central government and the country fell apart. Stephens's effort to be accredited by the national government failed completely, and, indeed, he and Catherwood spent months traveling from Belize to Guatemala and then to El Salvador, Nicaragua, and Costa Rica in a series of vain attempts to find and identify the legal government. Eventually, they gave up and moved on to Yucatán, where they explored and excavated the Mayan ruins of Palenque—their lasting merit and an enormous contribution to awakening the popular and scholarly interest in that almost forgotten civilization.

The traveling took place under extremely difficult conditions because of a lack of roads and means of transportation, and often Stephens and Catherwood found themselves in great danger, caught between the fighting parties, because the war was waged with utmost brutality and under conditions of disorder, shifting allegiances, and an absence of any regard for life and property of even the civilian population. Neither Stephens's papers nor his diplomatic dress, with a hat bearing the American eagle, were safeguards against the ignorant rabble soldiers of the warring parties. We find the American and his British companion alternating between a position of social, discursive, and, not least, economic superiority (if need be, Stephens simply buys some Mayan ruins in order to have free access) and almost complete victimization by the circumstances surrounding them. Different from "the great Humboldt" (*Incidents*, 1: 98), with whose work Stephens is familiar, he does not try to bring order and a system of relationships (however open and suggestive) to the chaotic material with which he is confronted, but in his often day-to-day account makes the reader follow him from one difficult and confusing situation to the next. We can follow his route on the map, yet there is rarely anything like a superior perspective in the text. Like the travelers, we are usually made to work our way through almost impassable wildernesses and equally irritating and confusing human encounters. Often, this makes for exciting reading, but not exactly for deep and detached insights. Where Humboldt describes the practice of crossing steep mountain passes by human carrier, that is, sitting in a chair strapped to the back of a native *carguero*, he remarks that this practice may appear to be degrading in our eyes (and it was in his), but is not for the locals, who consider it an honorable profession practiced voluntarily in spite of hardship and poor pay and not because of pure need (Humboldt, *Ansichten*, 36–38). This is at least an attempt to arrive at a balanced view. Such an effort is lacking in Stephens, who is forced by illness to try this transportation once, but finds it intolerable:

> It was bad enough to see an Indian toiling with a dead weight on his back; but to feel him trembling under one's own body, hear his hard breathing, see the sweat rolling down him, and feel the insecurity of the position, made this a mode of travelling which nothing but constitutional laziness and insensibility could endure (*Incidents*, 2: 276),

properties he attributes to many of the local population. He reports that "Though toiling excessively, we felt a sense of degradation at being carried on a man's shoulders" (2: 274), because the procedure unsettles his US American sense of civilized human interaction, not because it is considered degrading for the carrier.[15]

The material space of Central America thus does not interact with an imagined space that is governed by globally conceived geographical and geological structures, social systems, and patterns of sociocultural history as in Humboldt. Stephens's geographical imaginations consist, on the one hand, of aesthetic patterns in the European tradition that he applies to the grandiose landscapes and the tropical birds and flowers, and, on the other hand, of notions of an omnipresent decay and degeneration. He starts out describing nature and landscape in terms of the beautiful and the sublime (and, occasionally, the picturesque) as they had been defined in eighteenth-century Europe. They had now, in the period of a US American national culture defining its own range and specificities, been applied by Irving, Cooper, and the painters of the Hudson River School to the landscapes of North America, in order to demonstrate that these were not inferior to those in Europe even though they were almost completely lacking in historical associations. And just like some of the authors discussed by Leo Marx, Stephens deals with the conflict of the "garden" and the "machine" entering even here by assuming a position of aesthetically transforming detachment:

> Steamboats have destroyed some of the most pleasing illusions of my life. I was hurried up the Hellespont, past Sestos and Abydos, and the Plain of Troy, under the clatter of a steam-engine; and it struck at the root of all the romance connected with the adventures of Columbus to follow in his track, accompanied by the clamour of the same panting monster. Nevertheless, it was very pleasant. We sat down under an awning; the sun was intensely hot, but we were sheltered, and had a refreshing breeze. The coast assumed an appearance of grandeur and beauty that realized my ideas of tropical regions. There was a dense forest to the water's edge. Beyond were lofty mountains, covered to their tops with perpetual green, some isolated, and other running off in ranges, higher and higher, till they were lost in the clouds. (1: 26–27)

In later passages Stephens continues to draw comparisons with European sceneries, particularly the English park landscape, or with mythological scenes, and he credits the *indios* with possessing "that eye for the picturesque and beautiful in natural scenery which distinguishes the Indians everywhere" (1: 32). In such an environment, the Native is bound to be a noble savage.

However, closer observation produces difficulties. The jungle proves to be virtually impassable and the mountains as almost impossible to cross. When the pure-blood Carib Indians turn out to be "completely civilized" (1: 28), this is proved only by the fact that they appear as pious Catholics. Repeatedly, Stephens delights in what Pratt has called "the-monarch-of-all-I-survey scene" (201–8):

> At eleven we reached the top of the mountain, and, looking back, saw at a great distance, and far below us, the town of Chiquimula; [. . .] and, rising above a few thatched huts, another gigantic and roofless church. On each side were mountains still higher than ours, some grand and gloomy, with their summits buried in the clouds; others in the form of cones and pyramids, so wild and fantastic that they seemed sporting with the heavens, and I almost wished for wings to fly and light upon their tops. (1: 77)

But this ultimate elevation cannot be reached; the church ruins signal deterioration and loss. The jungle swallows pre-Columbian pyramids and Spanish-colonial edifices alike. At this point Stephens begins to complain about the lacking utilization of the country. "The scenery was grand, but the land wild and uncultivated, without fences, enclosures, or habitations" (1: 57). Rather than cultivating the external as well as human nature and making it subservient to technological and sociopolitical progress as is the custom in his own country, people here submit to their frailties: their indolence, but also their passions and violence. At the same time, they submit to nature as it surrounds them and by its climate conditions, by a vegetation all but impossible to control, by earthquakes and volcano eruptions appears to mirror or even support these negative human tendencies. The net result is decay and decline. The prehistoric ruins that must have been built by a completely different kind of people find their counterparts in destroyed or decaying churches. Stephens evokes the pre-romantic, melancholic tradition of the *ubi sunt* reminiscent of Goldsmith and the school of the picturesque when he speaks of "a picture of a deserted village" (1: 79), yet on the whole his is not a comfortable aesthetic but a critical point of view:

> At six o'clock we rose upon a beautiful table of land, on which stood another gigantic church. It was the seventh we had seen that day, and, coming upon them in a region of desolation, and by mountain paths which human hands had never attempted to improve, their colossal grandeur and costliness were startling, and gave evidence of a retrograding and expiring people. (1: 78–79)

Although living in republics, the people have no idea of democratic interaction as it is practiced in the United States, but seek the physical annihilation of their political opponents and thus live in a Hobbesian state of constant civil war. Following then current discourses of the degenerating effect of racial hybridity, Stephens sees the social order as corrupted by a mixture of many ethnicities. In one of the small towns, he finds "Indians, negroes, mulattoes, Mestitzoes [*sic*], and mixed blood of every degree, with a few Spaniards" (1: 37). Soon he has to realize that many of the couples are not married, that further inland the male and female population, regardless of race, walks around semi-nude, worst of all "a little white girl, perfectly naked" (1: 57). The clergy conforms to Anglo-American notions about the corruption and sexual immorality of the Catholic priests: "In the evening we visited the padre [. . .]. He was a short, fat man, [. . .] and we found him swinging in a hammock and smoking a cigar. He had a large household of women and children; but as to the relation in which they stood to him, people differed" (1: 66). Stephens has a hard time handling these impressions with a certain detachment, although with "people differed" he manages to produce an almost Twainian irony. And when he tells a hacienda owner at whose place they spend the night and who, it turns out, has two wives, that "in England he would be transported, and in the North imprisoned for life for such indulgences," he receives a lesson in cultural relativity: "he responded that they were barbarous countries; and the woman, although she thought a man ought to be content with one, said that is was no *peccato* or crime to have two" (1: 89).

While chastising what he considers a transgression of basic social and religious rules, Stephens is in fact guilty of a transgression of his own by transferring his set of rules to an alien culture. Without completely acknowledging it, he is in precisely the situation often encountered by ethnologists and described by David Signer. The cool observation of the Other, which presupposes a clear distinction of an object and a subject uncontaminated by what he or she tries to describe, as well as the potential reversal of the two positions, remains an illusion. Rather, and in tune with psychoanalytic tenets, we recognize the object only as far as it is part of ourselves and thus also the subject of a projection (Signer 102). The proximity of transference and transgression observed by Freud (cf. Knellessen, Passett, and Schneider, introduction) finds its realization in Stephens's disgusted comments about half-naked women and his falling in love with a local young woman, whom he desires because "her manner was so different from the cold, awkward, and bashful air of her countrywomen, so much like the frank and fascinating welcome which a young lady at home might extend to a friend after a long absence" (1: 390). The transgression he commits by first tempting her into closer contact than her society would normally permit is topped by the second when he leaves her the next morning: "I walked out of doors, and resolved that it was folly to lose the chance of examining a canal route for the belle of Guanacaste" (1: 392).

He regrets "that so beautiful a country should be in such miserable hands" (1: 86), and it cannot come as a surprise that just as he visits the wildest and most untouched region of Nicaragua, Stephens sketches the plan for an isthmian canal preferably to be built by US Americans. The project of a canal, which was to connect the Atlantic and Pacific Oceans, and to which

Stephens did in fact devote part of his later life, is not only to become a boon for world trade but also a means of saving Central America:

> It will compose the distracted country of Central America; turn the sword, which is now drenching it with blood, into a pruning-hook; remove the prejudices of the inhabitants by bringing them into close connexion [*sic*] with people of every nation; furnish them with a motive and a reward for industry, and inspire them with a taste for making money, which, after all, opprobrious as it is sometimes considered, does more to civilize and keep the world at peace than any other influence whatever. [. . .] I would not speak of it with sectional or even national feeling; but if Europe is indifferent, it would be glory surpassing the conquest of kingdoms to make this greatest enterprise ever attempted by human force entirely our own work. (1: 419–20)

The metaphor of the fertilizing streams of civilization coming from the urban center develops the biblical image of heavenly Jerusalem and the waters of life and the Puritan one of the "City upon a Hill" into a program of purpose for the future American commonwealth, secularizing the image and strangely exchanging the poles of nature and culture. It follows that in Stephens's opinion, the civilizing feat of the construction of a canal at the connecting point of the Americas should be carried out by the United States, possibly only by the City (!) of New York. Civilization, coming from the metropolis and epitomized in the steamship, will literally penetrate Central America; needless to say that Stephens's vision was to be realized more than seventy years later with the opening of the Panama Canal, fulfilling his economic hope, albeit hardly those of "civilizing" the country. As we also know, this aim was achieved by powerful intervention without changing the situation of most Latin American countries in the manner anticipated by Stephens.[16]

There are moments of regression when Stephens, quite in keeping with Freud's theory of culture and civilization, discovers in the natural scenery he encounters an island of wish fulfillment and thus a niche reserved for art in the system of sublimation required by civilization:

> [O]n a point above us was a palm-leafed hut, and before it a naked Indian sat looking at us; while flocks of parrots, with brilliant plumage, almost in thousands, were flying over our heads, catching up our words, and filling the air with their noisy mockings. It was one of those beautiful scenes that so rarely occur in human life, almost realizing dreams. Old as we were, we might have become poetic, but that Augustin came down to the opposite bank, and, with a cry that rose above the chattering of parrots and the loud murmur of the river, called us to supper. (1: 55)

The reality principle wins out against the dream, the poetic and the anti-language of the parrots.

IN VIEW OF THE comparative scarcity of nineteenth-century fictional texts on Latin America by American female writers, the following text stands out as an exceptional treatment of the encounter of a North American woman with nature, civilization, and cultural differences in Latin America.[17] Mary Peabody Mann's *Juanita: A Romance of Real Life in Cuba Fifty Years Ago* was published posthumously in 1887 but presumably written in large parts before the Civil War. The novel is based on a fourteen-month recreational stay at a friend's plantation in 1830s Cuba, where Mary Peabody had accompanied her sister Sophia, Nathaniel Hawthorne's wife-to-be, and thus offers perspectives usually not available to American women at that time.[18] If *Juanita* had been published in the 1850s, it might have become a major abolitionist text.[19] Peabody Mann might also have fulfilled the role of an "ambassador of culture" (Gruesz), and as such might have represented a counter-model to New England poet Maria Gowen Brooks, who inherited a plantation in Cuba and became a member of the slaveholding criollo class there.[20] Because Mann focuses almost exclusively on the horrors of slavery and on racial inequality, her book is less dominantly an example of Latinamericanism than other texts discussed here. Where she describes Cuba in general, she uses the conventional, stereotypical elements: church depravity, political corruption, civil disorder, immorality, all of which is made worse by the institution of slavery. In view of "a people so nationally ignorant as the inhabitants of the Spanish Colonies" (*Juanita*, 201), the only hope for improvement lies in an annexation by the United States; but Mann is afraid that this might strengthen racism even at home and thus echoes the fear of an infection. After all, the action of the novel is set about fifty years before slavery is finally abolished in Cuba in 1886 and about thirty years before the Thirteenth Amendment to the Constitution of the United States.

What makes the novel exceptionally interesting in the present context, though, are its detailed descriptions of nature and the way nature is perceived by the foreign observer. Nature appears as closely related to what makes Cuban society and culture of that period more different from and more similar to those of, respectively, the Northern and the Southern United States, that is, the peculiar institution of slavery. The central, focalizing figure of the novel is Helen Wentworth, an unmarried New England schoolteacher who comes to visit her former schoolmate Isabella Rodriguez, who has married a plantation owner. He is, as abolitionist Helen is horrified to find out, a slaveholder. It is Helen's observations (closely modeled after Mann's own) that we are made to follow. Right at the beginning, she notices the beauty of scenery and vegetation, but also the way the plantation houses are hidden from view:

> After leaving the white limestone formation that surrounds the city of Havana, and which is very dazzling and trying to the eyes, they passed into the deep, rich, red soil of the interior, which makes such fine contrast with the luxuriant foliage. No fences mar the beauty of the scenery, but the plantations are bordered with broad lime hedges, impervious, by reason of their spines, to man or beast, and often covered in their turn by a little blue convolvulus, whose delicate vine trails over them and the adjacent earth. No houses are seen from the road, but gates, sometimes of great architectural beauty, and always more or less pretentious, shut in long avenues of trees. (28)

The slight suspicion that is already here cast over the harmony of nature and culture grows deeper later on:

> Vegetation clothed the earth there [in New England] as here, but here its rank luxuriance, where untamed, typified the unbridled sweep of human propensities, while the curbs and restraints that a certain measure of civilization imposed upon it only concealed the fens and marshes that were the product of a decay as pestiferous to the physical as the corruptions of the heaven-born passions are to the moral atmosphere. (49)

And, indeed, corruption and decay mark slaveholding Cuba far more drastically than even the degeneration pointed out by Stephens.

The culmination of this darkening view of tropical nature against the background of the horrors of slavery is reached when Helen and others witness the opening of the gigantic, magnificent blossom of the night-blooming cereus cactus, which is described in great detail and leads Helen to the following observation: "This most glorious of all flowers, shining out upon the dark night, brought back her old faith, that God had not forsaken even the land of the slave" (114). However, when they return to the plantation house, "Helen's heart sank within her, for she apprehended some new calamity, and immediately she saw a tall, stout negro, with his hand hanging by the skin from his wrist, severed from the arm and spouting blood" (114). It is a fugitive slave whose hand the brutal overseer has cut off with a machete because the slave had injured one of his dogs used in the pursuit. The two scenes follow immediately, one after the other, and make abundantly clear that in this land of horrors, Helen's trust in a divine order is ill-founded. Sympathetic nature responds by sending a violent storm that creates great damage, as we are to find out later. The sum total of Helen's observations is that Cuban civilization, for instance as far as agricultural technology is concerned, is only weakly developed if compared to that of the United States

(158), that Cuban society is totally corrupt, and that "[t]he confusion created by a succession of rulers each following the policy his own self-interest suggests, gives rise to many evils that are not found in United States slavery" (209)—a comparative view of civilizations that sheds light on the fundamental divisions characterizing the United States and the US American perception of its neighbors that might be of interest for either the Southern or the Northern side of the divide.

The corruption of humans and nature in Cuba is made most glaringly obvious by the introduction of the embodied moral alternative, Juanita. The eponymous heroine of the novel is a light-skinned woman of "singular Moorish beauty, which bore no trace of the negro" (62)—although an abolitionist, Mann shares many of the racist conceptions of her age, down to her description of black slave Camilla's "long, orang-outang arms" (85). Juanita has Moorish and European ancestors and belongs to a group of slaves that were legally emancipated under British pressure, but whose status has been denied to them by the tyrannical Spanish Captain-General Miguel Tacón and the majority of the Cuban plantation owners. She is well educated and an accomplished painter. Although aware of her status as *emancipada* but in contrast to her rebellious brother, she makes no attempt to leave the Rodriguezes, partly out of loyalty toward some of the family members, partly because she is in love with Ludovico, the Marquis of Rodriguez's son, who also loves her and for whose children she is a surrogate mother. When Juanita is at last set free, Ludovico, after his horrible white wife has died, proposes to marry her, but she realizes that her role as a former slave would "'ruin his earthly life. His father will never consent to it or forgive him. It is enough for me that he wishes it. If I marry him, I shall be a dark cloud upon his life'" (211).

Juanita's noble self-sacrifice conforms to that of many female characters in nineteenth-century fiction. When she is caught together with her brother under the suspicion of rebellious activities, they and "twelve hundred other negroes, free and enslaved" (217) are herded together in a building. There, all of them perish when a furious mob sets fire to the house. That is, she suffers the fate of the tragic mulatto whose social role (albeit not racial background) she fulfils (Ard xxi). According to Patricia M. Ard,

> Mann used her own form of the romance to tell a story of slavery in the Americas and its corruption of what she valued most—marriage and the family. [. . .] But Mann unintentionally told another tale as well. By taking away Ludovico, her beloved, from Juanita, not once (when he married a white woman) but twice (when she dies), Mann re-inscribes the culture of ethnic dominance and rejects a vision of a racially harmonious future for the Americas. (xxxiii–iv)

However, this is an all-too-simple notion of the function of fictional literature to offer role models for real life. Juanita's fate abounds in ironies. She dies physically because she is taken for a slave, which she is not legally but through her fate, but she has already died symbolically when she renounced Ludovico because she realized that—even in view of all the cases of miscegenation that occurred in all slaveholding societies—the consummation of her erotic desire would bring about the collapse of the social, that is civilizational, status of her beloved and his children. She, the sensual (slightly) dark heroine, is the most culturally refined of all the characters in the book, overcoming her instinctual nature for the sake of fulfilling her role as savior of the core element of the official, European and North American civilization of her age, namely the family and parenthood. She is culturally superior also because of her art, by which she reconciles nature and the human spirit:

> [I]n Juanita's portfolios she [Helen] found abundant food for reflection. There was the history of a soul, as it were. The difference between Juanita's sketches, whether of a rare flower or tree or landscape, or of a head—of which there were innumerable specimens,—and the drawings of Ludovico, was the difference between talent and genius. Juanita's were not transcripts of anything, though portraits, but were expressive of the highest thought suggested by the image. (*Juanita*, 145–46)

Juanita's art has overcome the split between nature and culture, and that between the civilizations. More than the other characters who have contributed their share in Victorian home-created art—Isabella, Helen, Ludovico—she is the one who deserves to pursue her vision as a self-determined, gifted person, and the ironic, despairing message of the novel is that liberation needs other, economical, forces to succeed. As the last, retrospective pages of the novel make clear, in the final analysis poetic justice can be hoped for only in the afterlife. Religion is the refuge for those who are part and parcel of the cultural discourse but are powerless to step out of it, as it is the reward promised to those whose flesh and spirit are mutilated by this very culture.

MOST NORTH AMERICAN MENTAL constructions of Latin America at the end of the nineteenth and the beginning of the twentieth century focused not on a timeless paradisiac nature but on the usable, changeable environment. After the failure of the development hoped for on the Pampas, the pioneer or cowboy and, after 1849, the soldier as those character types who, emulating the winning of the American West, open the land for themselves, their civilization, and society, are replaced by the engineer, the planter, the merchant, and the entrepreneur; examples have been discussed in Chapter 4. The image of the Garden of Eden is now used only to lure American capital.

In his annual report for 1900–1, the first US governor of Puerto Rico after the Spanish-American War says, "Puerto Rico, the loveliest island washed by the ocean's waves, lies between the Atlantic and the Caribbean. [. . .] Nature has here 'planted a garden' and man has only 'to dress it and keep it' to make it blossom like another Paradise" (qtd. in Binder, "Tropical," 93). Reductionist literary texts of this period therefore did not even need to develop a suitable plotline in order to defend the marriage rules, that is, to defend white protagonists against the embraces of seductive, dark-skinned natural men and women, as James Fenimore Cooper and others had found it necessary. In Claude H. Wetmore's *In a Brazilian Jungle* (1903), the wedding between a young American woman and a British nobleman functions as the confirmation of a community of interest of the Anglo-Saxon master race. Remarkably, the component of sexuality is completely eliminated from the discourse on exotic, savage alterity. Anglo-Saxon cooperation is also required when US coffee importers and English marines jointly put a criminal Brazilian coffee planter out of action, a man who has been associated by the appropriate imagery with the treacherous side of tropical nature in the shape of snakes and tarantulas. Never is there a question about the validity of the imperialist discourse of superiority. Brazil is described only in its function as a potential supplier of natural raw materials that have to be produced and processed by competing North American and European businessmen.

AROUND THE MIDDLE OF the twentieth century, however, other perspectives appear. The escapist motif in Stephens is now taken up by a small but noticeable group of writers, among them the Beat Generation of the 1950s and 1960s. By now the political situation had changed dramatically since the days of classic imperialism. The Cold War had brought the idea of a Third World, and Latin America was considered to be part of it, a zone of influence that was now, for the first time after the role and investments of the European powers had been reduced to second place, seriously contested between the United States and the Soviet Union. Kennedy's Alliance for Progress sought to keep the Latin American countries firmly at the side of the West as it was then conceived of. New developmental measures were introduced by US administrations, and Latinamericanism, though still intact in its basic elements, for a while displayed a friendlier side that included respect for the various democratic and social movements in several countries, even while the support for anticommunist dictators continued. Such shifts in US policy vis-à-vis Latin America had occurred before, but now the discourse of socioeconomic development, in conjunction with the images that post–World War II mass tourism had brought home, created a mood for a less arrogant approach to the southern neighbors.

At about the same time, the disillusionment with capitalism and the materialism and technology orientation of the American way of life among many young people north and south, and the wish to escape from it; the enthusiasm for revolutionary movements for the underprivileged at home or abroad, and the fetishizing of leaders such as Malcolm X or Che Guevara; and the environmental movement and alternative lifestyles, like that of the hippies, brought about a heightened awareness of other cultures and differing forms of culture, now clearly distinguished from civilization as the ruling model for dealing with the Other in need of development. This also brought a new sensitivity for the conflicts or convergences of nature and culture. Recent studies such as María Josefina Saldaña-Portillo's *The Revolutionary Imagination in the Americas and the Age of Development* or Molly Geidel's *Peace Corps Fantasies* have revealed that neither government-created volunteer work in the "underdeveloped" countries nor the revolutionary movements could truly overcome the barriers separating the visitors from the target population, especially indigenous peoples, nor could they develop a true alternative to the developmental narratives of capitalist thinking in the period. Still, at the time such dreams were dreamed, and they find their representation in literary texts like the ones discussed in the last part of this chapter.

Real or pretended escapism presents itself in almost touching naiveté in the writings of the Beat Generation. However, this does not imply a diminishment of the claim of control, even where that control is not openly admitted, for instance when the young beatniks in Jack Kerouac's novel *On the Road* enter Mexico. The categories of description used in their approach to alterity stem from their own needs of projection, and thus of appropriation and internalization of the Other. Thus, the Mexicans the travelers see along the road are called "cats" (*Road*, 276) or "straw-hatted Mexican hipsters" (275). Kerouac also dehybridizes the local population by continuously calling them "Indians," a term that he then applies to a major part of the traditional human population on earth. In the eyes of Kerouac's fictional alter ego Sal Paradise, Mexico is a territory belonging to one part of that globe-encircling, archaic fellah population that will outlive the atomic apocalypse and guarantee the fresh start of natural man:

> The boys were sleeping, and I was alone in my eternity at the wheel, and the road ran straight as an arrow. Not like driving across Carolina, or Texas, of Arizona, or Illinois; but like driving across the world and into the places where we would finally learn ourselves among the Fellahin Indians of the world, the essential strain of the basic primitive, wailing humanity that stretches in a belt around the equatorial belly of the world from Malaya (the long fingernail of China) to India the great subcontinent to Arabia to Morocco to the selfsame

> deserts and jungles of Mexico and over the waves to Polynesia [. . .]. These people were unmistakably Indians and were not at all like the Pedros and Panchos of silly civilized American lore—they had high cheekbones, and slanted eyes, and soft ways; they were not fools, they were not clowns; they were great, grave Indians and they were the source of mankind and the fathers of it. The waves are Chinese, but the earth is an Indian thing. As essential as rocks in the desert are they in the desert of "history." And they knew this when we passed, ostensibly self-important moneybag Americans on a lark in their land; they knew who was the father and who was the son of antique life on earth, and made no comment. For when destruction comes to the world of "history" and the Apocalypse of the Fellahin returns once more as so many times before, people will stare with the same eyes from the caves of Mexico as well as from the caves of Bali, where it all began and where Adam was suckled and taught to know. (280–81)[21]

In opposition to traditional US notions, Mexico is being masculinized by this chain of associations, but its "fatherly" inhabitants display features connoting femininity. As in D. H. Lawrence three decades earlier,[22] the Indio-Mexicans are feminized: the keyword "soft" occurs repeatedly and is contrasted with a destructive masculine US American hardness. Or one might say that the pervasive body imagery of this text reduces the difference between the genders and makes the locals appear as belonging to a natural, Adamic state before the fall. Entering Mexico is also stepping out of history, which is seen as a destructive process. Timelessness or a cyclic return of the same are the marks of natural mankind before "civilization and its discontents." The central bordello scene thus appears like a fantasy of primal wish fulfillment: sex, drugs, dance, and music make a "long, spectral Arabian dream in the afternoon in another life" (289) come true, which even the pecuniary coda cannot ruin.

By recoding the traditional American auto- and hetero-stereotypes, the drifters come to regard Mexico as a natural paradise. What is usually held to mean cultural degeneration is here seen as a positive resistance against the American way of life, or as its shrinking to a more humanly acceptable measure, so that even economic weakness turns into something positive: "We gazed and gazed at our wonderful Mexican money that went so far" (276). The friends explicitly distance themselves from the earlier American invaders or importers of civilization, and in their enthusiasm they even shift the spatiogeographical proportions:

> Behind us lay the whole of America and everything Dean and I had previously known about life, and life on the road. We had finally found the magic land at the end of the road and we never dreamed the extent of the magic. "*Think*

> of these cats staying up all hours of the night," whispered Dean. "And think of this big continent ahead of us with those enormous Sierra Madre mountains we saw in the movies, and the jungles all the way down and a whole desert plateau as big as ours [. . .]. It's the world! We can go right on to South America if the road goes" (276–77).[23]

Their geographical imagination replaces what most observers agree on as real by dream and fiction ("the movies"); the process of cultural sublimation is reversed. Quite in tune with this inverted repression of their rejected identity components in favor of a view of nature as resistant, they never realize the contradiction of their own lifestyle on the road and the natural sedentary one of the "Fellahin." Perversely, even the traffic, noise, and bustle of Mexico City are presented as "Fellahin-childlike" (302) and thus as a sign of an existence close to the earth.[24]

LIKE THE THEME OF the Other in general, that of alien nature as compared to civilized society has often been used for cultural criticism in the twentieth century, and particularly after World War II. A decisive development of the potential range of this topic is presented in Paul Theroux's novel *The Mosquito Coast* (1981). As told by his son, Al Fox—a Yankee from Massachusetts—is an inventor and a sharp critic of the wastefulness and the social as well as ecological sins of American civilization, which he thinks is destined to come to a catastrophic end. Together with his family, Fox emigrates to Mosquitia, the most remote region in Honduras, to risk a new beginning in the jungle where he erroneously expects to find an untouched new world. With his wife and children as well as a group of natives (*mestizos* and *zambos*, that is, people of mixed Indian and black genealogy), he creates a community by using that which nature has provided in a seemingly optimal manner. "This was the distant empty place that Father had always spoken about. Here he could make whatever he pleased and not have to explain why to anyone" (*Mosquito Coast*, 164).

> "The Iron Age comes to Jeronimo," Father said. "A month ago, it was the Stone Age—digging vegetables with wooden shovels and clobbering rats with flint axes. We're moving right along. It'll be 1832 in a few days! By the way, people, I'm planning to skip the twentieth century altogether. [. . .] You look at Jeronimo and you can't tell what century it is. This is part of your original planet, with people to match [. . .]. What's a savage? [. . .] It's someone who doesn't bother to look around and see that he can change the world." (162–65)

A production plant for ice blocks turns him into a bringer of civilization —"'Ice is civilization'" (39)—and indeed Fox might fulfil the role of an "ambassador of culture," but when he tries to get rid of three armed intruders by freezing them in his ice machine, the plant explodes and contaminates the whole area. Even Fox now admits the destructive side of his paranoid ideas. "'All right, I admit it—I did a terrible thing. I took a flyer. I polluted this whole place. I'm a murderer.' He sobbed again. 'It wasn't me'" (275). His sorrow does not refer to the people he has killed, but to the dead plants and animals. From now on, accompanied only by his family and increasingly under the spell of his delusions, Fox tries possibilities of a fresh beginning with ever simpler means but is defeated by uncontrollable nature, with which to live in real harmony (as his children do in their playground camp) he is too proud and too technology obsessed. He will admit only his own, nonwasteful concept of a technological-scientific civilization, and finally meets his death when he tries to destroy the technical equipment of an American mission.

Ironically, yet also sympathetically, Theroux narrates the failure of the refugee from American civilization who represents this very civilization in archetypical purity: as a believer in progress even where he criticizes progress, as a loner and extreme individualist in spite of his role as father of a family, and, in spite of his notions of cooperation, a work fetishist who will not tolerate anybody by his side, let alone in front of him. Unmistakable intertextual references make him a reborn version of Mark Twain's Connecticut Yankee who, in the end, can also not improve but only (partially) destroy the alien and nature-oriented world he has entered. Fox's struggle against the superstition of Christianity may be as justified as that of Twain's Hank Morgan, but because both can replace it only by new myths of the perfectibility of mankind, myths that cannot be turned into reality with humanity as it is, the catastrophe is predictable.

Fox's fearlessness in facing the alien in man and nature may distinguish him from others: "'When a man says women are all the same, it proves he's afraid of them. I've been around the world. I've been to places where it doesn't rain and places where it doesn't stop. I wouldn't say those countries are all the same'" (84). But as he cannot yield himself to this Other, he does not develop a fruitful alternative position. In this context it is worth noticing that for the protagonist, sexuality is of no importance because outside this theoretical statement, it does not seem to influence his notion of the country to be opened up. It is exactly this point that puts him in line with a series of American heroes to whom Annette Kolodny attests immaturity:

> Our continuing fascination with the lone male in the wilderness, and our literary heritage of essentially adolescent, presexual pastoral heroes, suggest that we have yet to come up with a satisfying model for mature masculinity on this

> continent; while the images of abuse that have come to dominate the pastoral vocabulary suggest that we have been no more successful in our response to the feminine qualities of nature than we have to the human feminine. (*Lay of the Land*, 147)

It is significant that Fox speaks of the small model of his ice machine as "she," but of his plant in the jungle as "he" (*Mosquito Coast*, 31, 163). The closeness of his experiments to the products of the very civilization he tries to escape is verbo-satirically exposed when a native speaker of Creole calls them "'spearmints'" (165).

Theroux confirms and updates not only Twain's criticism of progress, but also his skepticism with regard to the possibility of an escape from civilization. His narrator is Fox's oldest son, a boy of the age of Huck Finn, who, together with the other children and in their own little refuge place, playfully explores the gesture of nudity and a life of and with nature:

> I felt that ours was a greater achievement than Father's, because we ate the fruit that grew nearby and used anything we found, and adapted ourselves to the jungle. We had not brought a boat-load of tools and seeds, and we had not invented anything. We just lived like monkeys. (177)

In the end, however, the son dreams of only one thing: a return to the United States where he would ironically find a well-stocked (factory-made) refrigerator. His father's claim to improve upon creation fails already because of the insufficiency of man's physical nature. At the end of his life, Fox is paralyzed by a bullet and can only drag himself across the sand on his belly, like a reptile: "Father was missing, but we could see the groove-mark of his body across the sand, like a lizard track, with handprints on either side" (380). Along the coast that is covered with the debris of civilization swept here by the sea, only the natives are able to survive, because they have learned to recognize their limits vis-à-vis nature and have adapted their lifestyle to a very small stock of cultural possessions. They are the representatives of a shadow economy, mixed-bloods not only of race and language, but also because they maintain an in-between status between wilderness and civilization. Theroux's critique is pervasive: while US Americans cannot escape their destructive culture qua civilization because it corresponds to their inner nature, a large part of Latin Americans exist in constantly shrinking niches of survival, dependent on a reconciliation of nature and culture that is constantly growing less probable under the pressure from the north.

For the late twentieth-century engagement of North American writers with the irritatingly ambiguous Latin American alterity, the paradigm of nature versus culture still plays an important role, but the poles have become confused. The achievement of culture now does not rest on a perfectly rational management of existence, but in the most complete adaptation to the given. "Scavengers"—the seagulls feasting on refuse both in Massachusetts and in Honduras, Fox himself, who at the end uses trash to create a new basis of civilization, and the vultures taking care of his remains—are the prototypes of a new world for which the border between Anglo and Latin America, between culture and nature, will not be relevant any longer.

# [7]

## GENDERED PERCEPTIONS OF LATIN AMERICA IN TWENTIETH-CENTURY US LITERATURE

[A] subtle differentiation on both sides of the biological barrier, structured by the recognition of a social law to be assumed in order ceaselessly to be contested
—Julia Kristeva, "On the Women in China" (79, qtd. in Minh-ha 103, 116)

AS WE HAVE SEEN in previous chapters, questions of gender are never far from inquiries into the nature of ethnic alterity. Stockton's and Davis's novels exemplify the binarist, masculine-feminine concept of the active, superior, invading United States and its representatives on the one hand and the passive, submissive, and at best sensually attractive south on the other. This finds its sequel in early twentieth-century primitivism, as in Porter's portrayal of María Concepción, whose activity amounts to a violent reestablishment of the old order. As the century went on, gender roles were often, but not always, seen as more complex. Sometimes, Latin American women, such as Beals's Esperanza, Hergesheimer's La Clavel, or Gonzales's Consuelo, gain considerable agency and demonstrate that feminism and changes in the concept of gender roles are not a North American privilege. When Consuelo becomes a sniper in the Mexican Revolution, and a cynic at that, she goes beyond the "tender violence" of the US female photographers in Laura Wexler's book by this title, who by their domestic-looking images, by masking the violence going on, in fact were accomplices of racism and imperialist brutality at the end of the nineteenth century.

The assumption in such texts and other cultural representations is that there are two genders and that they stand in some form of power relation. The rigid binarism implied here looks absurd in the age of Third Wave feminism with its emphasis on the constructedness and fluidity of sexual and gender identities beyond femaleness and maleness, and on the intersection of race and gender, resulting in the development of a variety of feminisms outside the one originating from and focused on the needs of white middle-class women, a charge often leveled against the Second Wave. Black feminisms like Alice Walker's "Womanism" come to mind, or Ana Castillo's Chicana "Xicanisma," which will be briefly addressed later in this chapter.

However, on a level outside of recent feminist theory, we have to admit that the primary division of humankind into two—and not a plurality of—genders is a basic element of the construction of social order around the globe. Its underpinning is an uneven distribution of power, and thus a Foucauldian discourse that has regional, ethnic, and class varieties. Thus, while the constructedness of gender is not questioned, it makes sense to see two discourses of alterity, namely race (and by extension, ethnicity and other-culturality) and gender in their interaction. This chapter, then, deals with such interaction as it manifests itself in earlier and later twentieth-century literary texts. My question is whether Latinamericanism is reinforced or complicated or even counter-discursively subverted by this interaction. As will be seen, this interdiscursivity is made virulent not only by the historical varieties of the discourse of Latin American alterity, but also by the changes in the gender discourse of the period. I will refer therefore to gender models where they inform the fictions under discussion, but do not aim to follow the debates on gender theory beyond that.

The description of ethnic alterity in terms of gender and sexuality has a long history. Although it can be traced back to antiquity, in the Western tradition it became general practice in the age of colonialism, notably in texts related to the so-called New World. The *locus classicus* for a systematic argument along such lines, and an example that is particularly revealing for the purpose of a study of North American literature about Latin America, is Ginés de Sepúlveda's application of so-called Aristotelian dichotomies of superiority and inferiority in the context of his debate with Bartolomé de Las Casas in the year 1550.[1] As I have pointed out in Chapter 2, Sepúlveda classifies the *indios* as the inferior contrary of the Spaniards in a chain of opposites such as body versus soul, animals versus humans, and, notably, women versus men. The conflation of ethnic and sexual differences almost always entails the explication of the unfamiliar by means of the familiar, the naturalization of an asymmetrical distribution of power, and, finally, the element of self-definition that results from the definition of the Other (Uerlings 20).

Much of this type of analogically linked hierarchical binarism has survived into later European and North American notions of colonized peoples, notably US notions of Latin Americans.[2] This continuity has been facilitated by specifically racist assumptions developed during the nineteenth and twentieth century. They complement and often overlay those on cultural difference. Mexicans, Guatemalans, and so forth were and often are collectively regarded as brown-skinned people, as "Indians," often also as unmanly if compared to American masculinity, and are presented as such in many literary texts, too. Race and gender are discursive constructions just like cultural identities, but they are still widely used in essentialist terms. Their intersection has long been a well-known phenomenon, but it was the coining of the term *intersectionality* in an article by law professor Kimberlé W. Crenshaw in 1989, and her own and others' work since that publication, that has made intersectionality studies an important branch of social science, political studies, gender studies, and others. The argument that the interaction of social and biological identity formation factors such as gender, race, class, or sexual orientation defines the forms of marginalization of individuals and social groups more precisely than the focus on just one of these categories, as had been customary before, is convincing. However, because the object of my study is not to describe marginalization as a social "fact," but the discursive construction of forms of otherness, I will use the term interdiscursivity rather than intersectionality.

The association of race and gender has been the focus of a number of critical studies, for instance Gail Bederman's *Manliness and Civilization* and Robyn Wiegman's *American Anatomies*, both dating from 1995. Notwithstanding their strangely reductionist tendency to equate race relations with white-black relations, such studies help to clarify the inherent contradictoriness of the identity discourse of (Western) civilization. Thus, for instance, the white fear of oversexed African males, of hypermasculinity, as it were, undermines the traditional association of whiteness with masculinity, control, and hence civilization. Human tendency to think in binary, linked pairs and the pitfalls inherent in such discourse was nicely illustrated by that old liberal slogan "blacks and women" used when speaking in favor of marginalized groups. An answer to this misleading binarism was given by Gloria T. Hull, Patricia Bell Scott, and Barbara Smith in their groundbreaking volume of 1982, *All the Women Are White, All the Blacks Are Men, But Some of Us Are Brave: Black Women's Studies*, that helped diversify the Black movement by a black feminist branch and the Women's Liberation movement by nonwhite feminisms.

During the last decades, many feminist critics have availed themselves of Jacques Derrida's critique of the dichotomous tradition in Western logocentric philosophy. In many of his works, the French philosopher pointed out the insufficiency of thinking in such binary pairs as presence and absence, speech and writing, identity and alterity, man and woman. Difference in this tradition, says Derrida, means inequality, with one term functioning as the ostensibly less positive counterpart of the other—but also failing to function, as one opposite "bleeds over" into the other whenever one tries to define it. Just as he uses his analyses of older philosophical texts, that is, the discursive tradition of Western philosophy, to point out the insufficiency of the dichotomous model to describe actual processes of thought, language and perception, so literary texts often subvert the very discourse they are part of. Derrida's own reading of Nietzsche, for instance, brings us close to the core of the topic of this chapter. In *Spurs* (1972), Derrida points out how Nietzsche, the woman hater, for whom femininity is tantamount to unreason, by linking "woman" to metaphor and literary writing makes her in fact an ally in his own project of undermining traditional Western philosophy with its very claim to reason, to logical truth. Similarly, the linking of the two discursive fields of ethnic and of gender alterity may reveal a deconstructive potential. Though these discourses look structurally similar and thus facilitate processes of converging differentiation, their interdiscursive interaction may not only yield a mutual reinforcement of patterns of world perception and description, but, not infrequently, also open up a contrary and subversive field of the imaginary.[3]

AS LONG AS GENDER is seen and represented only as analogous to the identity-alterity dichotomy referred to in perceptions of ethnonational alterity, the contrastive force of the alterity discourse remains unquestioned. It is only when gender appears as a discursive field in its own right that things may become more complex. That this is by no means always the case is shown by numerous adventure novels using both sets of stereotypes for a negative or else positive characterization of some Latin American country, group, or individual. What I propose to do here is to look for examples of a destabilization of the two discourses by their interaction in a given text, to see whether this discursive interplay may not subvert the analogy of the Other in gender and ethnicity terms, whether the intersection of the discourses may not even have been used intentionally by the authors for the breaking up of binary patterns. Once again, my selection is intended to present a spectrum of possibilities, not a systematic overview. I want to demonstrate the potential of interdiscursivity, sometimes in texts where one might not expect such complexities. Because gender is a pervasive, inevitable aspect of human life, most texts analyzed elsewhere in this study might be examined in this context, too, and in some cases I do indeed return to my previous analyses. I use twentieth-century, mostly US American fictional texts for exemplification but will start with a nineteenth-century classic by way of illustrating the potential inherent in this interdiscursive process.

Herman Melville's first novel *Typee* (1846) is not a text about Latin America but about the Pacific Marquesa Islands in the period of colonial expansion, yet also, in a way, about genderized perceptions of ethnic alterity in general. The starting point of the novel is familiar from numberless colonial texts: the masculine protagonist and representative of a white, patriarchal, and superior order enters the world of an ethnic Other semanticized as feminine. Early in the novel, Melville has his fictional alter ego Tommo and his comrade unintentionally descend into the valley of the ferocious, cannibalistic tribe of the Typees, whom they had hoped to avoid. In their preconceived notions, the Typees represent the ethnic Other, savagism at its worst, because they have a record of violence not only against other tribes but also against colonial intruders. In Melville's description, the descent of the two men through an unmistakably female genital topography can be read as a symbolic return to the womb. Subsequently, and following an old chain of analogy, the feminine in its Typee variety is made to appear as particularly close to nature. The beautiful Fayaway, who will be Tommo's female companion for the weeks of his semi-captivity, represents the natural, "savage" state in a particularly soft and none-too-alien variety. Here a Victorian sexual fantasy has found its lusciously physical embodiment.

And yet Tommo's dealings with this projection of male desire appear regressive rather than erotic. Due to a leg injury acquired during the descent, Tommo is helpless and has to be carried around like an infant—readers schooled in even a household version of Freudian psychology will recognize that he has suffered a symbolic castration. Thus the very scene that appears as the culmination of sexual wish fulfillment remains curiously ambivalent. Unbelievably, Fayaway has been released from the strict order defining the roles of men and women in her culture and, against the taboo, is lying in a boat with Tommo. Suddenly she gets up, takes her robe of tappa—the only piece of clothing she is wearing—from her shoulders and "spreading it out like a sail, stood erect with upraised arms in the head of the canoe. We American sailors pride ourselves upon our straight clean spars, but a prettier little mast than Fayaway made was never shipped a-board of any craft" (*Typee*, 134). The gender roles have been reversed, and vis-à-vis the feminine, Tommo finds himself once again on the level of what Julia Kristeva has defined as the semiotic, the pre-Oedipal stage of pre- and nonverbal drive articulation—after all, he cannot speak the language. By his return into the maternal *chora* he experiences the assault of the semiotic, which will restructure the symbolic order, that is, in Lacanian terms, the patriarchally defined linguistic-plus-cultural order, in this case the order of Western culture Tommo has been carrying along. The territories of the semiotic and the symbolic are linked by transitions in both directions. For Kristeva, the drive enters the universal order of signification, the "natural" language guaranteeing the social structure.[4]

However, when Tommo is not on the lake, sporting with Fayaway, he finds himself in a different, alien symbolic order using its own "natural" language.

What terrifies him is not so much the suspension of his sexual identity as symbolized by the transfer of the phallus to Fayaway and thus the undoing of his male individuation, that is, his self-alienation. What he is mainly afraid of is the prospect of being swallowed by the alien *culture*. He faces the prospect of being swallowed in a literal sense, namely as a potential victim of cannibalism. According to Kristeva, the act of sacrifice turns violence into a signifier. It is therefore structurally related to an alternative procedure Tommo finds hardly less threatening: the submission to the Other by undergoing the body tattoo, because this would mean—once again, literally—an inscribing into the symbolic, into the order of language where individuation occurs and hence into an alien culture. In continuation of the regression metaphoric of the earlier parts of the novel, Tommo would then find himself reborn into the order of the Typees—a notion filling him with horror and an eventually successful desire to escape. While he is thus allowed to retreat behind the walls of American masculinity, Melville, the author, in the rich symbolism of his very first novel demonstrates an awareness of the relativity of cultural and gender identity,[5] of the endless deferral of "truth" about the self and the Other, the masculine and the feminine, the outside and the inside, eating and being eaten. From the initial analogy between ethnic and gender alterity arises an interplay of the two alterity discourses that is productive of any degree of ambiguity, of a subversive questioning of both orders of social interaction: that of Victorian, patriarchally conceived gender relations and that of the superior Euro-American subject position vis-à-vis the "dark races."

INTERDISCURSIVE BORDER CROSSINGS can be perceived in much simpler terms, notably in such works of popular fiction seemingly intended to affirm all the binarisms the alterity discourse has in store. This applies to many novels in the context of imperialist expansion, even after World War I. And yet, there are surprising disruptions. In Rex Ellingwood Beach's *Jungle Gold* (1935), the action is set at the turn of the nineteenth to the twentieth century; Theodore Roosevelt's ruthless policy regarding the Panama question is alluded to and finds the protagonist's approval. The historical context is the establishment of the big American fruit companies in Central America. The protagonist, a handsome, blue-eyed giant with a name indicating his sense of mission, Steve Pentecost, founds a great banana plantation in the jungles of Honduras, becomes a railroad king, and manipulates local politics in conformity with his desires. He is a man without a past: "his origin was a mystery and his destination was uncertain. [. . .] He was [. . .] a man of peculiar detachment, at one moment as loving and at the next as ruthless as a child" (10).

A combination of Mysterious Stranger and American Adam, Steve embodies US American masculinity in a purely future-oriented, expansionist, go-getting, rugged individualist variety. Again and again he leaves Hannah, his submissive yet resourceful American wife, behind in order to follow what he considers his destiny—the taming of the jungle: the foundation of an agribusiness empire against such obstacles as the often violent political opposition and the equally violent and sometimes criminal business competition, an incompetent and backward local population, or the forces of a wild and overpowering nature with hurricanes and earthquakes, floods, and diseases that kill great numbers of his workers, including those he has brought from the United States. Part of this destiny is to be found in the beautiful and vitalizing shape of Mamatoca, a Mayan woman representing wild, tropical nature whom he needs as his female counterpart: the source and aim of his drives, waiting to be conquered by him, "for in the fire of her primitive passion smoldered the very life force of the forest itself" (116).[6] Steve thus turns into an increasingly savage robber baron reminiscent of Theodore Dreiser's Cowperwood. He who represents the American pioneer spirit in its various historical shapes, also symbolizes the noncontrollability of instinctual nature. In subjugating the wilderness, in opening and, eventually, exploiting it, Steve reveals "something wild, inexorable, and vastly menacing about him" (169). His untamed inner nature leads to destruction when he appropriates the resources of civilization.

Civilization, on the other hand, manifests itself in the resistance against one's desires. It is represented by Hannah, who also stands for the American past and tradition. She is of old pioneer stock and embodies a good deal of Calvinist belief and work ethics. She tries to fulfill the gender role allotted to nineteenth-century American women, that is, to exert a moralizing influence on her half-savage husband, an influence based on family values plus religion.[7] The maternal role accrues to Hannah exclusively: Mamatoca, the representative of maternal nature, is forced by her tribe to abort Steve's baby, an event that marks the beginning of her physical decline. Yet when the Pentecosts are increasingly estranged, Hannah grows to the additional public task of compensating for Steve's misdeeds by acts of charity and by spreading a benign civilization—she builds a hospital and founds a city on the coast where living conditions are more salutary for the people. That is, she assumes the civilizing and tempering role that the bourgeois gender discourse assigned to women, but with a power and efficiency denied to most women of that period, and thus assumes the role of founding *mother* for parts of the country. At the same time, her husband increasingly falls prey to his instinctual nature and is rational only in terms of a goal-oriented pragmatism, without the controlling social responsibility the nineteenth century expected male leaders in politics and business to personify. Steve agrees to his business partner's proposition: "'Let's make this a white man's country'" (129), but it is Hannah who is much more successful in introducing North American standards—a kinder, gentler colonialism, we might say.[8]

Gender borders are crossed again in the way Beach presents the careers of Steve's and Hannah's children: the girl follows the passionate ways of her father; the son resembles his mother, and as Steve's successor in the company introduces modern and more humane business methods. At no point does the novel indicate any doubt about the superiority of North American concepts of civilization over the "backward," dirty and disease-ridden, politically anomic conditions in Central America. Yet in the course of unfolding a story of personal and economic successes and failures, binary concepts of nature and culture, passion and rationality, superior and inferior peoples, all of them epitomized in the gender relations acted out in this novel, are increasingly destabilized. If discourses define that which makes sense in a given society, the normative surface, as it were, they also carry along a subversive, "nonsensical" underside that tends to become apparent when they intersect with other discourses, a fact that finds its symbolic expression in Steve's jungle death of a fever he has contracted from his dying "wilderness woman" (116). It remains anybody's guess as to which extent this subversion reflects an authorial intention. Beach, known for his adventure novels with settings like the Klondike or the Canal Zone and an unlikely candidate for symbolic complexities, may simply have let the power of discourse(s) do its own work.

BEACH'S BOOK IS STILL based on turn-of-the-century imperialist premises and late Victorian ideas of gender relations. It thrives on comparatively simple reversals, on an exchange of positions. The period after World War I, with its questioning of social, and in particular of gender norms, produced other and more ambitious fictions at the intersection of the discourses of gender and ethnicity that explore the changing, performative quality of discourses, cultures, identities, even bodies much more radically, whether the author does this intentionally or not. Reinhold Görling has shown how the differential aspects of cultures and societies are complemented by the production of interspaces or even non-spaces, heterotopias in Foucault's terminology, where intercultural dialogue can take place beyond the projection of what is cultural practice within one's own society. Often, in literary texts dealing with an internal alterity, the exotic is used as a heterotopic testing site for the study of alternate forms of existence and identity.

The most famous example of such experiments of the imaginary in the context of the European and North American discourse of Latin America, or, for that matter, of gender, is D. H. Lawrence's Mexico novel *The Plumed*

*Serpent* (1926)—a British text that served as a model and touchstone for many North American writers. As Annegreth Horatschek has pointed out, Lawrence uses a Mexico in concordance with the whole range of then current stereotypes concerning that country, its population and cultural forms of expression, to develop a highly gendered model of alterity. Lawrence's critique of post–World War I European society is developed in a series of ironic gender reversals. The British female protagonist Kate represents a male, logocentric European civilization that in Lawrence's opinion has become decadent, weak, and in this sexist sense, effeminate. She escapes from her private traumata to the postrevolutionary Mexico of the early 1920s, where she finds the men feminine in a double sense. The urban *mestizos* disgust her as "fattish town men in black tight suits" (13); they are "the mongrel men of a mongrel city" (25), according to the widely held Western association of racial mixture with decadence. The disappointingly unheroic toreros are "effeminate-looking. [. . .] With their rather fat posteriors and their squiffs of pigtails and their clean-shaven faces, they looked like eunuchs, or women in tight pants" (19). If this negative linking of an obtrusive physicality with cultural deficiency seems to be reminiscent of the way early Europeans associated the "dark races" (158) with inferiority, femininity, the body, Lawrence's reasoning is entirely different. These men appear as negative because of their intimate association with Western civilization. The pure *indio* men, on the other hand, are seen by Kate as overwhelmingly beautiful in a way that combines physical strength with features carrying primarily female connotations: softness, smoothness, relaxation, passivity: "Their very nakedness only revealed the soft, heavy depths of their natural secrecy, their eternal invisibility. They did not belong to the realm of that which comes forth" (131).

This association of female passivity with alterity has been described by Luce Irigaray and other feminist critics. Just as the patriarchal order regards woman as disruptive because with her supposed inaction she represents the "Other" of the male subject, of the male discourse, so Kate experiences these *indios* as disruptive of her Eurocentric concept of reality (Horatschek 677). When Kate joins the subversive indigenous movement founded by her Mexican friends, a movement urging the return to pre-Columbian cultural and religious practices, and when she ritualistically marries the *indio* general Cipriano, a "column of blood" (*Plumed*, 433), she takes part in the rediscovery of a dark race in more than one sense of the word, a "female" race, as it were, from which, in Lawrence's gender-plus-culture heterotopia, a redefinition of masculinity might take its beginning.

Lawrence's view of Mexico and his powerful descriptions of Mexican life have had a deep impact upon North American texts on Latin America.[9]

However, his tortured modernist-primitivist philosophy based on a mixture of essentialist notions on race, gender, and the sociopolitical appears dated, and his idealization of a strangely conceived femininity and the gender order he envisions have been regarded with disgust particularly by most feminists. But female writers have brought their ideas of the order of gender to bear on their writings about ethnic alterity just as much as their male counterparts; and so have those who question simple, binary models of gender: gays, lesbians, and bisexuals. Again, we have to recognize that fiction on ethnic alterity is genderized also on the level of the author's personal identity and the social discourses that shaped it, Latinamericanism among them.[10]

In a remarkable carryover from the sentimental fiction of the nineteenth century, the role of the teacher and governess appears as a recurring feature in North American fiction on Latin America, notably that written by female authors.[11] The failure of the protagonists' "civilizing" efforts because of the conflict of the discourses of ethnicity and gender is portrayed most brilliantly in the work of the great modernist Katherine Anne Porter. Porter admired Lawrence's portrayal of the visible Mexico but detested the particular brand of sexism she found in his writing, where the female characters achieve full self-realization only in becoming part of some male-dominated system of society. Look once again at her short story "Flowering Judas" (1930), which I have discussed in Chapter 5 in the context of fictions on the Mexican Revolution: Laura shares the frustration and aimlessness that characterize Lawrence's protagonist at the beginning of *The Plumed Serpent*, yet her failure has to be seen not so much as that of a representative of the declining West, but as a personal defeat in view of the discrepancy between high pretensions and insufficient fulfillment, both applying to her personal role as well as to the fate of the revolution. Although she has a freedom of action that goes beyond what was customary for women particularly in Mexican society, much of what she goes through is gender specific. A male character would not feel threatened by a macho society the way Laura does; just as little could a male protagonist be made to appear as betraying his sexual and social role by rejecting all potential partners.

Whereas most literary characters in North American fiction on the southern neighbor seem to have internalized the gendered version of Mexico as the country of desire, whether for sex or power or death, Laura does not, or not any longer, conform to a role model that fits this pattern and that seems to work for millions of tourists and any number of adventurers of both genders: "Nobody touches her, but all praise her gray eyes, and the soft, round under lip which promises gayety, yet is always grave, nearly always firmly closed: and they cannot understand why she is in Mexico" (*Collected Stories*, 95). However, rather than using her disillusionment for achieving the neutral position of an uninvolved observer, Laura finds herself in an intercultural situation where she is, as it were, paralyzed by the conflicting demands of several discursive systems. She can neither reject the Other of the revolution nor become an unquestioning part of it. She can neither assume the superior North American, quasi-masculine role of controlling her personal gender relations nor accept the submissive role of Mexican women according to the national cliché. Because she cannot retire to any form of either-or position, because binary differentiation as a mode of structuring reality is no longer sufficient, because there is no saving hybrid position, either, she remains in a state of painful transdifference. I will come back to this aspect at the end of the chapter.

INTERDISCURSIVE GAPS APPEAR MORE frequently after World War II, in the period of the Cold War, and sometimes make for highly suggestive texts. I return here to Michael Rumaker's short story "Gringos" (1966), which I have used in my introductory chapter to demonstrate the workings of Latin-americanism. The story, however, contains a second level of meaning that transforms it from a stereotypical to a deeply ironic text. Set at the historical moment when post–World War II beliefs in US military, economic, politi co-institutional, and cultural superiority defending the "Free World" against communism are beginning to be questioned by the Vietnam War, the student rebellion, ethnic and civil rights movements, and the new, Second Wave feminist movement, the story ironically undercuts US superiority beliefs by showing the dead end of a male chauvinist sex and gender discourse in conjunction with an equally dated idea of ethnic-cultural alterity.

What the protagonist, a young American man, whom we later get to know by his first name Jim, encounters in the Mexican border town seems to confirm not only ethnic but also gender stereotypes concerning the foreign country. There is the little boy who exploits his sister, there are the old churchgoing women exploited by the church, there are the shameless gender relations characteristic of a society where everybody can be bought, and they are linked with the physically repulsive. A young Mexican man whom Jim asks for directions flirts with two girls and lets his pants down in front of them; the girls simply giggle. Another urinates into the street. The young *gringo* and Harley, the American sailor, see a woman combing her wet black hair. "Her hair had the shine of a bird's wing, glossy and rich" (*Gringos*, 51). But when they approach her, this solitary specimen of stereotypical Latin American female allurement immediately lifts her skirt: "The flesh of her legs hung loose and pebbled in the stark afternoon sunlight, the skin greenish and laced with clusters of veins" (51). As in a medieval morality play, we are shown the hideous underside of carnal attractiveness. The discourse of the Latin American Other is exemplified by the sphere of gender relations. Treacherously alluring females are exploited by macho males, and both cooperate to exploit the visitors from the North, who nonetheless represent a nation whose manifest destiny it is to control and exploit the brown-skinned people, the racially inferior.

However, the intersection of race and gender here also serves to reveal the curious contradictions of discourses of alterity. At first glance Rumaker's story seems to conform to an American discourse of a gendered Mexico to be penetrated by American men bent on adventures, on escape from whatever restrains or threatens them at home, on sexual wish fulfillment, or on the acquisition of economic gain or political power: in a word, men pursuing a quest for self-realization and thus, identity. The pages of North American fiction by male white authors, whose picture of Latin America is shaped by their own genderized identity construction, are populated by such characters. In our case, the young protagonist is on a walking tour to Mexico City, "'walking away from trouble'" (44), as he says. The sailor is on furlough and is obviously taking advantage of the superior power he both represents as a member of the US Navy and embodies by his impressive physical strength. What they encounter across the border is a sterile Mexico whose feminine qualities have been reduced to commercialized sexuality, a wasteland rather than a subtropical paradise.

And yet the two Americans themselves appear as reductive forms of American self-perception: dirty, foul-mouthed, and without manners, they can hardly count as representatives of a superior patriarchal civilization. As the title indicates, they deserve the contemptuous Spanish epithet *gringo*. To make things even more complicated, there are at least hints of a potential interest in homosexuality, though both men articulate their reserve in this matter. Sexual identity appears to be fluid even in a vociferously binary order of genders. Another aspect calling clear divisions into question is the omnipresence of the abject, not only on the Mexican but also on the American side. Jim and Harley repeatedly expectorate, as do the Mexican characters, male and female. An American sailor is lying "in the middle of the road, his cheek resting in a pool of vomit" (38). The hotel bed the two Americans share is covered with "blood and come stains" (44), but Jim does not mind having sex with the same prostitute directly after the sailor: "'I don't mind sloppy seconds'" (58). Mexican workers carry sides of bloody, fly-covered meat into a butcher shop, but again the Americans share the physical experience: "Jim and the sailor stopped and watched, Jim idly leaning his shoulder against the rear of the van and staining his shirt with blood" (49). In Kristeva's definition, the abject—blood, urine, bodily fluids, the unclean—is associated with the maternal body and hence with the permeability of the border between the female, pre-individuation realm of the semiotic and the male-dominated, identity-establishing order of the symbolic (Kristeva, *Powers of Horror*). In this story, the abject unites Mexicans and Americans. Rumaker's mode of presenting his protagonist only from the outside resembles Hemingway's method and reminds us of his theory: Most of the iceberg remains under water, that is, for the reader to discover.

What emerges in the reading process is that the encompassing negativity of the world encountered by the *gringos* corresponds to their own negative traits. From here it is easy to see Mexico—abject in a general and also a psychoanalytical sense—as a projection of the protagonist and hence part of himself. In terms of Kristeva's later study, *Strangers to Ourselves*, we all bear the foreign, nay, the foreigner, within ourselves, as what is strange, disturbing, in Freud's sense *unheimlich*, uncanny:

> Foreigner: a choked up rage deep down in my throat, a black angel clouding transparency, opaque, unfathomable spur. The image of hatred and of the other, a foreigner is neither the romantic victim of our clannish indolence nor the intruder responsible for all the ills of the polis. Neither the apocalypse on the move nor the instant adversary to be eliminated for the sake of appeasing the group. Strangely, the foreigner lives within us: he is the hidden face of our identity, the space that wrecks our abode, the time in which understanding and affinity founder. By recognizing him within ourselves, we are spared detesting him in himself. A symptom that precisely turns "we" into a problem, perhaps makes it impossible. The foreigner comes in when the consciousness of my difference arises, and he disappears when we all acknowledge ourselves as foreigners, unamenable to bonds and communities. (Kristeva, *Strangers*, 2)

It is the negation of this foreignness in ourselves that leads to its projection onto the external Other, a projection notably of the abject, the desire, the drive, the uncanny.[12] The moment gender relations come into view not only as an illustration of cultural difference, but in their own problematic instability and as an area of projections, we are dealing with a story not only about two *gringos* in Mexico at a given historical moment, but about universal aspects of intercultural relations. The Mexican setting serves as a catalyst to bring the main character's nature into the open and functions as a mirror in its reflection of gender trouble. The mutual deconstruction of stereotypical notions of the ethnic Other and of gender binarisms can be overlooked only when we identify too closely with the protagonist's point of view.

NOT ALL RELEVANT TEXTS of the later twentieth century represent the discursive changes occurring at that time. And although in many popular novels by male writers, a male US American protagonist still represents the patriarchal order, in women's fiction this pattern is often modified in a way that is quite familiar from psychoanalytical discussions of Oedipal constellations: the female protagonist attempts to gain the affection of and then tame the *macho*. Because her national background enables her to carry patriarchal power in her cultural baggage, she finds Latin America a terrain where a complete gender reversal should be possible for herself and provide great satisfaction. Inevitably, however, she has to battle against the *machista* rudeness and infidelity of her Latin lover in a society where she finds little understanding even from female friends and in-laws. While trying to escape the limitations the gender discourse of her home country has put upon her, she encounters the more archaic gender constructions her Latin American environment has in store.[13]

Such is the case of the woman nicknamed Rubia (blonde), the first-person narrator of Christine Bell's popular novel *Saint* (1985), who manages to come to terms with her unfaithful Latin husband in a kind of disillusioned arrangement, but whose social reform efforts are thwarted by the heat and fertility of the surrounding jungle and the irresponsibility and irrationality of the uneducated local population. Although the female protagonist achieves the quasi-male position of the person in charge of their hacienda, she does not have the clout to enforce her rational, North American views and methods. Unsuccessfully, she tries to combine the roles of the angel in the house and the nurse and teacher that were assigned to women in nineteenth-century Euro-American civilization, two of very few escape routes from the wife-mother role prescribed by her society. What might have developed into a bridge transcending the boundaries of cultures and genders, a Bhabhaian "third space" of successful hybridities, succumbs to tropical nature, a development that seems to reaffirm the age-old association of the feminine with nature, whatever its shortcomings may be:[14]

> If heat had a smell, it would smell like this: layers upon layers of rotting vegetation steaming on the jungle floor. It is not an unpleasant odor by itself. It rises bestial and musklike. But in the hot moist air before the rains come, the jungle tries to cover it like a whore with sickening sweet wafts of frangipani and Spanish jasmine. (*Saint*, 3)

Rubia cannot achieve the synthesis that Beach's Hannah Pentecost created; she cannot control what oppresses her by the tokens of feminine, refined civilization:

> The air is heavy enough to hold in your hand. It should be cooler inside. The paths from the main gate leading to the stables and the main house are clean and neat. The low kept ground cover appears cool and green. The iced chan-

> deliers inside, the open windows and polished wooden floors, the crystal vases and silver tea sets appropriately spaced in the large rooms, the fans droning discreetly in every room, in every corridor—yes, it should be cooler inside. But this is the kind of heat that has substance, that clings and speaks. This is the kind of heat that knows the convoluted corridors of the house as well as it knows the jungle outside. (3–4)

On the contrary, male superiority in its North American version and hence the genderized binary inter-American distribution of power is reestablished when oil is found and the hacienda is turned into a provider of raw material, while the living quarters, the heterotopic site of Rubia's intercultural reform attempts, are reclaimed by the jungle.

IN THE UNITED STATES, the image of Mexico and other Latin American countries is gendered in order to accommodate aspects of the alterity discourse that are basically the same regardless of the *author's* gender. This is so even where gender roles and the North American cultural alterity discourse are questioned, namely in such Chicana fiction as contains descriptions of a visit to the homeland.[15] Hitherto, with the exception of Gonzales's *El Vago*, analyzed in chapter 5, I have not included Mexican American or other Latino texts because they belong to a somewhat different discursive system. However, I will discuss the following two novels because they represent the potential of interdiscursivity to an even higher degree than the ones analyzed before. By representing the foreign within US society and within individual US citizens, these texts provide particularly manifest examples for Kristeva's anti-xenophobic argument that we are strangers to ourselves.

Both books are road novels, not a rare phenomenon in fictions dealing with visiting Mexico. As Ronald Primeau has shown, road novels can be used to confirm dominant values such as the role of "the individual in a mass-dominated society," but may also be used to express the new, the emergent[16] that "is most often manifest as escape, political protest, or social reform and may be particularly evident in road works by women and ethnic minorities" (Primeau 4, qtd. in Ganser 42). In her excellent study of contemporary road fiction by American women, *Roads of Her Own*, Alexandra Ganser divides the texts under discussion into three groups: quest novels, novels about "para-nomadic" travelers, and picaresque novels. Obviously, overlappings are possible.

Sheila Ortiz Taylor's novel *Faultline* (1982) is the highly humorous story of a lesbian coming out. Because Taylor is a Chicana, one might expect that the return to the ancient land would serve as a catalyzing experience to bring this development about. However, the author uses the Mexican connection highly ironically. The novel is told from the point of view of a variety of major and minor characters and comprises events of 1959 and 1971–72, with considerable jumping back and forth in time. In 1959 young Arden Benbow, the Californian protagonist, accompanies her partially immobilized Aunt Vi(olet) who is escaping to Mexico from the nursing home where her newly rich husband has put her after she has suffered a stroke. The third in the party is Aunt Vi's dwarfish orderly Homer Rice, a failed magician, whom Vi calls Maurio Carbonara. Their flight to Mexico is in itself a parody of a pattern well known from (often popular) literature and Hollywood films (Pisarz-Ramírez 338). Arden makes a point of being "Indian" and sometimes reflects on what that may mean; in a "Character Reference" by an official, we get the following information: "It seemed her grandmother's maiden name was Benbow, that she was an Indian from somewhere in the northwest" (*Faultline*, 29).[17] Thus, Arden seems to have neither Mexican connections nor any specific cultural knowledge of the country, but this is of no importance because the Mexico the travelers encounter seems to be a holiday extension of the United States, a theme park prepared by the tourist industry.

Their first stop is a campground and trailer park on the Pacific coast near Guaymas that is run by Ruby, an elderly former stripper from Los Angeles who has found her subtropical dream-space here and runs it with the help of a Mexican employee, a place straight out of Tennessee Williams's *The Night of the Iguana*, and of course entirely dependent on US tourists. Here they are joined by Michael Raven, the private eye Aunt Vi's husband has sent after them. Michael also follows them to Guanajuato, where they stay for a month in an old Spanish castle that has been transformed into a luxury hotel. Like the catacombs of Guanajuato, with their well-known collection of naturally mummified bodies of cholera victims, the hotel is primarily an attraction to American tourists. Rather than being horrified by the distorted bodies, as had been the case with science fiction writer Ray Bradbury when he visited the catacombs (Bradbury xvii), Taylor's characters turn their visit to the site into a grotesquerie when Michael, who is ill, sways, grazes one of the pyramids of skulls, and makes it collapse: "The schoolteachers broke into a run, the guide screaming high-pitched directions. I grabbed Aunt Vi and Maurio grabbed Michael. We dragged them back, while three million skulls broke loose, bounding, crashing, and rolling down, thundering like the devil's own bowling alley" (*Faultline*, 73). Taylor thus deconstructs the US American discourse on the Mexican Other either by over-conformity or by burlesquing its most sinister element, the omnipresence of the theme of death.

Sure enough, the avalanche of skulls affects all four travelers, but their self-finding transformations are by no means consistent. Aunt Vi finds sufficient new energy to all but finish the gothic romance *Secret of the Skulls* she is writing. Her death while sitting in bed, writing, is her rather undramatic version of the death-in-Mexico motif. Arden, encouraged by her aunt, finds that she is a poet herself, and by writing the finishing three pages of Vi's novel, a prose writer as well. Michael and Homer/Maurio, failed detective and magician, respectively, discover their love and make a public announcement of their gay relationship. But the main character, Arden, counteracts the border-transcending tendency of their Mexican experience by giving in to her fellow student Malthus's request that she marry him. Malthus, who has also followed her to Mexico, "with a love as tenacious as poison ivy" (77), makes her give up her literary career. Instead, they have six children, and it takes the major earthquake suggested by the title, the San Fernando quake of 1971, to throw her off her tracks and into the arms of Alice, the wife of Malthus's colleague and superior. True, she had fallen in love with Ruby twelve years before, but that had remained in the range of a tender and appreciative affection. Thus, it is the tectonic structure of the Americas and not the trip to Mexico that brings about Arden's lesbian coming out.

The term *faultline* has other implications as well. It refers to the line dividing fault from non-fault, a fuzzy line, indeed, as a number of incidents in the novel reveal. It is only by proving that there is nothing wrong with being a lesbian and a mother raising six children that Arden can win the custody struggle with Malthus and thus bring about the plural happy endings of the book's conclusion. Gabriele Pisarz-Ramírez argues that

> Ortiz Taylor's Mexico emerges as a place of freedom, a space of spiritual and personal recreation, where identities become fluid and are open for refashioning [. . . ,] a symbolic backdrop against which a spiritual quest or cleansing is played out [. . . ,] a place where the exclusionary patriarchal logics which [. . .] are shown to be oppressive for Arden and her aunt Vi in the U.S., seem to be suspended. (337)

This observation has to be qualified, however. If, in the terms used by Ganser, *Faultline*, in its on-the-road parts, is a quest novel, the quests pursued by the individual characters are more often acts of chance, and the role of Mexico is fulfilled only in a comic confusion of directions and a debunking of clichés. Taylor pokes fun at the conventional Mexico discourse, but also at an equally essentialist discourse on gender and sexual orientation. It is in the strongest and in a sense most poetic passages of the book that this soft undermining of essentialism finds its best expression. In a scene also analyzed by Pisarz-Ramírez, Arden "reassembles an old motorcycle and muses about its possible re-conceptualization from an aggressive symbol of performed maleness into a vehicle for harmony and spirituality" (Pisarz-Ramírez 337).

> You are upset about the motorcycle. Or maybe motorcycles in general upset you, and the thought of a woman on a motorcycle, especially when she is not a mannequin passenger, drives you wild. Step to the rear of the bike, please.
>
> Well, part of your problem is that you are thinking about men on motorcycles. You are thinking of arrogant noise and sideways leers through tinted face shields. You are thinking of sprawling legs and phallic innuendo.
>
> Motorcycles do not need to be noisy. They can hum. The hum means they are well cared for and do not require your attention. And the rider does not require your attention. The rider's attention is elsewhere.
>
> The rider is watching for wild flowers. She is feeling the ripple of asphalt, feeling for the bank of a curve, listening for the bird call or the thunk of a manhole cover. She is with things, as things. She is reaching, at odd moments, for what they stand for. Between her and the wind there is nothing but her own calm mind. (*Faultline*, 66)

As other incidents showing Arden as a motorcyclist confirm, the novel redefines social roles as fluid, in motion. This involves gender roles, sexual preferences, family relations, but also ethnic identities. *Faultline*, then, not only is an ironic version of a quest (road) novel, but also contains elements of a picaresque view of society from the outside or underside. However, Arden as a modern *pícara* and her associates have a wider field of role-playing than their forebears in the history of picaresque fiction. For instance, the man whom Arden, after her separation from Malthus, hires to take care of the chaos created by her children plus three hundred rabbits whose fertility she had underestimated is a black giant who is also gay and a dance student. The interdiscursive and counter-discursive processes in this novel make it a high point in the comic questioning of the order of things. As such, it appears to be a farewell to the certainties, triumphant achievements, but also the black-and-white thinking so common among the members of Second Wave feminism and a step toward the more fluid gender and sexuality identity constructions and the recognition of ethnic pluralism in gender relations, too, that have been emphasized by Third Wave proponents such as Rebecca Walker and race-oriented feminists such as Cherríe Moraga and Gloria Anzaldúa.

Ana Castillo's epistolary novel *The Mixquiahuala Letters* (1986) is a much grimmer book. In the now fashionable scholarly terminology, it might be called *nomadic* because it presents the repeated trips of two young women to Mexico, a retracing of routes that might remind some of the repetition-structured movement through space that characterizes the lifestyle of true nomads. In the wake of Gilles Deleuze and Félix Guattari's *A Thousand Plateaus*, the term *nomad* has become immensely popular in postructuralist and postcolonial discussions of the role of the subject as moving through space and transcending boundaries. Rosi Braidotti in *Nomadic Subjects* and other critics have added a feminist perspective. A definition like that offered by Richard Osborne in his *Megawords: 200 Terms You Really Need to Know* points to its attractiveness but also reveals its distortions: "To be a nomadic subject is to be homeless, to exist in an imaginary and symbolic realm that subverts the accepted definitions of what is and replaces them with categories of fluidity and possibility" (195, qtd. in Ganser 165). The dire necessities of the life of true nomads, their marginalization in many geographical areas and nation states, is far from being just imaginary and symbolic, and therefore Ganser correctly introduces the neologism "para-nomadic": "In order to distinguish a more metaphorical nomadism from traditional nomads, *para-nomadism* might be a better terminological choice than neo-nomadism, expressing a 'close-to' relation between figural and actual nomads rather than echoing a questionable evolutionary development" (179). For a study of women's road novels, the term has specific attractions:

> From a strictly epistemological perspective, feminist para-nomads should be of interest not because they are supposedly free-roaming warriors, but because nomadism, even when characterized by a mobility that is premeditated, strained, or challenged, implicitly resists traditional Western binary structures such as departure and arrival, movement and rest, central and marginal, or public and private spaces. [. . .] Epistemological para-nomadism therefore offers to dismantle binary structures of center and margin in both a postcolonial and feminist context without denying the existence of a center altogether. [. . .] According to this reformulation of the nomadic as para-nomadism, the protagonists of the road stories in the following [Ganser's] analyses embody the opposite of the vanguards of freedom of mobility and the adventurous traveler: they are forced onto the road by external (economic) coercion, which frequently translates, by way of its discursive inscription onto the body, into internal pressures. (179–80)

In the case of *The Mixquiahuala Letters*, though, the characters' nomadism is not due to external pressure but to an internal desire to test one's limits, to explore the exotic and the erotic in a series of efforts to find sexual fulfillment, satisfying relationships, detachment from home, and a new home that may turn out to be some kind of ancestral belonging. Mexico serves as a catalyst and helps the protagonists to find their roles, their perspectives on life, society, love, and personal relations. In the case of the letter writer, Teresa, who travels to Mexico more often, a complex and fluid perception of the country is achieved. Her friend Alicia, on the contrary, experiences the Mexico of her two visits as a much more dominantly hostile testing ground. For both, nation and culture are encountered almost exclusively in the shape of the Mexican men they meet and who fulfill all US clichés of either aggressive or romantic sexism. While debunking idealizing Chicano notions about Mexico, the novel also confirms US stereotypes. This is not too surprising given the fact that the two women travel as backpacking *gringa* tourists, therefore evoking reverse clichés held by the Mexicans. The novel seems to be playing with several varieties of (para-)nomadism and simultaneously contains a strong element of the quest narrative. In this process, center and margin turn out to be fluctuating and potentially interchangeable.[18]

*The Mixquiahuala Letters* is the story of the relationship between two young US American women, Teresa and Alicia, over a period of roughly ten years, beginning when they are both around twenty years old. It is told in a series of forty letters—some of them in the form of poems—from Teresa to Alicia and thus returns to the old model of the epistolary novel that was so fashionable in eighteenth-century sentimental fiction, particularly among female writers. However, because we do not get Alicia's answers, not even by implication, and because Teresa's letters tell the story of the women's friendship, focusing on their joint travels to Mexico, events that are well known to the recipient, we may wonder if these letters may not be directed primarily at the sender herself. Some of the letters are not even signed and may never have been sent at all. They are not dated but apparently have been written at different times. What makes matters even more disturbing is that their sequence in the book does not correspond to the chronology we may—perhaps—deduce from the content. Instead, the author begins by addressing the reader:

> Dear Reader:
> It is the author's duty to alert the reader that this is not a book to be read in the usual sequence. All letters are numbered to aid in following any one of the author's proposed options. (*Mixquiahuala*, 7)

This is followed by three different lists of chapters, one "FOR THE CONFORMIST," one "FOR THE CYNIC," and the third "FOR THE QUIXOTIC" (7–9). None of these proposed sequences for reading contains all letters as they appear in the book, where they are printed in the numerical order 1–40. The author ends this disconcerting prologue by commenting, "For the reader committed to nothing but short fiction, all the letters read as separate entities. Good luck whichever journey you choose!" (9). In case this postmodern procedure of letting the readers assemble their own versions of the text should remind some of Julio Cortázar's *Hopscotch* (*Rayuela*), the book bears the dedication "In memory of the master of the game, Julio Cortázar" (6). Whether this dedication to the great Argentine novelist is respectful or ironic, this being a book casting doubt on patriarchal master discourses, remains anybody's guess (cf. Gonzales-Berry 115). Any reading sequence, though, will produce basically the same impression: the relations of women and men are doomed to end in disappointment or even disaster.[19]

Assuming that the novel contains some autobiographical material, the decade covered roughly corresponds to that between the early 1970s and early 1980s.[20] In Letter 9 we learn that Teresa's husband Libra goes to California at the period of the last flower children. He is joined in San Francisco by Teresa, who works in the Women's Liberation movement and the Chicano movement. In the poem forming Letter 10, she speaks of "our Aztlán period" (38), referring to the mythical homeland Aztlán celebrated by the movement, and also gives the years 1974 and 1976 as temporal orientation points. But politics play hardly any explicit role in this book. In Mexico, the friends are at one point suspected of having been involved in the assassination attempt against a presidential candidate, but the political background is never explained, nor are recent dramatic events such as the 1968 Tlatelolco student massacre in Mexico City even mentioned. Apart from the brief treatment of women's lib and the Chicano movement, the political situation in the United States remains equally obscure. That Alicia's lover Abdel, whose death is the main topic of Letter 40, is a traumatized Vietnam veteran may be seen as an indirect comment on the war, but it is Alicia's relationship with him, and his suicide as a final act of vengeance for Alicia's unwillingness or incapability to lend him the emotional support he needs, that is at the center of this letter. As always, Teresa also comments on her friend's behavior, culminating in her empathetically assuming Alicia's voice in the last lines of the book:

> *I DIDN'T KNOW YOU*
> *HAD A GUN! I DIDN'T . . . KNOW . . . !*
> *MOTHER OF GOD, HELP!*
> *TERESA . . . ? ABDEL, YOU SON OF A BITCH!*
> Motherfucker, why didn't you just leave? (132)[21]

This is the last instance of the battle of the sexes that makes up most of the content of the book. Teresa and Alicia's friendship defines itself as a mental and emotional grappling with one another's relationships with men because both women define themselves through such relationships. Their discussions, as they are presented by Teresa, thus fill the whole range from closeness and deep understanding to disgust, detachment, or jealousy. If the decade described eclectically in this epistolary series can be seen as the formative period of both women—Teresa finds her role as a poet, Alicia hers as an artist—their art never takes center stage. If we are to judge from those letters presented as poems, Teresa's poetry is focused on gender relations; it even includes a dramatic monologue by one of her lovers who has jilted her, a kind of poetic getting-even. Alicia's work is also centered around the gender roles of women. Teresa sees Alicia's mixed-media series *La casita* consisting of "angry dolls made of papièr maché [*sic*] with hair from your own head" (118) as an expression of Alicia's anger. As the Spanish title of the series indicates, the artist has had her Mexican experiences in mind. However, Teresa explains her own lack of tears by the fact that they are beyond all this now: "There were no tears. They dried with the remains of the fetus that had ended far away from oceans, casitas, dreams and follies of gringas and suave Latin lovers. It's past. The exorcism of the artist's rite serves only as a reminder" (118). What she refers to here is the fact that both women have had abortions. Teresa aborted a child in her twenties when she tried to keep her Spanish lover Alexis. He, however, was horrified when she told him, after which they broke up. Alicia had an abortion at age seventeen, her black lover Rodney not caring to take the responsibility for a baby. She could get access to the clinic only by using the papers of a Puerto Rican friend, a mistaken identity that leads to her (nonconsensual) sterilization, not an uncommon procedure at American hospitals of that time with respect to ethnic minorities.

In both cases, the absolutely traumatizing experience is to be seen in an ironic inter-American context: Teresa tried to hold on to her Spanish lover, acting against her Mexican Amerindian heritage that made her hate white men and women. Alicia, who has had a WASP upbringing and whose own Spanish, part-gypsy ancestors are denied by her family, undergoes the treatment intended for Latin American nonwhites. Thus, these experiences are chiasticly arranged. In each case, they have left the deepest wounds in the women's emotional life.

Their friendship, which Teresa calls a "love affair" in the sense of "an expression of nostalgia and melancholy for the depth of our empathy" (39), never turns into a lesbian relationship, but they are aware of each other's physical qualities. In a poem in Letter 11, Teresa tells how she watched Alicia getting a massage, which is turned into lovemaking by the masseur:

*the elastic waistband of your panties*
*pushed down over the swollen profusion*
                                        *of your buttocks*
*with the help of his confident hands*
*[. . .]*
*i closed my eyes*
                    *went on*
                    *with my nap* (40)

Voyeurism does not develop into involvement. Their mutual awareness changes from situation to situation, but it is when cultural contexts come into play that Teresa realizes that bodies are socially, discursively constructed. During their first stay in Mexico, as students "at a North American institution in Mexico City" (18) whose instructors do not speak Spanish, they live in a boarding house, where

> our hostesses giggled and fluttered attentively and with nervous apprehension about their latest American guests.
>
> Didn't they tell anything by my Indian-marked face, fluent use of the language, undeniably Spanish name? Nothing blurred their vision of another gringa come to stay as i nodded and shook hands during introductions and took my seat. (18–19)

Teresa is disappointed about not being recognized as belonging to the Mexican people. On the other hand, their Mexican teacher in copperwork, who is "enraptured" (20) by the blond American female students, doesn't like her because she is not gringa enough:

> i, with dark hair and Asian eyes, must've appeared like the daughter of a migrant worker or a laborer in the North (which of course, i was). i was nothing so close to godliness as fair-skinned or wealthy or even a simple gringa with a birthright ticket to upward mobility in the land paved with gold, but the daughter of someone like him, except that he'd made the wade to the other side. (21)

Thus, skin color is a matter of class rather than race, but in situations of competition it will be a distinctive feature. In the poem making up Letter 13, Teresa confesses, "Alicia, why i hated white women and sometimes didn't like you:/ Society had made them above all possessions/ the most desired" (43). She hates white women even more when they prefer dark, southern lovers and thus avail themselves of a sexuality that is superior to that of WASP men. In this context rife with ethnic stereotypes, she can see Alicia only as unattractive: "Meanwhile, you were flat-chested, not especially pretty and/ bore no resemblance to the ideal of any man/ you encountered anywhere" (44). However, in the very next letter, Teresa enters another discursive field, that of feminine solidarity, and beyond that writes as an intimate friend who can praise Alicia's beauty: "i wish i could have convinced you how beautiful you are, then perhaps you might not've gone through so much personal agony during that second journey to Mexico" (45), and she goes on to describe in loving detail Alicia's hair, her long legs, her small breasts, her neck, her fingers. In a way, Teresa presents an early exemplification of Judith Butler's theory of the discursive performativity of sex and body:

> To "concede" the undeniability of "sex" or its "materiality" is always to concede some version of "sex," some formation of "materiality." Is the discourse in and through which that concession occurs—and, yes, that concession invariably does occur—not itself formative of the very phenomenon that it concedes? To claim that discourse is formative is not to claim that it originates, causes, or exhaustively composes that which it concedes; rather, it is to claim that there is no reference to a pure body which is not at the same time a further formation of that body. In this sense, the linguistic capacity to refer to sexed bodies is not denied, but the very meaning of "referentiality" is altered. In philosophical terms, the constative claim is always to some degree performative. (Butler 10–11)

This discursive formation of the body extends beyond the sexual characteristics to the individual's contextual appearance. Alicia pointedly "said i'd acquired the body most desirable to men of the region" (*Mixquiahuala*, 56), but Teresa goes on eating rich food and gaining weight, whereas Alicia eats "with a greater appetite, and found it difficult to keep up [her] weight," demonstrating her inability to conform to the local norms. Teresa's comment "Having the choice, i'd prefer [your metabolism]" (56) is an ingenuous acknowledgement of the limits of individual choice. This amounts to a racial identification, an attempt to accept her ethnic heritage as fundamentally positive. Although Butler warns us of a conflation of racism and sexism as analogical systems of power exertion (18), in *The Mixquiahuala Letters* both work hand in hand, and the same applies to what one might call inverted racism and sexism, the willful identification with a group considered as one's own.

Teresa acknowledges the dominance of the discursive over the individual when she writes, "Destiny is not a metaphysical confrontation with one's self, rather, society has knit its pattern so tight that a confrontation with it is inevitable" (59). This confrontation will end in submission or, rather, in her case there has been some conformity with the discursive order all along. To a certain extent, Teresa can follow the motto "When in Mexico do as the Mexicans do," whereas Alicia will not accept this order. Hence her "agony," the series of futile attempts to find love for herself as an individual. What she encounters instead is a series of men who, if they are interested in her at all, try to have sex with her as a sign of their victory, as the conquest of a white woman, an interethnic getting-even and a national Mexican backlash against Yankee supremacy. That Alicia cannot be part of the national ritual game of love is made symbolically clear when she arrives in a town where she is to meet Teresa and, looking for her, walks the evening *paseo* around the square in the same direction as the men rather than the opposite one of the women, thus becoming an object of ridicule.

The two women's "gender trouble" begins at home, but it is a race, class, and gender trouble. Teresa, who grew up in Chicago, thinks "of the city i'd been brought up in, where dark skin and a humble background had subjected me to atrocities" (61–62). Her early marriage out of love goes to pieces because of poverty or else because of her new feminist insight: "i'd left him because i thought i was fighting a society in which men and women entangled their relationships with untruths" (127). In Mexico, Teresa believes, the children she would have "wouldn't suffer at the hands of the ignorant, but would be raised in a land where copper-colored flesh was the norm" (62). She accepts the marriage proposal of Sergio, a rich entrepreneur in Yucatán, and is ready to divorce Libra, although she is not in love with her suitor, because she tries to accept the Mexican social and gender discourse: "What did love have to do with the order of things? A woman didn't marry for love in that part of the world. She married out of necessity," because this was "the only door opened to me to escape the banal destiny planned from birth" (62). And yet she is deeply hurt when Sergio lets her know that he was never quite serious, and thus reveals her own inconsistencies.

If Sergio represents one example of Mexican *machismo*, there are many more, but the friends almost ask for such experiences, because they apply the role model of the Women's Liberation movement in this unlikely con text. They see themselves as modern, liberated women not at all adverse to erotic adventures, but insist on their freedom of choice. They posit a universal, egalitarian gender order and will not come to terms with the more archaic Mexican order dividing women into virgins, married women, and, on the other hand, tramps, a category in which they are put not only by the men they meet but also by the bourgeois ladies in whose houses they happen to stay (and overstay their welcome). The asset of the *gringa* soon loses out to the blemish of the unattached or separated nomadic woman:

> How revolting we were, susceptible to ridicule, abuse, disrespect. We would have hoped for respect as human beings, but the only respect granted a woman is that which a gentleman bestows upon the lady. Clearly, we were no ladies.
>
> What was our greatest transgression? We traveled alone. (59)

The list of men runs the gamut from the friendly engineers who invite them to live in their house (an invitation they accept, being short of cash) and will not exert too much pressure to go to bed with them; to the engineers' "bosses," who take them back to the capital in their limousine, expecting sexual favors; to the would-be rapist Alicia escapes only by Teresa's desperate intervention; to the transvestites whose drag queen Miss America competition they watch naively, Alicia even more naively letting herself be dragged to the dance floor, dancing being her form of bodily self-abandon; and finally to the ghost-like force of evil that visits them one night and can be stopped only by

Teresa's prayers. Having inherited her grandmother's superstition, she is better equipped than secularized Alicia to cope with the spiritual side of the country, although she remembers Catholicism as utterly oppressive.

They blame society: "i'd had enough of the country where relationships were never clear and straightforward but a tangle of contradictions and hypocrisies" (54), but for much the same reason Teresa had left her American marriage. They visit and revisit Mexico as a land of—primarily sexual—adventure and thus also of the (para-)nomadic freedom of choice, whether of places or people. The country is later epitomized in their memories by a series of sometimes attractive but almost always disappointing men, but it is also their own contradictions, their confusion of freedom with the safe passage of tourists, their backpacking braveness with the expectation that everybody should respect their inviolability not only as *gringas* but also as independent women, that let their travels, particularly the second trip, develop into a nightmare for which they blame the Mexicans but might also blame themselves.

WASPish Alicia is less willing to accept this order of things, whereas Teresa has at least an inkling of her own inconsistencies and manages to turn her divided experiences into a new order. She revisits her estranged husband and with him conceives a baby boy, Vittorio, with whom she returns to Mexico. Not to the idyllic, rural Mexico she had envisioned in a dream where she felt she belonged: "i was of that mixed blood, of fire and stone, timber and vine" (95–96); but at least to Cuernavaca, the city of international schools and universities, where she, and possibly also her husband, can teach:

> We're going home, Vittorio and i. Are you surprised?
>
> In Cuernavaca, Vittorio's grandfather will take naps with him in the garden on the hammock tied to two tamarind trees. He will tell him stories he never told me. Mami will call him "hijo," rolling a warm tortilla sprinkled with salt and wrapping his little fingers around it.
>
> My husband will be gone for hours on end. i'll read over students' assignments, eyeglasses hooked on the nose, feet propped up to pamper legs that threaten an outburst of varicose veins. (119)

This self-ironic letter, which can be read as a farewell to Alicia because the latter might never condone this lowering of their standards of independence, marks the temporary end of Teresa's nomadic wanderings, because she is also a quester having found what she considers her birthright.[22] In Letter 26 she celebrates Mexico City:

> Mexico City, revisited time and again
> since childhood, over and again as a woman. I sometimes saw the ancient Tenochtitlán, home of my mother, grandmothers, and greatmother, as an em-

> bracing bosom, to welcome me back and rock my weary body and mind to sleep in its tumultuous, over populated, throbbing, ever pulsating heart. (92)[23]

However, this mythical model of the maternal remains isolated. Hardly ever does Teresa mention encounters with other women. Beyond the suspicious mothers of momentary male friends and the rural "women washing clothes in public basins (a kind of laundromat without machines)" (48), there are no Mexican female characters, and Teresa's cynical remark about the reduction of women to washing machines does not reveal an active engagement with the role of women in that country, let alone any effort to spread the gospel of women's liberation.

If on their second trip, in Teresa's alliterative, poetic words, "[m]onths of miles of moving continuously away from the familiar had worked their evil on our minds and emotions" (69), one may wonder if this evil comes only from outside. In retrospect, Alicia feels "it all had to have meant something, that, if we were able to analyze, it would be pertinent, not just to benefit our lives, but womanhood" (47), but her own positive and negative exoticism, her analogizing of Mexican *machismo* with Mexican alienity precludes the development of anything but binary positions. Tellingly, for all we know, she does not return to Mexico.

Teresa, on the other hand, not only embodies everybody's inner alienity and uncanniness that Kristeva has analyzed in *Strangers to Ourselves*, but the social, cultural, and psychological heritage of two nations. Simultaneously colonized and colonizer, she is in harmony and at odds with both spheres of her experience and, to boot, with the reductive because sexist straddling position of the (male) Chicano movement. She is simultaneously independent and family woman, American and Mexican, intellectual and rooted in nature. That is, she has arrived at a position of transdifference. Her way of coping with this situation is less an intellectual analysis than an open-ended search for her splintered self in the open, explorative, sometimes contradictory structure of the book she writes. Its very form indicates that there is no final stability, no final role to be achieved. In this she represents Castillo's idea of a *Xicanisma*, a Chicana feminism differing both from the male Chicano *movimiento*, with its indebtedness to Marxism and Catholicism, and from white feminism with its Anglo-bourgeois roots, a Chicana feminism that involves a return to the, in her mind, prepartriarchal world of indigenous, notably Aztec, Mexico.

It should be mentioned, however, that Teresa's identity construction does not correspond to the picture of the Mexican Other developed in this novel, a Mexico that, as Pisarz-Ramírez critically remarks, "assumes the form of a monolithic other: exotic, backward, *machista*, and fixed in the past" (336).

The intersection of the discourses of gender and ethnic alterity need not work toward emancipation, openness, and fluidity in both discursive directions. The relationship of identity and alterity will often be quite asymmetrical, on the individual as on the national and cultural level. The reification of Mexican cultural and gender conditions and the rebellion against the gender relations there formulated in this novel takes Castillo back to older and more essentialist forms of feminism.

AS I HAVE ALREADY indicated, transdifference both on the experiential and on the descriptive level is a particularly frequent phenomenon where discourses interact and overlap, as is the case in the mutual application of the semantic fields of gender and ethnic identity and alterity. Consequently, some of the subject positions in the texts I have analyzed and the reading experiences they produce can best be classified as transdifferent. For instance, in Porter's "Flowering Judas," Laura's situation between two worlds defined by ethnic and gender boundaries is one of transdifference. Porter's story, and, in some way, each of the others I have mentioned, affirms differences between North America and Latin America as well as between women and men, although these differences need not be seen as those of essential, "natural" conditions but are discursive constructions of reality. But the intersection of the two sets of differentiation results in experiences, subject positions, or at least reading experiences that resist any construction of meaning based on an exclusionary and conclusive binary model. And this, exactly, is what the term *transdifference* refers to. The very irresolution of the texts I have talked about—in terms of emotional experience as of plot fulfillment—shows that transdifference does not mean synthesis, an overcoming of difference. It does not mean hybridity, either, because in no case is there a continuous and, in Bhabha's sense, open-ended deconstruction of difference, nor, in a more popular version of the term, a dynamic merging of opposites. Transdifference presupposes difference as a given, as not going away. Situations and experiences of transdifference are uncomfortable, yet intellectually and emotionally suggestive. Although transdifference in itself does not carry a subversive connotation, at the interface of gender and ethnicity, such situations and experiences can be used to move beyond the binarisms that have too long stratified the fictions and discourses of the Other with stereotypical encrustations.

# PART FOUR

# [8]

## THE POST-VIETNAM ERA: VERSIONS OF REALISM

The earth is round and flat at the same time. This is obvious. That it is round appears indisputable; that it is flat is our common experience, also indisputable.
—Jeanette Winterson, *Sexing the Cherry* ("The Flat Earth Theory," 81)

AS I HAVE SAID in my introduction, the period between the late 1970s and the collapse of the Soviet Union in 1991 and briefly thereafter was extraordinarily rich in North American fictional texts about Latin America. The situation after Vietnam and the late phase of the Cold War with the surrogate conflicts in Central America and beyond may have offered particularly much material and created a heightened interest in the hemispheric tropics. More complex reasons may emerge from the following discussion of a number of remarkable North American novels dealing with Latin America, among them *A Book of Common Prayer* (1977) by Joan Didion, a writer whose essays and novels analyze current social and ethical problems; *A Flag for Sunrise* (1981) by Robert Stone and *The Mosquito Coast* (1981) by Paul Theroux, both of them leading representatives of the neorealist novel in the United States; *The Sign of Dawn* (1981) by African American writer James Wylie; and finally, *Bodily Harm* (1981) by Margaret Atwood, arguably the best-known representative of late twentieth-century Canadian literature and an astute commentator on social developments. *The Mosquito Coast* has been discussed in Chapter 7. *Bodily Harm* will be analyzed in the last chapter; it is mentioned here proleptically because in some respects it seems to belong in the same category of fiction.

At first glance, the texts I have used as representative of late twentieth-century fiction on Latin America still appear to be governed by the reality model of Latinamericanism as described in Chapter 2. A survey of dominant elements will yield the following results: All male and female protagonists come from either the United States or Canada.[1] All enter Latin America on a quest for the meaning of their lives, a fresh orientation and self-realization, or they have spent some time there and now feel prompted by their environment to pursue such a quest for meaning. The aim they strive to reach, or that may become suddenly and surprisingly visible, may lie in their own identity in the context of a family harmony to be reconstructed, as is the case with Didion's female protagonist Charlotte; the reconciliation of technological progress and an escape from civilization, as with Theroux's Mr. Fox; the ideal of a racially mixed society that is strongly shaped by people of African descent, as in Wylie; the solidarity of the suffering, as in Atwood; or more or less strongly religious epiphanies, as in Stone. In a number of cases, these aims are missed and usually also revealed as illusionary from the start. In other cases they are actually reached albeit often only in the moment of death, because the majority of the protagonists and most of the other main figures die at the end of the respective novelistic action or else are expecting to die shortly.

All of these characters are loners or, better, isolates, people who have become alienated from their world or the world in general. Theroux's inventor Al Fox is the only complete representative of American individualism in its traditional, positive sense. In addition, he is the only one to tote his family along. The others are isolated by the lack of social bonds that is typical of modern North American societies, even if they are members of a religious order. They may have many erotic encounters, but they do not succeed in establishing a lasting human relationship. Nor do they get integrated in the society of the respective Latin American country—if they survive at all, the end of the novel will show them on the way back or out. They come as tourists, journalists, missionaries, colonizers, soldiers, agents, deserters; in three of the novels, active or former cultural anthropologists play a leading role. This range of occupations in itself is revealing about the characters' attitudes vis-à-vis the country they visit. One can call their visits a late form of imperialist or postimperialist invasion.

In each book it seems that the Latin American Other can be epistemically appropriated according to well-established patterns. It is reduced to the same stereotypical motifs as in more trivial texts (although often with reversed evaluation): political repression and corruption; social inequality; revolutions; the dominant role of foreign powers, for instance in the roles played by the CIA or Cuba; drug smuggling, violence, decaying cities; and an overwhelming tropical flora and fauna as well as natives experienced as primitive, dangerous, or sexually attractive. This should not surprise us, because these texts are not primarily concerned with the Other but with the Self and its own strangeness, for which the Other has to serve as contrast, parallel, mirror, or simply backdrop. What one can notice immediately is that the authors have assigned not just regionally specific but also generally human relevancy to their narrative plots. As Robert Stone has put it in an interview, the individual lives in his books can serve as metaphors for the "universal situation" ("An Interview" by Bonetti, 98).

Yet it is evident that this supposedly universal situation is that of members of a society that Christopher Lasch in his famous study has described as *The Culture of Narcissism*, as a stage of decay of Western and, specifically, North American society that is characterized by an uncertainty of the individual about his or her role in society and private life, the growth of a regulating bureaucracy, consumerism, an all-powerful entertainment industry, the dissolution of the family, the shallowness of personal relations generally, and a weakening of community values. In all of the five novels I have analyzed or will analyze, this society appears in a very negative light; its claim of superiority vis-à-vis what lies beyond the border, notably its rôle in the countries of Latin America, proves to have disastrous consequences. While the "sweet Canadians" in Atwood's novel are only made fun of because of their misguided engagement in the Caribbean, the United States appears at best as lacking understanding or as indifferent to the problems of its southern neighbors, often, however, as repressive and exploitative. All of the texts display a wide variety of negative North American characters, whether these are individual adventurers, gunrunners, members of the foreign service, or representatives of commercial companies or religious or secular NGOs.

A striking common feature of these texts is that they were written under the shadow of the Vietnam War. At least some of their characters either were actively involved in the war or at least bear testimony to the way American society was divided over its issues, to the military and political failures and the moral abyss that swallowed the country's ideals and idealists. Notably Central America was seen by many as a second Vietnam, an area that might be suffering under corrupt regimes but whose revolutionary movements had more or less strongly leftist leanings and were thus seen as in danger of being instrumentalized by the Soviet Union—after all, the Cold War was still going on, and Castro's Cuba continued to be considered a source of potential "communist infections" in the hemisphere.[2] The Sandinista toppling of the Somoza regime in Nicaragua in 1979 was rapidly seen as proof of this hypothesis, and the counter-insurgency policy of the US government followed the same domino theory that had drawn the United States into the conflict in Southeast Asia.[3] If there should be anything like a collective repetition compulsion, it seemed to be at work here. The wish for a second chance correcting the outcome, if possible with unquestioned moral legitimacy, on the one hand, and, on the other, the fear of another military defeat, of another political and moral failure, of another series of wrong perceptions of regional conditions and the needs of the local population, sometimes in odd combinations, have left their imprint on the debate about the policy with regard to Latin America.

As a consequence, the complexes, neuroses, traumata that the protagonists of the novels under discussion are trying to come to grips with in Latin America are also representative of the problems of a society deeply traumatized by the lost war and by the division of the population regarding its justification. Some of the characters have fought or worked in Vietnam, and now the political and military situation in Latin America or simply the tropical landscapes, sounds, and smells, and every so often the local people, remind them of Southeast Asia. These novels, then, are political novels inasmuch as they discuss American imperialism, Cold War issues and ideologies, Latin American regional politics, and the acceptance or even support of corrupt regimes by the US administrations as long as they contribute to warding off leftist movements and Soviet Bloc infiltrations, the interplay of economic and political interests, notably as concerns US investments in those countries, the role of agencies like the CIA, and so forth. Basically, what is at issue is the question whether US American policy in Latin America is part of the defense of the "Free World" or a more or less ruthless game of power and economic exploitation. (In Atwood's novel, these questions are put into the contexts of the moral responsibility of the individual and of a wishfully neutral Canadian position.) They are also psychological and sociological novels because they focus on North American individuals visiting Latin America and becoming actively or passively involved in the struggles there while trying to come to terms with their personal crises. What one would expect, in addition, is that local conditions are scrutinized, that the question of how to view the Other plays a major role.

By definition, the political novel refers to contemporary conditions, situations, conflicts. It need not be realistic but can be allegorical, utopian, or dystopian (think of Orwell's *1984*) rather than representing reality according to some variety of realism. However, the novels I have selected present their settings predominantly realistically, although the plot of *The Sign of Dawn* makes it utopian fiction. I will therefore make the question of realism one of the recurring aspects of my analyses in this chapter. If the experience of the Vietnam War has contributed significantly to shaping the image of the self and the Other, this should have consequences in the representation of the domestic and, particularly, the foreign reality. Indeed, these texts sometimes reveal the convergence of alterity discourses: Orientalism (in its Southeast Asia–directed variety) and Latinamericanism often appear as interchangeable.

In *Fighting and Writing the Vietnam War*, Donald Rignalda has presented the interesting hypothesis that many novels on Vietnam fail because the authors approach their subject with methods that are just as inadequate to the local conditions as those used by the military for the jungle war. There it was the reliance on a linear, technology-ruled procedure, on the possibility of mapping the terrain, of measuring one's own potential and that of the enemy quantitatively, and of classifying human beings, that failed so disastrously when applied to a seemingly chaotic alien reality. In fiction, it is the approach of traditional realism, that is, a view of time and action as linear, the assumption of a universal transparency of human motivation and the claim that any reality is given, principally similar and hence also describable, that makes the texts inadequate as representations of the war experiences of that time and degrade them to documents of a partial, wish-controlled perception. To all appearances, the North American novel on Latin America confronts the same difficulties when it is supposed to represent not only the confusions of the self but the complexity of the Other. This is so not simply because of the political echoes of Vietnam, but because it is always easiest to transfer established habits of thinking and imagining to new objects. How, then, can they be realistic and to what extent is realism an asset, to what extent an obstacle?

Literary realism, which was briefly discussed in Chapter 2, is a problem of communication between author and reader. Authorial, "intentional realism" (Villanueva) is not enough, because readers are capable of constructing as realistic even verbal signs not intended to reflect any given, that is, consensually accepted reality of the author's culture and society (what, in the terminology introduced by Alfred Schütz, might be called the assumptive world[4]). Darío Villanueva points out, summarizing Morse Peckham, "that we can no longer accept an essential realism, understood as a faithful and transparent reproduction by artistic means of a fully present and univocal reality which the poet observes and out of which he creates his work" (Villanueva 146), as William Dean Howells might still have considered possible and adequate. Epistemologically speaking, reality doesn't exist, if by the term we mean one and only one complete and coherent totality, because there is no way of approaching it from the outside. For humans, there are numberless realities depending on the context, the "field of meaning" (M. Gabriel) we are positioned in or vis-à-vis.[5]

Nonetheless, it is possible to distinguish several levels of literary *vraisemblance*, as Jonathan Culler, following a lead by Todorov, has argued. Culler's first levels are of interest here; the very first one might even function interculturally. He defines it as "a discourse which requires no justification because it seems to derive directly from the structure of the world. [. . .] The most elementary paradigms of action are located at this level: if someone begins to laugh they will eventually stop laughing, if they set out on a journey they will either arrive or abandon the trip" (Culler 140–41). One might object that there are cases like the Flying Dutchman or the Wandering Jew, but they would exist only in specific, culturally defined notions of what is real, that is, on Culler's second level. This level refers to culturally accepted knowledge, the meaning structure accepted within a certain community of communication. What is acceptable as probable on this level varies widely from one culture and one historical period to the other. The third level is that of textual conventions: in our period and in Western society, a novel presented in verse would automatically be considered a deviation from the accepted realistic norm; medieval fiction was read (or, usually, heard) under quite different premises.

All of the texts to be analyzed next conform to level one, even Wylie's utopian adventure story. It is level two that is the one most hotly debated. One aspect of considerable significance in this context is the respective value we attribute to the description of social, political, economic, psychological, religious, or topographic-biological facts or supposed facts. In the present context, social and political aspects seem to dominate, at least among North American and European writers and readers. However, in the novels under discussion, these aspects receive different treatment if they belong to the domestic or else to the alien reality; if they do not, as in the texts Rignalda has in mind, the adequacy of representation may become questionable even within the author's cultural group.

Rignalda's criteria for realism, that is, the givenness of reality, the linearity of time and causality of action, and the transparency of character motivation, derive from classic nineteenth-century models of literary realism. William Dean Howells's theory of (realistic) fiction as formulated primarily in *Criticism and Fiction*[6] can be summed up in the following main points: Reality exists and is unambiguous; humans are capable of correct observation and representation. Reality should not be seen through a religious or metaphysical lens; it is meaningful in and by itself; truth does not demand a higher authority. Realism deals with external, that is, physical and social as well as with inner, psychological reality; it implies "fidelity to experience and probability of motive" (*Criticism*, 15). Therefore its main focus has to be on contemporary, observable reality. Realism presupposes "the equality of things and the unity of men" (15), that is, it represents the detail, the local, the ordinary, including ordinary, average, or even lowly people—in this, realism is the true democratic art. The "fidelity to experience" also implies that reality should be represented according to its true proportions, which means, for instance, not prioritizing aspects such as love entanglements for their romantic interest. Reality, and particularly the human sphere, should be represented in its details, its complexity and variety. Emphasis should be shifted from plot to character and complex characterization, because character and social environment explain behavior and, consequently, action. Causality should therefore be presented as more important than chance. To achieve these ends, the author or narrator should step back and allow the reader the impression of immediate participation. Finally, style should approach ordinary language; symbols should be used only where they emerge from the elements of the represented world.

Twentieth- and twenty-first-century intellectual developments have made part of these claims obsolete: we are no longer sure what truth is and how it could be ascertained or represented, nor that people are capable of correct observation. Reality has turned into a maze of often conflicting realities that are constructed by individual or collective, discursive approaches. And yet we tend to believe in the existence of the real and in textual methods that are more realistic than others. Fiction dealing with one's own society can be and is classified as realistic if its characters and actions are plausible by a kind of social consensus, while other texts are called postmodern, fantastic, magical realism, and so forth, depending on the epistemological model applied and the freedom from probability granted. Although we concede the possibility of writing realistic historical fiction, the texts to be discussed here concern contemporary conditions at the time of publication. As it turns out, these texts follow conventional realism primarily in their representation of the observers through whose eyes we come to see the culturally or regionally Other.

ROBERT STONE HAS OFTEN pledged his allegiance to a contemporary variety of realism. In an interview with Allan Vorda, he explains the advantage of fiction over journalism: "Fiction is something where you create the illusion of life, the illusion of continuity, and the illusion of cause and effect" (Stone, "Stroking," 215). The illusion-evoking quality of a text is not exactly the same as its realism—readers can experience the illusion of witnessing a scene even in fantasy fiction—but the terms are related, because realist texts provide a comparatively high level of signs easily transformable into imaginations of an external or internal reality. Later on in the same interview, Stone describes the kind of psychological realism he is after:

> I'm a realist as a writer in a very limited way. I'm trying to accurately portray emotional and psychological states, so they can be recognized. I think you have to go beyond the level of naturalism in order to do that. The only way you can make words evoke psychological and emotional states effectively is by creating an altered state of consciousness. My way of doing that is to write a lot of prose that is close to blank verse and is evocative in the same ways

> that poetry is. I'm certainly not a naturalist or a conventional realist. I'm after another kind of reality: the kind of reality that is subjectively experienced from the inside. (219)

Stone's intended realism, then, is a psychological one, focusing on characters rather than action, on internal mood and emotion rather than external characterization. He presents his characters in certain exceptional yet typical situations and lets their behavior result from that, in a kind of causal way Howells would have found acceptable. However, what strikes many readers as being foregrounded in his fiction is action, often highly dramatic action. There is much violence, and Stone readily acknowledges that war is for him a fundamental and revelatory series of situations and at the same time a metaphor of human existence. *A Flag for Sunrise* thus has the appearance of an adventure story.

And yet the book is a political novel with a realistic setting. In a 1985 interview, Stone commented on Central America as a scene of conflict:

> That's been a sphere of influence we've exploited economically and dominated politically and militarily very much the way the French, with a bit more success, continue to dominate their former colonies in Africa. We've run that part of the world without a lot of respect for the people who live down there; we've looked down on them as racial inferiors. [. . .] We saw these places as banana republics peopled by gooks who somehow are not quite real people. Nobody thought it compromised American virtue to kick their ass if they got out of line. It was, you know, the white man's burden. And we have to remember that when Kipling passed that duty on to the United States there was no cynicism or irony intended. I don't believe this country has simply been some horror story of racism and murder. But we have incurred a blood debt and it *is* coming up for payment. The end of empire comes for everybody and it's coming for us. So now we're faced with this area close to our southern sea frontier where the people have it in for us and are only too eager to collaborate with our enemies. I mean, if there was an invasion of the United States and whoever it was wanted to have a Central American legion, they'd get plenty of volunteers. ("Robert Stone" interview by Woods, 17)

That is, *A Flag for Sunrise* was written as a realistic political novel, and we have to see how the symbolical and philosophical or religious level of the text is congruent with this aim.

The novel's main field of action is a missionary station and the town and beaches nearby, located in the fictive Central American State Tecan (strongly resembling Nicaragua just before the Sandinista takeover in 1979). It brings together the young American nun Justin May, who is in sympathy with the revolution; Father Egan, an old, alcoholic Canadian priest; the American anthropologist Holliwell, who is trying to get away from a personal crisis and also has a CIA errand to carry out; and the violent, drug-addicted Pablo Tabor, who has deserted from the US Coast Guard. All of them are searching for a definitive meaning of their lives. During the beginning revolution, Justin is tortured to death by an officer of the Guardia Nacional, and Holliwell flees in a boat together with Pablo, whom he kills on the way because he fears for his own safety.

All of the main characters are North Americans. Each of them turns the Other into an object, but it is not always the ethnic other they are concerned with. Sister Justin makes the Tecanecan locals the object of her idealism, and because she fails miserably in providing significant help for the poor and the sick, she is persuaded to support the revolutionary forces by acting as a nurse for the wounded. Father Egan fails even more miserably in his confrontation with the horror of pure evil when he succumbs to the threats of Guardia Nacional lieutenant Campos to hear his confession—Campos has murdered a young Canadian tourist girl—and to dispose of the body in the sea, and when he tries in vain to get through to the brain and heart of Weitling, a young, schizophrenic child murderer of Mennonite German extraction also hanging out in the area.

For Pablo, the whole world consists of people threatening to "turn him around," to take away his subjecthood, so in his drug-induced paranoia he tries to get power over people, use them and kill them. He begins his killing spree by shooting his beloved dogs, almost kills his wife and son, has sex with the accomplice wife of an elegant gunrunner, Mr. Callahan, onto whose smuggling boat he has signed on, and afterwards kills her, her husband, and the boatman. Finally, he intends to kill Holliwell on their boat before coming to see him as a friend, that is, shortly before Holliwell commits the preventive homicide himself. However, brown-skinned Pablo is part of the Other himself. "Son of a whore," never having known his father, a person of mixed ethnic descent, "Mex mestizo mulatto nigger spic. Malinche" (*Flag*, 124), Pablo embodies the exploited of the Americas *and* the exploiters, the invaded *and* the invaders. He insists "'I ain't part anything, [. . .] I'm American'" (98), but in this very pronouncement he reveals the asymmetry of American history and society. In a plot rife with evil characters, Pablo is given more space than any other figure except Holliwell. He is as evil as can be imagined, but his anger at just about anybody appears not only to be the effect of his dope practices, but also to come from a feeling of being hopelessly alone: "what the hell is the use of me? No use at all" (124).

Toward the end of the novel, Egan's sermonizing makes Pablo believe he has a purpose in life, after all, that he is indeed part of a larger plot, which makes him turn completely paranoid. On the boat, his ramblings about his role in life make Holliwell crazy with fear and bent on getting rid of him. Holliwell tells him of a dream—which may just be a ruse to get Pablo to utter a self-definition that will justify killing him: "'In my dream [. . .] I'm different from everyone else. Maybe I'm on the subway, understand, and everyone in the car is black except me. Something really lousy is about to happen to me [. . .]. Or else I'm on a ship. The crew are Chinese or Malays, Indians, anything, something that I'm not.'" And sure enough, Pablo identifies himself with this role of the complete outsider: "'that's me [. . .]. I'm Spanish, see? Or my mother was. She was . . . I don't know, Indian, Spanish blood. So I never been what anybody else was. And down inside me, I never been. That's why all these people turn me around'" (430).

Yet the message of the book is that people suffer not because of ethnic difference but because of human nature. Just before he stabs him, Holliwell tells Pablo the story of the scorpion that asks a buffalo to carry it across the river and halfway across stings the buffalo although this means that they will both drown, explaining his act by "'it's my nature'" (431). It is "'a story about how people are [. . .]. You used to hear it in Vietnam. They probably tell it in Tecan as well'" (430). We can gather from this that Pablo is not different at all, but only the epitome of man's nature: violence and treacherousness, but also self-delusion and vain, almost innocent hope. Pablo, who in a sense embodies the Other, is the alter ego of the Americas, which leaves little to hope for from the coming together of North and South. However, this symbolic aspect remains a faint thematic strand; it is not bolstered by any sociohistorical investigation. That he is also a victim of social conditions and of inter-American history is an aspect that the book does not explore any further.

It is Justin who engages with Latin America on the most direct level by trying to be of help to the local population. And yet, she is mostly just an onlooker, as in the long description of a religious holiday and fair in the nearby port town she visits in the company of Father Godoy, a priest in sympathy with the opposition.

> The road led them inland through banana and then pineapple, to the top of Pico Hill, where they could see the ocean again and the wharves of the distant port, then down again past acres of yellow-painted, numbered company houses, finally to the tin-and-crate-wood shacks on the edge of town. From the town center they could hear the report of exploding firecrackers and the blare of the sound truck the Syrian store-keeper had hired to publicize his holiday specials.
>
> There was a block of paved street where the houses had carports and painted fences, then the Gran hotel, the Texaco station—and they turned into the

> crowded plaza. [. . .] In the center of the square, a ceiba tree had been hung with paper garlands and an elderly band in black uniforms was ranged beneath its branches. There were Japanese lanterns strung between the trees at two sides of the plaza and the square itself was jammed with people. Men of property stood with transistor radios pressed against their ears, teen-aged parents in cheap cotton dress-up clothes clung to their several tiny children—and lone children puzzled their way through the crowd's legs. The shoeshine boys had given over their space by the fountain and sat together with their boxes at the park edge, watching for flung cigarette butts, fallen change, loose wallets. (42–43)

Here and on the following pages we have a fairly convincing picture of a Caribbean coast town fair in 1976,[7] including its social structure, its ethnic mix, and the economic presence of the United States: the endless company houses must be those of employees of the United Fruit Company; the Texaco station and the American T-shirts worn by the teenagers add to this impression. On the other hand, the religious fervor of the crowd when the figure of Christ is revealed as well as "the raw cane liquor, barely rum, that was being passed in Coke bottles" (43) indicate the escape routes open to the common population. The presence of the Guardia guarantees the continuation of this order. It is no coincidence that following these impressions, Godoy can win Justin for a part as nurse in the coming revolution. It is a realistic picture in the Howellsian sense of a great number of precisely represented details, but the selection and hierarchy of these details is that of a fairly well-informed, yet nonetheless foreign observer, be it the omniscient narrator or a character, Justin.

The discrepancy between what Justin observes and what she can do makes her hate herself, her body and its needs and desires, her loss of faith and a role in life. Her death wish is mentioned several times, but she is also ready for self-sacrifice, if this is the price of a more active role: "To do penance and to amend my life, amen. To struggle unceasingly in the name of history. Gimme a flag, gimme a drum roll, I'm gonna be there on that morning, yes I am. And it won't be the me you think you see. It'll be the worthy revolutionary twice-born me. The objective historical unceasingly struggling me. The good me" (264). When she has broken her vow and slept with Holliwell, she realizes that this is not the liberation she needs nor he the person to make it possible. She resumes the metaphor she has used before by quoting Emily Dickinson: "'A Wife—at Daybreak I shall be—[. . .] Sunrise—Hast thou a flag for me?'" (380). The fact that Stone has chosen this for phrasing the title of his novel shows that he intends to present Justin's search for a purpose in life and death in a positive light. The young nun is the most attractive seeker for and embodiment of idealism and altruism, whose quest cannot be satisfied by a mere act of sexual liberation. Dickinson's poem puts the metaphors of marriage and the flag for sunrise in a religious, resurrectional context, although other possibilities are also there: in Stone's words, "what awaits us all on the morning after the battle [. . .]. What will be there to claim our allegiance—the red banner of revolution, or some emblem we can't recognize but that we've somehow created[.] And of course I intend an ironic reference to the American flag" ("Robert Stone" interview by Woods, 15).

The religious aspect comes up again in Justin's dying words, "'Behold the handmaid of the Lord'" (*Flag*, 416). Quoting Mary's words at the annunciation, she may express that she has found her faith again and thereby humiliates Guardia officer Campos, who is torturing her to death. Her submission to God's will makes her join the numbers of the Tecanecan victims of brutal oppression. Yet there is the irony that Justin has been twice betrayed: first by Holliwell, who by lusting after her takes away her last defense against the authorities, that of being a member of a religious order, and who under pressure tells his interrogators about her political engagement; and second by the revolutionists, because the skirmish around the mission station has been intended mainly to distract the government forces from the main area of action in the mountains. Thus, the death of the local sympathizers has been considered a possibility that one had to accept. The ideals of the revolution cannot be pursued only by ideal means.

That this is so is shown in a kind of inter-chapter mostly disregarded by the critics or seen only as a break in narrative consistency. The chapter,[8] close to the middle of the novel, departs from the stories and points of view of the four North American main characters in order to show, however briefly, the world of the Tecanecan revolutionaries. What we get to see, first from an omniscient perspective, and later through the eyes of Aguirre, the elderly leader just returned from Prague, is a meeting of the inner circle—including one man having turned traitor—in a university room in the capital. It serves to make the novel's plot clear by sketching the insurgents' intentions. If the ending appears sometimes confusing, given the various changes of the luck of war, this chapter foreshadows what we can gather as fact: in the end the revolution has succeeded, the president has fled the country, and Campos is trying to escape after having forced Father Egan to give him another absolution, this time for the murder of Justin. But the chapter also serves to show us the revolutionaries as varied human characters with differing degrees of commitment, differing degrees of belief in Marxism or Christian socialism. Thus, again, the focus is not on local color or history, but on characters, culminating in Aguirre's realization that with Emilio Ortega Curtis, the American-educated former artist, he has found the true leader for the revolution and the establishment of a new, national order, irrespective of the role the Communist Bloc may want to play. When Aguirre takes Ortega's self-promotion to leadership as cynicism, the other replies in a manner that puts ideologists to shame:

> "Cynicism? That I—a plain man, a mediocre artist, perhaps even a mediocre fighter—take it upon myself to bring justice to our accursed suffering country? To bring health to her children, dignity to her desperate poor? To replace her absurdity in the eyes of the world with pride—to make housing, hospitals, schools for her masses of ignorant? To leave sound philosophy and engage life which we both know to be so vulgar? To dispense life to some and death to others in the name of a form of humanity which for all we know may never exist? [. . .] *Hombre*, [. . .] there is no Jesus Christ. There is no philosophy in a shack or in the gutter. There is not yet even such a thing as the People. There are only poor creatures like you and me, my comrade—and we propose to bring these things about. We propose unto death." (210)

Although Stone insists that he plotted the novel before the revolutions in Nicaragua and El Salvador (Stone, "An Interview" by Bonetti, 107), there is much in this scene that resembles the establishment of the Sandinista leadership,[9] and we are to see that the book is not simply taking sides but showing the seriousness of the cause of the other side. Ortega's irritation at Aguirre's constant references to the Spanish Civil War, that is, the older leader's personal war, indicates that the Tecanecan revolution is a specifically Central American war—a fact often ignored by US government agents who regard it as a continuation of the substitute wars against communism.

The figure that dominates the novel in sheer number of pages and that has found the most critical attention[10] is anthropology professor Frank Holliwell, who follows an invitation by his old friend Ocampo to Tecan's neighboring state Compostela in order to give a scholarly lecture. The lecture that Holliwell does deliver, though, is a drunken monologue, and yet it contains the central message of the book. Holliwell denounces American popular culture:

> "Uncle Sam developed the first leisured, literate masses—[. . .] working masses with the money and the time to command the resources of their culture, who would not be instructed and who had no idea of their place. Because Uncle Sam thought of nothing but the almighty dollar he then created the machine-made popular culture to pander to them. To reinforce, if you like, their base instincts. He didn't think it was his job to improve them and neither did they. This debasement of polite society is what we are now selling you. [. . .] Underneath it all, our secret culture, the non-exportable one, is dying." (108)

In Holliwell's view, the United States has been exporting, sometimes by force—"'ramming it down their throats'" (107)—what is worst in US culture. The non-exportable secret American culture is that of American exceptionalism, which has two sides. As the belief in the "more," it led to the creation of mass culture. The other side is idealism, as Stone answered the question of what he considered best in America: "A tradition of rectitude that genuinely does exist in American society and sometimes has been translated into government. [. . . S]o much that is best in America is a state of mind that you can't export" (Stone, "Robert Stone" interview by Woods, 18).

It is Justin who embodies such idealism, and it is she who witnesses the exported pop culture Stone regards as "a form of pollution. It's why you get Central American Indians with transistor radios glued to their skulls" ("Robert Stone" interview by Woods, 18), just as in the town fair scene quoted earlier. Holliwell, however, is incapable of living up to any idealism. Although in the scene just described he is the author's mouthpiece, his whole appearance makes him the representative of the failures of American leftist liberalism after the Vietnam War. Traumatized by what he has seen in Vietnam, disgusted with his former role of working for the CIA, he drowns his identity crisis in alcohol and becomes the embodiment of indecision. In his despair over the meaningless of the world, the failure of individuals and countries to learn from past mistakes, his lack of ideals and belief, he may be thanatotic, as when he comes near death when diving off the Tecan coast, but he always pulls back, which is why he becomes a murderer rather than risking being killed himself. He refuses to work for the CIA as he had done in Vietnam, and to spy on the Catholic mission in Tecan, but half passively, half actively this is exactly where he winds up. Both sides, Justin and the US, Tecanecan, Cuban, and other sinister characters working on behalf of the Tecanecan government and American business interests down there and who interrogate him when the fighting starts, tell Holliwell that it is not acceptable not to take sides, not to accept a cause. His helpless "'Damn it, [. . .] I don't know quite why I came'" (*Flag*, 394) only makes things worse.

Holliwell's indecision and finally his despair over the nature of the world make him the representative of modern intellectuals. As Fredrickson puts it, "After murdering Pablo, Holliwell, sunk deeper in his despair, faces the ultimate fear, that evil is nonexistent. 'He, Holliwell, was things. There was nothing better. The absence of evil was the greatest horror' (43[8]). To Holliwell what terrifies is that there is no history, no evil, simply the blank thingness of the universe. 'We look at us. The thing looks at itself' (439)" (327). But the absurdity of the situation is heightened because the rising sun reveals to him that the boat has drifted to the immediate vicinity of a Caribbean island and that he is being watched by American tourists fishing from another boat close to his own. While Justin's sunrise gave her the feeling of being accepted by divine grace, his brings the realization of his own insignificance in view of the banality of life. The novel's last sentences are "She has her sunrise, he thought, and I have mine. Holliwell knew that he was home; he had nothing to fear from the sun. A man has nothing to fear, he thought to himself, who understands history" (*Flag*, 440). But what is the lesson of history? This final sentence might be self-ironical, but it could also mean that the way to understand history is to acknowledge the recurrence of the same. In biblical terms, "That which has been is what will be, That which is done is what will be done, And there is nothing new under the sun" (Eccl. 1:9). In the present, inter-American case, it means that Holliwell is back home in a world governed by US interests and power, by American money and the American way of life.

The tension between the political and the philosophical or religious level of meaning of *A Flag of Sunrise* is one that defines the whole novel and may be responsible for some of its problems, such as the overlarge number of evil or paranoiacally deluded characters, for instance the presence of the child murderer Weitling. Yet the two levels belong together, as Stone has repeatedly argued:

> If I'm not concerned with myself in the universe first, why am I concerned with what's happening in Central America? Am I in favor of the cause of small, brown people because they are groovy? Because as an American, I like to see the little guy beat the big guy? Because some kind of received, pseudo-moral wisdom has rubbed off me from some institutional walls? [. . .] There is nothing that motivates the nuns, the activists in Central America, except their position in the universe. That's all there is. That is the only morality there is, you and the universe. ("Me and the Universe," 234)

That is, Stone is concerned about individual morality apart from any given ideology. But where does the material come from, what role does social and political reality play in the context of individual behavior? In his essay "We Are Not Excused," Stone tells us how he got involved in the issue of Central America when he was visiting Nicaragua in 1976:

> As I said, I was working on another book, and this was supposed to be a vacation. But the longer I stayed in Nicaragua, the more I began to hear stories. After a while the stories began to form a pattern that conformed to a sense I had of the history of Central America. This band of republics between the Andes and the Grijalva River seemed to be placed by their gods in a very fateful situation. They seemed to have drawn the most violent conquistadors and

> the most fanatical inquisitors. The arriving Spaniards had found holy wells of human sacrifice. There, racial and social oppression had always been severe. The fertile soil of the place seemed to bring forth things to provoke the appetite rather than things to nourish—rare baubles and rich toys, plantation crops for your sweet tooth or for your head. They were all labor-intensive, high-profit items: bananas, of course, and coffee, chocolate, tobacco, chicle, emeralds, marijuana, cocaine. And since my subject was America, and the United States had been involved there for so long, by the time I got back to the States I had decided to [. . .] begin a new [. . .] novel, my third political novel, *A Flag For Sunrise*. ("We Are Not Excused," 34–35)

These aspects of Central American history and current situation form the material for a long chapter in the first third of the novel. After his disastrous talk at the university of Santiago de Compostela, Holliwell (doesn't his name echo the holy wells mentioned in the last quotation?) receives phone calls threatening him with death. He accepts the offer of an American couple, Tom and Marie Zecca, to drive with him to Tecan, where he did not want to go before. The fourth person on board is a young journalist, Bob Cole, who intends to visit the Atapa Indians presently in revolt against the *caudillo* and attempts by the government and a US company to take and exploit their land. Cole is the moral spokesperson in the car, mentioning all the injustice that has been done to the population. (Holliwell and the Zeccas are doubtful whether this is just a ruse to cover his true role; as we learn later on, the Atapa forces try and then execute him as a spy.) The Zeccas are very nice people. Tom is a military officer affiliated with the American Embassy in the Tecanecan capital San Ysidro, and he and Marie have done duty in Vietnam, but both object to the dictator's and his underlings' treatment of the people, the cruelty of the Guardia, and the American support for the regime just because it is anticommunist and because it protects US business interests. The stories Tom Zecca tells about the *caudillo*'s luxury life and cruelty bespeak his disgust with the situation, and he is looking forward to his own replacement. Like everyone else in the car, Tom considers the Vietnam War "'the dumbest damn thing we ever did as a country'" (*Flag*, 165). But he is under no illusion about the fact that something similar will happen when the revolution in Tecan starts:

> "The Guardia will have American weapons and support. The support will be mealy-mouthed and covert but it will be there."
>
> "And what do honest folk like yourselves do then, Captain Zecca?" Holliwell inquired. [. . .]
>
> "It's too late. [. . .] The usual shit will go down. [. . .] If we don't back them now, we'll have a Russian submarine base in Puerto Alvarado—maybe a

> missile base this time. See how that goes over in Dubuque, in Congress, in the White House [. . .]."
>
> "Fucked again," Holliwell said.
>
> "I'll be gone," Zecca said. "My tour is almost up. Then they can send in the types who like the Guardia's style. The headhunters, the Cubans, the counter-insurgency LURPs. And the guys who enjoy saluting animals in tailor-made pink uniforms." (168)

Yet despite this open exchange of opinions, at the end of the evening Holliwell comes to distrust even Tom Zecca, who tends to retire behind his role of pragmatic and efficient soldier, and indeed, everyone distrusts everyone else at least a little: late consequence of the moral corruption brought on by the Vietnam intervention.

It is from the perspective of this group of Americans that we get the most comprehensive picture of Tecan and the stretch of the Pan-American Highway between the two capitals, the poverty and struggle for survival even among the children already in Compostela, the market scenes that remind them of Vietnam, hovels at the outskirts of town, the banana plantations, the modernization where American companies have brought industry. Cole tells the story of conquistador Martínez Trujillo's cruel treatment of the Indians in his efforts to extort gold from them where there wasn't any, and reveals a belief in the justice of history, whereas Tom Zecca is more cynical: "'You ever see the murals at Bonampak? These characters all deserved each other'" (143). When they stop at a "tropical-Bavarian" (144) lake resort lodge, Cole tells how American tourist interests converted the lake into a fishing resort and imported American bass, killing every native species, which has brought starvation to the local Indians; and Zecca adds an episode of native *gringo* baiting. Holliwell and Cole have to bribe the Tecanecan consul to issue them visas. The central scene is at the border where the Tecanecan Guardia Nacional harasses young, hippie-type tourists, and where a

> crowd of local boys, whose proper business was assisting tourists through customs, selling cold drinks or begging, were amusing themselves by stoning [a cow caught by the border wire] to death. [. . .]
>
> The animal had lost its footing and was lying with its back legs tucked under it, its hooves tearing ineffectually at the dirt and wire while the rocks crashed down on it from every side. The boys would exhaust their handful and then run off into the sandy fields to gather more. Each stone was received by the cow with a soft bellow. Its eyes and nostrils were beginning to show blood. (151)

At Marie's request, Tom intervenes by revealing his authority as an American officer to the border guard, who scatters the boys by shooting over their heads. As in Rumaker's "Gringos," brutality has been passed down from one social group to the next lower one, cruelty to animals being the final result. And there is an example of sympathetic landscape:

> They drove on in silence over the dusty plateau. The coastward volcano was abreast of them, a second, larger rose ahead. To Holliwell, they seemed freakish mountains; only malignant gods could inhabit or inform them. They rose solitary out of featureless tableland, bare, without harmony, unbeautiful enough to appear exactly what they were—burst excrescences on Tecan's pocked dusty hide. A geology lesson, he thought. They communicated a troubling sense of the earth as nothing more than itself, of blind force and mortality. As mindlessly refuting of hope as a skull and bones. The landscape was a memento mori, the view ahead like a dead ocean floor. (156–57)

Equally oppressive is the impression they get of the Tecanecan capital when driving through.

Anyone who remembers driving through Nicaragua or some other parts of Central America in the 1970s will remember such scenes, impressions, and pieces of historical or current information as are being filtered here through the eyes and minds of US travelers. This is the book's pinnacle of realistic representation of the Latin American Other. It is realistic not simply because of the probability or adequacy of many of its details, but because these are presented through a set of subjective North American perspectives. No claim is made that this is a complete or even a balanced view. It is a model of reality that people living in those parts might correct in many ways. It is worth remembering that what the revolutionaries in the chapter mentioned earlier have to say about their country remains fairly abstract. Stone does not pretend to enter their minds as he does those of his countrymen. He is specific enough to refute Frederick R. Karl's critique that he "cannot break through the familiarity of his material. Tecan is Conrad's Sulaco, or Greene's Haiti, Southeast Asia, Africa, and Mexico, or the *Times*'s Nicaragua, or some other repressive Central or South American republic" (Karl 117). Tecan and Compostela are fictions precisely because Stone wants to present models of a certain reality without having to verify every detail that he has from hearsay or from his imagination.

Still, we are made to realize that these countries are not identical unless seen from a highly aloof, arrogant outsider's point of view. As a piece of inter-American realistic fiction, *A Flag for Sunrise* belongs among the most successful. Where it is less successful is in the sheer accumulation of more or less burnt-out characters from outside succumbing to the forces of evil in or around them. *A Flag for Sunrise* is, finally, a kind of theological novel about the presence of evil and the nature of the universe.[11] These questions are pressed upon the characters in part by what they witness in Central America, but one might wish that there were more than a cursory glance at the role of religion for the Latin American characters, and that others than only Sister Justin had been given the ability to in some way engage actively with the political, social, and economic reality rather than withdrawing into a haze of drugs, alcohol, or paranoia. But perhaps this is part of the devastating message of the book. When asked by a woman in his audience whether there is "'a place for God in all this,'" Holliwell answers, "'There's always a place for God, señora. There is some question as to whether He's in it'" (*Flag*, 110).

CHARLOTTE DOUGLAS, THE PROTAGONIST of Joan Didion's *A Book of Common Prayer*, also gets to Latin America by way of escape or quest after her illusion of a stable personal situation has been destroyed by the disappearance of her daughter, who has joined a group of terrorists. Because Charlotte cannot find orientation in her other relationships, either, she spends some time in the fictitious Central American country Boca Grande, vaguely hoping that her daughter might someday appear there. She works for social institutions and has social but also sexual contact with the leading family of the country without being able to understand the political conditions that are characterized by a periodic change of power among the members of this oligarchic family. When the next so-called revolution occurs, Charlotte disregards all counsel and remains in the country. She is shot to death under unclear circumstances—an end she may have coveted consciously or subconsciously.

Charlotte's story is told by an American woman who has married into the ruling family, Grace Strasser-Mendana, *née* Tabor (interestingly, the same family name Stone would use for his character Pablo), who in the process reveals so much of her own thinking and feeling that she has to be considered the second main character. In an inter-American context, Grace is the more interesting one, which is why I will not devote much space to Charlotte, who has been often discussed by critics. Large portions of the novel are set in the United States, and because the picture we get of Boca Grande is extremely reductive, we may wonder if *A Book of Common Prayer* should be included in a list of inter-American books at all. Considering that so much space is given to private lives and delusions, we are also hard put in calling it a political novel. Vietnam does not yet play a role, at least not on the surface. The urban guerilla group that Charlotte's daughter Marin joins resembles the Symbionese Liberation Army, and although she was not kidnapped but joined voluntarily, Marin is like Patty Hearst in coming from an affluent family whose wealth she comes to see as unethically gained, which, together with some crude version of Marxist or Maoist thinking, makes her become an active member of the terrorist underground. The way Grace depicts her, Marin is naive and a rather primitive thinker, voicing slogans on audiotapes (like Patty Hearst) such as "'*We shall reply to repression with liberation. We shall reply to the terrorism of the dictatorship with the terrorism of the revolution*'" (*Book*, 78). The obvious dictatorship of the oligarchy of Boca Grande is not put into any direct connection with this political belief. In her scathing critique of Didion as a writer and person, "Joan Didion: Only Disconnect," Barbara Grizzutti Harrison describes the author as devoid of politics and believing only in the individual: "All virtue resides in acts so private that only the participants can understand their significance. Read *A Book of Common Prayer* again, and you will see that what is implied is that having politics paralyzes the potential for performing good deeds: to swallow Didion it is necessary to swallow the notion that all acts of virtue are—must be—divorced from politics" (8).

Interestingly, though, in her second *Paris Review* interview ("Joan Didion, The Art of Nonfiction No. 1") of 2006, Didion pinpoints her move from her earlier personal and social commentary books to politics at the writing of *A Book of Common Prayer*, rather than, as the interviewer had suggested, at her reportage *Salvador* (1983):

> DIDION: Actually, it was a novel, *Common Prayer*. We had gone to a film festival in Cartagena and I got sick there, some kind of salmonella. We left Cartagena and went to Bogotà, and then we came back to Los Angeles and I was sick for about four months. I started doing a lot of reading about South America, where I'd never been. [. . .] Then later I started reading a lot about Central America because it was becoming clear to me that my novel had to take place in a rather small country. So that was when I started thinking more politically.
>
> INTERVIEWER: But it still didn't push you into an interest in domestic politics.
>
> DIDION: I didn't get the connection. I don't know why I didn't get the connection, since I wasn't interested in the politics of these countries per se, but rather in how American foreign policy affected them. And the extent to which we are involved abroad is entirely driven by our own domestic politics. [. . .] I started to get this in *Salvador*, but not fully until *Miami*. Our policy with Cuba and with exiles has been totally driven by domestic politics. ("Joan Didion," 9–10)

Thus, we have a novel that takes its beginning in a personal crisis: the author gets sick in (and of) a Latin American country. She then tries to comprehend that experience, the (for her: sickening) otherness of such countries by doing research and having someone else do research for her: "I would say, Bring me back anything on plantation life in Central America. And she would come back and say, This is really what you're looking for—you'll love this. And it would not be plantation life in Central America. It would be Ceylon, but it would be fantastic. She had an instinct for what was the same story, and what I was looking for. What I was looking for were rules of living in the tropics" ("Joan Didion," 11). Phrases like "small country" and "the same story" indicate that Didion is trying to create a model, an abstraction of some basic elements of a tropical, plantation economy country being exploited by its ruling class and by foreign, US American, interests. It is this model character we have to study in order to understand in which way the book is political and marks the author's becoming aware, perhaps not quite consciously yet, of the connection between the alien and the domestic, after all.

The book may also be seen as an emancipation of the author from her narrator. Barbara Harrison writes,

> [A]bout Boca Grande [. . .], Grace, the rich narrator, says: "there is poverty here, but it is obdurately indistinguishable from comfort. We all live in cinderblock houses." Oh no. [. . .] One does not have to have lived in a Central American country [. . .], one has only to read *Newsweek* to understand that there are certain very real differences between the cinderblock houses of the rich and the cinderblock houses of the poor. Earthquakes, for example: the esthetically unpleasing cinderblock houses of the poor collapse during earthquakes; the esthetically unpleasing cinderblock houses of the rich do not. [. . .] (One might also mention plumbing. Didion does not.) (B. Harrison 4)

Yet this was Grace speaking, whose last words in the novel are "I have not been the witness I wanted to be" (*Book*, 280)—witness perhaps not only for Charlotte ("I WILL BE HER WITNESS," [3]). Although Grace's style may be similar to Didion's own laconic way of writing, her way and view of life are not. She introduces herself in the following manner:

> I have been for fifty of my sixty years a student of delusion, a prudent traveler from Denver, Colorado. My mother died of influenza one morning when I was eight. My father died of gunshot wounds, not self-inflicted, one afternoon when I was ten. From that afternoon until my sixteenth birthday I lived alone in our suite at the Brown Palace Hotel. I have lived in equatorial America since 1935 and only twice had fever. I am an anthropologist who lost faith in her own method, who stopped believing that observable activity defined anthropos. I studied under Kroeber at California and worked with Lévi-Strauss at São Paulo, classified several societies, [. . .] did extensive and well-regarded studies on the rearing of female children in the Mato Grosso [. . .] and still did

> not know why any one of these female children did or did not do anything at all.
>
> Let me go further.
>
> I did not know why I did or did not do anything at all.
>
> As a result I "retired" from that field, married a planter of San Blas Green coconut palms here in Boca Grande and took up the amateur study of biochemistry, a discipline in which demonstrable answers are commonplace and "personality" absent. (4)

In other words, Grace comes from a wealthy, privileged background and has early on shielded herself against loss and terror, which made it possible that she took the death of her husband with equanimity and the estrangement from her playboy son Gerardo with—ostensibly—only moderate regret. This traumatized, hardened, disillusioned, cynical woman of sixty who is slowly dying of cancer (a fact she does not sentimentalize nor make capital of) is the empathetic imaginative explorer, "witness" in the biblical sense, of Charlotte's character and life. Reconstructing these after Charlotte's death, she uses her own memories, what she heard from Charlotte herself, Charlotte's two husbands, her daughter, and a number of others familiar with her, but in scenically evoking key moments and stages of Charlotte's career, she uses her considerable power of imagination and her great literary skill, particularly in rendering dialogue. All of this has led to readers' impression that here we have a sympathetic narrative authority writing about a person who may be odious in the beginning but is slowly gaining complexity and even impenetrability in her observer's mind.

However, as in Mark Twain's *Puddn'head Wilson*, where the crucial piece of information—"Dawson's Landing was a slaveholding town, with a rich slave-worked grain and pork country back of it" (3)—is slipped surreptitiously into a general, very idyllic description of the town, a decisive element of Grace's role in life is mentioned by her by the way: "Edgar's death left me in putative control of fifty-nine-point-eight percent of the arable land and about the same percentage of the decision-making process in La República (recently La República Libre) de Boca Grande" (*Book*, 12). The irony of "Libre" must not be overlooked. Didion has often cited Joseph Conrad as one of her literary models, but in contrast to Conrad's imaginatively reconstructing narrator Marlow, Grace has enormous potential agency. She explains why Edgar and his father, the former president, had endowed her with this much power and wealth—the other members of the family clan are more or less irresponsible, impulsive, irrational:

> The day Luis was shot Elena flew to exile in Geneva, a theatrical gesture but unnecessary [. . .]. The wife of any other Latin president would have known

immediately that a coup in which the airport remained open was a coup doomed to fail, but Elena had no instinct for being the wife of a Latin president. [. . .] A few weeks later Elena came back. [. . .] She was wearing tinted glasses and a new Balenciaga coat, lettuce-green. She was carrying a matching parrot. She had not taken this parrot with her from Boca Grande. She had bought this parrot that morning in Geneva, for seven hundred dollars. (12–13)

The deeper reason for Grace's investiture with the job of indirectly running the country may have been that she is American. So was her father-in-law, the father of Edgar, Luis, Victor, and Antonio:

> [M]y husband's father was the rich man, the *millonario*, a St. Louis confidence man named Victor Strasser who at age twenty-three floated some Missouri money to buy oil rights, at age twenty-four fled Mexico after an abortive attempt to invade Sonora, and at age twenty-five arrived in Boca Grande. Upon his recovery from cholera he married a Mendana and proceeded to divest her family of interior Boca Grande. (10)

US Americans have taken over the country, which includes the American Embassy where the Strasser-Mendana clan is often seen.

Joan Didion may have experienced Latin America as alien, intestinal disease-bringing, and, as she describes it in *Salvador*, violent, a place of terror and political and social brutality. Her successful Americans in *A Book of Common Prayer* overcome or are immune to the diseases and hence by natural selection the born winners. For Didion, her trip to Cartagena

> was like a hallucination, partly because I had a fever. It seemed to me extraordinary that North America had gone one way and South America had gone another and I couldn't understand why. [. . .T]hey're not industrialized [. . .]. Also, in North America social tensions that arise tend to be undercut and coopted quite soon, but in Latin America there does not seem to be any political machinery for delaying the revolution. Everything is thrown into bold relief. There is a collapsing of time. Everything is both older than you could ever know, and it started this morning. [. . .] I was overcome by [García Márquez's *One Hundred Years of Solitude*] when I read it, but when I went down there, I realized the book was far more social realism than it was fantasy. (Didion, "A Visit with Joan Didion" by Davidson)

In her own novel, Didion is trying to come to grips with this Latin American strangeness, the phantasmagoric quality of her impressions, the contrasts and ambiguities, in order to find out about her own way of thinking, as she has repeatedly said. The result is startling. Stone's Tecan resembles Nicaragua at the time of the Somozas. Didion's, or, to be more precise, Grace's

Boca Grande resembles no Latin American country, not even Panama, which comes closest to it. It is a reduction, a caricature written by a woman bent on finding meaning by reducing complexity—pace Luhmann. The name Boca Grande "means 'big mouth,' or big bay, and describes the country's principal physical feature precisely as it appears" (*Book*, 9). This may be so, but in its first meaning, "big mouth" refers to a big eater or loud-mouthed person, a braggart—a satiric epithet fitting most of the clan's male members but also the US protagonists Warren and Leonard. Didion's impression of Colombia was that of a land of contrasts, and these are the exact words Charlotte uses in her "'Letters from Central America'" (5) to characterize Boca Grande, a North American cliché notion of Latin America. Yet Grace contradicts:

> Boca Grande is not a land of contrasts. On the contrary Boca Grande is relentlessly "the same": the cathedral is not Spanish Colonial but corrugated aluminum. There is a local currency but the American dollar is legal tender. The politics of the country at first appear to offer contrast, involving as they do the "colorful" Latin juxtaposition of *guerilleros* and colonels, but when the tanks are put away and the airport reopens nothing has actually changed in Boca Grande. There are no waterfalls of note, no ruins of interest, no chic boutiques [. . .] to provide dramatic cultural foil to voodoo in the hills.
>
> In fact there is no voodoo in the hills.
>
> In fact there are no hills, only the flat bush and the lifeless sea. (5–6)

Boca Grande does not even have a history because no one remembers a first settler. It looks like a plantation extension of the United States, which in fact it is. Didion takes pains to make it a heterotopian no-place by giving confusing details: the country exports copra, but also anaconda skins, yet these enormous snakes do not occur in Central America but only in South America and in Trinidad and Tobago. Are we to imagine something as weird as anaconda snake farming? Grace occasionally talks about its "equatorial" light, but even Panama is still at some distance from the equator. On the other hand, the air travel distances given seem to indicate this country rather than any other. Didion worked with a map of Central America against her wall; she cannot have constructed such imprecision, such nonrealistic combination of descriptive elements unintentionally. Grace emphasizes the unambiguousness of Boca Grandean reality: "Almost everything in Boca Grande describes itself precisely as it appears, as if any ambiguity in the naming of things might cause the present to sink as tracelessly as the past. The Rio Blanco looks white. The Rio Colorado looks red" (9), and so on. It seems that much of the country escapes her gaze or that she avoids looking at it. She lets the road to the abandoned American aluminum combine grow over, contrary to her dead husband's intention to maintain it because "the interior had things we might want access to. [. . .] What I wanted from the interior had nothing to do with access" (11). What is she after?

Her detachment from the country she indirectly runs, her contempt for its leading families, including her own son, seems unsurpassable:

> Gerardo embodies many of the failings of this part of the world, the rather wishful machismo, the defeating touchiness, the conviction that his heritage must be aristocratic; a general attitude I do not admire. Gerardo is the grandson of two American wildcatters who got rich, my father in Colorado minerals and Edgar's father in Boca Grande politics, and of the Irish nursemaid and the *mestiza* from the interior they respectively married. Still he persists in tracing his line to the court of Castile. (13–14)

Yet if Grace is honest in saying "I am interested in Charlotte Douglas only insofar as she passed through Boca Grande, only insofar as the meaning of that sojourn continues to elude me" (14), she must be prepared to face her own delusions. To characterize Charlotte, she quotes numerous dialogues that in realistic detail and thus in quite the opposite of the reductive, caricature-like, picture of Boca Grande she draws, reflect the superficiality, amorality, tastelessness, and lack of purpose of the US American upper class. The two sentences that stick out, and seem to expose Charlotte's total insensitivity, are uttered at the American Embassy's Christmas party in response to a question about her husband Leonard's profession: "'He runs guns,' Charlotte Douglas said. 'I wish they had caviar'" (31). Yet the same Charlotte during the cholera epidemic "volunteered to give inoculations, and did, for thirty-four hours without sleeping" (218–19), in contrast to Grace, who also helped, "but only for a few hours the first morning, because I had no patience with the fact that almost no one in Boca Grande would cross the street to be inoculated" (219). Charlotte's altruistic side far surpasses that of Grace, who does not pause to reflect on the cause of the epidemic that might have something to do with poverty and the lack of plumbing, after all. Grace's self-delusion of not being affected by what others do, of not being involved, collapses when Leonard lets her know that Edgar, the rightist *caudillo* of Boca Grande, had financed the Tupamaros, the leftist guerillas of Uruguay. She is shaken by her realization of her own blindness vis-à-vis her husband's playing "the same games Gerardo played" (247), by his having been part of an international alliance of power and money running the world irrespective of right or wrong causes, of the alleviation of social misery or the continuation of repression. She comes to see herself as not too different from deluded Charlotte, after all.

Charlotte, whom the people in Boca Grande call the *norteamericana*, is a mixture of total naivety and a good deal of practical competency. She cannot understand Marin's acts and is the horror of the FBI agents trying to get information from her because she always drifts off into some reminiscence or other that is not helpful in any way. On the other hand, she performs an emergency tracheotomy and kills a chicken with her bare hands. She has fantastic plans for improving Boca Grande but works reliably at a birth control clinic. When an army colonel stops her vaccination activities by robbing the serum in order to sell it, she is only briefly shocked and then constructs the incident as the army's effort to use the vaccine even more beneficially. As Victor Strandberg has argued, Charlotte is the embodiment of "the North American ethos" (Strandberg 231), believing that the world is "peopled with others like herself" (Didion, *Book*, 57). When she is warned to leave the country before the revolution starts, she replies, "'In any case I'm not affected [. . .]. Because I'm simply not interested in any causes or issues'" (240). And when she walks into the roadblock where she will be detained and later shot, she says, "*Soy norteamericana* [. . .]. *Soy una turista*" (276). Her body will be thrown on the lawn of the American Embassy. It remains unclear, however, which side did this, just as it is unclear whether the guerillas received their unexpectedly large number of arms, which makes the fighting last much longer than usual, from Victor, the defense minister to be ousted by his brother Antonio, or from Leonard, Charlotte's second husband, the clever lawyer for the underprivileged and arms dealer, or even from the American Embassy staff.[12] In the end this does not matter because the guerillas play the part expected of them in "revolutions" that turn out to be simply coups d'état, and are finally killed or driven back when Antonio assumes the role of the strongman.

All of this, on a small scale, resembles what Didion will describe a few years later in *Salvador* as the typical American players, driven by a mixture of political and personal motives and aims and therefore liable to get instrumentalized by the country's ruling group. They are as deluded as Charlotte or Grace about their possibilities. It is no coincidence that both Grace and Warren, Charlotte's first husband, a rudely outspoken liberal, selfish, womanizing, and professionally unsuccessful man, are dying of cancer. They are eaten "from the interior" by their own inconsistencies, while slick Leonard survives by remaining aloof: he lets his wife run away with her first husband and takes care of him when he is dying, generously, but in the final analysis uninvolved. Together, the US characters form a much more mimetically drawn counterpart to the satiric abstractions of Boca Grande's ruling class (the common people almost never come directly into view).[13] Collectively, the characters represent the sometimes admirable, sometimes invidious roles of North America in Latin America, caretaking but often deluded, ignorant but efficiently self-serving. To my mind, *A Book of Common Prayer* is a satire of US Americans' activities in the world, prompted by their self-centered, domestic competition for wealth, power, sex, and love. The US side is depicted with precise renditions of commonplace dialogues and a host of physical details. In this sense, it can be called realistic. The Latin American side appears only in its most basic political and economic structures represented by the caricatures of its ruling oligarchy. Didion does not pretend to know the Other, and her narrator, Grace, for all her control of the country and its affairs, pretends that there isn't any, so as not to be too closely affected. It is a political novel in the sense that the domestic games of the rich and powerful are shown to have consequences outside the United States, a model of international politics Didion was to explore more fully in her later books.

JAMES WYLIE'S *THE SIGN OF DAWN*, published in 1981, presents a fictional end of the Brazilian military dictatorship that lasted, in historic reality, from 1964 through 1985. The black mercenary officer Jordan Mallory (Wylie's indebtedness to Hemingway and Conrad does not end with this name), a US American now in the service of Fidel Castro, leads a group of exiled Brazilians, central figures in a grassroots, socialist revolution against the military, through the Brazilian jungle to Brasília, where two of them—a defrocked black Indian priest and a beautiful mulatta—take the leadership of a new, democratic Brazil. Mallory has been drawn as reluctantly into another people's liberation venture as Stone's Holliwell into another CIA errand, but he handles matters with such superior competency that he comes to represent North American claims of political, economic, and military leadership just as well as the Rambos of the opposite side. The novel is a romantic adventure story presenting exotic characters, incidents, and settings, much violence, and a love story that ends in resignation. It is conventionally told, with varying focalizing figures, although we witness the events mainly from Mallory's point of view. The text appears to have been written for a popular audience, and the cover quotation from the *Dallas Times Herald*, "'The best black novelist to emerge since James Baldwin,'" may make one smile.[14]

However, the novel deserves our attention because it differs from most inter-American texts in significant ways. It is a utopian novel set in the immediate future of its time of publication. Though published in the post-Vietnam period, its principal characters, whatever their personal catastrophes may have been, are not disillusioned hollow men and women like, for instance, those in *A Flag for Sunrise*, but idealists ready to stake their lives for their respective goals. Although the military government and its dependency on the United States are presented following the usual patterns, the novel allows Brazil a more positive future, a change for the better, and hence departs from the atemporality, the hopeless repetitiousness of political life in Latin American countries and societies that is characteristic of the discourse of Latinamericanism. The North American intruder here is a black soldier, a dissident who has the courage to act contrary to the policy pursued by his country, and in this sense is not only a conscientious objector but an active defector and rebel, that is, for the US government, a traitor. Race and the interaction of ethnicities play a major role, and, more than in most other inter-American novels, the multiethnicity of Brazil including its unsolved ethnic conflicts is a recurrent theme. For all its excess of romantic action, *The Sign of Dawn* is a political novel with a clear, emancipatory message. Finally, the novel presents Brazilian nature in such richness of detail as to surpass even earlier texts making use of a jungle setting, like Beach's *Jungle Gold* discussed in Chapter 7.

Characters are introduced by their outer appearance and their none-too-skillfully related biographies: their own memories or a confession to one of the others will suffice. Jordan Mallory, the novel's hero, is a fifty-four-year-old African American whose father was a doctor and writer, a member of the Harlem Renaissance who took Jordan to Paris to live in the black community. He has studied anthropology—a recurrent feature in so many inter-American texts, but here the stereotype is used to upgrade the character who, realistically, can get a teaching job only at Howard University. He is increasingly committed to anticolonial ideas and sympathizes with revolutionary movements. He leaves his bourgeois academic life and goes to Vietnam to join the Vietminh and fight the French.[15] Next he assists the Algerian National Liberation Front in its struggle against the French colonial power. His family is estranged from him, and he continues to fight for revolutionary movements, now for black Africa, his true inner home. He works as advisor for the Congolese prime minister Patrice Lumumba, and witnesses the coup sponsored by the CIA, the former colonial power Belgium, and other Western countries that ended in Lumumba's assassination.

By now, Mallory is wanted not only by the French, but also the American authorities; he escapes to Castro's Cuba, in whose service he fights for the MPLA in Angola. Thus, he is an obvious choice for leading the expedition through the Brazilian jungle that will take the designated democratic president Machado da Silva to Brasília as the concluding act of the people's revolution against the military regime. Wylie takes care to make Mallory a dissident, but less in a national context (he doesn't become a member of the Black Panthers); also, he does not fight his own country (he does not stay in Vietnam long enough to have to face the American engagement there). While Cuba is a refuge for him he remains aloof from the political machine there and even more from the Russians. When a Russian agent later calls him an individualist ("'Individualism is a bourgeois sickness'" [Wylie, *Sign*, 228]), this may be seen as a sign that he has remained true to American ideals, though not politics.

All of this is extremely unlikely though not impossible. What we have here is a black advocate for anticolonial and anticapitalist movements around the globe who refuses to turn communist but is nonetheless caught in the dichotomous politics of the Cold War. He is competent like Hemingway's code heroes, ruthless in killing traitors or opponents, but basically humane—a black anti-model to so many white adventurers. His belief in the potential of what he considers his own people, the Africans, leads him to see in the Javahes, a tribe whose territory the travelers have to cross, descendants of an expedition sent out in 1310 by the Mali emperor Abubakari. There are historic reports that such an expedition was indeed launched by Abu Bakr II, who may have disappeared with his fleet and, as some scholars believe, may have reached America, although no witnesses returned. In other words, Wylie uses historical and contemporary material to construct a postcolonial, black anti-history involving far more agency for Africans than is usually accorded them in European historiography and political theory. As one of Mallory's companions puts it, "'Now I know what truly brought you to Brazil. You're looking for pieces of your past, aren't you? Living out in your own life the adventures of those old Africans people like me weren't allowed to know about'" (103).

The same mixture of the realistic and the fantastic applies to the description of the Amazon jungle the travelers traverse by boat or on foot. We get detailed descriptions of the vegetation and, particularly, the fauna:

> Monkeys chattered and screeched in the trees. A giant blue morpho butterfly danced over the canoe. Insects, mostly mosquitoes and biting flies, were out in profusion; and with them came the hungry birds, tree birds who felt adventuresome for the moment, blue-headed parrots, barbets, flycatchers, and motmots. Above circled flocks of stately waterbirds, yellow-billed river terns, snowy egrets, and swallow-tailed kites. The air was filled with their squawks and screams, playing off against the harsh rhythm and anvillike call of the blacksmith frog. They passed a group of black caimans lounging on the river bank, the bony ridge between their eyes making them look bespectacled and whimsical. (47)

However, the Amazon jungle soon turns from a fascinating encounter into a hostile environment. Of the seven Brazilians, sixteen Cuban soldiers, and three Americans setting out on the trip, only a handful survive and finally reach the capital. Men are killed by anacondas, jaguars, and piranhas.

Infections by insect bites are dramatic and life-threatening. The first losses occur when their Cuban army plane that is to take them to Venezuela is attacked by US jet fighters; later Brazilian army helicopters and planes will attack them repeatedly on their way south. Even worse is their encounter with the indigenous tribes whose territories they cross. All of these tribes, the Kaserapi, the Javahes, the Xavantes, and the Yanomamos, are actual peoples living in the region. However, Wylie transcends the limits of ethnographic description and freely uses his fictional imagination to construct contrasts and conflicts that remind one of those between James Fenimore Cooper's Mohicans and Hurons. The chief of the Javahes, whose medicine man has miraculously healed the infected foot of one of the travelers, which the white doctor Harry Philpot was about to amputate, makes them pay their debt by joining him in his attack on their enemies, the Xavantes; this ill-advised venture results in a catastrophic defeat, the death of virtually all Javahe men, and the ritual killing of their chief, who dies heroically.

The rest of the expedition escapes only with the help of a "civilized" young Xavante after their Indian guide has sacrificed himself. The Xavantes, "small yellow men" (149) "fighting a battle of mean, controlled ferocity" (148), serve here as the bad Indians, completely without clothing and on a "primitive" stone-age level of technology, devoid even of the competency to build canoes, without knives and tools: "They could only work with their hands and teeth" (151).[16] For Philpot, who represents white rationality, "'[t]hey're beasts, Jordan. I hate them'" (150). The high point of their "beastliness" is reached when they—who are cannibals—trick the travelers into eating of the flesh of the dead Javahe chief. Clearly, the Xavantes are the extreme pole of alienity, but all the indigenes that Mallory and his group encounter are examples of the Other, with varying grades of contact with "civilization" that has brought them some knowledge of Portuguese, clothing, and metal tools, but also diseases and violent expropriation.

If the Xavantes are depicted with all the negative clichés of the European and North American discourse of primitivism and represent a radical going back in time, so, to lesser degrees, do the other indigenes: "Mallory turned to Tariri [the Kaserapi chief] and smiled, but he sensed an immense primordial expanse of mistrust and ignorance between himself and this man, a gap it would take centuries to close. He was frightened" (34). Indeed, when first asked by the Cubans to undertake this expedition, Mallory voices his doubts: "'It's not exactly fear [. . .]. It's deeper, more profound. The Amazon swallows up whatever goes near it—people, expeditions, civilizations. It's the beginning of the world. The Indians who live there are our ancestors. I don't want to go back in time. I don't want to die back in time'" (8). This remarkable inversion of the commonly acknowledged "out of Africa" genealogy of modern humans seems to stem from a fear of being associated as an African American with the "savagism" of older periods.

Otherness, then, is a central theme, and the novel explores it in many instances. Mallory and his radio operator Woodlief, who has fought with him in Angola, are both African Americans and strongly resent the injustices their people and Africans in general have experienced from the whites; but Dr. Philpot, a formerly famous heart surgeon whose alcoholism has cost him his job, family, and country, is white and feels uneasy in the company of so many colored people. The other white character in the group is Johannes Siemels, a former high-ranking SS officer who has fled to South America and serves as their guide. He still believes in some Nazi ideas of racial superiority and is a fanatic hunter of the treasures of the lost prehistoric jungle city of Kananka, an Indiana Jones motif Wylie would not pass up. Yet Siemels is married to an Indian woman and on good terms with many others. And he is absolutely loyal to Mallory and the group. That is, he represents whiteness of another, strangely mixed variety. The Russians stand for European, but specifically Soviet arrogance, and it is no coincidence that the Russian KGB observer Kirov, who tries to join them later, will be turned away and die at the hands of the military because he has betrayed himself foolishly. For the young Brazilian Josef traveling with him, Kirov has not only a "mechanical and cold" side, but also a "twisted spirituality" (230) reminding Josef of Russian books, a mixture he registers as dangerous. And in one of the most lyrical, nature-loving sections of the book, Kirov also displays a romantic side:

> Shortly after four o'clock they came down into a valley cut by a wide, beautiful river so still the clouds reflected clearly in it. They swam across it with their knapsacks on their heads, rested for ten minutes, then climbed the high bank and walked on. The country was open now. It abounded in beautiful flowers, butterflies in astonishing colors, and flocks of parrots and other birds, who took up whole trees.
>
> "It is like the beginning of the world here," Kirov said. (231)

For him, this seems to have a different meaning from that voiced by Mallory in the beginning of the book, a mixture of fascination and repugnance. Kirov hates Brazil and their whole enterprise because it appears to him to be confusing, decadent, populated with "mongrels" (227). But he cannot help being infatuated with Julia although he hates the ethnic mixture she represents.

Julia, the young revolutionist who joins the travelers together with Kirov is at the same time the most symbolic and most stereotypical character in the novel. A beautiful mulatta with green eyes, daughter of a white entrepreneur and a poor black seamstress, she experiences racist contempt in her young years, and studies law. She then joins the revolutionary leaders Mallory is trying to take to Brasília: the black and Indian João Durado, a Catholic priest who has been defrocked for his siding with the poor; and Machado, the designated future president, an elegant black intellectual. For Josef, "'She is Brazil. She has the black skin of Africa and the green eyes of Europe. She is a woman. She is compassionate, tender, and has killed for our people'" (228). Julia is desired by almost every man around and will wind up in Mallory's arms for no other reason than that he is the male and she the female protagonist. The military kill her son and her family, whom, in a weird twist of the plot, she had tried to save by betraying the group. She is saved by being called for by the revolutionary multitudes assembled before the presidential palace, and after soft Machado has conveniently died of a heart attack, she will lead the new democratic Brazil, at the side of tough Durado, in whose face Mallory sees "the face of the jungle Indian and the jungle African, and [sees] so much there he could never express in words" (343). Both leaders have sacrificed much for their country, and Julia will also lose Mallory because he is told to leave Brazil as, ironically, he is suspected of being involved in a communist grab for power and will go to Africa in order to join another revolution for the people.

Although none of the major characters is "round" in the sense of complexity and development as defined by E. M. Foster, they are all mixtures of positive and negative traits; even Mallory has his weak moments. What is more important is diversity, social mixture, be it in the shape of people of mixed descent such as Julia and Durado or in the congregation of those from different race, class, and gender background that makes the Brazilian People's Congress after the success of the revolution a model for multiply structured, multicultural, intersectional human societies:

> The Congress chamber, with its soaring walls of rosewood and steel, was packed. Both galleries were filled, and every seat on the sloping main floor was taken. The air reeked of sweat. Armed peasants in faded clothes sat barefoot in the aisles. There were men dressed in coveralls, and young people everywhere, obviously students. One man dressed like a sugar planter was sitting next to a beautiful woman in a pale-blue silk evening gown. Blacks from Rio were there, wearing red and yellow metallic shirts. There seemed to be hundreds of soldiers. Mallory saw a rich man seated among Indians, a woman nursing a baby, a blind man. African-looking women in the traditional hooped skirts of Bahia shook bundles of magic herbs while cowboys from the *sertão* sat impassively. And every shade of human coloring was in that room; every mixture of blood and hair, eyes and skin set delicately beside the next. (329)

The ensuing struggle over which individual or group demands are to be met first threatens to end in political chaos. It is only the leadership of Durado that saves the situation, and there is no certainty that the new democracy can be put on safe ground. Nor is it certain that the native and foreign holders of economic power will let it, or the United States, whose CIA representative Tanner turns out to be Mallory's true adversary and one of the most hateful characters in the book. What is more, the Other has to be included in a way hitherto unheard of: the new Brazil has to accommodate its indigenous peoples so that they are free to make the transition into modernity, and at their own speed, although the representation of the Xavantes has made it clear that total stasis, the radical, cannibalistic "primitive" is unacceptable. On their trip, it was Machado who realized his ignorance of these tribes, a failure that makes him unfit for the presidency:

> "I'm finding myself to be an ignorant man, foolish, vain, and shallow. [. . .] We are in Brazil, yet a Brazil I know nothing of. This region is a mystery to me, and yet it is half of my country. I had never heard of the Javahes, the Xavantes, or any of these people who are so good and so bad. And I must tell you, their condition appalls me. I used to laugh at Indians, Captain. Like many people in my country, I thought they were savages. [. . .] Now I know they are more human than I am, better in ways I cannot imagine." (186)

The utopia of *The Sign of Dawn* ends where most utopias begin: the structure of the new society will have to be worked out in the future, and helpers from outside will not be part of it unless they have humanitarian capacities like Philpot, who wants to become a jungle doctor. Still, this anti-mainstream picture of a major Latin American country is interesting as a political novel, as an attempt at postcolonialism from the perspective of a marginalized group. Wylie's literary means are not sufficient to develop a style and technique that will let the many types of the Other speak for themselves. His inability to deal with gender equality (which is a demand the women in the People's Congress make) is made evident in the case of token woman Julia. She is never more than a cliché figure, a sex symbol depending on the men she consorts with, and her role as a catalyst is never clearer than in the extremely melodramatic and totally unrealistic scene where she, the modern Brazilian Eve, naked and washing herself, is threatened by a big poisonous snake that climbs "on her body, winding itself around her" (257). In contrast to Machado, who is unable to save her, it is Durado who shoots the snake and thus proves to be the right man at the side of the Brazilian female, be it only symbolically. Clearly, he is no innocent (Latin) American Adam, and neither is Mallory, who is a homeless fighter for his ideals unable to find or found a new paradise.

The fact that Wylie's novel heaps up many details that are verifiable according to standards of scholarly knowledge of the 1980s, that is, that can be found to be politologically, sociologically, ethnographically, topographically, botanically, and zoologically "correct," establishes a positivist, factualist kind of realism. However, the fact that, at the same time, even the most improbable and strange occurrences are obviously representable without any problems and can be fit into the book's temporal and spatial patterns, the countdown and the map, makes for a curious kind of mixture that can be accepted as adequate only in the adventure literature this novel belongs to generically. This mixture will be experienced by many readers as de-alienating and prevents the experience of the Other as such, in spite of the extreme alienity of much that is shown and told. The most remarkable capacity of literary art in this context is thus thrown away.[17]

*The Sign of Dawn* was published at the heyday of postcolonial literature, and its material suggests some of the central questions of postcolonial theory: Who has agency? Can the subaltern speak? Who is native? Does it suffice to belong to a marginalized group to qualify as reliable observer of and commentator on another country's anticolonial struggle? How can the intersecting demands of multiple ethnicities and racially mixed people, the classes of a strongly stratified society, the genders, the aboriginal and the modern, and so forth be fit into a structure of emancipatory meaning? And what would be the adequate forms of cultural and specifically literary production to present such problems? Postcolonial critics and theoreticians such as Gayatri Chakravorty Spivak have addressed these questions and the concept of postcoloniality per se. In her essay "Postructuralism, Marginality, Postcoloniality and Value," originally published in 1990, Spivak argues against elevating the so-called magical realism to the status of the given form of Third World literature:

> It is interesting that "magical realism," a style of Latin American provenance, has been used to great effect by some expatriate or diasporic subcontinentals writing in English. Yet as the Ariel-Caliban debates dramatize, Latin America has *not* participated in decolonization. Certainly this formal conduct of magical realism can be said to allegorize, in the strictest possible sense, a socius and a political configuration where "decolonization" cannot be narrativized. What are the implications of pedagogic gestures that monumentalize *this* style as the right Third World style? In the greater part of the Third World, the problem is that the declared rupture of "decolonization" boringly repeats the rhythms of colonization with the consolidation of recognizable styles. (Spivak 202)

As will be seen in the next chapter, magical realism is even more problematic when it is applied from a North American perspective. Certainly, *The Sign of Dawn* does not present the formal and thematic complexity one might hope for in a postcolonial text. Rather, it contributes to "the consolidation of recognizable styles." But what is the adequate form of modern realism for inter-American fiction?

A STRICTLY DISCOURSE-CRITICAL APPROACH concerning the novels discussed in the present chapter as well as those by Theroux and Atwood would lead to the conclusion that the authors' self-distancing from the North American discourse on Latin America, represented by characters who are critical of the United States or by an authorial detachment from characters embodying this discourse, remains half-hearted. The superiority of one's own society is documented particularly by its very ability to self-criticize even though the protagonists may be weak and problematical characters; the inferiority of the Other by its reduction to a mere frame of experience. However, the critical self-reflection of the discourse is whittled down so much that it becomes part of the discourse. Apparently, the Other remains representable without difficulties and can thus be dealt with conceptually. Its strangeness, its disturbing unfamiliarity that might have served for the subversion of the ruling discourse, is at best occasionally alluded to.

Yet, as my analyses have shown, the success or lack of success does not rest on these authors' representation of Latin America, but on the development of other themes connected with the encounter with the Other. Apart from Wylie's book, which belongs to a different category, these novels succeed in showing what this encounter does to the self or where the limitations of the self prevent the encounter to unfold its potential. Although they may be disappointing in the reduction of the Latin American setting and characters to auxiliary elements, thus, in a sense, reduplicating the hierarchy of the discourse of Latinamericanism, they explore their self-critical themes along the edges of this intercultural situation. Their realism consists in a representation of points of view that offer a variety of gazes at the Other that are believable in the culture and period of the authors. One might even say that it is the very fact that they refrain from assuming definitive knowledge of the Other that saves these books from being only further versions of the ruling alterity discourse and from being fundamentally called into question by readers south of the border. In keeping with Rignalda's thesis, it is the very limitation of elements of traditional realism, such as linearity and the transparency of characters or a consensus of what constitutes reality in the first place, that makes these books significant contributions to inter-American fiction. The next chapter will analyze texts whose authors do not simply modify realism but do away with it altogether.

# [9]

## THE POSTMODERN RESPONSE: MAGICAL REALISM AND METAFICTION

Some day one of these stories is going to be mortal, it's inevitable. Storyteller Strangled By Own Yarn.
—Ronald Sukenick, "The Death of the Novel"
(*The Death of the Novel and Other Stories*, 49)

POLITICAL, SOCIAL, AND CULTURAL situations like that of the post-Vietnam era described in the previous chapter do not necessarily elicit only a literature of traditional realism—the overlapping of modernism and social realism between the two world wars presents an example for divergent paths in reacting to an overwhelming experiential context. As we have seen, Ana Castillo's *Mixquiahuala Letters* discussed in Chapter 7 is an experiment in feminist postmodernism. The neorealist novels discussed in the previous chapter are realistic only with significant qualifications, particularly as the adequate representation of the Other is concerned. One way to achieve more adequacy in this respect might be seen in adopting literary modes that have served the self-representation of the Latin American Other and have come to be considered as part of the cultural identity of Latin American nations or regions. The extension of realism into magical realism appears to be an obvious way to achieve such adequacy. The first novel discussed here exemplifies this approach and its problematics. Another reaction to the difficulties of realist representation is to programmatically and explicitly call it into question. Postmodern metafiction does just that, where it is not, as in texts of *littérature engagée* such as Castillo's or those by the Native American authors to be discussed in Chapter 10, bound to engage directly with the conditions it may hope to improve.

But where is the border separating committed from uninvolved literature? Among the three novels (by white male authors) to be discussed in this chapter, it is the one that, as it were, enters a supposedly Latin American mode of thinking and writing, magical realism, which is the most removed from the world it refers to and from the problems attached to discursively approaching the Other. The metafictional novels, on the other hand, deal with recent intercultural conditions by focusing on the question of understanding alterity. In an often-quoted passage from his short story "The Death of the Novel," Ronald Sukenick has summarized the situation of postmodern literature in the context of radical epistemological skepticism:

> Reality doesn't exist, time doesn't exist, personality doesn't exist. God was the omniscient author, but he died; now no one knows the plot, and since our reality lacks the sanction of a creator, there's no guarantee as to the authenticity of the received version. Time is reduced to presence, the content of a series of discontinuous moments. Time is no longer purposive, and so there is no destiny, only chance. Reality is, simply, our experience, and objectivity is, of course, an illusion. Personality, after passing through a phase of awkward self-consciousness, has become, quite minimally, a mere locus for our experience. In view of these annihilations, it should be no surprise that literature, also, does not exist—how could it? There is only reading and writing, which are things we do, like eating and making love, to pass the time, ways of maintaining a considered boredom in face of the abyss. (*Death*, 41)

The reality of the Other, therefore, cannot be an aim of adequate representation. However, in a number of fictions, the Other can serve as an obvious example of unrepresentability. As is often the case in postmodern literature, the questioning of the real opens new perspectives on the imaginative construction of the world that might even include commentaries on "real"-life political, economic, and cultural practices.

THE QUESTION OF TRANSCULTURAL perception is particularly tricky where North American hetero-stereotypes appear to correspond to elements of Latin American self perception, for instance, the Mexican cult of death. An interesting case of such integration of elements of the alien identity discourse is the spread of the so-called magical realism in the body of fiction under discussion. As Vittoria Borsò has demonstrated, the transfer of this term from European art history to Latin American literature has contributed to the stabilization or even to the formation of a regional identity discourse. In our context, the somewhat vague term *magical realism* refers to the combination of the genre-defining narrative methods of realism and the fantastic, of a mytho-magical with a rational, logocentric worldview, and of an oral tradition with a print culture (Borsò, *Mexiko*, 13–14). By adopting it, Latin American writers and intellectuals particularly of the "boom" period between 1955 and 1975, a period associated with Gabriel García Márquez and Juan Rulfo, among others, have made it part of a more complex identity presentation. It is characterized by the aspect of heterogeneity, the presence of otherness in the self, epitomized, for instance, in Octavio Paz's concept of *otredad* as the shaping feature of Mexican society. This kind of unreconciled *mestizaje* has thus become a central idea of Latin American existence (Borsò, *Mexiko*, 114–40). Although its defining features, its representativeness and applicability have remained highly controversial, it has served as a manifestation of cultural autochthony.[1] Foreign observers, on the other hand, have ignored the Latin American controversy and have adopted the concept as reliably representative of *the* world view of their Latin neighbors and hence as an addition to the existing alterity discourse of their own societies. Hence, internationality is claimed for the respective North American fiction on the basis of a hasty acquisition of what is conceived of as genuine—this time not on the level of the externally observable, but on that of a supposed penetration to the deeper layers of cultural identity.[2]

The consequences of such literary endeavors are by no means less problematic than those of earlier ventures into Latin American alterity. One of the most ambitious of these texts is John Updike's novel *Brazil* (1994). That one of the most renowned contemporary American writers and—after the completion of his *Rabbit* pentalogy, we may feel safe to say so—the outstanding exponent of a neorealist probing into the mind and manners of white middle America, should try his hand at magical realism may have been the result of curiosity, of the desire to test his limits. The reviewer in *Time* characterizes the result: "As a future dead white male, Updike makes mischief with a changing world that unsettles his sensibilities and excites his imagination" (Sheppard 73). In the context of the present discussion, however, the book needs to be seen as more than a literary spree.

The comprehensive title *Brazil* indicates that the novel is intended to convey essential aspects of the country, Brazil during a specific era, that of the military rule from the mid-1960s to the mid-1980s, but also Brazil "as such." This is done through the almost parabolic story of Tristão and Isabel, a modern-day version of Tristan and Isolde/Iseult with elements of Romeo and Juliet and other fated lovers added. Tristão, a young black from the *favelas*, son of a prostitute, who makes his living by theft and robbery, and Isabel, the blonde daughter of a wealthy diplomat belonging to the country's white elite, meet at the stereotypical place where class seems to dissolve into body: the Copacabana beach. Theirs is a love at first sight, ordained by destiny, as they come to realize, absolute and lasting all their lives. It entails emotional fidelity and the readiness to make sacrifices, as demonstrated above all in Isabel's willingness to give up her class, her race, and eventually (though unsuccessfully) her life for her love(r). Their attachment manifests itself primarily in sexual desire and sexual fulfillment; highly explicit scenes of lovemaking abound. In its absoluteness and exclusiveness, their love must remain childless. Although both have sex with other people as well, and Isabel will have six children by other men, this is of small importance, and the loss of three of the children causes only temporary pain.

Because the meeting of opposites is the central theme, the plot takes the lovers through starkly realistic and highly fantastic experiences. Their escape from Isabel's father, who will not permit a more than temporary transgression of class boundaries, is only short-lived. They are separated, but after two years Tristão finds Isabel again, and together they head into the interior, where his lack of success as a gold digger makes her resort to prostitution. When he kills one of her father's agents, they are forced to flee into the Mato Grosso, where hostile Indians murder their Native servant and steal Isabel's children. Close to death by starvation, they are rescued by a group of *bandeirantes*. These slave-hunting conquerors and explorers of the seventeenth and eighteenth centuries appear to have survived here into modern times. Quite in character, they immediately enslave Tristão; Isabel is made one of the leader's wives. Things get even more surreal when Isabel enlists the help of her lesbian Indian girlfriend to find a Native medicine man, who eliminates the fundamental cause of the lovers' separation by making her black and Tristão white. After this reversal of racial affiliation, that of class can be handled with ease. Isabel's father accepts both of them in their new shape and identity, Tristão has a career as an industrial manager, and for many years they live the lives of the upper bourgeoisie until Tristão visits the site of the story's beginning, Rio's beach, and is murdered by a gang of young blacks. In vain Isabel tries to follow him into death, Isolde-like, but at least her merging with her lover has become complete: formerly blue-eyed, she now has Tristão's dark eyes.

In Hawthorne's famous definition, the chronotopos of the romance is "a neutral territory, somewhere between the real world and fairy-land, where the Actual and the Imaginary may meet, and each imbue itself with the nature of the other" (Hawthorne, *Scarlet Letter*, 28; cf. Schiff 157). An adequate reading of texts of this genre therefore requires an acceptance of the possibility of an intrusion of the marvelous into the ordinary world, a poetic attitude that writers of the Age of Romanticism and the American Renaissance could still expect of most of their readers. Late twentieth-century readers, however, found it harder to bridge the gap between the *real* and the *maravilloso* according to the Latin American literary discourse. The radical "suspension of disbelief" they are willing to perform when dealing with fantasy literature or science fiction, for instance, cannot be taken for granted with respect to other narrative reading material.[3] For the literature of *realismo magico*, the communicative assumption is that Latin Americans, at least certain groups among the population, believe in magic and will see no exclusionary contradiction between a scientific and a marvelous order of reality.

In *Brazil*, this is not the case. Even though Tristão is said to believe in spirits—"He believed in spirits, and in fate" (*Brazil*, 4)—and experiences his first catching sight of Isabel as a stroke of fate, he is nowhere actuated by this belief but behaves according to the exigencies of the moment and the pragmatics of a man of his age, class, and experience. And Isabel is an educated young woman who scoffs at much of what she has been taught by the nuns of her convent school. Thus, their flight into the interior may be a trip into an area of cultural backwardness, but their meeting with the *bandeirantes* in their leather armor is surprising for the lovers and unconvincing for the readers even if they know Euclides da Cunha's *Os Sertões* (1902), one of Updike's sources.[4] Even worse is the Indian medicine man's miraculous transformation of the protagonists' racial attributes. Thus, it is not the use of a substratum of myth (Tristan and Iseult) or, more generally, of the globally known narrative motif of the origin-related love conflict that endangers the textual coherence, but rather Updike's effort to outdo da Cunha and others in their representation of the meeting and possible blending of heterogeneous elements as the essence of Brazil. This theme is present from the very beginning of the book: "Black is a shade of brown. So is white, if you look. On Copacabana, the most democratic, crowded, and dangerous of Rio de Janeiro's beaches, all colors merge into one joyous, sun-stunned flesh-color, coating the sand with a second, living skin" (*Brazil*, 3). The magic beliefs and practices of the aboriginal population and the everyday life of an industrial society, the people out of the seventeenth and those of the twentieth century are brought together in a manner that only partially fulfils the communicational contract of any variety of magical realism. Rather, one gets the impression of Brazil as a gigantic metaphor—of which more needs to be said next.

The tortured metaphoricity of the novel is already evident on the level of style and imagery. Updike's marvelously precise and detailed realistic descriptions have always used an element of metaphor when it comes to the characters' impressions and their emotional response to their experiences. In the *Rabbit* books, the resulting mixture of descriptive precision and metaphoric enhancement conveys a sense of what, according to Hemingway's literary ideal, the real feels like. But in *Brazil*, Updike's imagery does not achieve the merging of the real and the imaginative as it does in his earlier novels or, for that matter, in the literary tradition from Faulkner to García Márquez that his book seems to log into. Forced metaphors abound; a phrase like "this delicate mild smell, which felt stretched within him like a sleepy cry" (6) might serve as a textbook example of multiple catachresis. Stilted dialogues reminiscent of Hemingway's notorious failures in his attempts to imitate some kind of archaic Spanish in *For Whom the Bell Tolls*, and the many unexplained Portuguese expressions intensify the impression of a confusing and confused exoticism but contribute to the ruin of the narrative style, which, after all, is also meant to convey a sense of rebellious student conversations from 1968 or the atmosphere of an automobile plant. As R. Z. Sheppard put it, "Lyricism mingles with basic Anglo-Saxon in much the way that liberated clergymen in the 1960s flavored their moralism with four-letter words" (73).

What makes things worse is that the sphere of imagination and sense impressions evoked by this sort of metaphoric language and stylistic mix is often combined with a cloyingly sentimental sententiousness, as in "he had remained chaste in his soul, that spiritual organ where his life cried out for its eternal shape" (*Brazil*, 85). Frequently, such sentences articulate elements of social discourses whose origin and function remain unclear, as in "The female need to surrender always troubled his warrior spirit" (7). Does this patriarchal phrase serve to characterize a certain macho group of people in Brazil, or is it intended to carry a more universal message? Although many such sentences may be attributed to the limited perspective of the focalizing characters whose figural point of view is usually applied, there are not infrequently authorial intrusions like the one just quoted that seem to indicate a complicity of the author's narrating voice with his characters.

This handling of point of view is part and parcel of the power of narrative disposal claimed by the author. Different from most inter-American novels by US authors, there are no active American characters; the only one even mentioned is an elderly tourist lady whom Tristão had robbed before he met Isabel. Her ring bears the inscription "DAR," Daughters of the American Revolution, but Tristão and Isabel, who receives it as his first present, read the letters as *dar*, "'to give'" (5, 8). As a gift that will finally wind up in the hands of the Indian medicine man, it symbolizes not intercultural communication, but distance, incomprehension, and constant reencoding. It epitomizes the absence of North American views and institutions in this novel. The problem of alterity perception is thus simply brushed aside. The author unhesitatingly enters the minds and feelings of his Brazilian characters and claims the competence to evaluate and comment upon any, even the most exotic, phenomenon.

What, then, can Updike have had in mind when he handled the Other and the question of the limits of any alterity discourse so cavalierly? Although the book often resembles the assemblage of clichés characteristic of much popular US fiction on Latin America, its supposed status is indicated in the author's afterword, where he discloses his international, intertextual indebtedness to, among others, da Cunha's *Os Sertões*, Claude Lévi-Strauss's *Tristes Tropiques* (1955, but relating impressions of the 1930s and 1940s),

Gilberto Freyre's *Casa-Grande e Senzala* (1933), and Theodore Roosevelt's expedition report *Through a Brazilian Wilderness* (1914). An English translation of Joseph Bédier's *Le roman de Tristan et Iseult* (1900) "gave me my tone and basic situation. And I took courage and local color from the truly Brazilian fiction of Joachim Machado de Assis, Graciliano Ramos, Clarice Lispector, Rubem Fonseca, Ana Miranda, Jorge Amado, and Nélida Piñon" (*Brazil*, 263). A truly impressive list.

Bédier must have shown the author ways of retelling the medieval story material in a modern, more ambiguously psychologizing manner, of combining the high and the low, although Updike went far beyond him and pushed the tension between the ideal of an almost religiously conceived romantic love and physical lust to an extreme. Updike had written an admiring but also critical review of Bédier's *Love Declared* in which he sees Bédier's enterprise as an example of the, for him, typically French invention of "the Tristanian technique of containing Man's biological rage" (Updike, *Assorted*, 197). In a sense, *Brazil* is his answer as it demonstrates the attainability of the adored, after all. The other texts offer models of describing exotic nature and landscapes, but also people. They can be quite contradictory; whereas da Cunha is highly critical of the "intermingling of races highly diverse" (84), Freyre sees Brazilian culture as a fortunate blending of racial, but especially cultural, elements from the three major early groups of population: Portuguese, African slaves, and Indians. Where Freyre celebrates harmony, da Cunha elaborates on the economic, social, and cultural tensions between the advanced coastal area and the primitive backcountry in the Northeast. What they and other texts mentioned have in common, however, is the notion that the essence of a country like Brazil can indeed be captured, that there are (more or less deep) structures of the social and cultural order, a structuralist notion making Lévi-Strauss relevant beyond his ethnographic descriptions of Brazilian indigenous cultures.

*Tristes Tropiques* would have been interesting for Updike also because of Lévi-Strauss's epistemological concept of a "super rationalism" permitting the integration of the empirical into the rational without loss of the sensual qualities of the former. The transfer of insights from one field to another (say, love to sociology or vice versa) and the discovery of the basic potential (and, to a certain extent, the risks) of the meeting of ethnic, gender-related, social, economic, cultural, stylistic, and other opposites seem to be two fundamental principles at work in this novel. In this respect, Updike's claim is universal and his text is intercultural in a variety of aspects, notably in its narrative motif of love overcoming all obstacles and in its moral and philosophical message of the need to transcend borders. He has safeguarded his venture by positioning it in the context of literary and scholarly discourses propagating or exemplifying a crossing of boundaries. Most of his intertexts, if they deal with Brazil at all, refer to conditions having existed many decades before the time of the novel, which is set "years ago, when the military was in power in far-off Brasília" (*Brazil*, 3), that is, during the same period before 1985 as in Wylie's utopian *The Sign of Dawn*. But whereas Wylie's novel imaginatively transcends the historical moment, *Brazil* more or less ignores it, as the "far-off" indicates. Although the novel presents a political debate among Isabel's fellow students, they serve only to indicate the kind of political correctness that was considered chic among the young elite around 1968. Cultural essentials are seen as transcending the epochs. In this frame of reference, Brazil can indeed be regarded as a timeless metaphor for the reconciliation of opposites. It clearly functions as a screen on which the author projects aspects of race and gender that are equally pertinent for US society, but which he might have found difficult to handle on such abstract, fairyland terms in an American setting.

However, there is a more skeptical counter-theme. Whether Updike intends the love story as an exemplification of the boundary-transcending qualities of Brazil or the country as a symbolic background for the workings of perfect love, the result is less than ideal. As Isabel realizes, "a price for the intensity of their love was sterility" (236). The ideal remains without offspring and hence, possibly, without future. Even in Brazil it can survive only with the help of magic, and it cannot retain its perfection. When Isabel is incapable of Isolde's *Liebestod*, she comes to see that "[t]he spirit is strong, but blind matter is stronger" (260). The novel also brings together, but does not reconcile, "Brazilian romanticism" (260) and the reality principle. The lovers exchange their racial affiliation, but they cannot eliminate the racial differences that make them attractive for each other but also separate them. The result of the racial mix in Brazilian society in general is shown to be less than perfect. Gender as well as other social relations are based on asymmetrical power distribution, and the lower classes, for instance the servants, but also women in general appear to be almost naturally submissive, even to the point of their ready acceptance of corporeal punishment.

Here, the love theme rapidly becomes submerged in a European and North American discourse of superiority that is also at work in Updike's description of the country. Brazil is characterized by an untamable nature,[5] extreme class contrasts (hardly anyone but representatives of the extremes comes into view), a sexually highly permissive society that is shaped by sexism nonetheless, and a population often living in chaotic or anarchic conditions and interacting with barely restrained brutality. The country still harbors really "primitive" or even "savage" groups (in conventional, superiority-discursive terms), and in keeping with racist clichés, the supposed main qualities of the three major ethnic groups are revealed above all else in their physical behavior and body awareness, which for the protagonists change with their racial affiliation. Notwithstanding contemporary notions about the discursive nature of human attributes, race and gender seem to be derived solely from the body, the biological traits. Tristão may symbolize the future overcoming of *négritude* and the heritage of slavery: "'We are seeing the end of slaves and masters in Brazil, and I, who have little competence, can help here, having been both'" (238). But this is plausible only on the basis of the generalizations both of the Euro-American alterity discourse and of the Brazilian identity discourse: in this novel both seem to merge without major problems. For instance, Freyre's preconceptions about "higher" and "lower" cultures and about racial qualities crop up with hardly a trace of authorial detachment:

> Salomão heard a grim undertone as the young husband [Tristão, recently turned white] pronounced these insistences, but ascribed it to the well-known melancholy of the Portuguese race; no less an authority than Gilberto Freyre assures us that, had not the early colonizers imported Africans to cheer up their settlements, the whole Brazilian enterprise might have withered of sheer gloom. (*Brazil*, 229)

Seen in this light, the Brazilian metropolis is an aberration, because the world of business buries the country's "true life, the life of ecstasy and the spirits" (54). "The true Brazilian, they jubilantly agreed among themselves, is an incorrigible romantic—impetuous, impractical, pleasure-loving, and yet idealistic, gallant, and vital" (65). True, Updike also shows us the other side, the work-ethic world of São Paulo, but in either case he subscribes to essentialist notions of the other culture, some of which he may have found in the "truly Brazilian fiction" he mentions in his afterword, but the "truly" is never questioned.

In his "A Special Message" for the readers of the exclusive Franklin Mint Edition of *Brazil*, Updike defends himself against his critics:

> We can catch at a truth from a distance as well as up close; I refuse to disown my Brazil as unrealistic. A country's sense of itself is an activating part of its reality, and this sense derives in part from outsiders. Because others have romanticized and sexualized Brazil, Brazil is saturated in romanticism and sexuality. Sex, between masters and slaves, conquerors and indigenes, has shaped its identity as an image of the world that is coming, one world of many mixed colors. (qtd. in Ristoff 64)

It may be that the novel results from Updike's obsession with skin[6] and skin color,[7] and one can argue that it is "ultimately about America, not [. . .]

Brazil. More specifically, [it is] about the struggle in America for identity: personal as well as national," that is, worked out by "oppositions—black and white, male and female, rich and poor, American and foreign—that may confuse or alter identity" (Schiff 157). If so, it is all the more deplorable that Brazil should remain outside of "America," just as in James A. Schiff's undifferentiating sentence. It remains totally accessible and available as an exotic pole of alterity, including a *real maravilloso* whose miraculous side is reaffirmed in the face of an insurmountable reality when, in the last lines of the novel, the now "*dark-eyed* widow" (*Brazil*, 260; my emphasis) returns home, to whatever kind of future life she may have.

SOME READERS MAY HAVE wished that *Brazil* were a parody of exoticist fiction, of magical realism, of the love romance. Many phrases and passages are extreme enough to qualify as parodistic exaggerations, but the seriousness of numerous other parts and of the basic themes disproves such a reading. Nor can *Brazil* be seen as an exposure of stereotypical notions in the manner of Walter Abish's *How German Is It*. Yet there are such books about Latin America, and Daniel Curley's novel *Mummy*, published in 1987, is a case in point. Not surprisingly, it has found only a comparatively small audience; there is no Penguin edition, as in the case of *Brazil*. The book explodes current and former clichés about Mexico, magical realism included, and this is hardly a popular enterprise. At the same time, the novel self-reflectively undermines the literary forms of representation supporting such stereotypical discursiveness.

*Mummy* swims against the stream of convention by relating the odyssey of a certain Marc Williams not to but from Mexico, back into the United States. Williams has just served a seven-year sentence in a Mexican prison because he tried to drive his dead mother's car across the American border, not knowing that it was packed with drugs. His mother, officially an antique dealer in Mexico but actually a dope pusher, was buried in Guanajuato, where her body like many other corpses underwent a process of natural mummification. Because nobody claimed it, it was put on public display. Williams robs the mummy (in both senses of the word), hides it in the imitation of a knight's armor that he fixes on top of his car, and then tries to make his way back to his starting point Alpha, Illinois, in order to bury his mother in her hometown. He is pursued but sometimes also protected by police and drug agents of both countries, as well as by members of the drug mafia, but never learns who tries to find him and for what reason. When he finally manages to reach the United States in an ancient landing craft named *Styx*, a kind of Flying Dutchman vessel, he is joined by a young woman of mysterious background called Alice Jo, who claims the mummy for herself.

The United States turns out to be no less chaotic than Mexico. Identities remain fluid on both sides of the border. Alice Jo changes hers, for instance, by the use of body paint that transforms her into a black woman. When, at the end, a fan blows away the little mummy dust that is left, Alice Jo suggests a new measure of escape from their pursuers: "'We become Chinese and open a restaurant'" (*Mummy*, 241).[8]

Although published seven years earlier, in many ways *Mummy* seems like a response to *Brazil*, right down to the exchange of racial affiliation. This burlesque text is a postmodern answer to attempts to create "world literature" by combining the descriptive elements of the current alterity discourse with supposedly universal themes and the cultural concept as well as the literary technique of magical realism. Curley toys with the thematic material. The difficulty of getting rid of one's mother fixation is turned into obvious and hilarious symbolism. Almost all components of the North American discourse on the Latin American Other are called up and deconstructed by parody or by superimposing other, for instance literary, discourses. Indeed, the book indicates right from the beginning that there can be no access to the realities of self and Other that is not discursively mediated. Identity depends not on character and experience but on semiotics, as the changing and at the same time noncharacterizing names of the protagonist indicate. Marc (that is, the sign) Williams carries a family name derived from a Christian name and travels with forged papers carrying the names John Doe and Richard Roe.[9] Ironically, the narrator often uses these "non-names" for the protagonist, who also appears in the various roles he plays in order to deceive his pursuers: "Someone was being very resourceful, but it was hard to tell who—Roe or Doe or the gangster or the pilgrim or the tourist or the expatriate or even the drunken American novelist" (65), a metafictional reference pointing at the author himself, whose level of reality is thereby made to merge with that—or those—of the main text. The textualization of "facts" is made particularly evident when Williams's theft of the mummy from the Guanajuato museum is immediately turned into a popular myth that in turn has the sequel of "a cult [that] had begun to spring up on the spot" (25).

The arbitrariness of language is a constant aspect, as when Williams is trying to buy a car and the old man selling it comments that it belongs to his grandmother, who

> "[. . .] couldn't even drive it on Sunday because, pobrecita, she lives next to the cathedral."
>
> "What a pity," Williams said. [. . .]
>
> "Sí, qué lástima," the little old man said in English. [. . .] "Let me tell you, it is a Buick Electra—"

> "A Buick Electra," Williams said as if really impressed, although to tell the truth he didn't know a Buick Electra from a Toyota Orestes.
>
> "To be sure," the man said. "And it's loaded: PS, PB, PW, A/C, AM/FM 8 tr cass, mint cond, 40 mpg—"
>
> "40 mpg?" Williams said.
>
> "Hwy," the man said. "Blk/blk lthr int, mag wheels—" (11)

The question in which language the conversation is supposed to take place—often simply skipped in inter-American texts—is here solved in the sense of a bilingualism turned upside-down. Product names are parodically traced back to the (ancient Greek) cultural heritage, and product qualities appear in the series of abbreviations typical for newspaper ads.

The same relativization applies to place—"Everything that wasn't street was shop and everything that wasn't shop was street" (10)—and of course to personal identity:

> Williams stepped into the butcher shop. The little old man was not to be seen. There was one customer and the butcher, who was whaling away with a heavy cleaver at his block. *Thwack* [. . .]. "Señor," the customer said in the voice of the old man. "Señor, you are punctual." *Thwack*. Williams looked at him. He was twice the size of the old man and half the age. *Thwack*. He was wearing a T-shirt from South Dakota State University, black pants like a waiter's, and truck-tire sandals. *Thwack*. [. . .]
>
> "Shall we go?" the man said, now in the voice of the man whose clothes he was wearing. *Thwack*. (12–13)

The sound of the cleaver appears to be the only reliable acoustic element of the scene. Otherwise, the coordinates of reality perception are fluid. And this is not simply due to the alien environment but applies to reality per se, which is seen as a construction, poststructuralist fashion. However, though we are accustomed to such semantic and phenomenological instability from postmodern texts in general, here the added difficulty of approaching the cultural Other creates a constant uncertainty about whether the instability results from an intercultural or an ontological problem. The discourse of alterity becomes indistinguishable from any discourse. Race, gender, age, and other qualities appear to be fluid, and thus the question of identity applies to anybody on any side of any divide.

As one name refers to others, narrative incidents, motifs, and so on refer to other books. The novel is replete with intertextual references to myths and literary texts from classical antiquity to the present. The quixotic side of Williams's quest is indicated by the name given to the suit of armor: "Don Q." Allusions to Dante refer not only to the *Inferno* but also to Malcolm

Lowry's *Under the Volcano*, which in turn has the *Divina Commedia* as a pre-text. Williams's radical "on-the-road" existence reminds readers of the title and concept of Jack Kerouac's novel. When the protagonist sees his imminent death at the hands of angry *indios*, one of whom greets him with "'Buenas tardes,'" "he deduced that it was already past noon and that the last meal he wasn't going to eat was lunch" (41), an echo of many such logically twisted conclusions in Joseph Heller's *Catch-22*.

The cliché of the ready availability of Latin American women is alluded to in a manner that calls into question any need for more complex intercultural communication: whenever Williams is hungry, he opens his hood, and there will always be a woman offering food and sex. Fittingly, the discourse of magical realism is associated with indigenes: Williams stays with a village priest whose Otomi Indian housekeeper is an old witch who changes into a young nymphomaniac every night. At the end of this episode, witch and priest take him to a pyramid built of old car wheels in order to sacrifice him and his car to the gods; the revival of ancient Indian cults has been a staple element in fiction on Mexico since Lawrence's *The Plumed Serpent*.[10] Williams escapes the obsidian knife because the witch takes "Don Q" for Quetzalcoatl or Cortés, respectively—these and most other elements of "reality" are interchangeable because they are, first of all, elements of a virtually arbitrary discursive tradition.

In this respect, many of the fantastically humorous facets of the novel refer to serious problems; the effect is often disconcertingly two-sided. And so are any comments about so-called essential features of a given culture. Instead of the traditional refuge south of the border, Williams finds a veritable industry of persecution, but the United States is just as bad. It is presented as the playground of social absurdities with which we have become familiar from the texts of the New Journalism and from the post-postmodern novel. Before his first attempt to cross the US border, Williams imagines "that his first Howard Johnson's ice cream cone would give him terminal la turista" (49). The American customs officer has the "intense blue [. . .] eyes of a machine gunner" (54). In an ultimate inversion of cultural discourses, even the Mexican prison is seen as having its "comforting rigors [. . .]. He had never experienced an American prison. It might be worse. It might be beautifully worse where they had laws" (56). The familiar appears as alien, but as the novel unfolds, even the strangest occurrences evoke feelings of familiarity because all of them, and thus all reality, belong to the same discursive "order": "The country was as blank as anyone could wish. It looked like Mexico" (147). Anything can happen here, too, including a confrontation with his dead mother. The features distinguishing the United States from Latin America are of no real importance; if anything, Williams's home country, and particularly the corn-growing Midwest, is more threatening and more distant than Mexico:

> He was in the middle of nowhere as surely as he had ever been among the cactus and mesquite and rocks and the forsaken beds of dry rivers. Now only the sheriff's men stopped to speak to him, to ask him hard questions, to search his car, to rattle the Don's visor. They refused to believe that a car with Mexican registration could be free of marijuana. [. . .] No woman ever stepped out of a corn field to offer him a freshly cooked ear, a biscuit, or the smallest slice of the fatted calf. Sometimes he heard a voice among the corn, a woman singing because she was alone and hidden. He toyed with the latch of his hood but never popped it. Disappointment would have been too hard to bear here, for the truth was that wherever he was, he was home. (226)

The parody of the quest tradition, the negation of any North American superiority concerning order, rationality, and humane behavior all tend to explode the discourses of identity and alterity alike. However, deconstruction is more than just an intellectual pastime. The traditional elements of the discourses of alterity and identity concerning nation, culture, gender, and race are brought into focus one after the other and are exposed as adequate not for any given reality, but only for the discourse as such. However, given the relatedness of discourse and power structure, none of this is harmless. And thus, the parody of the quest and other literary patterns is used for counter-discursive purposes; obviously, it cannot crystallize into a new and better structure. The book does not offer a model for dealing with alterity but only for dealing with such models. If Updike's *Brazil* is a tour de force, so is *Mummy*, but Curley creates a new variety of Mexico fiction or, rather, metafiction, which, in its allegiance to international postmodernism, uncovers the facile handling of the epistemological, ethical, and aesthetic aspects of intercultural representation in most literature about Latin American alterity. However, as Arun P. Mukherjee has warned us in his essay "Whose Post-Colonialism and Whose Postmodernism?", the subversion of conventions that takes place in postmodern texts cannot be seen as a generally acceptable form of liberation; postmodernism and postcolonialism may be at odds for those not sharing the privileges of Euro-American mainstream culture. And this culture is the place both of Updike's archetypal and basically modernist novel and Curley's demythicizing postmodern text. Ideally, then, self-questioning should be a reciprocal effort.

WALTER ABISH EMPHASIZES SUCH reciprocity in his novel *Eclipse Fever* (1993). Whereas *Mummy* is primarily redirectional by its inversion of the south-of-the-border pattern, *Eclipse Fever* is bidirectional. Its claim, however, is not a higher, metadiscursive and transnational truth, but to put any truth claim in doubt. In an often deceptive manner, Abish turns self-questioning into questioning per se. From the beginning of his career, the defamiliarization of the familiar has been the prime object of his fiction. The highly artificial structure of *Alphabetical Africa* (1974) demonstrated the incompatibility of the order of the linguistic sign and "reality," and in a parallel move, the colonizing as well as the reductive aspects of a Western discourse applied to an alien world, as Klaus Milich has shown. The self-restriction of using only words beginning with the letter *a* in Chapter 1, those beginning with *a* or *b* in Chapter 2, and so on, so that the pronoun *I* is available only from Chapter 9 on, *she* only in Chapter 19, and *you* only in Chapter 25, the next to last before the process is reversed after Chapter 26, reveals how language creates reality. It does so just like maps, dictionaries, and names that were means of appropriating by deauthenticating, emptying, and then semiotically and conceptually refilling the "white" spaces of the African continent and thus clearing the way for the military, political, and economic appropriation by the colonial powers (Milich 195).[11]

Abish's *How German Is It—Wie Deutsch Ist Es* (1980) and *Eclipse Fever* (1993) are much less obviously not only metafictional but metasemiotic and, hence, metadiscursive texts. This has resulted in misreadings, as early reviews indicate, and "the realistic mode" Thomas Peyser attests to them turns out to be a trap (Peyser 245). To say, as does the *Oxford Companion to American Literature*, sixth edition, that *Eclipse Fever* "is a meditation on the cultural and societal malaise of Mexico and other third world countries" (Hart and Leininger 4) is to miss the very point of the book, which is not so much about Mexico as about "the everyday in a foreign setting," and "the foreign as a means of examining the familiar" (Abish, "An Interview with Walter Abish" by van Delden, 381, 384[12]). Indeed, it might have been another country serving this purpose; initially, Abish had Italy in mind. As in the case of *How German Is It*, Abish visited the country he wrote about only after finishing the novel: "I was afraid that a visit might destroy the Mexico of my imagination" (385). But this imaginary Mexico is one designed to question any cliché notions the readers may bring to the novel because of their acquaintance with travel and history books or with the fiction of other writers:

> I wanted to reject what many writers seem to allude to as Mexico's transformative emotive power. Reading Lawrence or Lowry, one is made to feel that the characters are destined to undergo a cathartic conversion. There is something sanctimonious about the way the turbulent social events are portrayed—the way the country is used as a divining rod to establish good and evil. As a result non-Mexican writers have become the conveyers of a Mexican mystique. (382)

Characteristically, Bonny, the almost seventeen-year-old US American runaway and one of *Eclipse Fever*'s two most prominent characters, does not grow more mature by the initiatory sex and crime experiences she has in Mexico, as do the protagonists of so many inter-American fictions. Under shock, she regresses, and at the end of the novel she has the mind of a seven-year-old. Bonny has always considered herself to be her writer father Jurud's muse and source of information about the reality he fails to see; she has regarded herself as a "book waiting to be written by . . ." (Abish, *Eclipse* 51; ellipsis in original), which is why her letters to Jurud "omitted nothing" (43). According to Abish's self-analysis, her regression therefore denotes "a desexualization and the destruction of the imagination, the spirit, the muse" ("An Interview," 389). And, referring to the meaning of the title: "A serious reading of the novel must take into consideration that it is the muse, the source of our inspiration, that is being eclipsed" (388). But this might serve to mobilize the reader's own imagination, perhaps to inspire her or him.

The other prominent character, the Mexican critic Alejandro, also gets into great trouble near the end when he is arrested by the "Department for the Prevention of Delinquency" (*Eclipse*, 330) and is interrogated and beaten. In Abish's reading of this episode, "Alejandro survives his ordeal because he is protected by his influential father-in-law. I guess that could be interpreted to mean that criticism will outlast the muse by virtue of its connections to authority and power" ("An Interview," 389). That is, the novel is very much about intellectual and writerly command, fictional narratives being superseded by metatexts.

*Eclipse Fever* is a multi-stranded novel. There is Alejandro, the critic, who takes his wife Mercedes to the airport of Mexico City. She will travel from there to New England, where she is to accept a teaching position, although her real intention is to join her lover, the Jewish American writer Jurud, whose works she has translated into Spanish. Real intention? Much of what takes place between Mercedes and Jurud is the product of her husband's jealous imagination. In the end, she will return to Alejandro, with much between them un(re)solved. There is Preston Hollier, a wealthy American entrepreneur and collector of pre-Columbian artifacts, who travels to Mexico in order to pursue his plan to sink an elevator shaft into the great Pyramid of the Sun in Teotihuacán so that it will be more easily accessible to elderly Americans for whom he plans to build a resort nearby. His wife Rita has an affair with Francisco, Alejandro's literary friend. As we have seen, there is Jurud's sixteen-year-old daughter Bonny, who cannot stand the presence of Mercedes in her father's household and runs away, eventually to Mexico in the company of a gay Mexican smuggler of pre-Columbian objects. Bonny gets into all kinds of sex-and-violence scrapes, only to be found battered and traumatized but alive on the pyramid of Tajín. Her title-giving plan to watch a solar eclipse in Yucatán falls flat because the place to see it from turns out to be Baja California, and thus, suffering from *la turista,* she has to watch it in her hotel room on CNN. A central event in the mythical world of ancient Mexico is thus reduced to its media representation. There is a crime story involving some of these and some other characters; that is, the novel has plot elements of a conventional thriller with a (partly) Latin American setting, including murders, stolen art treasures, erotic entanglements, thieves, rapists, killers, brutal police officers, a shady American entrepreneur, and corrupt Mexican politicians. Although many characters and plotlines converge, "the traditional sense of closure is replaced by what one of the last chapter titles calls 'an unfolding sense of unending'" (Peyser 258), mocking Kermode's *The Sense of an Ending* and its central argument about our hunger for conclusions. Ihab Hassan has neatly summed up the thematic levels on which the novel can be read:

> The book may be read as an international thriller (two murders), a geo-political fiction (Yanqui economic imperialism), a study of cultural contrasts (Mexico and America), a Proustian interrogation of sex, class, and society (on both sides of the border), a meditation on power, both public and personal (*chingar*, the constant Mexican jostling for superiority), a reflection on human obsessions (with homes, places, memories, iterative patterns), a quest for identity (of Bonny, the runaway American teenager; of Alejandro, the Mexican literary critic; and of the American and Mexican nations), a hidden portrait of the artist as fabulator (Abish himself), and a metaphysical novel about the yawning absence at the heart of reality (the titular eclipse). (Hassan 627)

As in a Pynchon novel, there is the sense of conspiratorial activities that might explain everything, but hardly anything is ever explained. Sense remains elusive. Like "Switzerland" for the protagonist of *How German Is It* (52), "Mexico" is a catchword evoking a series of stereotypical images, including of course the pre-Columbian past, pyramids, human sacrifices, and the supposed treachery of Malinche. What seems to be at stake is the way people (and this means US Americans at least as much as Mexicans) deal with personal crises, with the betrayals of their own lives, with the temptations of sex, money, and power. What is really at stake is the way they make sense of their experiences or fail to do so. Theirs is the familiar world defamiliarized and thus made conscious by projecting it upon the screen of an alien society and by technical devices we know from other Abish texts as well. As in *How German Is It*, the collaging of widely known stereotypical signs (Schöpp 249), the many left-out pieces of information, the gaps in plot and characterization, and Abish's characteristic use of inserted questions jostling the reader out of a fictional illusion make us reconsider what we think we know.

The interaction of language not so much as a means of realistic representation, but of titillating, hilarious stylistic indirection with stereotypical notions shaping people's view of reality is nicely demonstrated in a sex scene involving Mexican Francisco and WASP Rita:

> When he inserted the rigid upward-curving expansion of his concupiscence into that cunningly designed aperture at the juncture of her ever so white legs, so that the extent of their coupling positions was limited only by their imagination—when he repeatedly, moistly, with her active participation, as the mind clocked the rapid acceleration of the pleasurable to and fro, thrust himself forward, *into* her, *into* that often, on school toilet partitions, graphically replicated, iconically loaded opening [. . .], didn't Francisco, simultaneously, also enter that to him still elusive, paradisiacal American world in which she, a former cheerleader, had once been nurtured? Didn't she, as well, provide him with unlimited access to her convictions, to her identity, not excluding her sense of individual worth, which back in the U.S.A. well may have included (who could say?) the Buick and Pontiac in the suburban driveway. (*Eclipse*, 106–7)

Sex, like intercultural exchange, depends on the images produced by the mind, be they graffiti or cultural stereotypes. But who is thinking, imagining here? The paragraph ends with the following questions: "But how could he possibly appreciate the cherished values that unite Americans, rich and poor, black, Hispanic, and white alike? How could he, given his innate ambivalence, his forceful Latin passion, appreciate the American virtues that conditioned her?" (107). Is this Francisco ruminating? The author commenting? The implied reader reacting? And which of them are aware of how cliché-like these phrases are? Interpersonal as well as intercultural understanding is an exercise in preconceived notions: "Though he had no way of knowing what she was thinking, he was able to categorize her thoughts, her musings, as part of the American perfection, that unattainable, antiseptic perfection. You make me feel so Mexican, he admitted" (112).

Reconsidering, trying to decipher and communicate but also to conceal meaning is the principal activity not only of the narrator or author, but also of the characters, many of whom are intellectuals, artists, and writers. Take the critic, Alejandro, whose self-perception is rather limited. He hardly remembers anything from his childhood, for instance. In Abish's words, "In the novel, the critic is the prime interpreter, the analyzer, the questioner even as he goes out of his way to overlook everything that is injurious to the functioning of the self" ("An Interview," 384). This reading can be applied to the novel as a whole. Criticism can be seen as an exertion of power. As Alejandro puts it, "I equate criticism with energy. It's an assertion. A form of domination" (*Eclipse*, 176), but Abish insists that this statement, too, has to be qualified as resulting from a need rather than to be taken at face value ("An Interview," 386). The critical or other probing into the minds and matters of persons and texts—an invasion, as it were—and on the other hand the refusal to get involved when involvement would be essential (as when Alejandro stays aloof when a thief tries to escape with a stolen codex) are shown to be characteristic ways of interaction between individuals and societies.

Equally typical are deception and self-deception. Like Alejandro, Mexico appears blind to the nastier aspects of its past (cf. "An Interview," 382). Thus, Abish is not at all squeamish about criticizing aspects of the other country. But again, the alien is used to remind readers of what they are too familiar with even to notice: their own society's dealing with its history. US presence in Mexico is felt to be mostly exploitative. Similar to *Alphabetical Africa* and different from *How German Is It*, the discourse about the Other the text inscribes into and thus, in a manner, constructs in order to deconstruct it, is one of power, of superiority. The American industrialist and owner of "Eden Enterprises" Preston Hollier collects illegally acquired pre-Columbian art and would like to "penetrate" and then commodify the Pyramid of the Sun. And yet, as in the case of the Mexicans, Abish is far from simply criticizing what may appear as negative. Instead of solely denouncing the North American role in Latin America, he makes this interesting comment:

> It seems entirely appropriate that a large American enterprise in Mexico should be named Eden. I imagine that if the Garden of Eden were to exist today, it would be run by an institution. In the novel, the name *Eden* is intended to ironically evoke the story of Adam and Eve with its disquieting justification for God's action. It's an amazing piece of writing. From a writerly point of view it is necessary to see Eden as something created not for the habitation of Adam and Eve but only for the sake of their expulsion. ("An Interview," 385)

Whatever the moral justification may be, people can serve others by pushing them out of their respective imaginary paradises, by disillusioning them, by making them aware of their own desires, their own flaws, but also their own resources. Francisco, the lover of Preston's wife Rita, has this to say about her husband: "Preston [. . .] has provided us with a kind of fantasy of the future we can accept. [Rita:] He doesn't have a clue about the Mexican psyche. [Francisco:] Who does?" (*Eclipse*, 110).

Not surprisingly, literature is the only way of properly dealing with reality. Yet we are made to witness a violent quarrel between Mexican writers about the discourses governing Mexican literature and their perception of US writing:

> [Francisco:] In Mexico we aren't free to produce a paragraph that's devoid of our constricted Mexican symbolic content [. . .].
>
> Fuentes, for example, is free to locate his novels wherever he chooses, Alejandro [. . .] said.
>
> Wherever he chooses? Francisco expressed amazement. Our ceaseless contemplation of conquests, colonization, revolution, mass executions, betrayals, sieges, and the omnipresence of death, this loathsome celebration of death, dictates what we write, and foremost what we think.
>
> Bullshit, Alejandro said. Utter, total bullshit.
>
> [Raúl:] How not to envy that innate optimism of the writers to our north . . .?
>
> [. . .]
>
> Alejandro objected, Hardly the same . . . .
>
> [. . .] Unconvinced, Francisco leaned back, lighting a cigar. All the same, Jurud's virtuosity is the measure of an all-too-accessible world unfettered by the interlocking jungles, pyramids, peasants, and torments of our spirits. (172–73)

Intercultural cross-fertilization in an age of constant, palimpsestic overwriting of national identity discourses under the impact of ideas from abroad does not depend on factual information that can only be elusive, anyway, but on a mutual stimulation of the imagination. Thus, the characters' discussions about the respective virtues and characteristics of US American and Latin American literature are not meant as authorial judgments but as stimuli for a reconsideration of imaginative representations, of signification and its discontents. By calling into question not only the nature of representation of reality, but also the very dichotomies governing the discourses of self and Other, Abish has raised American self-questioning to the level of a universal reflection upon the power and the impotency of the cultural imagination.

As we will see in the next chapter, this questioning can also be directed at the core of national and cultural identity discourse formations, the foundational narratives where they involve the idea of the Other. Epistemological despair cannot be the final answer to the moral burdens of the past.

# [10]

## SPLINTERED FOUNDATIONS: POSTMODERN AND NATIVE AMERICAN VERSIONS OF COLUMBUS

Myths are the action, metaphors are tribal survivance.
—Gerald Vizenor, "Reversal of Fortunes" (*Shadow Distance*, 224)

IN THE AGE OF postmodernism and postcolonialism, not only the discursive construction of the Other has changed, but also that of cultural identity. Developments in US society since the 1970s have made the nation avowedly multicultural, multiethnic, post-consensus. They have brought to the fore conflicts of race, gender, class, and ethnicity, "diversity" being the common and often euphemistic denominator. Such changes can be seen as fundamentally disruptive or also optimistically, as in Annette Kolodny's comments on the situation at the beginning of the twenty-first century:

> Happily, Americans no longer—out of jealousy or insecurity—actively compete with Europe to claim a romantic and storied ancient past. [. . .] The antiquity of the continent and the long presence of its many First Peoples is already well established. [. . .] The nation is now unequivocally multiethnic, multicultural, and interracial, with those groups once labeled minorities moving rapidly into a new majority. As a result, we can no longer insist upon any single defining origin story that begins in Europe. (*In Search*, 330)

This optimistic view, however well-founded its hope for ethnic equality may be, does not do away with identity and alterity but posits a new awareness of their relativity. What this amounts to can be seen in versions of the myth of Columbus that were published in the context of the quincentennial. The novels to be discussed, two of which belong to the canon of Native American literature, have contributed to the development sketched by Kolodny and in part foreshadowed it. But they also show that the beginning dissolution of identity positions does not necessarily bring about a ready acceptance of alterity. While Stephen Marlowe's postmodern novel is a testimony of the insecurity of the period and the loss of truth and value systems, the equally postmodern but also postcolonial texts by Michael Dorris and Louise Erdrich, and by Gerald Vizenor, can find solutions to the ongoing interethnic inequality only in utopian projections.

*THE MEMOIRS OF CHRISTOPHER COLUMBUS* (1987) by Stephen Marlowe is a novel that demonstrates the deconstructive inconclusiveness of (hi)story-telling. Not only does the identity of the voyager disappear in the turbulently moving waters of a life that may be inconclusive in its own right, but national identities depending on a founding figure and a founding event cannot be established either. The novel is a testimony of US American self-doubts of the late twentieth century, and if there is any message to be derived, it is that of the moral and epistemological murkiness of all ages.

Stephen Marlowe (1928–2008) published a long list of mystery and science fiction novels as well as other works under this and a number of other pseudonyms, and also under his real name, Milton Lesser. If the confusion concerning his name(s) in reference works is any indication, he enjoys mystifying his readers. Thus, the phrasing on the title page, "*The Memoirs of Christopher Columbus* with Stephen Marlowe," hints at problems of identity and authority right from the start. That this novel, which should have put the author in the ranks of respectable literature,[1] was for a while left out of the lists of his works in reference books such as *The Writers Directory* may also point to the difficulty of placing this work.

The problem is one of genre, to begin with. Two-thirds through the long novel, there is the following imaginary conversation between Columbus and one of his discerning readers:

> Sooner or later some well-meaning critic is bound to ask, "Are you writing an autobiography, a historical novel, a romance or what?"
>
> To which I'll answer promptly, "Or what."
>
> He'll say, "But why all the anachronisms? Can't you at least stick to your own century?"
>
> I'll try to explain that my anachronisms are intentional. For isn't capturing the essence of a bygone day something like translating poetry? Doesn't the spirit of the original matter more than mere vocabulary? (Marlowe, *Memoirs*, 377–78)

Some reviewers have called this book a picaresque novel, and the first-person narrative, the rise of the protagonist from humble origins, the view of the various strata of society from an outsider's position, the ups and downs of his career, the wealth of details, characters, and episodes all seem to fit this genre. But then this is a book about a historical person, and many of the incidents Columbus relates are also historical, with varying degrees of verifiability. The book purports to be an autobiography, a genre holding particular prestige in the United States where it has been linked with the credo of individualism and with the success story. Thomas G. Couser summarizes this view in his comments on an advertisement for autobiographies of business leaders:

> Its [The ad's] claims [. . .] illustrate a pervasive lay habit of reading autobiography as an especially, even essentially, authoritative kind of writing [. . .]. Academic criticism [. . .] is never this naive, [. . .] but until recently much of it shared two of the advertisement's assumptions. The first [. . .] is that autobiography is nonfictional, since it records the experience of a historical person, not an invented "character." The second [. . .] is that the author is present in the text, that a pre-existent unique personality can be conveyed through—or despite—literary mediation.
>
> According to referential or transactional theories of language, autobiography has a kind of "authority" lacking in most forms of literary discourse—the authority of its grounding in a verifiable relationship between the text and an extratextual referent. (Couser 15)

However, as contemporary theories of identity have it, and as Couser proceeds to reveal with respect to some of the best-known American autobiographies, the unity of the self "is to be found in continuity of consciousness, not in consistency of behavior. Personal history is not the product of prior selfhood. Rather, selfhood is the product of an internal autobiography; identity hangs by a narrative thread" (17).

One might expect a pseudo-autobiography to follow the more classic definition and present a stable narrative self and an unquestioned version of past events, but in the case of Marlowe's Columbus, the "continuity of consciousness" extends to the present time, making identity a rather vast affair. In fact, Columbus's authority stems not only from the notion that this is *his* life story but also from the fact that his retrospective view is that of a modern person. But this creates problems of its own, as we shall see.

Columbus's double claim of presenting the truth and of translating the spirit of his age makes for contradictory demands. By his authority as agent, victim, or witness of the events of his life and times, he can fill in gaps and correct errors in the historical and biographical work of others. Thus, he never tires of poking fun at Morison and Madariaga (without ever mentioning them by name) for getting both the external events and his psychological or other motivation quite wrong: "Take the fellow [Morison] who flatly said he would leave my 'psychology, motivation and all that' to others. So what does he do, every chance he gets? Probes my innermost thoughts anyway, then presents his insulting speculations not as conjecture or psychohistory but as fact" (*Memoirs*, 127). Occasionally, he takes personal offense at some version of an episode in his life, as when he attacks Saul Bellow for reminding him that it was the hated upstart Amerigo Vespucci whose name was used for the new continent:

> A lot has been made of my return to Spain in irons, and more written about it than anything but my First Voyage. How are the mighty fallen: it's too tempting a subject to resist. I resent none of this excessive recounting of the low ebb—at least professionally—of my life.
>
> With one exception.
>
> Why did a latter-day novelist in John Cabot's part of the New or an Other World, a Nobel prizewinner, have to end his longest and most famous novel like this?
>
> "Columbus too thought he was a flop, probably, when they sent him back in chains. Which didn't prove there was no America."
>
> Sure I thought I was a flop. Who wouldn't? But using the Vespucci eponym is really rubbing it in. (480)

He insists on presenting all the details necessary for forming an opinion of his motives, his moral character, his successes, and his failures. He also corrects his earliest biographers and commentators, for instance Las Casas or his son Fernando, and he even acknowledges that his own known writings may be inaccurate:

> I wrote elsewhere (not altogether accurately) that I went to sea at the age of fourteen, implying that it was all very sudden, that, perhaps, I was one good offshore breeze ahead of the police [. . .].
>
> My own son Fernando put it otherwise. Young Fernando, unwilling to spring from the loins of a semi-literate nobody who ran off to sea at fourteen, sent me in his biography (a book I don't recommend) to the University of Pavia to study mathematics, geography and astronomy, so I could become a suitable father for the illegitimate son of the Admiral of the Ocean Sea.
>
> I was born at sea. (6)

Although Marlowe's version is quite fanciful here, in other instances the author has his hero propagate scholarly truth. For example, in keeping with what we think we know today, Columbus explodes the popular myth that it was he who had to convince the people of his time that the earth was round, whereas this was common knowledge at least among scholars and navigators.

Often, however, Columbus takes up (without admitting that he is doing so) all kinds of legends, traditions, and speculations concerning his person that have arisen over the past five centuries and weaves them into his yarn. Thus, whereas scholarship has confirmed Columbus's Genuese origin, Marlowe's Columbus follows the rumors made internationally known by the Spanish historian and biographer, Salvador de Madariaga, that he was really the son of converted Spanish Jews and was born on board a ship taking the family away from the threat of church persecution to their Italian exile.[2] After the (again unhistorical) violent death of his father, Columbus becomes a wine and food taster for his Spanish compatriot Rodrigo Borja, who, as Roderigo Borgia, pursues a spectacular clerical career that will make him Pope Alexander VI. Columbus is sexually initiated by Borgia's mistress and then (nonfatally) poisoned by her jealous husband, who sets the secret society of assassins, the "Brotherhood of the Golden Stag (or Hind)"[3] on Columbus's tracks in what turns out to be a lifelong pursuit.

Columbus, who—at Borgia's request—continues to be supported throughout his career by the banking firm of the House of Centurione, makes his escape to England by way of Portugal, where he first meets his later wife, Felipa. But it is in England that he meets a young student by the name of Tristram who soon turns out to be a woman in disguise—Isolde, of course. They have a highly romantic love affair and, when he follows her to Ireland, he gets to know that she is also the sister and lover of a slightly crazy young friar, who is called Brother Brendan like the legendary early discoverer of America and who frequently imitates St. Francis when he isn't active as The O'Gaunt, a descendant of John of Gaunt playing the role of an Irish Robin Hood. Columbus is present at the violent death of Isolde/Tristram and her brother at the hands of Padraic Lynch, well known in Galway tradition. He then travels to Iceland, picks up some information concerning the Vikings' settlements in North America, and meets Giovanni Gaboto, alias John Cabot, who has his own plans concerning the rediscovery of America.

Back in Portugal, Columbus marries Felipa but is cuckolded by a foppish new arrival from Nuremberg named Martin Behaim (the supposed inventor of the globe). After Felipa's death, Columbus works in the bookstore of Martin Waldseemüller (the German cartographer who produced the first maps showing the New World and naming it "America"), and meets his mistress Beatriz. He then disappears from sight because for two years he is active as a Spanish spy behind the Moorish lines, being instrumental in the conquest of Granada, before he succeeds in persuading Queen Isabella and King Ferdinand of his "Great Venture." The rewards he claims (the status of Viceroy, the title Admiral of the Ocean Sea, the percentage of the riches his discoveries will bring back to Spain) are those suggested by his *converso* mentor Santangel, who is trying to improve the future chances of the Spanish Jews, a detail that makes Columbus appear less greedy and ambitious.

Although the subsequent narrative roughly follows the known events of the voyages of discovery, numerous details do not, but remain within the pattern established so far. Thus, between voyages Columbus comes to know and falls in love with Petenera, the ravishing figure from Spanish folklore who turns out to be the Blue (!) Pimpernel, a key agent of a Jewish underground relief organization trying to save Jews from the Inquisition, whose horrors she is to experience and Columbus to witness in a memorable and moving account. And so forth—the scheme is clear enough: Columbus meets not only the people we know the historical Columbus met, but just about every other important contemporary; often, as in the case of Waldseemüller, by way of impossible anachronisms. But he also meets people from all kinds of myths and legends. And he interacts, confessedly in his imagination, intertextually with fictional figures such as Melville's Ahab—"Am I any less monomaniacal than Ahab? Isn't the fabled East my white whale?" (181). He wonders how the weeks before his first sailing might have been dramatically presented by Lope de Vega or Shakespeare, and he refers to Don Quijote in one of his amatory notes to Beatriz; that is, he places his life in the context of a world of texts written and oral, factual or fictional, legendary or contemporary of either his "real" life or a later day.

If the genre of the book as a whole remains uncertain, the types these incorporated texts belong to cannot be neatly distinguished, either, nor can the individual stories be kept apart—an insight Columbus shares with postmodern theory. If he cannot keep from becoming a legend himself, how is he to prevent the merging of his story with any other story?

> I became a legend in my own lifetime and, modesty aside, for all time in 1492. My every move from the moment I crossed the gunwale of the carrack *Santa Maria* in the port of Palos would belong to the ages. Before they did sums, small children in school would study the legend into which my life disappeared; for many I became their first undeniable hero. [. . .]
>
> I have often pondered what becomes of the man when the legend achieves its own life, when the myth becomes more enduring than mere flesh and blood. Must he become enslaved by that legend, trapped in that myth, forever denied a moment's privacy? This is the danger but, living legend or not, I intend to keep private those final few weeks with my united family [. . .], almost the last real privacy of my life, for the intervals I could steal later from that difficult taskmaster, history, were brief and rare. (156–57)

But this is pure nonsense, because right from the start he interacts with the legend, and the elisions are as much an element of any narrative as are the events and existents mentioned. His desperate attempts to construct a correct version of his identity are doomed from the beginning. His tale is at times ribald or uproariously funny, at others deeply moving. It often presents an interplay of moods as we know it from the later writings of Mark Twain. Like Twain's Connecticut Yankee, Columbus delights in his role of superman and then, again, is tortured by doubts and feelings of guilt, notably when he realizes his role in the establishment of slavery and colonial exploitation. His triumphant tour through Spain reminds us of Hank Morgan's triumphs, just as his visit of the prison of the Inquisition is a heightened echo of Hank's impressions of the feudal dungeons. And, like Hank Morgan, he is eventually incapable of changing the course of history as well as concealing his own destructive role. During a fight with the Natives, he speaks of the "enemy dead" and then corrects himself: "Enemy? *We are the enemy*" (356; italics in original).

What is happening, then, is that Columbus loses his original ideological orientation and hence the framework informing his narrative. Translating past events into a modern language used by a man who apparently has the freedom to let his mind roam, through not only his personal memories but also the history of the ages, necessarily implies moving through the discourses of the periods and cultures he appears to have at least observed, if not experienced. Columbus establishes countless parallels to events and characters past and present; he repudiates certain views and narrative constructions of historical reality in order to present "the truth," which nonetheless stays always beyond his grasp. None of the roles he keeps playing or telling us about—that of the picaresque drifter, the heroic seeker, the competent superman, the self-searching and penitent depressive, or the ironic and self-ironic commentator—enables him to retain control over his narrative. The selection he makes (for instance, he evades the question of who actually made the first sighting of the New World), the hierarchization of events (his love affairs gaining considerable importance), his establishment of new causal, emotional, and genealogical links in his narrative plot, and his consideration for his latter-day readers, create a new story of Columbus, yet a story that keeps carrying the burden of all the earlier ones as it unfolds. The message is clear. Because history is an open process, so is any event and any life story that is made the subject of narrative rendering.

Because Columbus's story is history and myth in all their unending multiplicity of development and ontological vagueness, the question of identity —the "Who am I?"—turns into a "'What am I?'" as soon as Santangel informs him about his Jewish origin, and then immediately into a "'*Why* am I?'" (146). But the recourse to teleological thinking is hopeless in a textual field where narratives of any variety keep streaming in, and not even Columbus's recurrent suspicion that there may be Pynchonesque conspiracies at work plotting his life (or death)—the Borgias, the Centurione bank, the Jewish "Movers and Shakers" in Spain, the Brotherhood of the Golden Stag or Hind—leads any further.

Not surprisingly, then, Columbus has to seek orientation from a higher sphere. During his identity-and-purpose crises in the newly founded colonies, he develops stigmata. In a series of dreams, he sees himself as St. Christopher (given his name, this association comes fairly naturally), but a St. Christopher who fails to fulfill his role of the Christ-bearer and hence turns into Cartaphilus, the Wandering Jew, who again turns into Herne the Hunter, who meets the (historic) Roger Wendover at St. Albans in early thirteenth-century England and saves the manuscript of Wendover's Wandering Jew story for posterity, thus also saving elements of his own future life (Wendover's text will be passed on to him through Tristram and Petenera). From this drifting through historical reality, myth, dream, and dream-within-dream, Columbus also salvages Cartaphilus's signature, which is identical with his own, the famous and mysterious arrangement of signs historians have so long tried to decipher. And eventually, in a mystic moment outside of time, a moment, that is, where Columbus is not the helpless victim of ever-unfolding time-plus-narrative, he comes to see God or what he suspects to be God in the shape of a ball of lightning. Naturally, Columbus asks the essential questions about his identity, his purpose in life, and hence the purpose of history.

> "Who am I?" I ask. "*Why* am I?"
>
> The ball of lightning pulses brighter yet. Wrong question.
>
> "Am I a Christian or a Jew or what?" He ought to know the answer to that one.
>
> —Or what, says the voice [. . .].
>
> "Are you Blind Chance?"
>
> —Some men call me that. I've been called worse [. . .].
>
> So I ask the ur-question, the question I figure will cover the most territory. I ask:
>
> "Why?"
>
> —Why what?
>
> "Just why." (542–43)

But God refuses to answer and only suggests that his omnipotence and omniscience are relative, that there might be worlds above his world—"Chinese boxes, my dear Colón"—and tells him, "Believe what you want. Anything is possible" (545). God leaves Columbus with the consolation that his discovery was instrumental in changing not only the outer but also the inner life of mankind:

> What had you to know—to explore, to discover? [. . .] Why must you know those things? The time had come for people to cross the seas and live on the

> lands of all of their world. The time had come for them to explore this Earth and, exploring it, explore inside themselves. Do you think a Don Quijote or a Hamlet, an Abraham Lincoln or an Einstein, would have been possible without your Other World? [. . .]. Would the rights of man have been heralded, without this Other World? Would people have found a new continent of wonders inside themselves, without this Other World? Would the wellspring of creativity have overflowed, without this Other World? And it was given to you, you with your faulty vision and confused ideas of geography, to find it. (546–47)

But of course, this return to a traditional teleological model derived from Western ideology and cultural values can no longer satisfy Columbus, who now wonders if God might not have been a symptom of the mysterious malady he has been suffering from for some time.

Can there be any higher authority in a world where divinity has become highly doubtful, where stigmatized Columbus, rather than carrying Christ, appears to be carrying the burden of human sin and failure himself and where he also appears to be his own creator and the creator of the historical or mythical past necessary for his later existence? Columbus is last seen on his deathbed, in the literary tradition sketched earlier, but at the very end he gets up and moves on to some other level of reality, trying to discover more clues about his life and those dear to him.[4] He finds himself in an Arab city and buys one of Piri Re'is's maps bearing a facsimile of his own signature, which he could not have used at the time he was a mapmaker himself, so that his later life must have left its traces on his earlier experiences. That is, he experiences the *mise en abîme* situation familiar from so much postmodern metafiction. But by this time, he may not even be Columbus anymore, but a narrative voice on a metalevel, for the book ends, "I run home carrying the chart and dreaming of far places. Not Columbus's places, not the Indies. But my own [. . .]—Venice, Jerusalem the Golden, Trebizond [. . .]—and I know I will see them all as surely as my name is . . ." (569), only to be continued overleaf by a remark concerning the author under his pseudonym: "STEPHEN MARLOWE studied philosophy at the College of William and Mary [. . .]." Columbus's identity and authority derive from the author's and merge with his: there can be no story apart from the storyteller. But, given the author's uncertain identity, the question is passed on to the reader, who is asked to construe his own author, his own Columbus, his own history.[5]

Marlowe uses one of the world's master narratives to call into question the very notions of event and person. By going back even behind the historians' solid foundation, the sources, and by revealing the ideological motivation or discursive patterning of earlier versions, his Columbus deconstructs all kinds of earlier narratives and tries to substitute his own, but he can never gain control over story and history, nor can he escape from them, not even in death. Thus, there can be no closure, no arrival, only a moving on to the next sphere. The novel is structured by the contrary movements of chronological order versus temporal indefiniteness, identity constitution versus identity dissemination, completion by supplementary information versus endlessness of new linkings, cause-and-effect sequences versus chance and fitful fate, closure versus openness and metaization, and teleology versus an infinite choice of the meanings of history. Given the epistemological uncertainty, the allusions not only to the bardic version but to the macro-stories mentioned in Chapter 3 remain indecisive. Surprisingly, this holds true of the tragedy of the Indians as well; even the Native chief Guacanagarí comes to the conclusion, "'Blind chance spins the world. No one is to blame'" (438)—a great relief to Columbus. There is no way of separating the story of Columbus from any other story and of clearly assessing it, and hence the voyager's example, Marlowe seems to say, has to be seen as that not of the triumph or failure of certain value systems governing the narrative construction of reality, but of the openness of narrativity per se, or, in the key metaphor governing the text, of discovery as a basic human (and narrative) impulse.

Marlowe's Columbus, then, is not another attempt at defining the historical and discursive beginnings of either America through the story of the Columbian voyages, but a demonstration of the impossibility of such attempts. However, in one sense it builds a bridge between the author's North and the South first touched upon by Columbus. *The Memoirs of Christopher Columbus* was published when the "boom" of Latin American writing had been in full fling for quite a few years. The concept of the so-called magical realism was well known in both Americas and all over the globe. One can argue that Marlowe's novel conforms to the magical realism that Latin American authors such as Alejo Carpentier have claimed to be specifically at home in their part of the world, nay, to be a natural form of expression for Latin American storytellers. The blending of two levels of "reality" referred to—the first being historically accurate and factual according to the given notions of mimesis; the second being fantastic, that is, factual only in the sense of an enlarged concept of reality—takes place in Marlowe's book as well. He may even have taken as one of his models Carpentier's concept of *lo real maravilloso* as exemplified in Carpentier's own Columbus novel. In *The Harp and the Shadow*, Carpentier brings together Columbus's own period and the nineteenth century when Pope Pius IX unsuccessfully tried to have Columbus canonized. It has Columbus tell his own story in which he appears as successful not because he "discovered" the New World or because he brought home the desired treasures, but because he invented himself in language. The novel, too, has a deathbed scene, and it brings into dialogue authorities as diverse as Las Casas and Marx, Voltaire and Washington Irving. In *The Memoirs of Christopher Columbus*, Marlowe plays with elements introduced by Carpentier and thereby creates the most pan-American US Columbus novel of the quincentennial years.

IN THE POSTCOLONIAL PERIOD, questions of identity versus alterity are complicated by the presence of the subaltern in the dominant society, nation, or textual space. The consequences of the Columbian voyages; the decimation and often extermination of the Native population; the dispossession, enslavement, forced assimilation and hence ethnocide in both Americas cannot be ignored by any Native American author dealing with American history and its impact on the present. Thus, a discussion of the founding story of the post-conquest Americas would be grossly incomplete if it did not include at least some Native versions of the event. They exist, even by witnesses of the conquest.[6] The texts that are most relevant for my undertaking, however, are contemporary narratives by Native North Americans dealing with Columbus and his aftermath. Predictably, such texts are meant to undermine the Eurocentric alterity discourse governing the non-Native narratives.

This can be done in condensed form, as in the poem "History Lesson" by Canadian First Nations (Okanagan) writer Jeannette C. Armstrong. The poem begins with a scene of chaos and destruction that devalues any claim of the purposeful, preordained course of action many had seen, at least retrospectively, in the history of conquest and settlement:

> Out of the belly of Christopher's ship
> a mob bursts
> Running in all directions
> Pulling furs off animals
> Shooting buffalo
> Shooting each other
> left and right
> . . . . . . . . . . . .
> Pioneers and traders
> bring gifts
> Smallpox, Seagrams
> and Rice Krispies
>
> Civilization has reached
> the promised land. (54)

And it ends with a reversal of the teleological view that had dominated most of the early US versions of Columbus:

> Somewhere among the remains
> of skinless animals
> is the termination
> of a long journey
> and unholy search
> for the power
> glimpsed in a garden
> forever closed
> forever lost.
> (*Seventh Generation*, 55)

Paradise, vestiges of which Columbus had believed to have seen, is a recurrent motif in Columbus literature, Native and non-Native. So is the search for wealth and power or even a better society as well as its futile ending, for instance in the US so-called termination policy of the years after World War II. Native writers are divided over the question as to what extent the victimization of the Native population of the Americas should remain at the center of indigenous texts concerning the history and present state of Native and Euro-American relations. While many continue to protest past and current conditions, others emphasize the achievement of Native survival and, indeed, survivance as defined by Anishinaabe author Gerald Vizenor: "The character of survivance creates a sense of native presence over absence, nihility, and victimry" (*Survivance*, 1). In narratives of both schools, ironies of European or Euro-American intention and failed or insufficient achievement abound. But the fact that these texts were practically all written by authors of mixed descent creates additional challenges to the discursive location to be found.

Marlowe's Columbus deals with his grief about the disastrous effects his voyages had on the American Indians by personalizing the problem in the figure of his adopted Native son, Yego Clone. The name is Clone's own unwittingly self-ironic attempt at imitating the name Columbus had given him, Diego Colón—could a Native American who considered the explorer a superior being and his master ever be more than just a clone? The devastating effect of smallpox on Clone's looks and his sacrificial death by a knife intended for Columbus make him a symbolic and tragic figure whose forgiveness and whose adoption of Guacanagarí's fatalistic "No one is to blame" lets Columbus off rather lightly. As was to be expected, the Native texts dealing with Columbus that were published around the quincentenary of the first voyage reveal a tendency to rewrite history in quite a different, more political direction. For instance, they ask what would happen if new documents were found that throw fresh light on the "discovery" and its sequel. This is the case in the two novels to be discussed here, *The Crown of Columbus* by the husband-and-wife team Michael Dorris and Louise Erdrich (1991),[7] and *The Heirs of Columbus* by Gerald Vizenor (1991).

WHILE THE COLUMBUS OF Marlowe's *Memoirs of Christopher Columbus* is quite abreast of recent historiographical and literary theory—"History flows not into but from the pen of the historian, so who can say that I am right and Las Casas wrong?" (21)—the characters of Dorris and Erdrich's *The Crown of Columbus* believe in history in the traditional sense. Although the protagonists are university teachers, for them history is the narrative reconstruction of the past based on documentary evidence. Their own story appears to be equally conventional, a story of love and adventure. *The Crown of Columbus* is not primarily a novel about Columbus but about some modern people from varied backgrounds in search of Columbus for personal, artistic, and professional reasons.[8] If Marlowe's book can be seen as an extreme example of an ironic, metahistoriographic type of history-telling, the novel by the two renowned Native American writers seems like a relapse into the romance model.[9] This, however, may turn out to be doubly ironic.

Most of the early reviewers of *The Crown of Columbus* were disappointed with the book. The upshot of their comments was that it was a potboiler suffering from a mechanically constructed plot designed to please an audience conditioned by sensational adventure fiction and movies. And, indeed, the plot bears all the marks of popular writing. Vivian Twostar, a part-Navajo assistant professor of Native American studies at Dartmouth College, falls in love with her renowned WASP colleague from the English department, Roger Vandyne Williams, who is also a well-known poet. When Vivian gets pregnant, they separate because she insists that he is not the person to play the role of a father, although she secretly hopes that he might convince her of the contrary. With the quincentennial approaching, Roger writes on his long Columbus poem, "Diary of a Lost Man," whereas Vivian, worried about her tenure, has to accept an assignment to do a Columbus article for an alumni magazine, written from the Native American point of view. Roger has all the important material from the library, but during her search for useful items, Vivian accidentally discovers some pages of Columbus's lost original diary.[10] These pages, plus some oyster shells bearing an inscription in Hebrew, contain clues to where to find a crown Columbus is said to have intended as a present for the Natives on his first arrival and that was considered the greatest treasure of late medieval Europe. The Columbus material was intentionally misplaced in the library by an eighteenth-century Mohawk student in revenge for what the whites had done to his people. It had originally been given to the university for verification of its genuineness by some early member of the wealthy Cobb family, whose descendants have tried to get it back ever since.

After the birth of their daughter Violet, Roger and Vivian resume their relationship, and together they travel to the Bahama island of Eleuthera, one of the possible sites of Columbus's first landfall, as guests of Henry Cobb, who owns the rest of the diary and hopes to find the crown in order to sell it and thus to escape his financial difficulties. When Vivian resists his efforts to get at the documents by a deal or by force, he tries to murder her. She escapes by using her knowledge of karate. Roger, who has been searching for her, is swept by an undertow into a hidden cave, where he is found by Vivian and Nash (her unruly son from a failed first marriage) after all hope had been given up. Naturally, the cave also hides the glass box with the crown everybody had assumed to be pure gold and jewels. It turns out to be Christ's Crown of Thorns, presumably fake, but at Columbus's time believed to be the true relic. The baby daughter Violet, who had been swept away on a raft,[11] is found (on Christmas Eve!) by Valerie Clock, a black Caribbean girl who henceforth feels a sense of mission and hopes to cross the ocean in the direction of Europe.

The crown indicates that Columbus wanted to present the Indians with the treasure and burden of Christianity rather than with earthly wealth, but also that his present was never given and never accepted. Vivian's manuscript find, on the other hand, reveals that the explorer considered the Natives as forming sovereign nations and therefore, with Vivian's skillful handling, gives a tremendous boost to Native American claims of sovereignty. At the end of the story, which is placed at a date more than one year after the publication of the novel (the action takes place in 1990, with a postscript dated 1992), Vivian has been given tenure; she is a great success. She, Roger, Nash (who had always before rejected his future stepfather), Violet, and even Vivian's Navajo grandmother all form a happy family.

Although the plot is contrived, it is captivating, as plots of adventure novels tend to be. That the book was such a success as a novel of love, mystery, and adventure can be attributed to the authors' conforming to the standards of such popular genres. Had they sold out to commercial interests, then? In a way, yes: a particular class of readers is given what it demands and another class of readers, the established critics, in particular those specializing in Native American literature, is antagonized—intentionally, I think. For what is being displayed here is an example of the strength of people's (the characters' and the readers') desire to get carried away. Narrative emplotment, the authors seem to say, distorts reality, and the more it does so, the more we are ready to suspend our disbelief. The narrative construction of reality will always have a strong element of wish fulfillment. The more contrived it is and the better (and the less realistically) all details fit together to form a strong chain of teleological causality, but also the more the plot appeals to our sense of (individual and historical) poetic justice, the more it will satisfy our basic instincts, our Kermodian hunger for closure and purpose.[12] Dorris and Erdrich emphasize the unreality of their story by having it end in the future, thus indicating the tinge of utopia coloring the whole. Fictionality, which, in a technical sense, is the result of a contract between writer and reader to suspend certain speech-act conditions (G. Gabriel), is here shown to result virtually inevitably from any kind of narrative and to become more prominent the better knit the story appears to be—a lesson to be applied to other texts as well. As investigations of reader response have shown, this artificial side of emplotment will not diminish our sense of participatory illusion but rather enhance it.

Thus, if chance appears to be the principal factor of history as an open process in Marlowe's novel, it functions here as a series of coincidental turns always eventually creating the results most needed and desired. But plot dominates also in another sense. When the crew members Columbus had left behind in the Caribbean at the end of his first voyage saw their impending death at the hands of the Natives, they hid the crown and left the clues necessary for its retrieval, and thereby started a plot. Cobb plots against Vivian in order to regain the missing part of the diary and hence access to the supposed treasure. Vivian plots to use Cobb in order to find the crown and thereby substantiate the claims of Native Americans generally. Again and again, the characters (and this includes the loving couple) try to entrap one another—for benevolent or less benevolent purposes. Not only does plot govern the narrative, but the characters try to control the events by constant plotting; they make their wishes the basis for the story they try to construct.

But this, as Theodore Sarbin and others have shown, is what we all do anyway. The authors appear to be aware of the similarity of popular fiction to everyday notions of the story quality of life. The seemingly most outworn feature of this novel, its romance plot, turns out to be its principal metafictional feature, a commentary on the nature of narrative that is hard to overlook if one manages to escape the suspense and emotional entrapment by the text. But that, exactly, is the problem.

To be sure, many elements of the novel have nothing of popular literature about them. The adventure portions may be a little too long, and the narrative voices of Vivian and Roger (most of the chapters are told by either one or the other, usually alternatingly), initially quite individual, tend to become less distinguishable as the book goes on, but otherwise this is a well-written literary text. In the first and last chapters, which are subdivided into four sections each, the authors introduce third-person narrative (figural and authorial) and, besides the two protagonists, also have Nash and Columbus enter the list of first-person speakers. Point of view, therefore, is shown as a decisive factor in storytelling, and although most of the telling is chronologically progressive (with some necessary flashbacks), we are sometimes confronted with differing versions of the same event as seen by either Vivian or her lover. The use of dates for some of the chapters and subchapters indicates the basic sameness of narrative as a reporting of events in a temporal continuum, whether referring to the immediate or the remote past or even to the future. The novel sets in at a relatively late point in its chronological development—Valerie's discovery of the baby, Violet, and the discovery of the nearly drowned Cobb by friends of the protagonists—but also in another introductory subchapter, at a very early point, Columbus's first landfall. This double beginning creates suspense concerning the contemporary events and raises questions of the past's impact on the present as well as the present's role in defining the past. Most of the scenes and episodes are rendered with skill, the narrators giving proof of their wit, their ability to play with language and ideas sometimes in order to voice their anger or frustration yet more often their self-irony, of which Vivian has the larger share. But they also demonstrate their capacity for precise observation: in spite of its romance aspects, many parts of the book are completely realistic.

In addition, as befits a text purportedly written by two university professors of literature or cultural studies, the novel teems with intertextual quotes and allusions. Roger, in particular, gains pleasure and mental stability from referring to his favorite authors Donne, Herrick, Spenser, Shakespeare, and Milton, among others, while Vivian, quite in character, feels closer to Maxine Hong Kingston's *The Woman Warrior*, and even Cobb is reminded of Joseph Conrad's *Heart of Darkness* as he describes his situation. The protagonists know their Samuel Eliot Morison, of course, and Roger has studied Columbus's sources from Pliny to Mandeville. When pregnant Vivian is locked in the Dartmouth library one night and there inadvertently finds her first clues to the Columbus mystery about to unfold, this carries overtones of Borges and Umberto Eco. Her enclosure in and rebirth from the labyrinthian womb of the nightly stacks (shortly before she gives birth to Violet) find their later counterparts in Roger's entrapment in the cave and the subsequent discovery and deliverance/delivery of himself and the crown. In both cases, words and acts are seen as inseparably linked. Vivian's search in the world of texts confronts her with the daring act of that eighteenth-century Mohawk Peter Paul,[13] to remove the Columbus material from its place and hence to cut off the whites from an important source of historical information. Roger, in comparison to his lover the more bookish, contemplative type of person, is brought into his predicament when he acts in order to save the infant Violet; he, in turn, is saved by his words, his repeated recitation of his Columbus poem, which stirs up the bats infesting the cave—their untimely swarming out of the opening leads to the discovery of the entrance by the others and to the acts of rescue and recovery.

If the world of texts and the world of action are hard to keep apart, their relative merits remain doubtful, too. Much of what the principal characters plan to do turns out to be a failure because of adverse circumstances or because they miscalculate their partners and adversaries. The protagonists succeed only in a world ordered by authorial arrangement of chance, cause and effect. And this success, much as they—and we, the avid readers—may desire it, is hard to imagine outside the world of the book. Thus, didn't Peter Paul's act keep the world from knowing that Columbus had quite different views of the political status of the Natives he encountered than is usually assumed? But then, would the world have been prepared to treat them any differently if it had known sooner? And would it do so now? The ending of the novel is a piece of sheer and glaring make-believe and wish fulfillment—that the United States, Brazil, Mexico, or New Zealand would change their stance on aboriginal rights after the discovery of some additional pages of Columbus's diary is as preposterous as the whole plot.

Peter Beidler has defended the novel on account of the serious themes it pursues almost in spite of its plot: themes like that of discovery, which is omnipresent in the text and concerns human relations just as much as new worlds, historical knowledge or poetic procedures just as much as material gain; themes, too, like the type of Native American literature and politics adequate both for the quincentennial and for the future status of Natives everywhere. Although such themes are indeed important parts of the novel's argumentative structure, I think that the powerful tension between its popular fiction appeal and its thematic and aesthetic complexity points to one of its most central questions, namely, what is the right kind of story.

And here, metafictional and, for that matter, metahistoriographic hints abound. Right at the beginning of her narrative, Vivian comments on the famous Orozco murals at Dartmouth:

> They were a jaw-dropping, nightmare gallery: conquistadors and peasants, Aztecs and Jesuits. The only major female figure in the whole damn epic was a vicious-looking schoolmarm with her hair pinned back in a bun, yet Orozco somehow spoke to me. Vivian Ernestine Begay Manion Twostar. Coeur

> d'Alene-Navajo-Irish-Hispanic-Sioux-by-marriage. I liked to think a version of American history was contained in that logjam of names.
>
> [. . .] There was, actually, one other woman character in the Orozco saga. She was pregnant too, a skeleton wearing a black gown, or actually, she was in the throes of delivery, her head on fire, watched by an unimpressed row of emaciated, gray professors. Her chitinous offspring—fetuses packed in bell jars—wore mortarboards. [. . .] Ahead of its time, it could have been the emblem for Native American Studies, my so-called discipline. (*Crown*, 11–12)

Will her version of Indian-white history be equally vitriolic? It will be pan-American, emerging from a feeling of solidarity with the Natives of all parts of the Americas, although she hardly devotes any space to the indigenous peoples of Latin America.[14] It will also be anti-academic establishment, to be sure, and hence stand in opposition to Roger's, who insists that he should concentrate on the exceptional figures and on the narratives or narrators immortalizing them. While Vivian is after new facts that might reveal new aspects of real history, Roger accepts history as the sum total of previous scholarship and imaginative or poetic reconstruction. But if her way seemingly wins out, it also undergoes a number of modifications. In the beginning, she indulges herself

> in a fantasy of that fateful event from the alternative perspective.
>
> On the tiny island of Guanahani, a few families of Lucayans are asleep, swaying obliviously in their hemp hammocks. They're a healthy, pleasure-loving group, laid-back beach bums and surfers, with absolutely no aptitude for destruction. If they and their neighboring Carib rivals fight at all, they throw wooden fishing spears at each other. There's not much to argue about anyway, since they share a land with plenty of food, great weather, and fabulous scenery.
>
> [. . .] Nature lovers that they are, they prefer to go au naturel. Life's a beach from one day to the next. People grow up, make love, give birth, eat, die. [. . .]
>
> Then one particular dawn, there's a novelty. The sails of three Spanish caravels appear on the horizon of the world. [. . .] They've got no reason to expect it's not more good news. (24–25)

But this naive and simplistic version is a fantasy in more than one sense and a reaction to the bardic version, which, in the shape of an emotional paragraph from Morison, Vivian has quoted just before. If she would stick to this fantasy, it would be part of a Native American version of Latinamericanism no less simplistic than that of the North American settler nations. It is not at all in keeping with Vivian's character and her position in general, and it is hard to see how this piece of retrospective dreaming can be taken as mirroring the beliefs of the authors. The passage is another trap, just like the overall plot of the novel, a trap baited by the myths of the noble savage and an earthly paradise.[15] Later on, Vivian is quite capable of presenting the economic, nutritional, and, particularly, the demographic stories of the Columbian voyages mentioned earlier, in Chapter 3, when she talks to her students. And rather than simplify the world of the Natives on the eve of contact, she here correctly emphasizes the degree of their diversity that distinguished them from the comparatively homogeneous European culture: "'Over here you had hundreds of societies, millions of people, whose experience had told them that the world was a pretty diverse place'" (82).[16] The Europeans won because they had "'[o]ne god, one family from which all their languages originated, one creation story, one agenda: to rule the world. [. . .] They absolutely believed that the earth was their oyster'" (83).

However, as Vivian's reflections of the Orozco murals have indicated, there can hardly be an uncontaminated Native American view of the Columbian events today. As a mixed-blood and as a person in a transdifferent, multiply mixed and torn position, caught between various social roles, notably as a woman in the academic world, she can

> relate to Columbus, stranger to stranger. There he was, no matter what version of his life you believe, pushing and pulling at the city limits of wherever he found himself. An Italian in Iberia. A Jew in Christendom.[17] [. . .] He didn't completely fit in, anywhere, and that was his engine. He was propelled by alienation, by trying to forge links, to *be* the link, from one human cluster to the next. [. . .]
>
> The more disparate and contradictory the facts I accumulated about Columbus, the more I understood the man, both identified with him and hated the failure of understanding he'd come to in the end. [. . .] He was a certain kind of man in court, another in the Caribbean; a mercenary, a saint, a scholar, a fanatic, and, of course, a slave trader. [. . .] He was a nexus of imaginary lives, of stories with but a single foot in fact, and when by accident he was at last truly a part of the greatest, most farfetched tale of all, he didn't know what to make of it. (124–25)

Consequently, Vivian identifies not only herself but Roger (as the would-be superior white male) and even Cobb (as the embodiment of reckless entrepreneurism) with Columbus, and so, in their respective ways, do the other major characters: there is a Columbus for and in everybody. Given such problematizing of self and of history, given other metafictional and metahistoriographic remarks, given the equation of the invasion of a territory with that of a story, when Roger's apartment is broken into by Nash, who steals Roger's diary and tries to make it public, given all that, it is hard to conceive how the main plot could be taken as anything but another lie, another fiction to be recognized as such.

And there are other indicators. Like Stephen Marlowe, the authors present a piece of handwriting in facsimile, thus providing what is usually the bedrock of history-telling, the source. But the two pages allegedly taken from Columbus's missing diary and a letter are here presented in Vivian's handwriting with corrections and comments by Roger, the whole supposedly based on the translation produced by Vivian's grandmother, who has some knowledge of Spanish. The second document, describing the situation Columbus encountered on his return to his first settlement during his second voyage, bears the date "the twenty-eighth of January in the year fourteen hundred and ninety-two" (145), which is obviously absurd, because it would place the scene long before the discovery but also ignores the fact that the Gregorian calendar was introduced only ninety years later. Nor do the places fit: if the now dead followers of Columbus hid the crown in their vicinity, it should have been in Hispaniola, not Eleuthera. In other words, while in a mystery novel the conclusiveness of the evidence and the eventual clarity of the information given form essential parts of the story as it is finally unraveled, *The Crown of Columbus* rings true and consistent only for the inattentive reader.

To be sure, the novel is not completely playful. Indeed, often seriousness and playfulness alternate in a breathtaking manner. When Nash and Vivian sing parts of the Navajo Blessing Way as the glass box with the crown is hoisted from the cave, it sounds strangely apt, as if here, eventually, Natives, by relying on their holistic and harmonious religious heritage, were capable of gaining control of the alien religious system imposed on them. But when Vivian then breaks the box with a karate chop, the scene appears to be turning into parody, although none of the participants sees it that way. Another stumbling block is Roger's poem, an impressive dramatic monologue recreating the mind and mood of Columbus, a text the authors had previously published in the journal *Caliban* under Roger's name. It is quoted in its full length of sixteen pages and is certainly no laughing matter. But then, Roger recites it to the bats, and again we are torn between conflicting modes of response.

The rage of contemporary Native Americans and their wish to take history back are all there—in a way, the whole plot is a testimony of the effort. On the whole, and in spite of the soap-opera outcome, the interpersonal problems of the characters are considerable and believable. Also, and this is more important in the present context, *The Crown of Columbus* is an inter-American novel. As in so many other narratives of this kind, the novel takes a group of US citizens to a Caribbean setting where they act out their conflicts before they return home. The descriptions of the island setting are realistic enough:

> I saw no long sand beaches, no royal palms or coconuts, no paradise. Unfinished construction frames, skeletal and hollow, appeared from time to time. The clustered settlements we passed consisted of one store with a gas pump, a small restaurant, and houses of cement block painted lime green, magenta, powder blue, or yellow. No one sat on the iron grillwork porches, no customers walked in and out of the stores, few cars passed us. Farther on, a solitary, tall, thin man stood in a cleared field, just stood there, an attenuated Giacometti figure, burnt expressionless and still beneath the high sun. (188)

The scene reveals the ongoing exploitation of the Caribbean by North Americans. In contrast to many other inter-American novels, however, Vivian links the contemporary situation to that of the Native Americans at home as a consequence of the historic European expansion:

> "This place reminds me of a reservation," I mouthed to Cobb.
>
> And it did. Poor soil, bright colors, dark people, junked automobiles. In the variety emporium where we finally stopped, there were the same kind of long-shelf-life staples that rural Indians depended upon. (188)

Columbus, the founding figure of the identity discourses of North and Latin America, the impressive, doubt-ridden yet purposeful solitary individual in Roger's poem, is also the founder of misery for the Native population then and now, and for the descendants of African slaves as well. Vivian, though fully aware of this, cannot escape her role of the North American visitor. Her impressions of the Caribbean are in no way more complex than those of countless others. To redeem the situation, to lift the Natives of the Americas out of their marginalized situation but also to make the transdifferent position of simultaneously belonging with the invaded and the invaders a fruitful, creative, and change-inducing one, to unveil all the ambiguities of the Black Legend and its discursive aftermath—all this would require a miracle, and that is what this place of discovery has in store, not only for the protagonists. But of course, this miracle is and remains an outrageous fiction, a Native utopia.

Like Marlowe's novel, *The Crown of Columbus* is a book about discovery —of treasures, persons, facts, worlds, ideas, and modes of perception. But where Marlowe ironically reveals the eventual hopelessness of goal orientation, this book ironizes such irony by making us feel the power of our obsession with goals, with the things to be found. It is therefore also a book about desire and seduction. It demonstrates that, in Roger's words, "the present is a sponge that sucks history dry" (375), yet it is not only ideology, the discourse we are part of, that shapes historical narration, but also our primary desires, our vicarious wish for the characters' success in love, in parenthood, in career, our hunger for a primitive division of the good and the bad, for justice, albeit poetic. Numerous details remind us that side-taking would be all too simplistic, that truth remains elusive, that no (hi)story has definitive validity. As Nash summarizes Grandma's Navajo philosophy, "Truth was all in the story, in the way it was told and in who was doing the telling. It could change in a minute or remain the same forever. A truth lasted only until a better one came along and replaced it" (362). Yet the overall plot and numerous other details make us partisans, nonetheless.

Using a term coined by Gerald Vizenor, we might call this text trickster discourse. How else but by reference to the trickery of narrative told, lived, or read can we explain the entrapment of characters and readers in the belief that Columbus, whose principal errand was to bring back gold and other riches to Spain, should have carried gold (the crown) to the Indies? Where the postmodern stance applied in Marlowe's book undermined the notion of self, the equally postmodern awareness informing *The Crown of Columbus* questions that of the Other as well, and deflates simple models of cultural alterity. Both Columbus and Vivian, "the European" and "the Indian," are examples of multicultural transatlantic and eventually inter-American fluctuating identities. But the book also demonstrates how hard it is to keep such awareness alive, how the deconstruction of the notions of person or event will lead to their reconstruction, if only the affective stimulus is strong enough. And that is a metafictional and metahistoriographic lesson, too. If Marlowe shows us that there is no escape from a world of stories, Dorris and Erdrich point out that the stories are the escape. There is no need to assume that there is less longing for such an escape among Natives than among other people, they seem to add.

REWRITING HISTORY, THAT IS, declaring the conquest and the claims to the New World made on the basis of the supposed superiority of European civilization(s) invalid, can be done by a simple, starkly ironic inversion of this claim as in Osage writer Carter Revard's satiric short piece "Report to the Nation: Claiming Europe" in which the speaker describes the reaction of the European "tribes" to his claim that their countries were the property of the Osage Nation. He proposes to collect some of the weapons and skeletons of the European wars for an Osage museum, but then decides he might just as well "cram most of Europe into a word-processor and bring it back to deal with on our own terms, far more efficiently and cheaply than by trying to load all that geography on our backs the way Ameropeans have done" (*Earth Power*, 170). At the end, he hopes that "some better fate befalls me than fell on the European conquistadores" (179) and comes to the conclusion that

> Europe, being second-hand and badly used, ought not to be priced so high as Louisiana when Jefferson took the land on which, as he maybe didn't know, our people happened to exist; and freeze-dried as in these words Europe won't be worth things of value. So don't let any of us offer language, traditions, beadwork, religion or even half the Cowboy and Indian myth, let alone our selves, this time. (179–80)

Gerald Vizenor's novel *The Heirs of Columbus* reclaims Europe with a different argument reaching back to early history. It is a more serious and, in a postmodern way, even more playful book than *The Crown of Columbus*, more serious in its aesthetic complexity but also in the way it addresses contemporary issues, more playful in the way it reinvents history and invents future developments. Vizenor, of Anishinaabe (Ojibway) and French descent, rephrases questions of authenticity and group affiliation. The novel also deals with property rights concerning cultural objects. There is the further issue of the status of narratives, of the truth of myth as well as of supposedly factual stories of discovery, in a word, the nature of narrative truth and cultural meaning as it is developed in narrative texts. *The Heirs of Columbus* deals with such questions in a more convincing way than many other literary texts that were published in the context of the Columbus quincentennial in 1992. It pokes fun at the dominant Western version of the history of the so-called discovery of the New World, and in addition at Native American essentialist counter-histories, the type of history that cannot but be a narrative of victimization. Yet humor and satire also have a very earnest side. The novel challenges what Vizenor seems to consider all-too-glib narrative representations of what it means to live as a Native American and in particular as a person of mixed descent in contemporary Euro-America, and yet to partake of portions of the indigenous cultural heritage.

*The Heirs of Columbus* abounds in intertextual allusions and *roman-à-clef* elements. The villain of the novel, Doric Michéd, a stylish member of the Brotherhood of American Explorers and a mixed-blood of vague Native ancestry, shares most components of his name with the late Michael Dorris, as Christoph Irmscher pointed out in one of the best pieces of criticism on this book (Irmscher 93). One might add that Michéd seems to share some elements of Dorris's public role as well.[18] *The Heirs of Columbus* is therefore to be read as a novel dealing with many unsolved conflicts in contemporary ethnic North America and beyond. It reveals that David Hollinger's concept of postethnicity as the freedom of the individual to choose between a variety of ethnocultural affiliations may be too optimistic and therefore less adequate than Vizenor's own notion of the *postindian*, which acknowledges both the existence and the inadequacies of the Columbian "simulation" *indian* (Vizenor, *Fugitive Poses*, 15). The simultaneity of absences and presences (to echo the subtitle of Vizenor's book) in the context of interethnic relations and discourses, and the omnipresent practice of binary differentiation in spite of its shortcomings, result in a network of tensions. They belong to the sphere of *transdifference*, the simultaneous relevance of conflicting properties or affiliations.

In *The Heirs of Columbus*, elements that normally serve to bring order cannot fulfill this function but contribute to ambivalence and, indeed, create a reading experience of transdifference. One such element is genre. Generally speaking, literary genres are important ways of structuring communication and hence of meaning construction. To say that *The Heirs of Columbus* is a postmodern novel, and therefore inevitably combines a large number of genres or textual types and modes, is begging the question. What deserves our attention is the function of this very combination. In Vizenor's text the play with literary and extraliterary genre components and traditions, the oscillation between fiction, nonfiction, and metafiction does not lead to the total relativity of meaning and values that we find in a great number of postmodern texts. Rather, the author manages to have it both ways: the skepticism regarding the stability of order and evaluation systems is offset by an insistence on the ability of human beings to distinguish between the good and the bad, the useful and the useless.[19]

Perhaps in the first place, *The Heirs of Columbus* is a *historical novel* because it deals, among other things, with historical events such as Columbus's voyages of discovery and the fate of Pocahontas or that of the Sephardic Jews. It is also a *mock-historical* novel because in a surprise twist, Vizenor avails himself of the thesis of Augustus Le Plongeon concerning the Maya as originators of all civilization. The novel presents Columbus as a descendant of the ancient Maya, who are said to have brought their culture and their genetic "signature of survivance" (*Heirs,* 3) to the Old World, so that Columbus's voyage can be shown to be a return to his origins.[20] But the difference between history and mock-history may be negligible when we consider that in Vizenor's opinion, the distinction between good and bad stories is much more important than their generic category and their factuality.

When we turn to the contemporary plot, *The Heirs of Columbus* moves through a whole range of genres. It is a *postcolonial* satirical novel because on the level of its main action, a group of tribal people, the Heirs of Columbus, by means of their trickster methods, subvert and ridicule the power, practices, and representatives of the dominant society. Like their leader, Stone Columbus, they claim to be genetic heirs of Columbus by way of his sexual union with a beautiful shaman and tribal healer, Samana, and hence they are crossbloods, to use Vizenor's term. The postcolonial subversion involves the economic exploitation of non-tribal people: Stone runs a bingo hall on board their flagship, the *Santa María Casino* (named after Columbus's ship), anchored on the international border between Canada and the United States, which makes his venture an inter-American one, fitting for a book on the heritage of Columbus. Stone's partner Felipa Flowers acquires not only, in Pierre Bourdieu's terms, economic but also cultural capital by "repatriating" (8) stolen cultural objects from museums, art collections, and so forth.

The world of the culture capitalists is *satirically* exposed when she meets the elegant but shady art dealer Doric Michéd and, with the magic tricks of a young tribal shaman (an element of fantasy? Or myth?) manages to get hold of not only several medical pouches, but also a portion of the bones of Christopher Columbus. The heirs bury these at their headquarters, the so-called Stone Tavern near the headwaters of the Mississippi—an act that one may read as a narrative rejection of any essentialist ownership claim the Maya or other tribes involved might make. The action is turning *utopian* when Michéd's legal action against Felipa is just as unsuccessful as that of the state against the casino because the heirs win the help of a federal judge, Beatrice Lord, a representative of a better US social order (the novel also contains elements of that popular American genre, the *courtroom narrative*). An element of *tragedy* enters when the casino ships sink in a storm and especially when Felipa tries to recover the bones of Pocahontas from England and is killed by Michéd. However, *comedy* must prevail, so Stone and the others buy land at Point Roberts between Seattle and Vancouver Island, another Foucauldian heterotopia after the ship and the stone tavern. They call it Point Assinika[21] and, on October 12, 1992, 500 years after Columbus's landing in the New World, declare themselves a sovereign tribal nation. There, they finance genetic research that will heal disabled children by the "genetic code of tribal survivance" (132), an even stronger utopian element, which is emphasized by Vizenor's having the final part of the book take place in 1992, one year after the publication of the novel.

Because the reform model envisioned at the end, namely of endowing all of humanity with tribal qualities, requires a scientific innovation, *The Heirs of Columbus* is also a *science fiction* novel. The book also contains qualities of traditional *myth* because the action is presented as part of the age-old fight of good versus evil, enacted on the contemporary, symbolic level by the struggle of Felipa and Stone against Michéd and his like, and on the level of traditional Anishinaabe mythology by the moccasin game the Heirs have to play against the *windigo*, the Anishinaabe evil spirit, a contest that can never be won but where the catastrophic, nay, apocalyptic defeat can always be put off. Finally, *The Heirs of Columbus* is a postmodern piece of *metafiction* because its genre mix and its high degree of intertextuality continually amount to a reflection on the nature of literary and other narratives.

Obviously, this genre mix creates narrative ambivalence, for instance when our ordinary sense of the progress of time is called into question by the sudden shifts between historiographic passages, contemporary action, and proleptic excursions into a utopian future. It is no oversight that the narrative past tense is sometimes exchanged for the present or perfect, as in "Since the *Santa María Casino* sank Felipa has lived in a house trailer [. . . .]" (46), thereby taking us outside the world of fiction altogether and tying the action to our real-life temporal order—at least if we follow narratological theory in the distinction of, on the one hand, narrative past as a fictionality marker where it occurs in a novel and, on the other, (nondramatizing) present or present perfect as references to the "real" world, again when they occur in a work of fiction. Thus, the truth value of the second part of the sentence has to be measured against other reality statements. The simultaneous experience of fictionality and nonfictionality appears to refer to a drastic case of ontological transdifference.

The collision of genre aspects of history, fiction, and myth may be the novel's most interesting formal feature. Hayden White has commented on the relatedness of myth, history, and fiction, which he explains on the basis that

> the systems of meaning production shared by all three are distillates of the historical experience of a people, a group, a culture. And the knowledge provided by narrative history is that which results from the testing of the systems of meaning production originally elaborated in myth and refined in the alembic of the hypothetical mode of fictional articulation. (White, *Content*, 45)

In Western society and thinking, however, myth, history, and fiction are often associated with typical forms and rules of communicational pragmatics. If taken not in a metaphoric sense but according to their respective position in the order of genres and speech acts, they are hard to reconcile. All three occur as narratives in one sense of each term. And yet, in Western literary communication, they differ because of the respective notions of truth and the real as well as the corresponding speech-act patterns at work.

I have already said that the decimation or extermination of the Native population, the dispossession, enslavement, the forced assimilation and hence ethnocide in both Americas cannot be ignored by any Native American author dealing with American history and its effects on the present.

Or can they? In *The Heirs of Columbus*, there is very little mention of this aspect. Consider a quotation from the very beginning: "The Admiral of the Ocean Sea, confirmed in the name of the curia and the crown, was an obscure crossblood who bore the tribal signature of survivance and ascended the culture of death in the Old World" (*Heirs*, 3). Columbus's title "Admiral of the Ocean Sea" is best known from Samuel Eliot Morison's monumental biography *Admiral of the Ocean Sea: A Life of Christopher Columbus*. In the sentence quoted, is it used affirmatively, in bardic recognition of Columbus's rise from obscure origins to the status of explorer with access to royalty and ecclesiastical leaders? Or ironically, either as an allusion to the later negative reversal of his fortune or to indicate the relativity of his greatness in view of its aftermath? The "tribal signature of survivance," we find out later on, may be Columbus's major asset and legacy, a feature that might redeem the world. So, may there be greatness in his career, after all, albeit contrary to his beliefs and aims? That is, did he not only *as*cend, but *tran*scend what is here summarized as "the culture of death," the sum total of the negative effects of European domination? The Columbian voyages are a particularly good example for the observation that it is not the higher or lower degree of scientifically verifiable factuality that turns facts into events and thus into story elements, but the systems of sense making and evaluation informing this process. But again, what kind of narrative do we have here?

As will be remembered, Hayden White avails himself of Northrop Frye's types of narrative emplotment, macro-genres, as it were: tragic, comic, romantic, or ironic. However, the sentence from *The Heirs of Columbus* just quoted seems to indicate that Vizenor is writing in all of these macro-genres at the same time. For him, the choice of focus does not depend on the historian's perspective, but apparently all approaches are valid and therefore applied simultaneously. The question of which history *The Heirs of Columbus* has incorporated is relevant because this is a historical novel dealing, albeit only in some portions of the text, with historical people and events and containing numerous quotations or paraphrases from historiographic texts such as Morison's biography or historical sources such as Columbus's diary. But of course, this is not a conventional historical novel in the tradition of Walter Scott. Rather, like Marlowe's *Memoirs of Christopher Columbus*, it belongs to the type of novel that Linda Hutcheon has called *historiographic metafiction* and that I prefer to name *metahistoriographic fiction* because it reflects on the very conditions of writing history. In this as in other respects its demands on the reader are extraordinary because the text constantly runs against our expectations. The result is not another novel of victimization but a narrative of survivance, to use Vizenor's terminology.

The material on Pocahontas provides a good example. It consists of very few pages of biographical information from contemporary and modern sources, often as quotations with sources given and without authorial commentary, for instance this passage concerning Pocahontas's reception at the English court:

> Pocahontas was presented at a performance of *The Vision of Delight* and *Christmas, his Mask*, by Ben Johnson, on Twelfth Night at the end of the Christmas season in the Banqueting Hall of Whitehall Palace. King James and Queen Anne danced at the masque in honor of Rebecca Rolfe. Prince Charles, the new Earl of Buckingham, the Earl of Montgomery, Sir Dudley Carleton, ambassador to the Netherlands, John Chamberlain, and others in royal favor attended the masque. Chamberlain wrote to Carleton that "the Virginian woman Pocahontas, with her father's Counsellor hath been with the King, and graciously used. And both she and her assistant well placed at the Masque." (*Heirs*, 97)

The brutal Eurocentrism of the event is left for the reader to discover. Only rarely do we find direct evaluative statements, as in "Felipa Flowers [. . .] was determined to rescue the remains of a young tribal woman who had died in service to the religious politics of the colonies; she had died in tribute to the noble fashions of the seventeenth century and would be buried at last in the tribal House of Life" (97). Even this sympathetic approach may be attributed either to an authorial voice or to Felipa's point of view. Although Felipa's solidarity with victimized tribes or individuals moves the reader to sympathize not only with Pocahontas but also with her, the novel as such progresses beyond situations of victimization and will not let us rest too long on such sentimental feelings. If we want to find out about an authorial perspective behind the mosaic of quotations and paraphrases of historical and historiographic material, we have to notice, for instance, that Vizenor's version of Pocahontas's biography skips the most notorious episode: Captain John Smith is not even mentioned. By selecting and by adding his own imaginations, Vizenor moves away from the stereotyped versions common in popular notions of history. By creating a collage of quotes, he gives the impression of historical factuality. In an interview, he said, "I don't consider Columbus a good story and I don't consider it healthy after such a long time to continually tell a bad story that victimizes me" ("Gerald Vizenor: The Trickster Heir of Columbus," 102). To turn this bad story into a good one, Vizenor combines the borrowed material with his own additions and replacements, which thereby claim an authority of at least equal weight to that of the historiographic tradition.

The first narrative paragraph of the novel gives a good impression:

> Christopher Columbus saw a blue light in the west, but "it was such an uncertain thing," he wrote in his journal to the crown, "that I did not feel it was adequate proof of land." That light was a torch raised by the silent hand talkers, a summons to the New World. Since then, the explorer has become a trickster healer in the stories told by his tribal heirs at the headwaters of the great river. (*Heirs*, 3)

The first fictional word in this text is "blue," a significant addition to Columbus's testimony because blue turns out to be the leitmotif color of the novel. But drastic things follow two lines down: Vizenor's fictional hand talkers are given the same semantic status as Columbus's observations and their classification as "journal to the crown." The author makes us jump back and forth between history and fiction, between real (but possibly false) and pretended (but possibly true) assertions. By adding silent hand talkers or by making Columbus a descendant of the Maya, the generic binaries he makes us digest in one dish contain history of the most factual, place-and-date-governed kind and fiction of an overwhelmingly fantastic variety.

If fiction and historical narrative are sometimes difficult to unite, so much more are fiction—be it historical or other—and myth, if the unification involves not just the mythic worldview of some fictional character but also the conflation of the contradictory claims of "truth" in both types of text. The worldview of myth is characterized by the undividedness of reality (cf. Cassirer 39–77), by the unity of "subjective" and "objective" truth as well as of the physical and metaphysical spheres. Whatever philosophical, anthropological, and psychological theories of myth have come up with, on a pragmatic level, myths have to be believed and are therefore true. The myth background for *The Heirs of Columbus* is Anishinaabe,[22] so it is an evil *windigo* who threatens to annihilate the tribe if Columbus should win the final moccasin game. He is stopped only by Stone's hint that this would mean the end of the world and thereby of the game, too, because Stone is in possession of a powerful war herb whose use would bring about total destruction, and which he has made part of the contest of good and evil. "'The game never ends,' said the wiindigoo. He paused over the blue moccasins, raised his hand, and then moved back into the shadows" (183). Vizenor bluntly yokes (fantasy) fiction and—tribally specific—myth together, and in addition, as we have seen, history. This yoking amounts to a parody of the respective genre-defined textual traditions, but a parody that is less destructive than constructive in that it makes us engage in considering solutions for the problems addressed.

As readers, we have to accept the simultaneous validity of all three types of genre discourse. We can find no escape in saying that "this is only a novel" because what is at stake is the survival of the human race and a number of lesser but none the less significant issues such as the chances of the genome project, the question whether cultural memory can be transmitted by "the blood," the benefits and dangers of Indian casinos, the question of cultural property, and the responsibility for the genocide in the New World. For those who have the right view of reality, these things go together, although not without considerable tension, just as animals like Memphis the panther can appear "'disguised as humans'" (70) but remain animals if only you have the proper perception. In a court hearing exchange, Judge Lord insists that the "'[e]vidence is rational and reason has precedent,'" but Lappet Tulip Browne, one of the tribal group, counters:

> "The rules of a legal culture rule out tribal stories and abolish chance in favor of causative binaries."
> "Even languages must have rules," said Lord.
> "The languages we understand are games," said Lappet.
> "Language can be a prison," said Lord.
> "Trickster stories liberate the mind in language games," said Lappet.
> "Touché," said the judge. (82)

In this play on Wittgenstein and Jameson, the position favored by the tribal speaker and obviously supported by the author is that of openness, chance, play, but that does not mean replacing the binaries of the "either/or" by a synthesis, the harmonious blending of some model of hybridity, but by another binary, the "either AND or," the persistence of difference in all its shortcomings and its suspension.

This is to say, once again, that the textual structure as a whole, and particularly those elements of meaning construction that are carried by genre are shaped by transdifference. As Lappet Tulip Browne asks the court to "'strain to understand'" (80) the transdifferent status of the trickster, who in this novel turns out to be a "real" figure, a mythic character, and a figure of speech, so we must strain to understand, and feel, the simultaneous validity of genres, ideas, social affiliations, or moral positions that are ordinarily thought of as mutually exclusive. It is a text where oppositions mean healing; where the antinomies of biography versus fantasy, history versus myth, history versus utopia, tribal versus postethnic and universal, of gambling income and humanitarian spending, genetic engineering and chance, power and imagination, gender and transgender, are all brought together in a combination of manifold transdifferent ambivalences, or, as Vizenor would say, a complex of stories and humor, humor that eventually even keeps the apocalypse just one sentence away. Accepting such transdifference will not allow us *not* to take sides, but in a further step, acceptance makes choice not just a causal necessity but an act of liberation. To see reality as simulation and yet to assume and act on the premise that the human condition can be improved upon turns the strain of undecidable elements into a creative force. The free acceptance of the transdifferent nature of many aspects of human reality, but also of individual decisions for one aspect over the other, makes *The Heirs of Columbus* a text of multiple liberations: of language, culture, people, land, objects, and ideas. Although not another gospel, it contains messages for a whole generation of wanderers in the intercultural contact zones of not only the New World.

One such contact zone is the utopian tribal healing center at Point Assinika, whose foundation at the inter-American border between Canada and the United States is described in a parodistic version of Columbus's own description of his first landfall, as several critics have noted:

> Point Assinika was declared a sovereign nation on October 12, 1992, by the Heirs of Christopher Columbus. "At dawn we saw pale naked people, and we went ashore in the ship's boat," said the adventurer [Stone Columbus] on an exclusive talk show radio broadcast. "Miigis unfurled the royal banner, and the heirs brought the flags which displayed a large blue bear paw." (119)

The point about Point Assinika is that it is tribal and global, local and hemispheric, transracial, a case of ethnic transdifference.[23] The celebration of mixed descent—"It is the 'crossblood wild bounce' that the novel celebrates, insisting that 'the best humans' are mongrels—crossbloods like Columbus and Jesus, Mayans, Jews, and Moors" (Krupat 170)—is not to be confused with that of a homogeneous mix, a concoction of the melting pot. As Christina Hein has shown, the Heirs'

> strategy [. . .] calls to mind those focus-shifting movements in Postcolonial and Subaltern Studies that have called for the constructive treatment of the borderlands, third spaces and other phenomena at the fringes of formerly clear-cut conceptual centers. Rather than falling in with a great number of voices deploring their status as "neither this nor that," then, they construct themselves, first, as the bearers of the world formula to heal all ills and redress all wrongs; and second, as an avantgarde center—as being the mixed descendant of either Sephardic Jews, Mayas, and/or Christopher Columbus turns out to be a universal trait, available to and imaginable for all. (Hein 129)

By naming the central creative mongrel living among the Heirs Caliban, Vizenor alludes to the Latin American postcolonial adoption of the name of Shakespeare's wild man as a symbol of resistance and Latin American self-definition (Hein 131). In the wake of the study *Calibán* by the Cuban

Marxist intellectual Roberto Fernández Retamar, numerous writers and critics have further developed his argument.[24] Vizenor's Caliban defies any facile identification:

> [A]s a "mongrel," he is decidedly mixed in one way or another, even if, symptomatically, it is hard to determine which. Is he dog as well as human; white as well as indigenous; Mayan as well as Ashininaabe? Stone as well as panther, bear, and mongrel, since "he remembered the same stories of imagination as the panther and the shaman bear" (16)? As a "great white mongrel," is he white in terms of skin color, or fur color, for that matter?
>
> Thus tossed back and forth in such a complex web of identification, "white" all but loses the privilege it usually connotes in the context of race. Rather than the signifier of facile access to power and various capitals (in the sense of Bourdieu), it is here a dubious signifier that points in several directions at once, speaking of plurality and the absence of purity and unequivocalness. (Hein 131–32)

Latin American theories of creolization and *mestizaje* come to mind. That is, Vizenor creates the most radical antidiscursive view of the Americas conceivable. The Maya discovery and cultural infiltration of Europe far in the past deflates any binarist, hegemonic discourse of identity and alterity, wherever it may have arisen. The Heir, the Heir, is everywhere. Or could be, if the healing powers should have their way.

# PART FIVE

# [11]

## CANADA AND LATIN AMERICA: MALCOLM LOWRY AND THE OTHER AS SYMBOLIC FIELD

Denn das Schöne ist nichts
als des Schrecklichen Anfang, den wir noch grade ertragen,
und wir bewundern es so, weil es gelassen verschmäht,
uns zu zerstören.
—Rainer Maria Rilke, "Die erste Elegie" (*Duino Elegies*, 4–5, lines 4–7)[1]

CANADIAN TEXTS ADDRESS the same general issues as US American ones: Columbus and the conquest of the Americas, other historical events such as the Mexican Revolution, nature, gender, and so forth. Their sheer number and quality makes these texts essential objects of a study of North American perspectives on Latin America, and to place these chapters here means regarding them not only as a highlight of this study, but also as important intertexts for US American books of the last fifty years. At the same time, the books to be discussed fill in significant historical gaps of this study. Malcolm Lowry's *Under the Volcano*, which is the main subject of this chapter, historically refers to the period leading to World War II and was published shortly after the end of the war. It shows North American and European visitors in Mexico at this ominous historic moment, and its mood is quite different from the texts referring to the postrevolutionary period of disillusionment, like Porter's or Beals's, but also from those referring to the 1950s, notably the escapist immersion into the Other we have seen in Kerouac's *On the Road*. In *Under the Volcano* there is no escape. The next chapter begins with fictions under the shadow of the Vietnam War and the social uncertainties of the 1970s and after, similar to those US texts discussed in Chapters 6–10, but it continues into the beginning of the twenty-first century and thereby brings us virtually up to date.

Looking for a specific Canadian inter-American position involves overcoming the prejudice that Canadians are not interested in what goes on south of the Rio Grande/Río Bravo. On the occasion of Prime Minister Harper's visit to some Latin American and Caribbean countries in the summer of 2007, the Toronto *Globe and Mail* quipped, "Every Canadian prime minister discovers 'Latin America' and then forgets about it. Perhaps Stephen Harper will be different, although it's hard to know why." The writer continues to comment on the lack of interest and information and argues, "Canada's foreign-policy interests are not seriously engaged in the hemisphere, except for a few issues in a few places. To describe Latin America [a]s Canada's 'back door' is simply wrong" (Simpson A 15). In particular, for many Canadians it is the presence of the United States that seems to prevent a proper perspective on the countries further south. In the introduction to their collection *Desde el invierno: veintitrés cuentos canadienses*, Margaret Atwood and Graeme Gibson wrote, "When we look south (which we do rather often in Canada), our gaze is blocked by the United States. The same thing happens when Latin Americans gaze far enough to the north."[2]

Not surprisingly, the Canadian alterity discourse refers, first of all, to the United States. Beginning with the American Revolution, the exodus of American loyalists to Nova Scotia and other areas, and the defense of those British colonies that would later become part of Canada in the War of 1812, Canadian writers have developed often very critical perspectives on the neighbors to the south: their material, economic, and technological success and their form of government that was often seen as chaotic, and above all their expansionist tendencies. Sometimes, for instance in Margaret Atwood's novel *Surfacing*, the destroyers of nature and of social coherence are called "Americans," no matter what nationality they belong to: "they're what's in store for us, what we are turning into" (*Surfacing*, 129). This critique of US American materialism (not so much of the ecological as of the cultural destructiveness) resembles Latin American comments on the "moloch" of the North, for instance the Uruguayan essayist Enrique Rodó's attack on US utilitarianism mentioned in Chapter 1. And again, as in Atwood's well-known poem "Backdrop Addresses Cowboy," the "American" is portrayed as a hyper-masculine invader of the more passive, receptive, feminine country beyond the border, "the space you desecrate/ as you pass through" (*Selected Poems*, 71), in this case the Canadian space.

As in many statements by Latin American authors, Canadians often see their country as "the better America" in danger of being overrun by the superior demographic, economic, and political power of the United States. Such asymmetrical relations have been thematized for instance in connection with NAFTA, the North American Free Trade Agreement among the United States, Mexico, and Canada that was extolled as serving integration and pan-American unity but in fact highlighted the existing and persisting differences. "US, Mexican, and Canadian narratives have all as emerging literatures addressed the here/there, Old World/New World, problematic. Yet a postcolonial consciousness toward and into the twenty-first century may increasingly view not only Europe but the US as an overwhelming presence" (Smorkaloff 92).

The lateness of Canadian nationhood and the comparatively weak self-perception as a nation have made it difficult for Canadian scholars to join the trend toward transnational hemispheric studies that are seen by many to be another form of US cultural imperialism. The problem is addressed in Winfried Siemerling and Sarah Phillips Casteel's introduction to their excellent anthology *Canada and Its Americas*.[3]

> There is a danger [. . .] that a defensive Canadian nationalism and self-protective instinct vis-à-vis the United States may inhibit the development of alternative paradigms of hemispheric American studies that Canadianists, with their historically weak nationalism and acute awareness of the imperial tendencies of the United States, are uniquely positioned to produce.
>
> For indeed, it is crucial to note that the almost off-handed dismissal, on the part of many literary theorists, of the "nation" or the "nation-state" as a category of literary and cultural analysis remains problematic, despite all theoretical arguments against essentialisms, for literatures that had to fight under postcolonial circumstances for national status as late as the 1960s. Are not the projects of "Canadian literature" and "*littérature québécoise*," for instance, on the verge of being remarginalized after having existed as fully institutionalized fields for only a few decades? (Siemerling and Casteel 10–11)

The contributors to *Canada and Its Americas* try to deal with this problem by exploring the possibility of "counter-worlding" (Leahy)[4] the imperial culture, that is, by focusing on specific Canadian areas of attention such as Canadian multiculturalism, the trans-border history of dealing with African slavery, internal forms of center and margin (notably the position of Québéc but also the situation of the First Nations), migration, and Canadian interaction with parts of Latin America, for instance the Caribbean. All in all, this emphasis on problems of the marginalized both in the theoretical and the analytical parts of the anthology provides Canadian perspectives for the new field of international and transnational hemispheric studies. However, as some of the contributors recognize and as David Leahy formulates it,

> in characterizing the political-economic relationships between the US and Canada or Quebec as imperial/colonial dyads, I am flattening out or erasing the multiple ways that Canada and Quebec have been or are imperialist in their own right and participate in and benefit materially from the imperialistic aspects of Canadian and Québécois capital, from the profitability of our international agencies, or from our national and foreign policies—for example, vis-à-vis First Nations in Canada and Quebec, the alienation of peasants from

> the land in Chad and the Yangtse Valley to the benefit of Canadian and Québécois corporate interests, or cheap labour from Jamaica or Trinidad. (Leahy 64)

The two chapters on Canadian texts try to consider this doubleness: the implication of the Canadian discourse on Latin America in a general and basically hegemonic Latinamericanism *and* the counter-discursive potential of literature in general and literature from a specifically Canadian perspective in particular.

AN ABUNDANT NUMBER OF Canadian literary texts deal with the—also inter-American—issue of US-Canada relations and perceptions. However, there also exists a significant body of texts on Latin American topics, encounters, and experiences, texts that bespeak a growing interest. The double issue of the journal *Canadian Literature* devoted to "Hispanic-Canadian Connections" as early as 1994 indicates this tendency, as does the anthology *Compañeros: An Anthology of Writings about Latin America* edited by Hugh Hazelton and Gary Geddes in 1990. *Compañeros* contains poems, short stories, and selections from novels and travel writing by eighty-seven authors. About half of the texts have been translated from French or Spanish; that is, they were written by Québécois or Hispano-Canadian authors, the latter a large and growing group due to the increasing number of people migrating north. Tendencies observed in both publications have continued since then. One is the role that immigrants and refugees from Latin America play in Canadian intellectual life. These writers figure prominently in both books, but I am not concerned with them, because their perspective on their countries of origin is necessarily different from what one might call the mainstream. Another is the strong interest that writers from Québéc have taken in Latin America—not too surprising given the fact that their own province in terms of language is also some version of "Latin" America, and that their postcolonial views of center and periphery might find equivalents in Latin America proper.[5] I exclude them here as well because what interests me most is the Anglo-Canadian as part and variant of a North American perspective.

Most obviously, and notwithstanding huge Canadian economic investments in Latin America, the Canadian discourse does not openly involve hegemonic thinking because it is part of the Canadian self-image that one is in about the same position of comparative weakness vis-à-vis the United States as, for instance, Mexico. Indeed, it might be this very position of solidarity that could subvert any claim to Anglo-Saxon superiority and make subject positions more complex. Thus, is there a specifically Canadian variety of interdiscursive tensions and ambiguities? I will begin with a novel that makes

Canadian remoteness from the field of action a constituent of the transformation of this field into a symbolic space.

IN THE FIELD OF inter-American literature, Canada has produced some heavyweight titles. Arguably the best novel set in Latin America and written by a non–Latin American author is Malcolm Lowry's *Under the Volcano* (1947). It is certainly the best North American one, if one wants to regard Lowry as a Canadian writer although he was born in England and died there. *Under the Volcano* is one of the masterworks of twentieth-century world literature and one of the most complex late modernist texts. The protagonist's fatal experiences in Mexico have a symbolic, that is, religious, philosophical, and political reach far beyond any simple representation of alterity. Yet the book contains descriptions of Mexican landscapes, towns, people, and customs from the point of view of *gringo* visitors that have led to some angry Mexican reactions. For instance, Lazlo Moussong, in his devastating critique of *Under the Volcano* as an artistic failure, argues that

> in Lowry's perception of Mexico, instead of values, we find unbearable weaknesses; heavy-handed distortions; excessively narrow compartmentalization; and, in the smug, petty, superficial way in which he views Mexico and its people, we discover the same point of view as is common among the thousands of North American ne'er-do-wells and European pensioners who settle in Cuernavaca and various other paradises and subsequently proceed to depict the immitigable mediocrity of their lives in exotic hues (217).[6]

Moussong does not proceed to exemplify these points, but instead quarrels with Lowry's use of symbols, his characters and so forth, that is, the book's qualities that have granted it its present international status.[7] It is exactly these general qualities that have made other Mexican writers canonize Lowry —"San Malcolm," as Óscar Mata has called him. The renowned author and critic Hernán Lara Zavala has devoted a lengthy essay to *Under the Volcano*. He comments on Lowry's life, alcohol addiction, literary influences, and aesthetics, and the complex, multilayered symbolism of the novel, a "magnificent and monumental" work that also "describes the intimate tragedy of a whole country, Mexico, by way of the personal experience of an artist like Malcolm Lowry."[8] Lowry is said to have identified with this tragedy, but Lara Zavala neither explains what is tragic about his country, presumably because he thinks this is obvious, nor does he describe at length in which manner Lowry makes use of Mexican settings, characters, and customs. This simply does not appear to be problematic. But what about the "Mexican local colour heaped on in shovelfuls" (qtd. in Day 316) that publisher Cape's reader objected to in his report on the manuscript of the novel? Although an in-depth and general analysis of this much-discussed novel would far exceed the scope of my study and although, on the other hand, a reduction of the text to the category of a novel about Mexico would be like reading *Moby-Dick* as a novel about whales, some comments on Lowry's use of Mexican material are appropriate.[9]

*Under the Volcano* is a novel about the fall of one man, Geoffrey Firmin, the British consul in the Mexican city of Quauhnahuac, or Cuernavaca.[10] Geoffrey's death at the end of the book occurs at the same hour as that of Yvonne, his estranged wife who has just come back to try a fresh start of their relationship. The twelve chapters of the novel give us the last twelve hours in the life of the Consul on the Day of the Dead, November 2, 1938, enriched by many flashbacks and digressions, and, additionally, information about the activities of those closest to him. Apart from Yvonne, these are his much younger half-brother Hugh and Geoffrey's French boyhood friend Jacques Laruelle, both of whom have betrayed Geoffrey by having slept with Yvonne. The events of Chapters 2–12 are presented from the point of view of Geoffrey, Hugh, or Yvonne. Laruelle is the focalizing figure in Chapter 1, set on November 2, 1939. This chapter presents his and the local physician Dr. Vigil's memories of the catastrophe that took place exactly one year ago, gives a general introduction to the setting, and sets the tone, especially when Laruelle reads a letter from Geoffrey in which he desperately implores Yvonne to come back, a letter he never posted. The central cause of Geoffrey's decline and the breakup of his marriage is his progressive alcoholism. During much of his last hours, the Consul is drunk on pulque, tequila, and especially mescal, at times so suffering from delirium tremens that, for instance, he has to ask his brother to shave him. One might say that Geoffrey quite intentionally drinks himself to death, although he is factually killed by the bullets of rightist police officers who take him for a spy.

There is hardly any dramatic outer action in the course of Geoffrey's last day, before the end, that is. A summary of Chapters 2–12 requires but little space: Yvonne and the Consul meet for the first time after her return to Cuernavaca and walk to their home; they try to make love, but Geoffrey proves impotent and continues drinking. Hugh and Yvonne meet, have an outing on horseback through a pastoral landscape, and visit the desolate area of Maximilian's palace, which reminds them of the tragic fates of the emperor and his surviving wife Carlotta. In his garden, Geoffrey talks to his American neighbor and is then visited by Dr. Vigil, who invites Geoffrey, Hugh, and Yvonne to his hometown Guanajuato, an invitation rejected by Geoffrey. Hugh shaves the Consul and discovers Geoffrey's Cabbalistic and alchemical books. Geoffrey and Yvonne visit Laruelle's place; Laruelle quarrels with the Consul about his treatment of Yvonne, and they then visit the fair, where Geoffrey steps on the Ferris wheel, is turned upside down, and loses his identity because his papers fall from his pockets. They take the bus to Tomalín and see a wounded and dying Indian lying in the road, but submit to the hint of the locals that they must not help him because this might implicate them in the affair. At the bull ring, Hugh wrestles a bull. While Yvonne and Hugh take a swim, Geoffrey drinks and after a quarrel, sets out for Parián. Yvonne and Hugh are looking for him in the forest; Yvonne hurries in the direction of the bar El Farolito in a beginning storm and is trampled to death by a runaway horse. During the same hour, the Consul reads Yvonne's letters, has sex with a prostitute, gets into an argument with police officers and some local officials, apparently fascist Sinarquistas[11] who accuse him of being a communist and spy, and is eventually shot and thrown into a ravine, one of Cuernavaca's *barrancas*.

The bulk of the novel consists of conversations, memories, dreams, hallucinations, and long passages in which the focalizing character experiences his or her surroundings. All of the characters are guilty: Geoffrey for his inability to love and to accept Yvonne's love, for his—as it often appears, willful—inability to overcome his addiction, but also for his inactivity, his *acedia*; for his Faustian readiness to surrender to his devils, to accept as fact that he is already in hell and wants to fathom its depths of despair; for his search for the knowledge of the abyss; additionally, also for having perhaps been involved in the war crime of literally sending captured German submarine officers "to hell" by not preventing (or worse) the stokers of the British ship ironically named *Samaritan* from burning them alive in the furnaces. Yvonne is guilty for having left Geoffrey (who had of course given her sufficient cause), for her failure to save him, and for her infidelities. Hugh is guilty for having betrayed his half-brother with Yvonne, for failing to save both Geoffrey and Yvonne because he is absent during the decisive moments, but also for his failures as a leftist intellectual who lacks seriousness and true devotion, and as a partisan of the Spanish loyalists—he has missed the decisive final Battle of the Ebro as he misses the scene when Yvonne gets killed. Laruelle is guilty, too, for having betrayed his friend and for his inability to create the films he wants to make and that need to be made. As in an ancient tragedy, they come together on the stage of Mexico and meet their death or their final failure.

This means that for the main characters, the Other is not Mexico or the Mexicans but the foreign, the uncanny side of the self. Not only are they guilty: they *feel* guilty, and it is this part intellectual, part emotional estrangement from their better selves that makes them suffer. Undoubtedly, this suffering is self-centered, even if it acquires Faustian dimensions as with the Consul. Unlike Rumaker's "Gringos," hardly ever do they project the strange part of themselves upon the Mexican Other; rather, they blame each other, but also themselves. They are or feel unable to do anything for the suffering local people around them. The dying Indian's appeal, "'*Compañero*'" (*Volcano*, 290), remains without answer. It is obvious that they are not ready or able to accept the claim of the Levinasian Other, which also means the divine, absolute Other revealing itself through the face of the other human being. If, according to some religious beliefs, despair and sin can be defined as remoteness from the Supreme Being, then this means that their Other has been replaced by their selves, that is, the devil within. This is what they are trying to come to terms with when they realize that failing to attend to the Other will cost them their essential identity, as in Hugh's obsessive, "idiotic syllogism: I am losing the Battle of the Ebro, I am also losing Yvonne, therefore Yvonne is . . ." (280). When the old fiddler bends over the dying Consul and uses the same "'*Compañero*,'" (414), there may be a hint that, if outer alterity can be overcome, so, too, the inner estrangement, but the end is and must remain inconclusive.

This looks as if Moussong were right in his assessment. There are a *gringa*—Yvonne is American—and three *gringos* in the looser sense, all of them falling or failing, all of them caught in their own private problems. However, as Lowry points out in his famous forty-page letter to his publisher Jonathan Cape, "the four main characters [are] intended, in one of the book's meanings, to be aspects of the same man, or the human spirit, and two of them, Hugh and the Consul, more obviously are" (*Volcano*, 10). That is, their "mediocrity" is an intentional representativeness, Geoffrey and his entourage are Everyman; or, as the author puts it, "This novel then is concerned principally, in Edmund Wilson's words (speaking of Gogol), with the forces in man which cause him to be terrified of himself. It is also concerned with the guilt of man, with his remorse, with his ceaseless struggling toward the light under the weight of the past, and with his doom" (17). On this quasi-allegorical level, even the minor Mexican characters have a symbolic function. For instance, the drunken horseman whom Laruelle observes in Chapter 1 "is by implication the first appearance of the Consul himself as a symbol of mankind" (21).

In spite of the considerable degree of psychological realism in the depiction of the Consul as an alcoholic truth-seeker, Lowry does not attempt to write a realistic novel, nor, in spite of a number of pertinent observations the main characters make, does he attempt to present a picture of contemporary Mexican reality. Instead, as he puts it in his letter, Mexico appears as a symbolic realm:

> The scene is Mexico, the meeting place, according to some, of mankind itself [. . .], the age-old arena of racial and political conflicts of every nature, and

> where a colourful native people of genius have a religion that we can roughly describe as one of death, so that it is a good place [. . .] to set our drama of a man's struggle between the powers of darkness and light. Its geographical remoteness from us, as well as the closeness of its problems to our own, will assist the tragedy each in its own way. We can see it as the world itself, or the Garden of Eden, or both at once. Or we can see it as a kind of timeless symbol of the world on which we can place the Garden of Eden, the Tower of Babel and indeed anything else we please. It is paradisal: it is unquestionably infernal. (19)

Mexico is a projection surface. Although this in itself might be linked to discursive patterns I have discussed in this book, and although this is not to say that Lowry is exempt from the North American or European assumptions about Latin America, an analysis of the novel in terms of its subscribing to a dominant Latinamericanist discourse would not be particularly rewarding.

What Lowry provides, instead, is a demonstration of the relativity of discourses, of the fuzzy edges of meaning construction. Chapter 10 of the novel is a very good example. Here, the Consul is sitting in the toilet of a bar, reading a tourist brochure on the city of Tlaxcala, a text giving topographical and historical information from which we get lengthy quotes, interrupted by fragments of a conversation between Hugh and Yvonne overheard by drunk Geoffrey. They recapitulate the scene with the dying Indian by the road, Hugh putting it into a political context, arguing from a communist position, explaining Cárdenas's policy vis-à-vis the agricultural cooperatives and the fascist danger, linking it to the conquest and a long history of exploitation, whereas Yvonne tries to de-politicize the incident, turning it into a sheer accident of a drunken peon. The Consul from his toilet position chimes in with dissenting opinions. The whole scene amounts to a cacophonic concert of voices giving their diverging opinions of things Mexican: its social and political situation and its history.

All of the characters involved in this scene (with the exception of the barkeeper Cervantes) are foreigners or, as we may assume in the case of the writer of the travel folder, cater to the tastes of foreigners; all have assimilated portions of prevalent discursive constructions of Mexico. And in each case, other factors such as the Consul's drunken hallucinations, the idea of treason that connects the historic Tlaxcalans (who sided with Cortés) with the treacherous couple Hugh and Yvonne and makes Geoffrey angry and jealous, the personal situations of Yvonne and Hugh informing their political opinions, color their versions of these discursive constructions. The Other cannot be grasped by a single approach, Lowry seems to say, but he has no intention of introducing anything like a superior view. Instead, the whole scene is symbolic of the confusion and downhill movement of all the main characters, but also of the country and the world at large, and part of an overall web of symbolic levels. To claim that the characters establish a coherent albeit reductionist picture of Mexico would miss the point of this work, which stands in the tradition of modernism and of symbolist American Renaissance writing Lowry alludes to so often: "In its frantic attempt to distil meaning out of this chaos the symbolistic work may resort to layers upon layers of learned historical and cultural allusions only to make us realize as in *Moby-Dick*, or in *Under the Volcano*, for that matter, that all these strata of literary, religious, political, or philosophical sense do not finally cohere among themselves" (Friedl 187).

This symbolic and symbolist approach applies even to the physical and political reality of Mexico, which I will take as my main example. Lowry uses spatial references that point to several levels of meaning: (seemingly[12]) objective, cartographic space; the symbolic space between heaven and hell that demarcates the scene of the novel as a whole; the discursive space that is the result of societal claims and descriptions, in this case the political, historical, and cultural orderings of Mexico; and the geographies created in the characters' minds.[13] The book begins with a detached authorial—or celestial—view from outer space, gradually zooming in on the place of the first scene, the conversation between Laruelle and Dr. Vigil at the Hotel Casino de la Selva:

> Two mountain chains traverse the republic roughly from north to south, forming between them a number of valleys and plateaux. Overlooking one of these valleys, which is dominated by two volcanoes, lies, six thousand feet above sea-level, the town of Quauhnahuac. It is situated well south of the Tropic of Cancer, to be exact, on the nineteenth parallel, in about the same latitude as the Revillagigedo Islands to the west in the Pacific, or very much farther west, the southernmost tip of Hawaii—and as the port of Tzucox to the east on the Atlantic seaboard of Yucatan near the border of British Honduras, or very much farther east, the town of Juggernaut, in India, on the Bay of Bengal.
>
> The walls of the town, which is built on a hill, are high, the streets and lanes tortuous and broken, the roads winding. A fine American-style highway leads in from the north but is lost in its narrow streets and comes out a goat track. Quauhnahuac possesses eighteen churches and fifty-seven *cantinas*. It also boasts a golf course and no fewer than four hundred swimming-pools, public and private, filled with the water that ceaselessly pours down from the mountains, and many splendid hotels.
>
> The Hotel Casino de la Selva stands on a slightly higher hill just outside the town, near the railway station. It is built far back from the main highway and surrounded by gardens and terraces which command a spacious view in

> every direction. Palatial, a certain air of desolate splendour pervades it. For it is no longer a Casino. You may not even dice for drinks in the bar. The ghosts of ruined gamblers haunt it. [. . .]
>
> Toward sunset on the Day of the Dead in November 1939, two men in white flannels sat on the main terrace of the Casino drinking *anís*. [. . .] As the processions winding from the cemetery down the hillside behind the hotel came closer the plangent sounds of their chanting were borne to the two men; they turned to watch the mourners, a little later to be visible only as the melancholy lights of their candles, circling among the distant trussed cornstalks. Dr Arturo Díaz Vigil pushed the bottle of Anís del Mono over to M. Jacques Laruelle, who now was leaning forward intently. (*Volcano*, 49–50)

This shifting of the perspective from the, as it were, objective and remote to the subjective, attentive, immediate is handled with consummate skill. The seemingly neutral positioning of the town on a global map raises the question of why precisely these points of reference are mentioned. Mountain ranges and valleys belong to physical geography but will later find echoes in the more symbolic mountains and valleys of memory and longing. What appears as innocuous turns out to be endowed with deeper meaning. Revillagigedo Islands and Tzucox simply signify the westernmost and easternmost points of Mexico on the nineteenth parallel of latitude, that is, territorial, political inscriptions of space, yet Hawaii is Yvonne's birthplace, and India that of the Consul, and therefore have strong personal connotations. "Juggernaut," however, evokes not so much a town but an overwhelming force that will crush those in its path, like Geoffrey Firmin.[14]

These places are part of a wider, globe-encircling band that comprises the area in the Pacific where the *Samaritan* destroyed the German submarine, and those northern parts of the Indian subcontinent where Geoffrey grew up, Kashmir, and where his father disappeared in search of a holy mountain, the Himalayas. The lateral positioning of the town is later supplemented by an additional line connecting it to the north, that is, Canada or, more precisely, Greater Vancouver where much of the novel was written, an area of salvation that the Consul dreams of in his unposted letter to Yvonne: "some northern country, of mountains and hills and blue water" (82), a lost utopia where lightning is seen from afar, but no thunder heard, as Geoffrey writes, and where he owns an island as Yvonne tells Hugh in Chapter 4. Canada forms a symbolic alternative to heaven and hell as represented by the Mexican topography and functions as a place of mental and emotional escape. However, there can be no discernible Canadian perspective on Mexico because Canada itself is only a projection or at best a memory of two of the characters.

There are other geographical rays connecting the town with the world. The first extends to Spain—Granada, where Geoffrey and Yvonne first met, and the Spain of the Spanish Civil War that is coming to a close between the two dates of the novel. The word "republic" rather than "country" in the very first sentence refers to Mexico in its fragile postrevolutionary state, certainly not an "empire" as under the reign of unfortunate Maximilian. However, it refers also to the Spanish Republic that was supported by Mexico and whose cause was lost while Hugh was still dreaming of fighting for it. Another such ray extends from Quauhnahuac/Cuernavaca to England, where orphaned Geoffrey was raised in a family of alcoholics. Again, the personal connections have geopolitical connotations: the action of the novel takes place at a time when the British Empire is still in existence, and countries mentioned—Canada, India, British Honduras—are parts of it, that is of an old order that is soon to collapse. Ironically, Firmin is a British ex-consul because Britain had severed diplomatic ties after the Mexican president Cárdenas had nationalized the petroleum industry in an effort to stabilize the Mexican economy and to put the national resources into the hands of the Mexican people.

Thus, Mexico is at the center of the world. Its physical topography is the result of the geological forces bringing about the Americas and provides the material for making it a natural paradise but also a natural inferno. Its political geography is to a large degree the result of outside forces: American and British economic interests, and German fascism and its local offshoots trying to gain influence and to subvert both the Cárdenas government and the role of the Anglo-Saxon powers on the eve of World War II. This political situation forms a backdrop for the private story and is symbolized by the Indian on horseback who appears several times and who is obviously one of Cárdenas's messengers carrying money to the agrarian cooperatives under the *ejido* system. In Chapter 7, the messenger is robbed and severely wounded, presumably by anti-Cárdenas forces, and the rest of his money is stolen by a disgusting petty thief, a *pelado*, the representative of Mexicans exploiting other Mexicans, while Geoffrey, Hugh, and Yvonne are watching helplessly. Before the rightist *Sinarquistas* kill the Consul, he has released the messenger's horse, which then tramples Yvonne to death, the final element of this symbolic concatenation. Of course, one might say that Geoffrey's uselessness as a constantly intoxicated Consul helps the antagonistic forces to gain supremacy. Just as the political interacts with the personal, so do both levels interact with the higher forces of destruction symbolized by man and his institutions just as much as by exterior nature. As Laruelle observes, again linking physical topography with the political and the metaphysical, "It was still raining, out of season, over Mexico, the dark waters rising outside to engulf his own *zacuali* in the Calle Nicaragua, his useless tower against the coming of the second flood" (75).

The same mixture of factuality on the one hand, and fictionalizing and psychologizing fact-bending and symbolizing on the other, that we have seen applied to Mexico as a whole also occurs on the local level. Quauhnahuac is made into a biblical or Puritan "city upon the hill" in a way that is hardly warranted by the actual topography of Cuernavaca, and the walls encircling this ideal place are made to appear as high as they might at best have been in the historical past (Ackerley and Large, Malcolm Lowry Project). The evocation of the town's ideality is undercut by the curious, ironic mixture of contrastive elements—"eighteen churches and fifty-seven *cantinas*" —that evaporates the echoes of a travel brochure by the ironic "boasts a golf course," and particularly by hints of the decay and neglect of the streets and roads that are supposed to facilitate communication and progress. This impression carries over into the smallest topographical entity, the hotel, where the signs of hopelessness accumulate. The town is a mental construction even where we still hear the authorial narrator. This tone corresponds to the mood of the people there: the mourning Mexican citizens in their procession and the depressed foreign visitor. Yet throughout the book, such correspondences work both ways. If Mexico stands metonymically for the world, Quauhnahuac stands for all of Mexico and the individual for all humanity. Therefore, Laruelle's reflections confirm the value of the individual in the face of anonymous mass warfare: "One would have thought the horrors of the present would have swallowed [the events of last year] up like a drop of water. It was not so. Though tragedy was in the process of becoming unreal and meaningless it seemed one was still permitted to remember the days when an individual life held some value and was not a mere misprint in a communiqué" (51).

There are other geographies on a smaller scale than the mapping of the opening pages, for instance the arrangement of the towns alluded to, that are symbolically associated with betrayal (Tlaxcala), hell (Oaxaca), and the possibility of salvation (Guanajuato). It is important to notice that the symbolic range of the centrally located town of Quauhnahuac/Cuernavaca, where the novel is set, fluctuates between the Garden of Eden and the Inferno, in a sense collapsing the two.

Notwithstanding his weakness, his lack of commitment—"He had few emotions about the war, save that it was bad" (55)—Laruelle is a keen observer, and what he observes is the disquieting effect of the unfamiliar but also the familiarity of the Other:

> The leaves of cacti attracted with their freshness; green trees shot by evening sunlight might have been weeping willows tossing in the gusty wind which

> had sprung up; a lake of yellow sunlight appeared in the distance below pretty hills like loaves. But there was something baleful now about the evening. Black clouds plunged up to the south. The sun poured molten glass on the fields. The volcanoes seemed terrifying in the wild sunset. [. . .] A sense of fear had possessed him again, a sense of being, after all these years, and on his last day here, still a stranger. Four years, almost five, and he still felt like a wanderer on another planet. [. . .]
>
> How continually, how startlingly, the landscape changed! Now the fields were full of stones: there was a row of dead trees. An abandoned plough, silhouetted against the sky, raised its arms to heaven in mute supplication; another planet, he reflected again, a strange planet where, if you looked a little farther, beyond the Tres Marías, you would find every sort of landscape at once, the Cotswolds, Windermere, New Hampshire, the meadows of the Eure-et-Loire, even the grey dunes of Cheshire, even the Sahara, a planet upon which, in the twinkling of an eye, you could change climates, and, if you cared to think so, in the crossing of a highway, three civilizations; but beautiful, there was no denying its beauty, fatal or cleansing as it happened to be, the beauty of the Earthly Paradise itself. (55–56)

This is a wonderful example of our dealing with the Other.[15] Alterity is subject to individual perception and projection and entails the double process of attempted familiarization and, on the other hand, rejection, alienating. Mexican landscape in places resembles what Laruelle knows well, but the series of comparisons emerges into what by its sheer, sublime extension remains unknowable: the Sahara. From here it is only one further step to make it extraterrestrial, totally alien. This double direction of familiarizing and alienating is stylistically marked by oxymoronic phrases like "plunged up" and metaphorically visualized by the two "arms" of the plough, a common and familiar object here anthropomorphized and pitied for having been "abandoned" in a world of increasing and hostile strangeness. There is the opposition of green and black, but even the pretty and familiar, the nourishing ("loaves," "plough") is subject to a destructive process—"[t]he sun poured molten glass on the fields"—that in turn, like the country as a whole, can be stunningly beautiful. The description in its antonymic evocation or naming of hell-fire and paradise is representative for the novel as a whole in its continuous double movement between these two poles and in its continuous ambiguity, its metaphoric condensations creating, paradoxically, semantic openness and constant fluctuation.

Mexico, then, is a "place" in de Certeau's terms only on the simplest level of observation and description: where there is a volcano there cannot be a city. Almost immediately, though, it becomes a "space" that "occurs as the effect produced by the operations that orient it, situate it, temporalize it" (de Certeau 117). Where de Certeau is thinking more of discursive, that is historical, political, and social inscriptions of space, Mexico is here seen also and primarily as a projection of individual minds that may be more or less oriented by discursive traditions but are themselves part of an overall multilayered symbolic order, or rather a multiply connected rhizomatic process. The mountain chains form "between them a number of valleys and plateaux" (*Volcano*, 49)—indeed, some of the "thousand plateaus" described in Deleuze and Guattari's study. Nowhere is this more obvious than in the volcanoes. Popocatépetl and Iztaccíhuatl are the tragic lovers in indigenous myths and thus symbolize Geoffrey and Yvonne's fate. Although they are static topographical elements of "place," in the novel they seem to shift about, hide behind each other, and, although this is completely unrealistic from a location in Cuernavaca, in the perceiver's eye change size and proximity: "Popocatepetl towered through the window, its immense flanks partly hidden by rolling thunderheads; its peak blocking the sky, it appeared almost right overhead, the *barranca*, the Farolito, directly beneath it. Under the volcano!" (380). The Consul promptly remembers that Tartarus is located right under Mount Aetna and, once again, realizes that he is in hell and that his hopes of ascending Popocatépetl and thus divine heights will remain in vain.

There is no space here to point out similar processes connected with symbols like the garden, the *barranca*, the bars, the wheel, water and thirst, and so on. It is the multiple interconnectedness of the text, including its pervasive intertextuality both on the authorial and the figural level, that prevents the novel from becoming "a hideous and intolerable allegory" (Melville, *Moby-Dick*, 205). It is only on the symbolic level that an appearance like the following escapes what Moussong has called "unbearable weaknesses" and "heavy-handed distortions" in Lowry's perception of Mexico:

> Bent double, groaning with the weight, an old lame Indian was carrying on his back, by means of a strap looped over his forehead, another poor Indian, yet older and more decrepit than himself. He carried the older man and his crutches, trembling in every limb under this weight of the past, he carried both their burdens. (*Volcano*, 321)[16]

This, we may assume, is the epitome of what Lara Zavala has referred to as Lowry's identification with "the intimate tragedy of a whole country, Mexico."

# [12]

## POST-VIETNAM AND TWENTY-FIRST-CENTURY CANADIAN VISITORS

for reading north depends on south, and south, north: the idea of here discovers there . . .
—W. H. New, *Touching Ecuador* (74)

WITH MARGARET ATWOOD and Graeme Gibson we return to the publication period of the late 1970s to the early 1990s that produced so many interesting US American books on Latin America. Here, again, Vietnam is in the background, and the social changes and conflicts at home—and this now includes Canada—play a significant role. Gender problems are central for Atwood's *Bodily Harm* (1981). Questions of gender and sexual orientation will resurface in the novels discussed in the second part of this chapter, but now with points of reference bringing us up to our own, contemporary moment in history. It will be interesting to see if and how the Other and the discourse concerning it have changed, too.

If Canada in *Under the Volcano* is only a faint echo, a place of imaginary escape, the case is different with another chef-d'oeuvre, Margaret Atwood's powerful novel *Bodily Harm*. Here, Canada, Canadian life and perspectives are constantly present even in the foreign place where the protagonist tries to overcome her domestic traumata. Here, too, the inter-American plot pattern is rather simple: Rennie, a lifestyle journalist from Toronto, has several traumatic experiences, among them a partial mastectomy, the collapse of her love relationship, and her unsuccessful affair with her physician. She escapes to a fictitious Caribbean island state, where she wants to write a piece of travel journalism and hopes to recover emotionally. She has an affair with Paul, an American contraband runner, who helps her overcome her detachment from her own body. Mainly through Paul's ex-mistress Lora, she gets involved in the violent politics of the country and an aborted uprising against the repressive regime. She is arrested and from her cell witnesses the torture of members of the opposition and the brutal beating of Lora, whom she then nurses and comforts. What Rennie has learned is the interconnectedness of all sufferers; she is capable of putting her own woes into perspective. The open ending describes her possible release through the intercession of the Canadian Embassy, but, alternatively, she may never get out.

In part, the book is a feminist critique of patriarchal society, but Atwood transcends this level by making Rennie herself part of a culture of superficialities, a culture of narcissism. The picture of modern Canadian society is Atwood at her sardonic best. Her satire includes the well-intentioned but basically uninvolved Canadian policy regarding the Caribbean. An opposition politician Rennie meets on the plane pokes fun at the "'sweet Canadians'" (*Bodily Harm*, 29) and their ignorance about the real conditions. Indeed, it turns out that their purely touristy interest is another form of Western imperialist exploitation, less violent than the US American, CIA-managed intervention thematized by Asturias, but structurally not too different. In the final analysis, the oppressed people of that island country are seen as examples of feminine vulnerability and victimization. Thus, difference is represented mainly in terms of gender. Gender relations are a version of the power game, and as such reveal great similarities between the Caribbean and Canada—the Other is a mirror image of the self, and there is no escape from this very self. Fruitful reflections must take their start from this sobering insight.

Most critics have seen the novel as in line with other, earlier Atwood texts, such as *Life Before Man* or *Surfacing*, that is, as "Another Symbolic Descent" (Carrington), the story of a young urban woman trying to find or redefine her identity in the context of contemporary Canadian society. As in those other texts, the deep structure underlying the surface of consumerism and all-too-flippant interpersonal relations is the gender discourse defining the continuing asymmetrical binary relationship between men who, however "enlightened" and "emancipated" from traditional gender roles they may consider themselves, are nonetheless the heirs of patriarchalism, and women who will play modern variants of their inherited role of the comparatively less powerful. The motto from John Berger's *Ways of Seeing* that the author has put above the text seems to confirm this reading: "A man's presence suggests what he is capable of doing to you or for you. By contrast, a woman's presence . . . defines what can and cannot be done to her" (Atwood, *Bodily Harm*, 7). As in, for instance, Atwood's novel *Surfacing* or her writings on the position of Canadian culture and society vis-à-vis external pressure, *Bodily Harm* also addresses the question of the accomplicity or at least co-responsibility of the victims, their sustaining role in the system that seems to control them. The emphasis on gender relations turns the novel into a demonstration of universal structures of human, societal behavior and brings the question of cultural, Latin American alterity into the context of intergender alterity that might diminish the international aspects of the question of the Other. It will remain to be seen what relevance the theme of the cultural Other has, after all.

It is one of Atwood's great achievements that characters and events are and remain believable, although she doesn't aim at complex characterizations and although so many elements are symbolic or satiric abstractions. "The meaning of 'Renata,' 'born again,' and perhaps even of 'Wilford,' 'will ford' or 'will cross over,' suggests the symbolic significance of [. . .] questions about identity: this is the beginning of an inner journey" (Carrington 49), and this observation can be applied to symbolic elements that have been amply analyzed by critics: motif chains such as hands or touch, cameras and eyes; or symbols such as ropes and chains; verbal ambiguities such as (prison and cancer) cells.

Rennie Wilford is a lifestyle journalist living in Toronto with her partner Jake, a packaging specialist, with whom she has a relaxed, rather superficial relationship whose erotic side is enlivened by the slightly sado-masochistic games Jake likes to play with her. This relationship cannot survive the partial mastectomy Rennie has to undergo after breast cancer has been discovered. Their shared attention to surfaces is shattered, and Rennie feels dissociated from her body. She falls in love with her surgeon Daniel, her savior for the time being, whom she tries rather unsuccessfully to entangle in a love affair. When Rennie returns home and finds two rather macho police officers sitting in her kitchen and is informed that an unknown man has climbed into her apartment and waited for her before he was disturbed and got away, leaving a coil of rope on her bed, she is ready for a vacation in some tropical paradise. She gets an assignment to write a travel piece on the Caribbean island state of St. Antoine and St. Agathe. Here she has an affair with Paul, an American drug runner, gets to know Lora, Paul's former mistress and now the lover of Prince, an evangelical candidate for the office of prime minister. Another such candidate is Dr. Minnow, whom Rennie has met on the plane and who tries to make her write not about her touristy surface impressions, but about the political corruption under the government of Prime Minister Ellis. Ellis is said to appropriate much of the foreign aid for himself and his underlings while exploiting the population, all the while relying on a US Cold War interest in his strategically positioned country between Cuba and Grenada.

When the people realize that Ellis has rigged the elections and try to overthrow his regime, he quells the revolution by armed force. In the course of these events, Prince and Minnow get killed, and Rennie, who is suspected of involvement in the uprising, is incarcerated with Lora under horrible conditions in a cell in the old British fort. This is, as we learn only at the end, where the two women tell their respective life stories to one another, while the many third-person and present-tense passages serve to relate Rennie's current experiences, also using her as the focalizing character. At the end, after the two women have witnessed the torture of other prisoners, and after Lora has been brutally beaten and may be dying in Rennie's arms, Rennie imagines herself being saved by the intercession of the Canadian government—an escape, though, that may remain illusionary.[1] However, she has finally reached an awareness of what unites her with suffering mankind and has overcome her psychological detachment from other human beings. In this respect Rennie has been saved, whatever her fate may be.

Less than one-third of the pages are devoted to the women's Canadian memories, most of them Rennie's. These include other traumatizing experiences, notably her childhood in the ultraconservative town of Griswold, where her cold and distant grandmother was the dominating person. This woman succeeded in estranging Rennie from her body and making her unable to enjoy more than superficial physical intimacy. Another experience was Rennie's assignment to write about pornography, in the course of which she had to watch film material at the police department, culminating in a scene where a rat emerges from the vagina of a black woman. Whereas Rennie had thus far been able to ward off the sadistic violence of the material as unreal, here she feels "that a large gap had appeared in what she'd been used to thinking of as reality" (*Bodily Harm*, 210) and reacts with violent physical nausea. Lora, who is also Canadian but comes from an underclass environment, contributes memories of her stepfather's cruelty and hints at other encounters that have made her the hard-boiled woman she is.

Critics have emphasized the gender thematics because Rennie's essential life experiences consist of relationships with men and with the frustrated and petrified women of her family. Her realization of the vulnerability of her female body can also be associated with the expectations society has with regard to women's physicality. Much attention has also been given to Rennie's inner rebirth, to her recognition of her role as part of suffering, mortal humanity, and to her overcoming her distance from the Other:

> She doesn't have much time left, for anything. But neither does anyone else. She's paying attention, that's all.
>
> She will never be rescued. She has already been rescued. She is not exempt. Instead she is lucky, suddenly, finally, she's overflowing with luck, it's this luck holding her up. (301)

However, this does not mean that the Caribbean is simply a set of stage props for the moral issues discussed in this novel: social and, in particular, gender inequality. Indeed, some scholars have described Atwood's development in the direction of political fiction and have used her revisions to show

how these aspects gained greater prominence and were presented more and more drastically (cf. Patton; Reichenbächer). In one of the best studies of the novel published thus far, Simone Drichel examines its status as a postcolonial text and as a representation of a Levinasian ethics:

> [B]oth ethics and postcolonialism share an interest in the figure of "the other." However [. . .] the postcolonial other appears incompatible with the ethical other insofar as both "others" conceptually pull in conflicting directions. Where the postcolonial other invokes a certain ontological closure of politicized identity categories, the ethical other demands an opening up of such categories and pushes us beyond essence. (21)

For Drichel, *Bodily Harm* should not be regarded as a deficient postcolonial text not sufficiently presenting "the 'voice' of the Other" (Tiffin 130; Drichel 23). Instead, the novel reflects the murky postcolonial do-goodism of former settler colonies like Canada, whose role is not so much that of the (former) victims of colonialism than of the accomplices of neocolonialism, although they share a common colonial "mother country" with the plantation colonies in the Caribbean. It is precisely the policy of ill-advised foreign aid that Dr. Minnow ridicules in his frequent comments on the "sweet Canadians." Drichel applies to the novel Sartre's concept of the gaze as a means of de-subjectifying the Other, that is of turning her or him into an object. She points out that Rennie, victim of the male gaze of Jake, of the stranger who entered her apartment, of various policemen and others, is also a perpetrator: "a male gaze of which Rennie is the object in Canada is replicated in the neocolonial gaze of the tourist that Rennie brings to the islands" (Drichel 27).[2] Rennie, who is trying to regain her subjectivity by becoming "invisible" (*Bodily Harm*, 39) will for this purpose "train" her gaze and particularly her camera on others and the Other, "turning the violent gaze around and claiming the 'gun' for [her]self, [. . .] becoming complicit with the violations carried out by the gaze" (Drichel 29). This approach is supported by other "instruments" Rennie brings to bear on the Other: notebook and travel guide and, one might add, the components of the Canadian alterity discourse she is part of, Edward Said's "textual attitude" (Drichel 30), and that helps her to nostrify whatever she sees.

What saves her—in the metaphorical sense—is the collapse of this scopic regime of subject versus object when from her prison cell she watches the torture of an old deaf and dumb man who had formerly tried to bring her good luck by offering her his touch: "the hurt man's face is on a level with Rennie's own, blood pours down it, she knows who it is, the deaf and dumb man, who has a voice but no words, he can see her, she's been exposed, it's panic, he wants her to do something, pleading, *Oh please*" (*Bodily Harm*,

290). As Drichel points out, this scene of mutual looking amounts to an encounter with the real behind the gaze. It is at this point that Rennie becomes part of a Levinasian ethics of acknowledging "an 'other' who exceeds my conceptual grasp and therefore calls into question my self-certainty: 'The other person stands in a relation to me that exceeds my cognitive powers, placing me in question and calling me to justify myself'" (Drichel 44, quoting Critchley, "Deconstruction," 32). The achievement of the position of being-in-question, as Levinas calls it, requires traumatization, a corporeal and emotional exposition to the demands of the Other through the encounter with the real.

If Rennie's final vision of her return to Canada should come true, she will write about her experiences: "She will pick her time; then she will report. For the first time in her life, she can't think of a title" (*Bodily Harm*, 301). She will write about the real. However, we have no way of knowing what she will or would write—unless it would be the novel *Bodily Harm*!—and what response she would receive. We do not know if Lora will survive—after all, she is Canadian, too, so why isn't she present in the rescue fantasy? All that remains of her is a memory, and that bespeaks loss and closeness at the same time: Rennie "can feel the shape of a hand in hers, both of hers, there but not there, like the afterglow of a match that's gone out. It will always be there now" (300). In all likelihood, though, we have to take Rennie's fantasized rescue by the Canadian Embassy for what would probably happen, including the diplomatic efforts of hushing up the "incident" (294) of her incarceration. Thus, Atwood manages to turn what may be wish ful fillment even on the part of the reader into a mini-dystopia.

Even if the climax of the book is what Drichel has described as Rennie's coming face to face with the Levinasian Other, most of the novel consists of representations of what Rennie sees while she is not yet sufficiently called into question. The decisive events that bring about her rebirth, her reconciliation with her body and her mortality, and, above all, her opening up for the needs of other people, take place in an alien Latin American location. The fictional state of St. Antoine and St. Agathe is apparently vaguely modeled after St. Lucia and St. Vincent.[3] That is, it has a history of changing colonial ownership, but since the eighteenth century it was British until its very recent independence, which may be assumed to have been achieved in the late 1970s like that of the neighboring islands. Rennie's visit would have to have taken place in 1980—Paul explains the damaged trees by referring to "'Allan. [. . .] The hurricane'" (98)—Hurricane Allen ravaged that part of the Caribbean in that year. And when the Canadian official who takes Rennie out of the country in her final fantasy comments on the irrationality of local politics and on the need to humor Prime Minister Ellis, he tries to make her promise that she will not make her harrowing experiences public in order to prevent further political unrest: "*entre nous* we wouldn't want another Grenada on our hands" (296). This clearly refers to the bloodless overthrow of dictatorially ruling Grenada prime minister Eric Gairy by Maurice Bishop and his New Jewel Movement in March, 1979.[4] Bishop's attempts to introduce social reforms and to achieve more political, economic, and cultural independence by establishing balanced relations with the United States and the Soviet Union plus Cuba was regarded with great distrust by the US government that divided the countries in its "backyard" along the lines of Cold War divisions into friends and enemies.[5] Pinpointing the geographical setting of the novel and the approximate date of action helps us realize the political urgency of a text beyond the very limited insight of the traveling protagonist:

> I wanted to take somebody from our society where the forefront occupations are your appearance, your furniture, your job, your boyfriend, your health, and the rest of the world is quite a lot further back. And so your planning is, what am I going to do next year and the year after that, and if I stop smoking now, I won't get cancer in twenty years. That's not the way people in those countries think, because they can't afford to. They are thinking what is going to happen tomorrow or next week or how they will get through the immediate time. I wanted to take somebody from our society and put her into *that*, cause a resonance there. (Atwood qtd. in Ingersoll 227)

Most of *Bodily Harm* presents Rennie's tourist or travel writer construction of the Other and her defenses against anything that might call this view into question. That she (and the reader) gets any information about the islands, their history, their current politics, the corrupt government, the role of the CIA and the Cubans, the misplaced foreign aid, the abysmal social conditions, and so forth, is not her merit but Dr. Minnow's. He teaches by telling and by showing her what he thinks she should see, while she continues to refuse his request to write a report: "'I just don't do that kind of thing. I do lifestyles'" (*Bodily Harm*, 136). That Minnow is later killed by Marsden, the CIA *agent provocateur*,[6] gives his message the necessary seriousness. To complain about the book's lack of information and the missing "'voice' of the Other" (Tiffin 130) is to miss its point. As far as the Latin American Other is concerned, *Bodily Harm* is a novel about the shortcomings of the tourist view as a new version of imperialism. One of its ironies is that the negative components of this view, that is, sweeping stereotypes of Caribbean corruption, environmental pollution, and the threat of violence, turn out to be exactly true, although many specifics and additional details continue to escape Rennie's notice and remain absent.[7]

That this is intentional should be obvious from the many details that remain open but that belong to the discursively informed set of stereotypes often applied to the Caribbean islands or that are present in numerous works of fiction dealing with this area, notably thrillers, a genre with which *Bodily Harm* shares quite a few elements. Thus, Paul, a US American with a presumably traumatizing background as an agricultural adviser in Southeast Asia in the early stages of the Vietnam War, is the man who touches Rennie as she has never been touched before and enables her to reaccept her body; but he is also, or so Lora says, a drug runner and therefore a shady character occupying a strange position between the parties active on the island. There is, indeed, no reliable information concerning Paul nor any of the other characters because there is no authoritative source. Rennie is caught in a net of often conflicting hints, for instance concerning the risks of associating with Paul, Lora, or Minnow. Unlike in most thrillers, these uncertainties are never cleared up.[8]

Aspects of the Caribbean that escape Rennie's attention include, for instance, race. She notices there is only one white man on her plane from Barbados. And on St. Antoine, "[s]he's beginning to feel very white. Their blacks aren't the same as our blacks, she reminds herself; then sees that what she means by *our blacks* are hostile ones in the States, whereas *our blacks* ought to mean this kind. They seem friendly enough" (*Bodily Harm*, 39). For her, they are remote, and by refusing to further consider skin color, she skips the history of African slavery that has made the island population what it is, namely almost completely black. Just before the doctor's assignment that led to her operation, she "was working on a piece about drain-chain jewellery. You could [. . .] wear [drain chains] on any part of your anatomy: wrists, neck, waist, even ankles, if you wanted the slave-girl effect" (23–24)—this is as "close" as she ever gets to the issue of slavery. She never comments on the fact that the woman from whose vagina the rat was emerging was black, although she will remember the film document at the end when she compares this form of brutality with the torture routines of the police on St. Antoine. Black skin makes her uncomfortable insofar as it makes her stand out and thus prevents her desired "invisibility."

Another element of strangeness that hardly finds any attention is language. After all, one would expect people to speak some Creole version of English, but Rennie has difficulties understanding them only at the very beginning. When a police officer approaches her because he wants to sell her a ticket for a police benefit dance, she doesn't understand him:

> So they're only police, not soldiers. Rennie makes this out by reading the ticket, since she hasn't understood a word he's said.
>
> "I don't have the right kind of money," she says.
>
> "We take anything you got," he says, grinning at her, and this time she understands him. (36)

Henceforth, she understands perfectly well such utterances that she finds threatening. The form of English spoken on the islands is indicated by slight elements of substandard usage. Most of the time she associates with other foreigners, anyway. The problem of communication isn't one of language but of cultural codes, and there she has great difficulties. This is made most obvious in the scene with the deaf and dumb man who is trying to make her shake his hand because this means good luck. She does not understand his gestures and his following her; she feels increasingly threatened by what appears totally alien, until Paul shows up and saves the situation, while "she feels both rude and uncharitable" (75). "'Alien reaction paranoia,' says Paul. 'Because you don't know what's dangerous and what isn't, everything seems dangerous.'" (76).

Nature is another aspect that remains alien and, if noticed by Rennie at all, is experienced as increasingly threatening. She has come to the islands in order to "do a good Fun in the Sun" (16) article, and indeed in the patio of the best hotel in town, "there's a tree covered with red flowers, huge lobed blossoms like gigantic sweet peas; a dozen hummingbirds swarm around them. Below, on the other side of the curving stone wall, the surf crashes against the rocks just as it is supposed to, and a fresh wind blows off the Atlantic" (90). But before, she has discovered a centipede in her sink, "ten inches long at least, with far too many legs, blood-red, and two curved prongs at the back, or is it the front? [. . .] It looks venomous" (60). And she has been down to the beach, which turns out to be not "one of the seven jewel-like beaches with clean sparkling iridescent sand advertised in the brochure. It's narrow and gravelly and dotted with lumps of coagulated oil, soft as chewing gum and tar-coloured. The sewage pipe runs into the sea" (79). When she drives through the forest with Paul, she sees "huge hothouse trees draped with creepers, giant prehistoric ferns, obese plants with rubbery ear-shaped leaves and fruit like warts, like glands" (98).

That is, the elements of alterity Rennie encounters and takes note of—nature, language, touch—appear as dangerous or abject, disgusting. So does the food, from the "airplane sandwich, slightly rancid butter and roast beef, rotting meat" (49) to the "guava jelly, too sweet, dark orange, and of the consistency of ear wax" (62). Fear and disgust are always closely related:

> The number of things Rennie thinks ought to happen to her in foreign countries is limited, but the number of things she fears may happen is much larger. She's not a courageous traveller, though she's always argued that this makes her a good travel writer. [. . .] Someday, if she keeps it up, she'll find herself beside a cauldron with an important local person offering her a sheep's eye or the boiled hand of a monkey, and she'll be unable to refuse. (127)

Yet what are external, alien sources of fear and disgust soon turn out to be aspects of the self. The camp of hurricane refugees in the fort that Dr. Minnow makes her visit, people who have been neglected by the government, has "the smell of bodies, of latrines and lime and decaying food" (125). Soon enough, Rennie will find herself imprisoned in a cell in this very fort together with Lora, and the bucket containing their own urine and feces will smell much worse.

As in Rumaker's "Gringos," the discourses of gender and alterity meet in the abject, but the theme is developed much more radically. Reading the first chapters of Julia Kristeva's *Powers of Horror: An Essay on Abjection* leaves the impression of holding a psychoanalytic tool kit for an analysis of *Bodily Harm*. The abject as what "does not respect borders, positions, rules. The in-between, the ambiguous, the composite" (*Powers* 4), the breakdown of the internalized Puritan order of Griswold is what bothers Rennie's system of surfaces. Her distinctions include lifestyles, genders, ethnic alterity, and also class, as becomes apparent when she meets Lora and dislikes her for her underclass manners. Yet Lora, being turned into an object by Rennie's gaze, reveals some elements of the abject that puts the subject-object distinction and, indeed, that of inside and outside into question:

> "You smoke?" says the woman. The fingers holding the cigarette are bitten to the quick, stub-tipped, slightly grubby, the raw skin around the nails nibbled as if mice have been at them, and this both surprises Rennie and repels her slightly. She wouldn't want to touch this gnawed hand, or have it touch her. She doesn't like the sight of ravage, damage, the edge between inside and outside blurred like that. (*Bodily Harm*, 86)

Repeatedly, Rennie has the fear of being turned inside out herself. When "the scar is pulling [. . .] she's afraid to look down, she's afraid she'll see blood, leakage, her stuffing coming out" (22). She tries to keep Lora at a distance, but the end of the novel shows her cradling Lora's battered face in her lap, a pietà scene, in which Rennie realizes the maternal as closely connected with the abject: "Abjection preserves what existed in the archaism of pre-objectal relationship, in the immemorial violence with which a body becomes separated from another body in order to be" (Kristeva, *Powers*, 10). Going back to the rejected maternal abject means going back behind language, behind the symbolic, behind signification, to what Kristeva calls the semiotic, the *chora*, the motherly body as a "receptacle" (14). In accepting Lora's unrecognizable face as that of the Levinasian Other, she identifies the situation with that perverted birth scene of the rat, "something small and grey and wet" (*Bodily Harm*, 210), coming out of the black woman's vagina. That is, she identifies with the tortured woman, the tortured animal. And whereas she threw up when she saw that film, she doesn't now:

> Very carefully, this is important, she turns Lora over [. . .]. She hauls Lora over to the dryest corner of the room and sits with her, pulling Lora's head and shoulders onto her lap. She moves the sticky hair away from the face, which isn't a face any more, it's a bruise, blood is still oozing from the cuts, [. . .] the mouth looks like a piece of fruit that's been run over by a car, pulp, Rennie wants to throw up, it's no one she recognizes, she has no connection with this, there's nothing she can do, it's the face of a stranger, someone without a name, the word *Lora* has come unhooked and is hovering in the air, apart from this ruin, mess, there's nothing she can even wipe this face off with, all the cloth in this room is filthy, septic, except her hands, she could lick this face, clean it off with her tongue, that would be the best, that's what animals did, [. . .] she can't do it, it will have to do, it's the face of Lora after all, there's no such thing as a faceless stranger, every face is someone's, it has a name.
>
> She's holding Lora's left hand, between both of her own, perfectly still, nothing is moving, and yet she knows she is pulling on the hand, as hard as she can, there's an invisible hole in the air, Lora is on the other side of it and she has to pull her through, she's gritting her teeth with the effort, she can hear herself, a moaning, it must be her own voice, this is a gift, this is the hardest thing she's ever done.
>
> She holds the hand, perfectly still, with all her strength. Surely, if she can only try hard enough, something will move and live again, something will get born. (298–99)

In this scene, Rennie is born again, and perhaps Lora, too, when Rennie calls her by her name: "'Lora,' she says. The name descends and enters the body, there's something, a movement; isn't there?" (299). The encounter with the abject, the identification with the primal birth scene, does not prevent a return to the level of signification, but we learn about the permeability of the border between the semiotic and the symbolic, between the maternal and the patriarchal, between self and Other. It is important to notice that the tortured old man is deaf and dumb, and therefore his appeal to Rennie is without language. However, his gift of the touch of hands is one that will enable Rennie to overcome her disgust of the abject, to accept it as part of herself. "Abjection is a resurrection that has gone through death (of the ego)" (Kristeva, *Powers*, 15).

It is also important to remember that the abject is not simply to be equated with morality nor with victimhood. If "[t]he abject [. . .] neither gives up nor assumes a prohibition, a rule, or a law; but turns them aside, misleads, corrupts" (*Powers*, 15), that also functions on the social level: "Corruption is [. . .] the socialized appearance of the abject" (16). The corruption of the island government is what Minnow and Prince resent and try to resist, and it is Lora's realization that Prince has been murdered that brings her to her violent, self-destructive confrontation with the prison guards, a scene in which Rennie is helpless but that she has to see—"why isn't someone covering her eyes?" (*Bodily Harm*, 293)—and thereby experience the final breakdown of her objectifying gaze. And yet she will remember that what is reflected in the tinted glasses of the policemen is her own face, her own gaze. Her rebirth is not simply a switching to the other side but a realization of her border situation: "We may call [the abject] a border; abjection is above all ambiguity" (*Powers*, 9).

And Rennie is only at the beginning. After all, Lora is her compatriot; Rennie does not, and does not have to, take care of the Latin American Other unless by her future writing, should she ever get to that. The man who gives her back her body is a US American, not a local person. Rennie remains within the context of North American voices on the Caribbean,[9] and she keeps at a distance from the one local spokesperson who is trying to change her perspective, Dr. Minnow, until it is too late. However, if Atwood succeeds in representing the limitations and perversions of the tourist gaze, she also succeeds in having her protagonist reach the border of her self-other distinctions as related to gender, class, and ethnicity, which might make her capable of writing about the island situation with indignation and compassion but without further nostrification of the Other. The novel shows human suffering in Canada and the Caribbean, in the north mainly as a consequence of a discourse of gender inequality, in the south in the perpetuation of a colonial discourse on the "natural" social and economic inequality between those in power and the majority of the population. Rennie realizes that wherever she is, she has to be "afraid of men because men are frightening, [. . .] there's no longer a *here* and a *there*" (*Bodily Harm*, 290). What she is beginning to see, however, is that gender inequality is a form of patriarchally generated social inequality and cannot be reduced to nor excused as some kind of male "nature." Social inequality is a practically universal phenomenon, but its manifestations differ widely, as Atwood's interview comment quoted earlier insists. When Rennie recognizes her own implication in this system, her own ambiguity, as it were, she may, nay might, yet turn into a model for a better Canadian approach to the southern neighbors. In this sense, she overcomes the half-heartedness discernible in the US novels of the post-Vietnam era of covert warfare discussed in Chapter 8.

ATWOOD'S ACHIEVEMENT IN REPRESENTING the encounter with the Other through the contacts of bodies, through physical fear and desire, through the interplay of power and powerlessness connected with the gaze, is rarely matched in inter-American literature. One other such text is the brilliant short story "Pancho Villa's Head" (1986) by Atwood's partner Graeme Gibson.[10] The nine-page story is set at Palenque in 1972,[11] at a restaurant where a local rancher plays the role of host. His grandiloquent comments on King Edward's abdication in favor of his love relationship with an American woman cease with the arrival of his nephew, a local police officer who intimidates all of the guests and finally has the young father of a small Indian family at one of the tables arrested and led off. No reason is given, although the officer mentions "*guerilleros* and hippies" ("Pancho," 26) and calls his action "*solamente una precaución*" (27). The whole event is witnessed by a "tourist," who serves as focalizing figure.

The other characters around are a middle-aged US woman, a young Canadian whose angry remarks about police violence make the others afraid for his—and their own—safety, and the Indian family consisting of the wife, two young daughters and a baby—a harmonious group the others hate to see broken up by the arrest. The tourist's perception is restricted by his drunkenness and his insufficient command of Spanish that allows him to understand only fragments of what is being spoken. In a lengthy flashback, he remembers his and his wife's train ride here, during which she mentioned that someone had stolen Pancho Villa's head[12] and they were disturbed by the noises of lovemaking from the adjacent compartment where a Mexican army officer and his girlfriend spend the ride. The story marvelously conveys the incredibly tense atmosphere, the alienity of the country (Why would anyone steal the head of the revolutionary leader? What is going on at the restaurant?), the fears and desires arising from the situation. The tourist was annoyed but also aroused by the amatory noise on the train that set his imagination going. He now feels faintly attracted by the American woman, and when he creeps into the hotel bed where his wife has been sleeping, he wants sex with her, only to encounter her disgusted refusal.

However, sexual desire, the alternation of attraction and revulsion, is only one strand connecting the impressions of the night. Noises—the small animals in the thatch overhead, the laughter from the table of the Indian family, the quality of voices and articulation ("'Hippies!' Coughing the glottal H, a small, derisive explosion" [26]), the presence or absence of music—and sight impressions—"As the rancher shook his head, admiringly, highlights flashed in his eyes. One side of his moustache appeared in meticulous detail, then retreated into shadow" (20)—shape the picture. What is even more impressive are gestures and touch that accompany or sometimes replace spoken communication or expression: the rancher "was pivoting slowly in a frozen shrug; his forearms were raised in front of his body, the palms of his hands upturned, as if to receive an answer" (21), and then he grasps the tourist's hand as if to enforce his request. Ambivalent gestures between physical aggression and tenderness occur several times. The American woman "tossed her head, rolling her eyes in mock horror at the noise. As the tourist stared at her thin, sharp mouth, the column of her throat, she ran her fingers through her hair, briefly uncovering a delicate ear. He imagined taking the lobe of it gently between his teeth" (22). The climax of such ambivalence is reached when the police captain approaches the Indian family where the mother is breastfeeding her baby.

> The policeman didn't sit, but leaned over the young mother, as if to admire her baby. "*Buenas noches*," he said, and then, after a pause—"*Señora*." The Indian woman bobbed her head without raising her eyes. Her hair, the colour of gun metal, was drawn with white ribbons into a braid. Puffing lightly, without inhaling, her husband held his cigarette between thumb and forefinger, as if he didn't hear the insinuating voice.
>
> The officer placed his hand on the baby's skull, with his fingers around it, as if he were selecting a melon. [. . .] When the Captain turned the tiny head until its face appeared, a moist brown nipple slipped from its mouth. The woman moved to rearrange her blouse, but the policeman brushed her hand aside. "*La cena*," he laughed explosively. Supper, don't interrupt its supper. The tourist desperately wanted a drink but the American had seized his arm, her nails cutting into the flesh beneath his sleeve. (23)

Perhaps better than any other text discussed in this book, this story presents the immediate goings-on, what is gripping, mentally and physically exciting beneath all the clichés, of which there are many: police brutality, the Mexican fascination with death, the silly, excitement-bent behavior of the foreign visitors ("the tourist only stayed in the vague hope that something might happen" [20]), the rancher's ruminations about the ideal form of love, and so on. The captain's contempt for the tourists is justified: "'Your Canadian comes here. His fingernails are dirty, but not from work. His hands are soft like a woman's'" (28). The visitors do not understand what is going on but experience it as a drama that conforms to their stereotypes. However, beyond all that appears as stereotypically alien, there is the revelation that human behavior follows certain patterns, no matter how remote the participants of a constellation may appear from one another. The gaze can be reversed and is reversed. Deep structures are revealed in the spontaneous emotions expressed by gestures more than by words, and by sense impressions not yet sufficiently filtered by cultural predispositions. The mystery of Pancho Villa's head seems to point in the direction of mortality as a human condition:

> The Captain's round, dark face, its eyes languorous now, contemplated the tourist with apparent interest. What could he mean, dangerous? How was he different?

> But the Captain only shrugged. He knew it was absurd, that the game somehow continued, but the tourist sensed the way shadows played upon his face. It was as if his expression no longer concealed the skull beneath its flesh. (28)

Who, here, is "he"? Intercultural communication has a level of deep, bodily knowledge that is intercultural, indeed appears to be universal and undercuts any discursive formation.

THREE DECADES LATER WE may ask how the Canadian discourse concerning Latin America as reflected in fictional literature may have changed, may have moved beyond the stasis indicated by the *Globe and Mail* comment quoted at the beginning of the previous chapter, that is, the lack of serious political interest, and beyond the self-criticism characterizing Atwood's novel. After all, Canada's role in the world has grown, NAFTA has brought a shared economic market with at least one major Latin American country, and Canadian society has grown multicultural due, also, to the influx of immigrants from Latin America and the Caribbean. And Canadian culture has become much richer and diversified. At the same time, things in Latin America have changed dramatically: the enormous growth of populations; the rise of at least Mexico and Brazil to the status of semi-industrial countries and, in the case of Brazil, of a coming world power; the demise of most military dictators; the greater political freedom of action due to the end of the Cold War; the accelerated destruction of natural habitats; the worsening situation in the field of drug production and trafficking; the rise of new leftist leaders and movements in Venezuela, Bolivia, Ecuador, Mexico, and other countries; and the reawakening of indigenous populations are just a few factors that have changed the social and political landscape in major parts of Latin America. How does literature respond to these developments?

Space does not permit an analysis of George Szanto's impressive Mexican trilogy beginning with *The Underside of Stones*, initially (1990) published as a "story cycle" and later reclassified as a novel when *The Condesa of M.* (2001) and *Second Sight* (2004) were added, the latter a novel filling in the temporal space between the other two texts. *The Underside of Stones* is somehow positioned between Mexican American writer Josephina Niggli's story cycle *Mexican Village* (1945) and postmodernism, with elements of magical realism added. It establishes the figure of the narrator, Szanto's somewhat fictionalized alter ego Jorge, a Canadian criminology professor spending a year in the fictional Mexican village Michoácuaro in the real state of Michoacán in order to get over the death of his wife. Michoácuaro as a world of physical locations, characters, and events is constructed by stories that find their way into the second-level stories written down by Jorge.

The wonderful balance and ambivalence between the factual and the (cultural) imaginary, between what Jorge can accept as real and another reality he is exposed to and that enters his awareness of the Other, is not kept up the same way in *Second Sight*, which is more of a political crime mystery, nor in *The Condesa of M.*, where the intertwining of a historical and a present-day thread of narrative, as well as the experienced presence of characters from the past, create a form of romance (in the Hawthornian sense) and shift the balance in the direction of magical realism. In all three books, we get abundant information about contemporary Mexico, the roles of the church and the PRI (Partido Revolucionario Institutional, the Mexican Institutional Revolutionary Party), folk practices and the clash of tradition and modernity. What makes the books particularly rewarding is the oscillation of Jorge's role as the superior, all-knowing rationalist and criminologist from "Norte America"—people here do not seem to make much difference between Canada and the United States—and as the ignorant, fumbling foreigner not knowing if he can trust what he sees and, particularly, hears. This oscillation makes for wonderful situational ironies that are in many cases exemplary for the encounter of North and Latin Americans.

I will focus instead on novels published since 2007. My first example, *The Buenos Aires Broken Hearts Club* (2007) by Jessica Morrison (aka Jessica Raya), is chick lit, pure and simple, and might be seen as a watered-down version of *Bodily Harm*. In a single day, the twenty-eight-year-old protagonist Cassie loses her job, her apartment, and her fiancé. During a drunken spree, she books a six-month stay in Buenos Aires. After her initial panic is overcome, she finds most people friendly and the city not really that different from what she is familiar with. She has an affair with a fantastic Latin lover, sleeps a few times with a perfect but finally boring American, and eventually winds up in the arms of Mateo, an Argentine painter. She has used her blog to tell the world about her troubles and goes on to create a commercially successful website for broken hearts exchanges, which enables her to stay with Mateo for good. The worst bodily harm Cassie complains about is that she hasn't had sex for four weeks. She gets to know very little about Argentina because all she cares for are personal relationships. Thus, if *Bodily Harm* reveals the sameness of the Other in terms of oppression and victimization, *The Buenos Aires Broken Hearts Club* shows the Other as similar because the needs of young women concerning love and a good income are the same throughout the hemisphere. Morrison avoids the question of a specifically Canadian perspective by making her protagonist come from Seattle rather than from her own city, Vancouver, but that doesn't lead to sharper conflicts. Thus, in another way than in Atwood's novel, the gender discourse reduces cultural difference and leaves only that of men and women. Both genders are lovely and lovable, at least in the shape of quite a few individuals Cassie meets.

Cassie remains more on the surface than even Atwood's Rennie in her life in Canada. Although the Argentine metropolis has its specific architectural and cultural attractions, the Other appears as more or less the same, at least on the level of personal relations, which is what counts most for the protagonist. The one moment when Cassie might get involved more deeply is when she sees *Las madres*, the weekly march of the mothers of those who "were disappeared" during the period of the Dirty War against leftist dissenters. After learning what this is all about, she gets a closer look and has to admit, "It is a truly heartbreaking sight. Yet also one pouring out hope and love" (*Buenos Aires*, 134). However,

> I step into the shadow of a tree, feeling that I am somehow intruding on a private moment, a glimpse into their country's great grief not meant for my foreign eyes. But mostly, I am suddenly, deeply, to-the-core-of-my-bones ashamed of the way I've been acting about Antonio. Such self-indulgent behavior, and over someone I barely know. What is his [temporary!] disappearance compared to the loss they have suffered? I spot a nearby table with pamphlets and a collection jar. I take out all the paper money I have in my wallet and shove it into the jar. (134–35)

This is the level of profundity and social responsibility Cassie is allowed to reach. She sympathizes with the women, she writes about her encounter in her blog and also raises money for *Las madres*, and on a later occasion she is even pulled into the circle of the marching women by an Argentine friend and experiences a warm "'Well come'" (283), but the question at the core of *Bodily Harm*, the universality of suffering and guilt, remains alien for Cassie. If the Other turns out to be much like the self, what remains truly different has to be repressed or safely pigeonholed in a slot called, for instance, "commiseration." It never occurs to Cassie that as a US citizen, she has inherited some national historic guilt in this matter because of the support of the American government for the Argentine military dictatorship during its Dirty War against the leftist opposition. Her sympathy, much like a donation to a beggar at the corner, may contribute to making her appear a nicer character, but this is simply not her world, not her generation.

In a sense, however, this might amount to a welcome break in the discursive association of Latin America with violence. It remains to be seen if other texts will pursue this course in a more complex manner. Amanda Hale's *The Reddening Path* (2007) isn't one of them. On the contrary, it explores the topic of political repression far beyond what Atwood tried to do in *Bodily*

*Harm*. The ambitious novel tells of the search of Paméla, the twenty-two-year-old adopted daughter of a lesbian couple from Toronto, to find her biological, her Maya mother in Guatemala. The mother, Fabiana, a victim of the genocidal war of the rightist Guatemalan government and military against the indigenous population during the last decades of the twentieth century, turns out to have survived first as the mistress of a member of the ruling class who exploits the fourteen-year-old girl sexually and is, indeed, Paméla's father, and later as mistress of Ernesto, a high-ranking army officer, one of the killers. Paméla fails to take her mother back to Canada but is instead joined by Guadalupe, a young nun, another Maya war orphan, with whom she falls in love. As a parallel narrative, we get a fictionalized version of the life of Malinche, the Native mistress, guide, translator, and eventually victim of Hernán Cortés during and after the conquest of Mexico; that is, part of the book is a historical novel. Prologue and epilogue are rendered by Ixchel, the ancient Mexican goddess of weaving, water, the moon, and childbirth; she knows all, laments, and accepts.

Thus, the fates of the present-day Maya women are shown to be part of a 500-year-old war against the Native population and, also, an age-old war against women. Canada remains sketchy, as do Paméla's foster mothers Fern and Hannah; it appears as a clean, well-lighted place playing a positive humanitarian role in contrast to the United States, which is involved in the Guatemalan atrocities. Two rationales for the intrusions into Mexico and Central America are schematically opposed: male conquest and exploitation versus female search for one's mother and for love in general. The feminization of Latin America here reaches its peak. Where *The Buenos Aires Broken Hearts Club* all but negates cultural difference, *The Reddening Path* emphasizes it, but, much more strongly than *Bodily Harm*, analogizes it to the difference between victims and victimizers, which is here shown to be primarily that between women and men but also between the indigenous population and the European conquerors.[13]

*The Reddening Path*, a novel clearly related to ideas and topics of Third Wave feminism, is an important book because it drastically addresses the horrors of what is euphemistically called the "human rights violations" during the civil war in Guatemala, and because it points out the continuity of the power structure even today and hence the fragility and, sometimes, superficiality of the peace accord of 1996. It thereby reminds the North American reader of what occurred on the same continent and often with the approval and support of US governmental institutions and agencies.[14] And because this is a Canadian novel, it might serve to remind the Canadian public of the infamous role played by Canadian mining companies in their collaboration with the Guatemalan government and the military, for instance in the eviction and silencing of Maya farmers on land coveted by the companies, although this issue is not mentioned in the book. The novel is also important because it shows the identity problems of the thousands of indigenous children from Latin America who were adopted by Canadian or US American foster parents.

However, one might wish that these topics had been handled with more literary skill. Rarely is the language up to the complexities of Paméla's situation. There are vestiges of a somewhat clichéd *écriture féminine*, for instance in the importance of dreams and other nonrational modes of approaching reality, but one has the feeling that the dreams of the characters are props to connect the various strands of the book and do not really open a symbolic level as they do in *Bodily Harm*. Hale's introduction of the narrating, weaving goddess in the book's frame resembles Leslie Marmon Silko's use of the Pueblo Indian creator deity Thought-Woman in her novel *Ceremony*. However, while even Silko's use of traditional sacred material was sometimes regarded as a problematic handling of religious taboos, even though the author is a tribal member, in Hale's case the use of Maya mythic material amounts to cultural appropriation and epistemic violence. Similarly, modern indigenous characters such as Guadalupe's village friend and advisor Chavela are used as focalizers just as easily as any others. Cultural alterity does not seem to be insurmountable in Hale's view, and real alienity does not exist.[15] Clearly, the parallelization of the fates of Malintzín/Malinche with those of the modern Maya women Paméla, Guadalupe, and Fabiana serves to demonstrate the continuity of the victimization of indigenous women and children, of genocidal violence, and of acts of betrayal.

For this purpose, the character of Malintzín is fictionalized and psychologized. As a child betrayed by her own mother and sold into slavery, she is in a way exculpated for her choosing Cortés as a protector and for committing treason against other indigenous populations, only to become a victim of betrayal once again when Cortés discards her. Yet the second function of this character is to make her the mother of *mestizaje*, the hybridization of races, peoples, and cultures, a process that is here anachronistically accelerated: "Everywhere he [Malintzín and Cortés's son Martín] looked there were people like himself, mestizos with golden skin and almond-shaped eyes, not quite Spanish, not quite Indian" (*Reddening Path*, 305).[16] In addition, Cortés's sons already prefigure Creole resistance against the Spanish "motherland." In this way, the ending is conciliatory even if Fabiana cannot escape her enthrallment by her captor—the complex psychology behind this or behind Ernesto's laying his guilt complex at rest in her arms is only hinted at. The motif of hunger and the craving for food is well developed, and that of weaving as a metaphor of feminine and divine forms of creativity, though somewhat cliché-ridden, is also put to good use, but on the whole there remains a feeling of disappointment about the unassimilated material and the unexplored depths of the alterity theme that offers itself for instance in the topic of adoption. The conciliatory, in some sense even escapist tendency of the book is made abundantly clear in the scene of Cortés's death:

> He knew himself scalpel of the king, scourge of the Gods, his greed and passion for power used to effect an inevitable evolution in which culture supplants nature. [. . .] As he rose above the earth, above the ocean, he saw the small part he had played in a great design, and he knew himself finally as essential and expendable. He was forgiven. (299)

Apart from the sheer sentimentality, this is an exoneration not only from the atrocities committed by Cortés and his troops, but from the European conquest of the Americas with all its consequences. "Nature" is here clearly associated with the indigenous population, a notion that one would have hoped had been long overcome, just like the nature-culture dichotomy. When Guadalupe joins her lover Paméla in Canada, we may discover a fictional glorification of a Canadian multiculturalism that would include not only Native and immigrant populations of any variety, but also sexual minorities and so forth, a northern vision that allows one to forget the intergroup horrors of the past and the present.

Although listed as detective fiction, Anthony Hyde's *A Private House* (2007) is much more satisfactory as a work of literature. The novel repeats the pattern of sending female visitors to Latin America. This time there are two: Lorraine, an elderly Canadian widow who has to fulfill the somewhat unlikely wish of her and her husband's deceased gay friend of handing a large sum to his former Cuban lover, Almado; and Mathilde, a youngish French journalist who has come to Havana to interview Bailey, a former Black Panther who has escaped to Cuba, and to hear his comments on Cuba in the twilight of the Castro regime. Mathilde falls in love with Bailey and they have a fulfilling affair before her return. Temporarily, she is under the influence of a beautiful lesbian and tourist-exploiting guide, Adamaris. Mathilde also helps Lorraine in her increasingly mystery-ridden quest for Almado, who turns out to be not only a male prostitute but also a petty criminal who may or may not have committed a murder in order to get hold of the passport of a young Canadian, Hugo, who has an uncanny resemblance to Almado.

Lorraine finds herself unable to unriddle the mysteries of identity and possible crime, but nonetheless leaves the money for Almado before her return to Canada. What is more important is that she overcomes her fits of agoraphobia in view of the strangeness and heat of the Cuban capital as well as her narrow religious background with the help of Santería doctors and priestesses. This is part of the strength of the novel: its depictions of many aspects of contemporary Cuban life and society, from the urban topography to the rites of black religion, from the political atmosphere to the aesthetic impressions of the city, above all its sordid decay. Whether all these details are correct is beside the point: they are rendered as observed by outsiders—a Canadian woman, a French woman, and a black US American man who has spent decades in the country. But fortunately, Hyde commands a literary style that is capable both of incredibly precise realism and of metaphorical openness and indirection.

While the political complexities—Black Panther revolutionary ideas then and now, the fate of Castroism, and the disastrous impact of the US embargo on the common people—are mainly left to the conversations between Mathilde and Bailey, it is the Canadian Christian widow Lorraine who experiences the Other most drastically. Given the economic situation, it cannot come as a surprise that just about everybody the visitors meet is a hustler of some variety, but when Lorraine buys powdered milk for a young couple who claim to need it for their baby and then returns to the store only to witness how the milk is reexchanged into money, with a percentage for the saleswoman, she is overwhelmed by shame and revulsion but unsure whether these feelings are directed against the people who perpetrated the scam or against herself—as a gullible person but also as a person not willing to give unconditionally. Her conflicting impulses toward the Other and herself bring her to the brink of collapse as her agoraphobia overwhelms her:

> All these streets ran into the labyrinth of the ancient city, Habana Vieja. O'Reilly. Obispo. Obrapia. One was as good as another; whichever one she took, that was where she ran. But the street was jammed with people, talking, walking, pushing, looking. She tried to get by. More lay ahead. And the road was so rough, so broken, so cracked, so cut across, so holed, that now she couldn't run, she could barely walk, and all the horror that her steps had fled now caught her, seized her by the legs, wrapped round her thighs, crushed her buttocks and her back—she was rigid now. She staggered. She looked around. She wanted to cry out, I need help. Her voice was still. Voices, faces, pressed upon her. Signs: *No Arrojar Basura . . . Un Mundo Mejor Es Possible . . . La Cita Es Con La Patria . . . Giron Triunfo del Pueblo*—they seemed to be everywhere. She stumbled into a cross street. She was gasping. She was so afraid. (*Private House*, 69)

What saves Lorraine shortly afterward is a group of schoolboys playing marbles whose rules of game she manages to decipher. Alienity isn't total;

some communication is possible. She is later courageous enough to explore the whereabouts of Almado on her own. When she enters the derelict building he is supposed to inhabit, she encounters "a dark, Gothic fantasy world" (227) where the abject seems to be the distinguishing feature: "It was an odour infinitely older than anything she might encounter in her native land; poverty, misery, and death distilled into the stench of eternity" (226). And then she inspects Almado's mattress:

> It was an awful sight. And yet now she knelt, sinking down through her own astonishment, and placed the palm of her hand on it and then forced herself to clench her fingers, seizing a fold of the cloth. Pity flowed into her, when she might have expected disgust. She reached out again, and with the tips of her fingers touched a dark, stiff patch of the fabric, like a scab or the lesion of some ghastly disease. [. . .] She knew she wasn't pitying Almado, certainly not, not even Hugo. Was it Murray? Dear Murray, lying on this bed. He had lain with this man. He had shared his body, on some bed. And wasn't it only chance, or the grace of God, that had placed Murray in his bed, and Almado here? But then that was true of everyone, including herself. She reached out, trailing her fingers across all the dreadful stains she could reach, blood, shit, semen, whatever they were; but they were what everyone was, even if their feather beds and their silk pyjamas allowed them the delusion that they were deserving, and something else. She closed her eyes. *You can pray anywhere*, Don used to say, but no, I can't, I can't pray here, she thought. It was too terrible a place. (228)

When she then discovers what she thinks are vestiges of Hugo's murder, Lorraine's panic returns. What saves her now and in a more fundamental way is her encounter with an alien religion. As a devout Christian North American, she yields herself to the rituals of Santería and thereby experiences in a positive, healing and liberating way the effects of a situation of religious transdifference. And she realizes that the causes of her panic are not only things "'out there'" but "claustrophobic spaces" like that "horrid room" (242) as well: "So she was afraid of something horrible and murderous inside herself, presumably Freudian—she was trying to flee it, deny it—but even if she'd wanted to murder her mother, she hadn't. Had her mother murdered her? Was there a dead body inside her, lurking—was she really a zombie?" (242–43). Lorraine encounters the abject as the ambiguous core of the real and can henceforth, after her healing ceremony, accept the union of the self and the Other in the ambiguities of identity, murder and rescue, home and abroad.

In this novel, for once, we have the Other in its finally indecipherable strangeness, and it is the experience and not the complete correctness of the observation that is important. Identity positions are fluid, shifting: white and black, gay and straight, Native and non-Native, European, Canadian, US American, and Cuban are no fixed categories. Near the end, Lorraine even wonders whether the Almado she has met may have been Hugo, the Canadian, in disguise, whether he may have killed Almado rather than the other way around. Now she and, in a different way, Mathilde, too, are capable of accepting the openness of existence in all its constellations. Differences are not explained away, but allegiances may go in several directions at the same time. The superimposition of ethnic, gender, and sexual discourses creates transdifference, the simultaneous experience as conflicting subject positions. Both protagonists return home with a changed identity, and in this respect the book follows an old pattern in inter-American fiction. However, the metaphor of agoraphobia or, more generally, the fear of other places, and the overcoming of this fear, may be the author's message for his Canadian compatriots in these days of global connection, change, and fluctuation.

HERE, AS IN INTER-AMERICAN literature at large, some such message seems to be represented best not in fiction but in the condensations of poetry, as in William H. New's lovely volume *Touching Ecuador* (2006):

> Colour: it rustles
> everywhere,
> *which way to look first*, everything is
> unfamiliar, tourist
>
> becomes traveller
> in the slow upheaval of connecting:
>
> touching difference as soon as familiarity: laugh, you cry; travel, you stay at home: nowhere is without the way you see it, words, words, corruptibility:
>
> *Learn by seeing*, the monks averred: *I turn, I look,*
> *I see*—how architects built llamas into the walls of
> the new church, tortoises and condors among
> the saints and gargoyled demons:
>
> Boundaries: who knew how far the flock would stray—
>
> (16)

# POSTSCRIPT

READING AND, YES, CRITICISM, are encounters with the Other. The vast body of inter-American fiction is only an example of this universal condition. We have seen the limits of identity-thinking both present and dissolving. Fictional characters have experienced situations and conditions of transdifference in multiple ways. Usually, their epistemological uncertainty, the ambiguities of the familiar and the foreign, outside and within, goes hand in hand with some moral problem, the need to decide and the undecidability of the issue, or the contamination, the insufficiency of any position. My preferences lie, clearly, with those writers, those works that do not conform to the binarisms of the alterity discourse but dive into the jungle of uncertainties. This is hardly a new approach—seven or more types of ambiguity have been landmarks in the exploration of literary greatness for a long time. However, transdifference goes beyond semantics. To represent the exposure of literary characters to conflicting but simultaneously present conditions, affiliations, or perceptions, to represent cognitive or affective dissonance, demands highly complex literary techniques and stylistic means. The empathetic reader or critic will share some such experiences of transdifference. She or he will also experience transdifference of a second order: the irruption of the alien into the conceptual framework of both the aesthetic and the ethical in these texts leads to an intertwining of both, to a simultaneous, tension-creating presence of the criteria of aesthetics and ethics. The conflicting pull of the differentiating, identity- and alienity-defining discursive order on the one hand and counter-discursive confusions, irresolvable ambiguities on the other is apparent in any text of a certain degree of complexity. Such complexity is the result of complex literary structures, that is, an adequate employment of aesthetic means. But all of these texts ask questions concerning the moral order, the social fabric, the rules of intercultural and international relations, questions that seem to demand clear and unambiguous answers but are made to appear as confounding and not so clearly decidable by the ambiguities of literary representation—a situation of transdifference on the reader's side.

The moral sympathies that have been apparent throughout my book are thus unfounded and yet, I think, necessary. The systems that used to found decisions and actions appear to have foundered. Yet (tremulous) decision and (unassured) action are still called for, in literature as in life. It is one of the great achievements of Herman Melville, to cite him as my model of good writing, to convey epistemological (notably in *Moby-Dick*) and ethical (notably in *Pierre*) uncertainties in adequate literary structures while yet demanding us to make value judgments, to posit norms in the face of their impossibility—in order to make human interaction and social structures possible at all. Although the characters of inter-American fiction may be groping for the right answers, the proper way of acting, as in Atwood's *Bodily Harm* or Stone's *A Flag for Sunrise*, and although they may utterly fail in this, as in Lowry's *Under the Volcano*, the reader is called upon go beyond that, to think about answers while smarting from the transdifferential tensions on the textual and metatextual levels alike.

# NOTES

*Preface*

1. Ralph Bauer (in his *Cultural Geography of Colonial American Literatures*) and others have done an excellent job in analyzing colonial literature, and that even with a comparative perspective.

*1. Introduction*

1. Most of the poems in *Questions of Travel* deal with Brazil, where Bishop spent more than sixteen years.

2. Cf. Manfred Siebald, "'Questions of Travel,'" 623–35.

3. I will discuss the terminology and theory used in this study in Chapter 2.

4. I prefer *discourse* to *myth* (as used by Eldon Kenworthy in his *America/Américas: Myth in the Making of U.S. Policy Toward Latin America*) because the latter term carries a host of unnecessary connotations and, other than *discourse* in the Foucauldian tradition, is not traditionally linked with the issue of power.

5. Wallace Stevens, "The Idea of Order at Key West," *The Collected Poems*, 130. Morse Peckham, *Man's Rage for Chaos: Biology, Behavior, and the Arts*.

6. The same applies to political ideas: "The 'anarchy of empire' [. . .] suggests ways of thinking about imperialism as a network of power relations that changes over space and time and is riddled with instability, ambiguity, and disorder, rather than as a monolithic system of domination that the very word 'empire' implies." Amy Kaplan, *The Anarchy of Empire*, 13–14.

7. The only suitable alternative, "Anglo-America," is far less common, carries the connotation of including constant references to Britain, and is therefore used here only occasionally where the *Anglo* aspect is indeed significant.

8. Other concepts are possible. In her *Continental Divides*, Rachel Adams points out the relativity of maps, regional divisions, and national boundaries. She sees the whole of North America, including Canada, the United States, and Mexico as one geographical space crisscrossed by borders and borderlands, that is, by cultural networks, contact zones, and groupings of influence and inspiration-getting. The result is a fascinating picture of North American and at the same time inter-American literary and other cultural contacts, self-searchings abroad, and imaginations of the diverse Others.

9. Cf. Gloria Anzaldúa, *Borderlands/La Frontera*.

10. For a more extended reading, see Chapter 7.

11. See also his pervasive use of the term in *The Exhaustion of Difference*. For other definitions of the term (in a variety of spellings), cf., for instance, Román de la Campa; John Beverley, *Latinamericanism*.

12. The dictator Manuel Estrada Cabrera (1898–1920) had finished the process by

which Guatemala became a banana republic in the literal sense by practically turning over the country to the United Fruit Company (see Gruesz on the origin of the term and concept of *banana republic*). The series of *caudillos* was interrupted in 1944 by the success of a revolutionary movement. The first free elections in the history of the country took place in 1945. However, in spite of the establishment of democratic parties and unions, the presidents Juan José Arévalo (1945–50) and Jacobo Arbenz (1950–54) failed in breaking the power of the traditional oligarchy and, especially, the US company controlling the economy and social structure of the country. When Arbenz began to redistribute agricultural land that was not used to the landless farm workers and *indios*, he was accused of communist leanings and his opponents easily won the support of the American foreign secretary John Foster Dulles and his brother Allen, director of the CIA. With US military and especially media support, an army of mercenaries under Colonel Castillo Armas invaded Guatemala in July 1954, and established another series of military dictatorships. The ensuing civil war was to end only in 1996 and left hundreds of thousands dead, mostly among the rural, strongly Indian population that was decimated by death squads and official counterinsurgency forces. The United Nations–sponsored Truth Commission stated in 1999 that the Guatemalan army had committed genocide against the Maya people. The American involvement is described and analyzed in Richard H. Immerman, *The CIA in Guatemala*. See also Lars Schoultz, *Beneath the United States*. For a study of Central American literary reactions to banana imperialism, cf. Ana Patricia Rodríguez, *Dividing the Isthmus*, 44–75.

13. "Americans All" became a popular slogan during the 1940s as part of US efforts to strengthen the idea of a pan-American identity as a defense against Nazism and later Communism. Cf. Uwe Lübken.

14. The term was reintroduced by Gerald Vizenor and for him denotes more than passive survival, namely an active and creative overcoming of victimization. For recent discussions of the term and its implications in the context of Native American self-positioning, see Vizenor, ed., *Survivance*. There he also refers to some instances of Derrida's use of the term (20–21). "Survivance" in both French and English is one of Derrida's central concepts referring to the inconclusiveness of, for instance, life and death (cf. his early use in "Living On. Borderlines"). Vizenor's collection of essays, *Manifest Manners* (1994), shows his extensive reading in poststructuralist thinking. His debt to Derrida and others, but also his inventive rephrasing of his sources and inspirations, have often been discussed in Native American criticism. See, for instance, James Mackay in Vizenor, ed., *Survivance* (255–59).

15. *Week-end en Guatemala*, like many other works of the Nobel laureate Asturias, is available in many languages but not, to my knowledge, in English. Discursive and ideological constraints can be formidable obstacles to intercultural communication. An extended version of my comments on Asturias can be found in my "Native Survivance in the Americas."

16. Of the many Latin American novels that come to mind in this context, Gabriel García Márquez, *The Autumn of the Patriarch*, José Agustín, *Ciudades desiertas*, and Carlos Fuentes, *The Crystal Frontier*, offer a remarkable spectrum of perceptions of the northern neighbor. For a discussion of the Mexican perspective on the United States, cf. Linda Egan and Mary K. Long, eds., *Mexico Reading the United States*.

17. Deborah Treisman, ed., *20 under 40: Stories from the* New Yorker.

18. The ethnologist Christoph Antweiler has presented a less period-based view of universal elements of human nature and culture. Cf. *Heimat Mensch: Was UNS ALLE verbindet.* The new situation in the age of globalization is discussed in his *Inclusive Humanism.*

19. There are numerous historical and political studies on such topics, for instance Lester Langley, *America and the Americas*; Thomas F. O'Brien, *Making the Americas*; and by way of a counter-perspective, British historian Felipe Fernández-Armesto's *The Americas: A Hemispheric History.*

20. Bauer makes the transnational aspect of inter-American studies visible by listing European critics in the field. I should like to mention here the book series Inter-American Studies/Estudos Interamericanos, edited by Josef Raab, Sebastian Thies, and Olaf Kaltmeier, and published by WVT Wissenschaftlicher Verlag Trier/Bilingual Review Press, Tempe, as well as the impressive output of the Center for InterAmerican Studies at the University of Bielefeld, Germany.

21. Although this is a timely warning for scholarship, literary writers have not hesitated to use binary models in writing about other parts of the Americas.

22. This is a problem even a sophisticated study such as José David Saldívar's *The Dialectics of Our America* cannot handle without undue generalizations.

23. Let me only mention the work of Will Kymlicka and Néstor García Canclini.

24. Some aspects of these concepts of the (American) South can also be traced back to the idea of a Global South that was a major incentive for the fifteenth- and sixteenth-century voyages of exploration. I refer to these at the beginning of Chapter 3.

25. *The Constitution of Society: Outline of the Theory of Structuration.*

26. Publications such as *Close Encounters of Empire*, edited by Gilbert M. Joseph, Catherine C. Legrand, and Ricardo D. Salvatore, have paved the way to a more multiperspectival approach to inter-American relations.

27. Canadian books of this period are also represented, but on the whole, the Canadian inter-American production appears to come a little later. This would bolster my argument that Vietnam and post-Vietnam were decisive factors for the rise in US publications.

2. *Alterity and Identity*

1. Personal communication by David F. Krell, who pointed out this passage to me, and who comments on it in his *Derrida and Our Animal Others*, Chapter 2, particularly 58–63. The problems addressed by Derrida in his seminar in this session, notably mortality, the (dead) body, thingness, need not concern us here. Not just yet.

2. The "we" in this chapter and in this book in general means myself and a supposed group of "informed readers" much like those Stanley Fish has in mind. Cf. *Self-Consuming Artifacts*, 406–7. The subjectivity of this approach cannot be avoided.

3. Cf. Klaus Lösch's excellent comprehensive discussion of "the Other and Its Description" in his essay "Das Fremde und seine Beschreibung." Lösch not only comments on many more aspects of this topic than can be alluded to here, but also names an impressive range of scholarly works from various fields that are devoted to it.

4. Waldenfels points out that the German *fremd* has a wider semantic range: "*Fremd* is firstly that which occurs outside of one's own region as being exterior, in opposition to being *interior* (compare ξένον, *externum*, *extraneum*, *étranger*, stranger, foreigner). *Fremd* is secondly that which belongs to others (ἀλλότριον, *alienum*, alien, *ajeno*), in contrast to

one's *own*. [. . .] Thirdly, *fremd* is that which belongs to a different kind, which is uncanny, peculiar, strange (ξένον, *insolitum*, *étrange*), in contrast to the *familiar*. The opposition exterior/interior points to a *place* of the alien, the opposition alien/own to *possession*, and the opposition strange/familiar to a *mode* of understanding" (71–73). To me, such semantic fluctuations point in the direction of a deconstruction of terminological and dialectical binarisms. One should not forget that etymologically the original meaning of *fremd* is *vorwärts* ("forward") in some direction, remote, a dynamic aspect noted by Heidegger in *Unterwegs zur Sprache*.

5. See, again, *The Order of Things* and, as a specification with regard to the socio-institutional aspects of the term *discourse*, *The Archaeology of Knowledge* (*L'archéologie du savoir*, 1969). Foucault's later books about social institutions like the systems of punishment thematize the rise of power structures in connection with the formation of discourses. We need not concern ourselves here with the fact that Foucault (in his preface to *The Order of Things*) speaks of a basic cultural and, as such, discursive order more fundamental than cultural codes and scientific theories and only later turns to the analysis of specific discourses that are on the same epistemic level as the alterity discourse discussed here, with the fact, that is, that his usage of the term *discourse* undergoes certain changes in the course of his life.

6. Cf. Chapter 6 in this volume for a more extensive discussion of the term *culture*.

7. "Wenn schon die 'eigene' Kultur eine[] komplexe, dynamische und heterogene Prozessualität darstellt, muss man akzeptieren, dass Kulturhermeneutik zwar Selbst- und Fremdverstehen vermittelt, dass aber auch in ihr Selbstverstehen und Fremdverstehen asymmetrisch bleiben" (my translation).

8. This is one of the central results of the advanced interdisciplinary doctoral and research program "Cultural Hermeneutics: Reflections on Difference and Transdifference" at Erlangen University from which the volume just quoted proceeded.

9. Slavoj Žižek has offered a Lacanian approach to the question of ethnic hatreds. In his discussion of the resurgent animosities between the post–Cold War nations of Eastern and Southeastern Europe, he uses Lacan's term of *jouissance*: "The element that holds together a given community [. . .] always implies a shared relationship toward a Thing, toward Enjoyment [*jouissance*] incarnated. [. . .] This Nation-Thing is determined by a series of contradictory properties. It appears to us as 'our Thing' [. . .], as something accessible only to us, as something 'they,' the others, cannot grasp, but which is nonetheless constantly menaced by 'them.' [. . .] We always impute to the 'other' an excessive enjoyment; s/he wants to steal our enjoyment (by ruining our way of life) and/or has access to some secret, perverse enjoyment" (51–54). The examples he presents come from everyday culture, work ethic, and national myths. I owe this reference to David Krell.

10. Cf. Chapter 3 for the sequels of the Black Legend to accomodate people of either European, Native, or mixed descent. In this context, the respective colonial histories and the shift of colonial power from Europe to North America should also be considered. Cf. Walter Mignolo and his concept of "colonial difference" in his *Local Histories*. As Sandhya Shukla and Heidi Tinsman point out, Latin America thus emerges not as the West's "Oriental Other but as stepchild and malformed version of its Anglophone sibling to the north" (19).

11. "ein hochkomplexes, aus objektiven, subjektiven und soziokulturellen Faktoren integriertes Modell eines Wirklichkeitsausschnitts" (my translation).

12. "[einer] grundsätzlichen Verständlichkeit aller menschlichen Äußerungen auf der Basis des gemeinsamen Menschseins" (my translation).

13. For a discussion of supposedly universal qualities in an age of globalization, cf. the studies by Christoph Antweiler mentioned earlier, p. 325, n. 18. See also Stagl's more recent short statement, "Der Universalienstreit in der Ethnologie."

14. "gewisse charakteristische Wertorientierungen Lateinamerikas und der USA einer kontrastiven Analyse zu unterziehen" (my translation).

15. "die menschliche Natur sei grundlegend böse, aber der Vervollkommnung fähig" (my translation).

16. Other contrasts listed by Göhring comprise, for instance, the control of nature versus one's submitting to it; an emphasis on time as passing versus living in the present; the orientation toward becoming versus that toward being; competitive individualism versus a thinking in stable hierarchies, and so on. For a more comprehensive but nonetheless generalizing, comparative study of the societies and cultures of the Americas from a European perspective, see Edmund Stephen Urbanski. The collection of essays edited by Knud Krakau, *Lateinamerika und Nordamerika*, is an excellent, concise comparative survey of society, politics, and economics in North and Latin America in their historical development until 1990.

17. Cf. Raffael Gutiérrez Girardot's "Kritische Bemerkungen zu Heinz Göhring" or Darcy Ribeiro's radical rejection of such classifications of Latin Americans (*Americas*, 25–26).

18. See Hofstede's URL: http://geert-hofstede.com/national-culture.html.

19. For Latin American perceptions of the United States in the course of history, see, for instance, the studies by Aguilar, Biles, Dean, Haring, Merrill, Rama, and Reid listed in my bibliography.

20. This is a simplified version of some elements of Levinas's ethics, which, in its radical position, demands a surrender to the Other that has qualities of the numinous. Levinas's ethics is grounded in a fundamental religious belief and can therefore not be taken as a general model. Rather, it represents an ideal position depending on the judgment of God as the absolute Other.

21. Uta Liebmann Schaub has shown that the counter-discourse implied in his texts is that of the Orient itself and thus not that of Orientalism. Cf. Liebmann Schaub 1989.

22. See Anderson's chapter "Old Empires, New Nations," 50–65.

23. Homi K. Bhabha, ed., *Nation and Narration*.

24. "DissemiNation: Time, narrative and the margins of the modern nation," originally published in *Nation and Narration*; here quoted from the revised version in Bhabha, *The Location of Culture*, 145.

25. See Chapter 5 of this volume.

26. Examples include the foundational figure of Columbus and narratives of conquest.

27. The Black Legend was a mixed bag of British or Dutch anti-Southern/Mediterranean and anti-Catholic prejudices. In particular, after the conquest of the Americas, it referred to Spanish greed, cruelty, and hypocrisy (in their claim of bringing the true religion and a higher civilization). Cf. Maria DeGuzman, Charles Gibson, David S. Shields.

28. This discursive/counter-discursive differentiation can be compared to the "doubling" of the discourse of nationness addressed by Homi Bhabha ("DissemiNation"). Amy Kaplan sees the need for a similar distinction between the domestic and the foreign

when the question of US imperialism is discussed. Contrary to the claims of the multiculturalists, she insists that "[t]o reconsider the meaning of imperialism in American studies is to make statehood unavoidable as precisely the site of the monopoly of power and the production of ideology." But the multicultural complexities of the domestic scene, that is, the "internal categories of gender, race, and ethnicity," and the more unified and linear "global dynamics of empire-building" are interrelated. "The binary opposition of the foreign and the domestic is itself imbued with the rhetoric of gender hierarchies that implicitly elevate the international to a male, public realm, and relegate the national to a female, private sphere" (Kaplan "'Left Alone with America,'" 16). Ironically, as can be seen in the discourse on Latin America, this gender hierarchy finds its echo in the respective categorization concerning North America and the foreign Other. Kaplan has further elaborated her ideas of the doubleness of the domestic and the foreign in her brilliant study *The Anarchy of Empire in the Making of U.S. Culture.*

29. Not all US American writers, journalists, and politicians of that time shared Everett's view, but it is a prominent example for the formation of Latinamericanism. For a discussion of more enthusiastic reactions to the Latin American revolutions in the early nineteenth century, cf. Caitlin A. Fitz's study *Our Sister Republics: The United States in an Age of American Revolutions.*

30. In a paper delivered at the 2013 conference of the German Association for American Studies, Rogelio Saenz pointed out that the US population at large has little knowledge of Latinos/as even today. This does not mean that the situation in ethnically mixed middle-class areas or at institutions of higher learning may not be considerably different.

31. See Streeby's argument mentioned earlier, p. 14.

32. That this gender discourse also plays a major role in the US American identity discourse has often been pointed out, for instance by Annette Kolodny in her *The Lay of the Land.* Seen from this angle, Latinamericanism is a continuation of the US discourse on nation building.

33. José E. Limón devotes his study *American Encounters* to the topic of genderized perceptions informing inter-American cultural relations.

34. "imaginierter Bedeutungen, die zur Artikulation drängen, [. . .] und zugleich Fundus von Bildern, Affekten und Sehnsüchten, die das individuelle Imaginäre [. . .] stimulieren" (my translation). Winfried Fluck, *Das kulturelle Imaginäre*, 21. Fluck's concept is based on Wolfgang Iser's and Cornelius Castoriadis's respective notions of the imaginary.

35. How intentionally this is done will often remain uncertain, just as the question of which role the subject might play in discourse formation found different answers in Foucault's theory as it developed over the years.

36. I think it is significant that even ethnography as the field programmatically devoted to the study of the Other has discovered the higher adequacy, nay, inevitability of literary forms of representation for its own uses. See, particularly, Clifford Geertz's concept of "thick description."

37. I cannot discuss here the semantic reach of both *representation* and *reality*. For the latter, I want to posit a constructivist sense—the whole discussion on discourses conforms to that—and an essentialist, positivist sense—I do not doubt that the Americas exist as physical and political entities nor that historical events like the Spanish-American War actually took place. Literature cannot represent positivist reality directly, "mimetically," but only prior models of reality, as Yuri Lotman has pointed out. Literary representation

may encompass a wide range of approaches depending on the reality models and techniques available at a given time, from "realism" to postmodernism. The authors discussed in this study employ or "represent" a considerable variety of such models and develop their own. One should note, though, that representation also has a performative side: the actualization of a representation by the reader is open to ambiguity. Cf. Wolfgang Iser, "Representation."

38. "Sinn dient der Erfassung und Reduktion von Weltkomplexität und erst dadurch der Orientierung des Erlebens und Handelns" (Luhmann 1970, 116; my translation).

39. "Sinn ist Selektion *aus* anderen Möglichkeiten und damit zugleich Verweisung *auf* andere Möglichkeiten" (ibid.; my translation).

40. I confess to having been one of them.

41. Cf. Eric Sundquist for a detailed presentation of the historical background. A number of critical studies explore further contextual aspects. The issue of Melville's dealings with the topic of slavery that was comprehensively treated by Carolyn Karcher has been expanded to include the Black Atlantic and questions of colonialism (Gesa Mackenthun). Markus Heide, who cites many of these studies, puts the story in the context of inter- and pan-American issues.

42. The effect of cultural and political values on the perception of "reality" in this story is analyzed by Tuire Valkeakari.

43. Cf. Guy Cardwell's groundbreaking essay, "Melville's Gray Story."

44. Cf. Yuri M. Lotman's fundamental reflections on the nature of art as a secondary model-forming system.

45. I owe this source to Stephan Kohl, whose own *Realismus: Theorie und Geschichte* remains a valuable survey for readers of German.

### 3. *Foundational Narratives*

1. It should be borne in mind that, as Terence Martin puts it nicely, "'Discovery' (then and now) was in the eyes of the discoverer" (17). In fact, the Americas have been discovered and rediscovered (and, in Edmundo O'Gorman's sense, invented and reinvented) again and again, over many thousands of years, first by waves of immigrants from East Asia (unless they emerged in America, as many Native traditions have it; aboriginal populations have always resented the idea of their having been "discovered"), and tens of thousands of years later by Scandinavians, probably also by Chinese or people from southeastern Asia, possibly by Africans, and almost certainly by Polynesians. Columbus's "discovery" was only the latest and in recent history the most consequential in a long series, and hence the Eurocentric, post-Columbian view of the Americas is only one among several possible.

2. "If the nadir populations for Amerindians of the various regions of the New World were added (nadirs were reached in the Caribbean islands by about 1570; in North America not perhaps until 1930), the sum would be about 4.5 million" (Crosby 24).

3. Although marred by some deplorable gaps, a number of inconsistencies and the uneven quality of the entries, *The Christopher Columbus Encyclopedia*, edited by Silvio A. Bedini, can give an idea of the range of historical information available in our time—for belief or further investigation.

4. In order not to complicate the issue of factual truth beyond what is necessary here, I would prefer to use *fact* for what is given and verifiable by cultural consensus and *event*

for the status of such facts in a narrative context—which is just the opposite of Linda Hutcheon's "distinction between the brute *events* of the past and the historical *facts* we construct out of them" (*The Politics of Postmodernism*, 57). It goes without saying that the selection and delimitation of facts also depends on aspects such as the method of approach, evaluative hierarchization, or the at once limited and yet (in the Derridean sense) endlessly open possibilities of textual description. Thus, even scientific facts are constructions.

5. Cf. Robin George Collingwood, *The Idea of History*; Arthur C. Danto, *Analytical Philosophy of History*.

6. See, in particular, Hayden White's *Metahistory: The Historical Imagination in Nineteenth-Century Europe* and *The Content of the Form: Narrative Discourse and Historical Representation*.

7. *Time, Narrative, and History*, cover text. Edmund Burke's argument is aptly summarized by Harold Toliver, 47–55.

8. See Jackson G. Barry's survey article "Narratology's Centrifugal Force" and many entries in the *Routledge Encyclopedia of Narrative Theory*, ed. David Herman, Manfred Jahn, and Marie-Laure Ryan.

9. The term used by Jean-François Lyotard in the context of questions of legitimation of scientific knowledge has come to be applied for other fields as well.

10. Cf. White, *Metahistory* and *Tropics of Discourse*. White in turn refers to Northrop Frye's system of four basic narrative myths in *The Anatomy of Criticism*, that is, (1) comedy, (2) romance, (3) tragedy, and (4) irony and satire.

11. This is a principal argument in Richard Rorty's "Texts and Lumps."

12. White develops this argument in the articles collected in his *Tropics of Discourse*. See also Heinz Ickstadt's application of White's theory to the postmodern historical novel in "Plot, Komplott oder die Herrschaft des Zufalls."

13. Detailed research in a fictional text's historical accuracy or intertextual groundwork has been done, for instance, by Mónica Calvo-Pascual concerning Marlowe's *The Memoirs of Christopher Columbus*. See Chapter 10 in this volume.

14. Hegel gave these lectures five times during the 1820s at the University of Berlin. The first, posthumously published, divergent book versions appeared in 1837 and 1840.

15. Surveys of US American literary and cultural constructions of Columbus and his period are provided by John P. Larner and Terence Martin.

16. The fact that both Stanley T. Williams (I: 41) and Lewis Leary (*That Rascal Freneau*, 47) see only a positive image of Columbus in this poem proves the power of discourse, here: the dominance of the bardic Columbus myth even in the twentieth century, a myth against which Freneau had shown remarkable resistance. Eric Wertheimer points out the presence of the Black Legend: "For Freneau to assume this story in the role of poetic and political myth-maker is to see himself as redeemer of not just Columbus's legend, but the slavery of conquered Incas and Aztecs—'Tell of those chains that sullied all my glory— / Not mine but theirs.'" (Wertheimer 47). I see Columbus's image here as much more ambivalent.

17. For Robertson's role for the American representations of Columbus, cf. Alice P. Kenney.

18. For a discussion of both aspects, see Thomas R. Preston. Barlow's linear concept of history is pointed out by John Griffith.

19. This historic inaccuracy is justified by Barlow by poetic necessity.

20. Thus, in Richard Snowden's anonymously published narrative poem *The Columbiad: or, A poem on the American war: in thirteen cantoes* (1795), the Americans fighting for their independence are addressed as citizens of "Columbia."

21. Cf. Robert D. Richardson, particularly p. 41.

22. Arthur L. Ford has pointed out that the fifth edition of *The Vision of Columbus* of 1793 already reflects Barlow's changed political, religious, and philosophical opinions (68–74). The limits of Barlow's progressivism can be seen in the fact that he dropped his original plan to discuss gender discrimination and to propose women's emancipation already in the first version (Ford 47). Helen Loschky traces a chain of influence from *The Vision* through Snowden's *Columbiad* and *The Columbiad* by James L. Moore to Barlow's own *Columbiad*, but the thematic elements I have pointed out are all Barlow's own.

23. One of the very best discussions of Barlow's achievement is Hans-Joachim Lang's, unfortunately available only in German.

24. See Ralph Bauer's seminal essay "Colonial Discourse and Early American Literary History" on the Creole position Barlow took in unfolding a postcolonial pan-American view of teleological history in opposition to the Buffon-Robertson Eurocentrism. Bauer shows Barlow as influenced by his reading or (secondhand) knowledge of Spanish and Spanish (Native) American counter-narratives: Alonso de Ercilla y Zúñiga's *La Araucana* (1569) and the Inca Garcilaso de la Vega's *Commentarios reales de los incas* (1607).

25. Wertheimer emphasizes the ethical benefit Barlow received from using the Inca myth: "Barlow's act of commodification of the native Other is also an internalization of nativeness, a self-Othering by the imperialist that brings with it an ethically self-serving dimension. I want to argue that one of the crucial implications of this identifiction is to draw the Americas more absolutely, and, Barlow hopes, more ethically, into commercial domains" (54). See also his comments on the contradictions in the "republican narrative of historical progress" (88). On the other hand, neither the contemporary Incas of Tupac Amaru nor their northern brethren could be allowed equal rights in the modern nation states, least of all in the rising United States.

26. Whether, as Joseph Tusiani has it, *The Columbiad* is also a piece of expiation for the European conquest, with the American rebellion symbolically undoing the injustice in the consequence of the discovery, seems doubtful because there is little indication that Barlow wanted the rights of the aboriginal population fully restored (34). The continuing conquest in both Americas was to create the need for a Native American or *indigena* version of the Columbus narrative of which there will be more to say in Chapter 10.

27. Rolena Adorno's valuable long article "Washington Irving's Romantic Hispanism" provides the contexts for placing Irving's *Columbus* in relation to the work of his contemporaries, and describes his use of source material and the response the book found among his readers. She emphasizes the national character of Columbus as a self-made man and thus a romantic role model for US Americans. She also mentions the historical and political context, notably the announcement of the Monroe Doctrine only three years before Irving's book (Adorno 94 n. 8).

28. As is well known, the boundaries between the two remained fluid before the advent of "scientific" historiography. However, Irving saw his own work as more imaginative and as stylistically more polished than that of, say, William H. Prescott.

29. It may be more than sheer coincidence that Irving later wrote the history of the fur-

trade establishment Astoria, founded by the first American big capitalist, German-born John Jacob Astor. Columbus and Astor, a fascinating connection. Cf. also Adorno, "Washington Irving."

30. Cf. Wertheimer's impressive chapter on Prescott, 91–132.

31. Unlike Cooper's *Mercedes of Castile*, *Vasconcelos* presents a successful union between a European hero and a Native queen and thus shows the prospect of ethnic hybridity less negatively than most nineteenth-century intellectuals would have considered possible.

32. In their *Sinking Columbus*, Stephen J. Summerhill and John A. Williams provide a survey and an analysis of the political and cultural approaches to the quincentenary in the United States, Spain, Italy, and parts of Latin America. In a particularly interesting section, they describe how in Mexico, due to its strong indigenist tradition, the term *encuentro*(encounter) was introduced to replace the discredited *discovery* and to avoid the more drastic *invasion*, and how, ironically, the Spain-oriented, discovery-focused approach finally won out nonetheless (172–78).

4. *Invasive Methods*

1. For the connections between foreign policy and domestic developments, cf. Amy Kaplan, *The Anarchy of Empire*; Gretchen Murphy, *Shadowing the White Man's Burden*; and Shelley Streeby, *American Sensations*.

2. *Filibuster* is used here in the sense of a person going to war in or against a foreign nation without being authorized by his or her own government.

3. For a recent critical assessment both of US imperial history and of the scholarly work done in this field, cf. Matthew F. Jacobson. Jacobson emphasizes the role neoliberal capitalism has played in the formation of imperial policies that he considers to have been neglected in earlier studies such as Kaplan and Pease's *Cultures of United States Imperialism*.

4. For examples of the rich connections between Latin America and other parts of the world that existed nonetheless, cf. Charles C. Mann, *1493*.

5. Pratt may not have been aware of Rolena Adorno's previous use of this term in a Spanish publication. Cf. Adorno, *Polemics*, 23, 329 n. 2.

6. Edward Soja has termed these categories "Firstspace," "Secondspace," and "Thirdspace."

7. The sailor's cross-dressing appears to be symbolic of Cooper's growing doubts in the masculine conquest jargon of his day. As Streeby has pointed out, cross-dressing and other forms of transcending gender boundaries was also a popular motif in the story papers and other types of mass fiction, although there this blurring takes place among the Mexican characters and does not question the basic situation of pitting masculine US America against feminized Mexico (cf. *American Sensations*, Chapters 3 and 4). Cooper seems to have been disenchanted with this kind of hierarchy.

8. The connection of American expansionism in Latin America and the movement for an extension of slavery to newly won territories is hardly ever made explicit. Again and again during the period before the Civil War, the South argued for territorial expansion into Mexico or the Caribbean with the aim of gaining more territory for a slave labor-based agricultural economy. Cf. Lars Schoultz, passim.

9. Streeby in *American Sensations* devotes a complete chapter to "George Lippard's 1848" and puts his Mexican romances in the context of his writings and ideas on class and

race politics, Catholicism, the Black Legend, and so forth. Her thoughtful analysis shows that Lippard is a good example for what her study demonstrates in general: the convergences and parallel developments of what I would call the discourses of identity and alterity.

10. "The heroines [of popular romances about the American empire] prove their own modernity by at once freeing themselves from traditional hierarchies and voluntarily subduing themselves to some 'real live man,' just as imperial subjects, like the loyal Olanchan general in *Soldiers of Fortune*, prove their capacity for liberation through their alliance with American power." Kaplan, *Anarchy*, 108.

11. Gretchen Murphy sees it as "an amalgamation through which Davis constructs a general and mythic relation between the United States and its southern neighbors" (*Hemispheric*, 122).

12. This narrative technique was not entirely new and had been used in more complex modernist ways in John Dos Passos's *Three Soldiers* (1921). It was to resurface in the sophisticated telling of Norman Mailer's *The Naked and the Dead* (1948).

13. For a debunking view of Roosevelt's role in the Cuban war, see P. Samuels and H. Samuels. Amy Kaplan's splendid article "Black and Blue on San Juan Hill" convincingly places the battle and Roosevelt's role in it in the context of the racial relations debate after the Civil War. Symbolically, in his narrative of the battle, *The Rough Riders: A History of the First United States Volunteer Cavalry*, Roosevelt defines black American soldiers as useful US citizens as long as they are under white command, while the Cubans, like the populations of other territories coveted by the US American empire, are first defined as black and then as incapable of self-government. The Spanish-American War thus appears as a continuation of the Civil War "in an imperial national discourse of the United States at the turn of the century" (Kaplan, "Black and Blue," 219). Kaplan extends her argument in the chapter under the same title in her *The Anarchy of Empire*, 121–45. In Chapter 3 of his *Trans-Americanity*, José David Saldívar widens the context in which we can see the Rough Riders episode by comparing Roosevelt's account with *Biografía de un cimarrón*, a *novela testimonial* by Miguel Barnet and Esteban Montejo (1966), that is, with the Cuban point of view.

*5. Representations of the Mexican Revolution*

1. Jürgen Link has shown that several specific discourses—here we can think of those on race or gender—can have certain elements in common, for instance symbols, myths, stock phrases, and so on. Cf. "Literaturanalyse."

2. Linda B. Hall and Don M. Coerver analyze the relations between the United States and Mexico 1910–20. John A. Britton describes the American political and intellectual reaction to the Mexican Revolution and its aftermath through the major part of the twentieth century.

3. For various competing Mexican interpretations of the revolution and its consequences as well as for competing versions of the Mexican discourse of identity, see Vittoria Borsó, "Images." John S. Brushwood lists and briefly describes a long series of Mexican novels on the revolution. Lancelot Cowie provides plentiful material on the representation of *indios* in Mexican and Guatemalan fiction that can be compared to texts by Katherine Ann Porter and others, whether in the context of narratives on the revolution or other contexts.

4. The connections between US radicalism and the events and movements in Mexico

are extensively discussed by Streeby, *Radical Sensations*, notably Parts I and II, 71–172. Streeby points out how the discursive and rhetorical elements of sentiment and sensation are used to move the masses. Her analysis of John Kenneth Turner's *Barbarous Mexico* as "a sensational exposé of Porfirio Díaz's Mexico that contemporaries compared to Harriet Beecher Stowe's *Uncle Tom's Cabin*" (24) is important for an understanding of the connections between the radicals on both sides of the border and the handling of the sympathies of readers of muckraking journalism. "As Turner compares Yaquis and other workers in Mexico to slaves in the United States before the Civil War, a host of other comparisons are suggested: that the horrors of the Porfiriato are like the horrors of the U.S. Southern slaveocracy; that Mexican rubber and henequen plantations [. . .] are similar to antebellum plantations [. . .]; and that the conflicts between Díaz and his opponents should be understood as another version of the U.S. Civil War" (133). Streeby also comments on the ambiguity of Turner's title, which fits nicely into the tradition of Latinamericanism: "Although in Turner's preface [. . .] he was careful to say that the word *barbarous* in the title was meant to 'apply to Mexico's form of government rather than to its people[,]' a form of government, he insisted, for which the United States was partly responsible, the title resonates with sensational U.S.-Mexico War-era formulations of Mexican savagery and unfitness for democratic self-governance" (137).

5. Cf. the critical discussion of Reed's approach in John A. Britton (36–40), who also mentions other American commentators on the events. *Insurgent Mexico* is given a more positive reading in Christoph P. Wilson's "Plotting the Border" that also provides a useful overview of the role of US war correspondents. For a complex assessment of Villa's life, contexts, and legend, see Friedrich Katz's monumental *The Life and Times of Pancho Villa*.

6. See Steffens's "The Sunny Side of Mexico" (1915) and "Making Friends with Mexico" (1916) (*World*, 4–31) and the somewhat more detached reminiscences in his *The Autobiography of Lincoln Steffens* (1931, 712–43).

7. *Sic.* Beals means Tlaloc.

8. The world of the muralists and other famous Mexican artists is depicted with much insider knowledge. Obviously, the German Mexican artist Lida, for instance, is a fictionalized version of Frida Kahlo (cf. *Stones*, 306).

9. Remarkably, Donald Pizer's extensive analysis of the trilogy, *Dos Passos'* U.S.A.*: A Critical Study*, contains hardly any references to the Mexican episode.

10. See Hartwig Isernhagen (161–201) for an excellent discussion of Dos Passos's handling of history and narrative. Isernhagen also points out the function of the passages related to Mexico.

11. The terminology is explained in Isernhagen (249 n. 1).

12. Even so, literature has the power of evoking the horror of what has been erased from history. There is, for instance, as David Krell has reminded me, "García Márquez's treatment of the workers' strike [in *Cien ãnos de soledad*], their rebellion, their slaughter, and the disappearance of the corpses in the sea—such that the event never occurred" (personal communication).

13. Thomas F. Walsh (71–83) gives detailed information about the background of the story and also locates it as being set at the village of Azcapotzalco in the vicinity of Mexico City. However, Porter was not to be completely fettered by her own experiences; her stories repeatedly evince her capacity for abstraction.

14. One might compare the narratively enhanced self-portraits of a Mexican family in Oscar Lewis's *The Children of Sanchez* to get an idea of the complex and differentiated way of thinking, feeling, and acting among the Mexican rural poor, and that includes situations of personal crisis and violent conflict.

15. Rachel Adams, who devotes Chapter 3 of her *Continental Divides* to Porter, Anita Brenner, and Tina Modotti as female mediators between Mexican modernism and the US cultural scene, sees the conflict of the two Marías as one between a traditional lifestyle and the liberations the revolution had promised but failed to bring. However, I cannot discover the necessary authorial-narrative detachment in this early story.

16. One of the most comprehensive discussions of the text is Darlene H. Unrue 52–59, 75–83. For the genesis of the story, see also Joan Givner 152–56, 217–19; and the comprehensive biographical background analysis in Walsh 121–33.

17. "Lover of Mankind" is the title of the section at the beginning of Dos Passos's *The 42nd Parallel* devoted to a positive portrait of the socialist politician Eugene Debs. The contrast of the two men couldn't be stronger.

6. *Nature and Civilization*

1. The English translation of Freud's term *Kultur* as "civilization" carries semantic implications I will comment on shortly. The translation of *Unbehagen* as "discontents" is equally dissatisfying. "Discomfiture" would convey the far more emotional connotations of the German term much better.

2. Cf. Freud, *Civilization and Its Discontents*. Freud argues that our need to accommodate the societal demands for a restriction of instinctual gratification involves both the love instinct and the aggressive instinct. In contrast to the former, the death drive cannot be used to strengthen the ties of society but must be repressed or else directed outward, against another, rivaling culture. Freud's theory here acquires an intercultural dimension.

3. Ulla Haselstein 402; my translation. The essay analyzes Freud's use of the metaphorics of the dichotomy of nature and culture and Jean Baudrillard's (culturally) critical reinterpretation.

4. On the complexity of these terms, cf. Raymond Williams, *Keywords*, and the revised version, *New Keywords*, edited by Tony Bennett, Lawrence Grossberg, and Meaghan Morris.

5. Cf. Donna Haraway in, for instance, *The Companion Species Manifesto* and *When Species Meet.*

6. Cf. the more extended discussion in my "Introduction: Culture, Economy, and Identity Locations" as well as in Breinig and Lösch, "Introduction: Difference and Transdifference."

7. James Strachey's translation of Freud's term *Kultur* as "civilization" follows this tradition.

8. This is the way Mark Twain represents it in his novel *A Connecticut Yankee in King Arthur's Court*, which will serve as a point of comparison in my discussion of Paul Theroux's *Mosquito Coast* at the end of this chapter.

9. Cf. the relevant interpretations of this process by Henry Nash Smith, Hans Huth, Howard Mumford Jones, Frieder Busch, Annette Kolodny, Cecelia Tichi, Marcia B. Kline, among others.

10. Heinz Göhring has termed the (supposedly) dominant Latin American attitude

toward the natural environment as "submission under nature," and with respect to the much more visible Amerindian population there as "harmony with nature," in contrast to the US "control of nature" (91–93; my translation). Frederick B. Pike's *The United States and Latin America: Myths and Stereotypes of Civilization and Nature* contains a wealth of valuable material on the US American myth of Latin America as primitive and uncivilized. Unfortunately, his own study suffers from a rather unsophisticated approach to social, psychological, and philosophical concepts. David A. Brading's *The First America* offers material for a more complex view of Latin American conditions through the nineteenth century.

11. Concerning the problematic notion of "primitive peoples," cf. Terry Goldie, particularly 19–40.

12. Regarding Anglo-Saxon prejudices about the Hispanic world, cf. Charles Gibson (1971) and Philip W. Powell (1971).

13. See also Vera Kutzinski and Ottmar Ette's defense of Humboldt in the introduction to their new critical English edition of his *Essai politique sur l'île de Cuba*, notably their polemic against the distorted view created by John Thrasher's cannibalizing translation of 1856, which turned Humboldt into a defender of slavery and colonialism. For a differentiated analysis of his achievement from the point of view of a historian of Latin America, see Brading's chapter on Humboldt, 514–34.

14. This is Pratt's short version of the title, an attempt to do justice to the descriptions of both nature and cultural artifacts. A critical new English edition, *Views of the Cordilleras*, was published in 2013, but in a much smaller format. I refer to the new and excellent German folio edition whose reproduction of the plates is admirable.

15. The cover illustration of Pratt's *Imperial Eyes* shows this Latin American practice as an example of colonial exploitation.

16. Current plans to build a second canal, this time through Nicaragua, and now financed by China, add another ironic note to Stephens's vision.

17. Concerning the role of gender and race in spatial perception, Gillian Rose gives a short version of the feminist argument: "Only white heterosexual men can usually enjoy such a feeling of spatial freedom. Women know that spaces are not necessarily without constraint; sexual attacks warn them that their bodies are not meant to be in public spaces, and racist and homophobic violence delimits the spaces of black and gay communities. There's also a sense of powerful knowledge of space—the space of that kind of geography is constructed as absolutely knowable" (160). This argument (which Derek Gregory quotes and discusses critically, cf. 126–28) is powerful and yet not universally valid. In our context, it should be mentioned that Alexander von Humboldt was gay, that there were American women directly supporting the filibustering movement (cf. May), and that public discourses are shared even where a female author (Mary Peabody Mann) approaches the subject of Latin America from a different angle. It is worth mentioning that Mary Mann corresponded with the Argentine writer and future president Domingo Faustino Sarmiento and translated his *Facundo* into English (Ard xiv), thus showing a certain familiarity with alternative, Latin American views of nature and civilization. That hers was nonetheless a perspective severely limited by her New England notions both of slavery and the superiority of anything US American over Latin American societies is discussed in Julia C. Paulk's "Visions of Cuba." See also the chapter in Iván Jaksić devoted to Mann, 109–24.

18. In her chapter on the inter-American contexts of Hawthorne's "Rappaccini's Daughter," Anna Brickhouse reports that Mary suggested to her brother-in-law that he should "write a novel of slavery and Cuban plantation life" (199) but did not mention her own novel, which does just that.

19. According to Patricia M. Ard, who did the new edition of the novel in 2000, "Mary Mann did not wish to publish her book during the lifetimes of the Cuban family on which she based the fictional Rodriguezes" (xvi).

20. On Brooks's transformation into María del Occidente, cf. Kirsten S. Gruesz, *Ambassadors of Culture*, Chapter 2.

21. This motif of the universal fellahin occurs in other works by Kerouac as well, as Rachel Adams and others have pointed out. Adams devotes her chapter on Kerouac to his role as a continental, transnational traveler and mediator between the French Canadian world his family came from, the United States, and Mexico. Cf. *Continental Divides*, Chapter 4.

22. See Chapter 7 in this volume.

23. Compare this to John Dos Passos's different, more realistic geographical imaginary quoted in the previous chapter: "On the map you see Mexico being pushed into the small end of the funnel of North America with the full weights of Yanquilandia crushing it down."

24. One might here envision the next step of a literary processing of the material, namely the transformation of Mexican nature and topography into a symbolic and metaphoric interior space of the individual as well as the collective subconscious. The Anglo-Canadian Malcolm Lowry successfully did just that in his great novel *Under the Volcano* (1947), where Mexico functions as both paradise and hell in the psychological, sociopolitical, and philosophical-religious sense. See Chapter 11 in this volume.

*7. Gendered Perceptions*

1. In fact, Aristotle only quotes the "Pythagorean Table of Opposites." He "cites these dichotomies in chapter five of the first book of his *Metaphysics* (at 986a); he does not affirm or adopt them, but merely cites them as an example of the widespread use of contraries or opposites in our thinking" (David F. Krell, personal communication) and thus can be seen as supporting the present argument.

2. It is complicated by an innercultural binarism described by Amy Kaplan in the context of empire: "The binary opposition of the foreign and the domestic is itself imbued with the rhetoric of gender hierarchies that implicitly elevate the international to a male, public realm, and relegate the national to a female, private sphere" ("'Left Alone with America,'" Kaplan and Pease, *Cultures of United States Imperialism*, 16).

3. The creative and epistemic potential of interdiscursive and, in Deleuze and Guattari's terms, rhizomatic networks, notably in the symbolism of literary texts, was pointed out long ago by Jürgen Link. Cf., for instance, his "Literaturanalyse als Interdiskursanalyse."

4. Here and for the following, cf. Julia Kristeva, *Revolution*.

5. This includes a hint of homosexuality in Tommo's relationship with his male guide.

6. The mythicizing of the untouched jungle and the Indian woman representing it is a topos in this type of literature. Remarkably, it can be found not only in European or Anglo-American texts, but also in Latin American literature, as soon as the wilderness is

no longer seen as the enemy per se, but only as the enemy of a deficient civilization. See, for instance, the Colombian writer José Eustasio Rivera's novel *La vorágine* (1924). Cf. Harald Wentzlaff-Eggebert, 1992.

7. The classic, comprehensive survey of gender roles in Britain and the United States during the nineteenth century is to be found in Elizabeth K. Helsinger, Robin L. Sheets, and William Veeder.

8. As I have mentioned before, Amy Kaplan has analyzed this interplay between the foreign and the domestic in the age of imperialism in her *The Anarchy of Empire*, notably in the chapter "Manifest Domesticity," 23–50.

9. One such text is Alan Harrington's adventure novel *The White Rainbow* (1981). Here, however, the "Community of the Sixth Sun," a neo-Aztec fundamentalist cult and colony started by a crazed man of mixed Castilian and Indian heritage, is shown as a completely negative attempt to achieve a kind of "regeneration through violence," a regeneration serving first and foremost the charismatic leader and not the downtrodden people on whose behalf he pretends to be acting. The American anthropologist visiting the community in order to study its order and behavior is therefore not integrated, but becomes the intended victim of the renewed Aztec practice of human sacrifice. He is rescued at the last minute by his loyal wife, both experiencing some sort of personality healing in the process. Harrington uses a great number of negative anti-Mexico stereotypes from the repertoire of Latinamericanism, including that of sexual license. The positive acceptance of their bodies that the protagonist's wife notices among the inhabitants of Mexico City is not made part of a fresh view of the coming together of the physical and the spiritual nature of mankind, as in Lawrence's novel. Cf. Anita Grassl's unpublished master's thesis "Die Mexiko-Darstellung in der neueren amerikanischen Romanliteratur und der Einfluss D. H. Lawrences."

10. Obviously, this is true of nonfiction writing as well (cf. June E. Hahner xvii).

11. This role has become so stereotypical that Carlos Fuentes adopted it for his purposes when he introduced the American female protagonist of his *Gringo Viejo*, discussed earlier in Chapter 6. At the same time, Fuentes's remarkable text, which, as we have seen, is meant to expose the foundations of both the US American and the Mexican alterity and identity discourses, indicates the way in which the female teacher's sense of mission converges with male versions of gaining control over what both *gringos* and *gringas* regard as an inferior culture and society.

12. Cf. Slavoj Žižek: "the fascinating image of the Other personifies our own innermost split—what is already 'in us more than ourselves'—and thus prevents us from achieving full identity with ourselves. *The hatred of the Other is the hatred of our own excess of enjoyment*" (57).

13. This generalization is, of course, also another simplification and, as such, part of the discourse about the Latin American Other itself. For complicating alternatives, see for instance Ana Patricia Rodríguez's comments on "transfronterista feminisms" (145).

14. Carol P. McCormack provides a critical analysis of such stereotypical dichotomous analogizing.

15. I take my examples from Gabriele Pisarz-Ramírez, who has emphasized this point.

16. In the terminology of Raymond Williams, *Problems*.

17. That she is (also?) a Latina can be deduced from her appearing as such in Taylor's later novel *OutRageous*, but in *Faultline* this doesn't seem to play a role.

18. Stephen Park (Chapter 5) points out that the novel is also an echo of earlier women's pan-American travel narratives and that revisiting is one of its principal methods of approaching the theme of Pan Americanism from a female, Chicana, perspective.

19. Hector A. Torres provides a good analysis of the narrative structure of the novel, of Castillo's method of developing her narrative authority, and of the way the individual unit (in his case, Letter 3) relates to the rest in spite of the fragmentation of time sequence and the disruptions of individual identities.

20. Castillo was born in 1953. The autobiographical aspect as well as the fragmented nature of the self is hinted at in an interview with Bryce Milligan, where Castillo says, "[I]n *The Mixquiahuala Letters*, I used the lowercase 'i' throughout because I feel—and I may be wrong about this—I feel that I am talking about a lot of people. So I also wrote in things that I had heard from other people" (Castillo, "An Interview," 26).

21. Erlinda Gonzales-Berry suggests that the very last, lowercased line is Teresa speaking in her own voice, and that in the use of the "crass, masculine phrase" it explodes the language traditionally associated with the Oedipal father-son situation (Gonzales-Berry 121).

22. Given her previous relationship with Libra, though, it is doubtful that this micro-utopia will ever come to pass.

23. Cf. Castillo, *Massacre of the Dreamers*. See also Maria-Cristina Ghiban.

8. *The Post-Vietnam Era*

1. The one exception is Julia in Wylie's *The Sign of Dawn*, if one may call her a true protagonist.

2. There were more than twenty civil wars and other armed internal conflicts in Latin America from 1945 through the end of the century. This is not counting international conflicts like the Falkland/Malvinas War or the "Soccer War" between El Salvador and Honduras. In many cases of internal conflict, the United States intervened directly or indirectly, primarily because it saw a danger of the country's falling into leftist hands.

3. Robert S. Leiken and Barry Rubin, eds., *The Central American Crisis Reader* contains much useful primary material for the study of the issues and contexts of that period. William M. LeoGrande's *Our Own Backyard: The United States in Central America, 1977–1992* is a comprehensive study of US policy in Central America in the sequence of the Vietnam War.

4. The great Austrian sociologist developed the concept in the context of his phenomenological typology of knowledge in *Der sinnhafte Aufbau der sozialen Welt* (1932).

5. See Markus Gabriel's entertaining gallop through some of the central questions of (epistemological) philosophy, *Warum es die Welt nicht gibt* (*Why Reality Doesn't Exist*).

6. The best summary of Howells's theory I have seen is Ulrich Halfmann's "'A Faithful Representation of Our Experiences of Life': Zur Romantheorie von William Dean Howells."

7. In the beginning of the novel, Paul Robeson's death (Jan. 23, 1976) is mentioned (18).

8. The American edition does not have numbered chapters as the British (Picador) does.

9. That Ortega reminds Aguirre of "the Old Man" (209) may be a concealed reference to Augusto César Sandino, the leader of the armed resistance against the US military oc-

cupation of Nicaragua in the late 1920s and early 1930s. The "Atapa Indian" leader a la Torre, one of the revolutionaries, resembles Sandino in his physical description and also his adherence to Adventism.

10. For extended analyses of this character, cf., among others, Robert S. Fredrickson; Brady Harrison.

11. Gregory Stephenson's detailed analysis of the characters and their perspectives as well as of the central symbols is overly positive as far as Justin's and particularly Father Egan's developments are concerned—the latter fails to convert any of the serial murderers Campos, Weitling, and Pablo—and overly negative as to the opposition's leaders, whose revolution "must inevitably end in a Stalinist-style tyranny: the man whom Aguirre has chosen to lead the revolution—the ruthless and self-righteous Emilio Ortega Curtis—is the very type of an aspiring tyrant" (80). Neither the Sandinista nor even the Cuban revolutions have resulted in anything coming close to Stalinist despotism. Just like virtually all of the criticism I have seen, Stephenson largely sidesteps the sociopolitical, inter-American aspects of this novel.

12. Patricia Merivale offers the intriguing options that it might have been Grace playing the power game or even Charlotte who saw to it that the guerillas would receive an extra shipment of arms. In the second case, this would have enabled Charlotte to quasi-join her daughter's revolutionary activities and to die for them (Merivale 103–4).

13. Of course, we get to know both sides only through Grace's rendering. She explains her extensive depiction of Charlotte's life and contexts in the United States by her fascination with Charlotte as a person.

14. Wylie is not mentioned in Richard L. Jackson, *Black Writers and Latin America*, a book that contains much information about the cross-cultural influences of black literary and political movements, for instance the impact of the US Civil Rights movement on Brazilian blacks, 102–6.

15. This move is almost but not quite as unlikely as that of the English hero of H. Rider Haggard's nineteenth-century novel *Montezuma's Daughter*, who joins the Aztecs in their fight against the Spanish. Not quite, because we have to remember the fates and careers of dissidents in the period of the Civil Rights movement and the Vietnam protest, for instance real-life black activists such as Assata Shakur, who also found asylum in Cuba.

16. That this extremely wild tribe in their jungle holdout should use banana leaves for camouflage and get high on banana syrup is one of the many cases where Wylie uses the facts with much poetic license. Bananas are not native to Brazil; they come from Southeast Asia and were introduced in Brazil by the Portuguese.

17. The novel still does better than Marc Iverson's *Fire Storm* (1992), which uses a comparable setup and is the first inter-American novel after the collapse of communism to take the new situation into consideration: after the loss of Russian aid, Cuba has to rely on drug money, to secure which it sends troops to Peru in support of a general revolution staged by the Sendero Luminoso. When the Senderistas take over Lima, they provoke massive American involvement, which, of course, solves the crisis. The novel is unmistakably a political pamphlet in disguise. Its symbolic action presents Latin Americans as wicked or helpless and demonstrates the continued need for US military strength even after the end of the Cold War. Interestingly enough, the novel shows the Cuban soldiers as disciplined and capable of strategic planning, whereas the Senderistas conform to the usual image of unreliable, uncontrolled, and unnecessarily brutal *mestizos*. That is, Latin

American competency, where it does exist, comes with an evil purpose or is the result of other-directedness. Countless spy and drug novels before 1990 also represented Cuba as the exponent of all that was negative (read: anti-American) in the world. However, the conspiracies and revolutions described in so much popular fiction on Latin America do not result in any significant change. As I have argued in Chapter 2, the discursive construction of Latin American societies sees them as essentially static, and in this respect *The Sign of Dawn* is a positive exception.

9. *The Postmodern Response*

1. For an analysis of the controversy over the term, cf. Graciela Maturo 167–84.

2. Amaryll Chanady, author of an important earlier study on magical realism, devotes a recent essay to discussing the current use of the term. She begins with commenting on the limitations of her former distinction of the fantastic, where the supernatural enters as the terrifyingly logical impossible, and magical realism, where the rational and the magical simply exist side by side in the same cultural context (a concept I still find useful), and then gives a survey of contemporary definitions. She now emphasizes the usefulness of the term for a cultural self-definition under the auspices of postcolonialism. Such an approach makes experiments like Updike's *Brazil* appear as even more problematic. See Chanady, "Magic Realism Revisited."

3. This is not to say that a meeting of the realistic and the fantastic is acceptable only where Latin American narrative material is involved; Updike's own *The Witches of Eastwick* is a case in point. But the use of magical-realistic elements in a work set in Brazil cannot be seen without taking this tradition into consideration.

4. The *bandeirantes* were members of armed colonial Portuguese expeditions exploring the hinterland of what was later to become the state of Brazil during the sixteenth through eighteenth centuries. Their primary aim was to capture Natives for enslavement; later, another goal was to discover precious minerals. In *Os Sertões*, da Cunha writes about a rebellion of religiously fanatic backcountry people in the late nineteenth century; the leather clothing of the *vaqueiros* involved is described in somewhat similar terms to that of Updike's *bandeirantes*.

5. The parts of the country shown are those familiar from *National Geographic*: "Brazil for tourists is shown: Brasilia [*sic*], Ouro Prêto, the Manaus opera house, the Mato Grosso or large scrubland in the country's middle; in Rio, the Copacabana apartment and the shanty of the Hill of Babylon no bigger than the apartment's bathroom" (Jay Prosser 86).

6. His psoriasis certainly pressed the theme upon him; cf. Prosser 87.

7. Updike published a letter to his two mulatto grandsons in *Self-Consciousness* (1989). Cf. Dilvo I. Ristoff's comprehensive discussion of Updike's handling of the theme of race.

8. The Chinese characters concluding the book are said to signify "marinated vegetable" and "tofu soup."

9. These terms are used in American English to indicate a party in a legal case whose name is unknown, or, more generally, a person of no clear identity or individuality, an Everyman.

10. A particularly gruesome example is Alan Harrington's *The White Rainbow*, mentioned here in Chapter 7. The pyramid as a focal point of plot and symbolism figures

prominently in many texts including those by Mexican writers. Cf., for instance, Carlos Fuentes, *Cambio de piel.*

11. Charles Caramello has shown that Kenneth Gangemi's also alphabetically arranged, postmodern Mexican travelogue *The Volcanoes from Puebla* does not achieve the same complexity as Abish's book or Michel Butor's *Mobile.*

12. This interview provides remarkable evidence of Abish's insistence on a nonrepresentational reading of the novel, quite contrary to the interviewer's efforts to elicit clear comments on content and message.

*10. Splintered Foundations*

1. Although most of the reviews of the novel were positive, it has received little scholarly attention. Apart from my early article, which forms the basis of the present subchapter, Mónica Calvo-Pascual in her published dissertation lists one article of her doctoral advisor and some papers of her own that she used in her book (3–4). Hans-Joachim Lang discusses Marlowe's image of Columbus in the context of the American literary tradition concerning the explorer. He emphasizes Marlowe's postmodern depersonalizing and dehistoricizing of the historical person ("Kolumbus," 566–69).

2. Calvo-Pascual devotes a whole chapter (57–90) to tracing the verifiable historical facts and sources and putting them in relation to both the legendary material and Marlowe's fictional inventions, thereby revealing the textual complexity of the novel, which she then, in the next chapter (91–113), tackles with chaos theory.

3. This is one of the many jokes about the vagueness of any piece of historical information. Because the *Golden Hind* was the name of Drake's ship, this is also one of the countless historical allusions and cross-references in the book.

4. The American tradition of having Columbus have a deathbed vision of the future is here jokingly referred to when Columbus steps into the street and finds it quite dark—"But my vision clears" (567). The next step, not only to have Columbus make a deathbed confession but to have him comment on later events (in this case the futile attempts to have him canonized) from a modern point in time, was taken by Alejo Carpentier in his *El Arpa y la Sombra* (Havana, 1979), which may have been one of Marlow's pre-texts.

5. Calvo-Pascual points out that not all subsequent editions carry this note—but it is quite unclear who authorized these later versions, and thus the question or joke remains open.

6. Examples are, for instance, the Native texts dealing with the invasion of the New World in Gordon Brotherston, *Image of the New World: The American Continent Portrayed in Native Texts*, and Ralph Bauer's edition and translation of Titu Cusi Yupanqui, *An Inca Account of the Conquest of Peru.*

7. Dorris and Erdrich collaborated also in the texts they published under their individual names. Their respective roles are hard to determine as long as the manuscripts are not accessible.

8. Here they resemble their authors, both of whom are or were of mixed descent. Erdrich is an enrolled member of the Turtle Mountain Band of the Anishinaabe. Dorris claimed to be part Modoc and, during his lifetime, was considered part of the Native American literary scene. I am not concerned here with the debate about his background and life that arose after his death in 1997.

9. Cf. Hayden White's typology in *Tropics* referred to earlier, Chapter 3 n. 10.

10. The diary has not survived but has come to us only in a possibly bowdlerized copy.

11. It was a yellow raft in blue water, to be sure, and thus an unmistakable reminder of Dorris's best-known novel, *A Yellow Raft in Blue Water*, which describes the fate of another mixed-blood daughter.

12. Cf. Frank Kermode, *The Sense of an Ending.*

13. Like "Roger Williams," this is one of the many referentially loaded names in the novel.

14. She is not the first Native American intellectual to engage with the situation south of the border. Cf., for instance, James H. Cox, *Red Land to the South*, which delineates the interest of American Indian writers of the 1920–60 period in revolutionary indigenous activities in Mexico.

15. Even Dorris's book of juvenile fiction about a Taino girl on the eve of discovery, *Morning Girl*, presents a much more complex picture of indigenous society.

16. The same point was made by Michael Dorris in a talk he gave at the 1992 conference of the European Association of American Studies at Seville, Spain, April 4, 1992; we may therefore assume that this is a position shared by the authors.

17. This refers to the de Madariaga theory mentioned above.

18. Hans Bak even sees an anagram of the names Michael Dorris and Erdrich. However teasing such speculations may be, they have lost much interest after Dorris's suicide in 1997. The quality of Vizenor's book does not rest upon a potential cryptic engagement with the factions among Native writers, though, but on the convincing way it deals with its major issues

19. I will use the term *genre* here in the loose sense of a category for a set of texts sharing significant components of form or content, or certain societal functions (like the postcolonial novel), or of their reality status (like fiction), but also as a category for certain modes of presentation such as satire or romance.

20. "[T]he French-American self-styled archaeologist Augustus Le Plongeon (1826–1908) [. . .] in the course of his extensive travels and excavations in Yucatán and after living for years in the midst of the Yucatec Maya, came to see the Maya not just as the founders of Atlantis and colonies in the Nile Valley, Mesopotamia and Egypt more than 11,000 years ago, but as the 'source of all world civilization'" (Irmscher 89, quoting from Desmond and Messenger).

21. "Many stones"; cf. Irmscher's cultural contextualization, 174.

22. Benjamin V. Burgess has commented on the way storytelling in the Midewiwin medicinal society in Anishinaabe culture has a healing function that is particularly efficient if the healer has the power to elaborate on a story. Thus, "the story of Columbus can be seen as the creation story of European dominance in America. Vizenor's novel is a level of elaboration to the Columbus story. Before he can elaborate the story, he must capture it. He does this by not setting the novel up as an opposition to the dominant narrative. The dominant narrative is very much alive in his novel; it is the levels of elaboration that make it a story of healing" (22–23).

23. Point Assinika could therefore fulfil the hopes for a global change giving tribal people agency instead of ongoing and equally global colonialism. Cf. Jodi A. Byrd, *The Transit of Empire: Indigenous Critiques of Colonialism.*

24. José David Saldívar devotes the third part of his *The Dialectics of Our America* to "Caliban and Resistance Cultures," and discusses the relevant publications.

*11. Canada and Latin America*

1. "For beauty is nothing/ but the beginning of terror, which we can just barely endure,/ and we stand in awe of it as it coolly disdains/ to destroy us."

2. "Cuando miramos al sur—lo que en el Canadá hacemos con bastante frecuencia—los Estados Unidos bloquean nuestra mirada. Lo mismo ocurre cuando los latinoamericanos levantan la vista hacia el Norte" ("Introducción," 11; the English (presumably the original) version comes from Atwood's old website (http://www.web.net/owtoad/desde.html) that is no longer accessible. Curiously, Atwood's new website does not mention this volume. I owe this quote to Barbara Buchenau and am much obliged to Hans-Herbert Räkel for getting hold of the extremely rare and hard-to-come-by Cuban publication. A reciprocal Latin American view was already formulated by the Brazilian writer and cultural anthropologist Darcy Ribeiro in his study *The Americas and Civilization*, where he describes Canada as "hidden behind the USA" and indeed only "a transplant of Europe—still so folded in the British flag," that is, the old and small world (388).

3. An ambitious earlier attempt is Alvina Ruprecht and Cecilia Taiana, *The Reordering of Culture: Latin America, The Caribbean and Canada in the Hood* (1995).

4. David Leahy uses Gayatri Chakravorty Spivak's term "worlding" for the "violent impact of imperialism on colonized spaces and peoples as well as the forms that inscribe imperial discourse on colonized space" (Leahy 62) as a basis of his own concept of "counter-worlding."

5. One such text is Francine Noël's novel *La conjuration des bâtards* (1999), which takes the main characters of her Montreal-based *Maryse*-cycle of novels to contemporary Mexico City and metahistoriographically refers to historical events such as the Spanish conquest as well. Cf. Catherine Khordoc, "Looking Beyond the Elephant."

6. "Así, en la percepción que Lowry expone acerca de México, más que valores hay aplastantes deficiencias, pesadas distorsiones, una estrechísima parcelización y la cómoda mezquina superficialidad con que mira a este país y este pueblo cualquiera de los miles de holgaz[á]nes norteamericanos y europeos pensionados que radican en Cuernavaca y muchos otros paraísos con que pintan de un tono exótico su irremediable mediocridad" (Moussong 205–6; English translation Penny Georgionis, ibid. 217. The article appeared in the trilingual journal *Ruptures*).

7. In my opinion, his critique of "too much attempted symbolism" (216), of stylistic commonplace sentences, and of Lowry's character drawing misses the essence of the intricately woven tapestry Lowry unfolds before us. Not surprisingly, American Latino/a critics have also voiced negative opinions about Lowry's representation of Mexico. Thus, Daniel Cooper Alarcón correctly writes that "[t]he inhabitants of Lowry's Mexico fall easily into well-defined categories" (*The Aztect Palimpsest*, 70). However, his perception is obviously also clouded by bias: "Curiously, these Mexicans are all characterized by their use of broken English, and here Lowry illustrates another of the racist moves typical of the adventure novel: classifying the Other as inferior through inferior speech. Yet, why should any of these characters be speaking English in the first place? Equally ludicrous is the fact that the Consul, Hugh, and Yvonne all speak excellent Spanish" (71). Wrong on both counts: the Consul mistranslates the sign in the public garden bordering on his own, "¿LE GUSTA ESTE JARDÍN? ¿QUE ES SUYO? ¡EVITE QUE US HIJOS LO DESTRUYAN!", into "You like this garden? Why is it yours? We evict those who destroy!" (Lowry 172), in line with his fear of being evicted from paradise. And Geoffrey's old confidante, Señora Gregorio, whose English is indeed "inferior," commands beautiful, poetic

Spanish (that Lowry renders in translation): "'*Adiós*,' she added in Spanish, 'I have no house only a shadow. But whenever you are in need of a shadow, my shadow is yours'" (273).

8. "obra magnífica y monumental [. . .] que tan bien describe la tragedia íntima de todo un país, México, a través de la experiencia personal de una artista como Malcolm Lowry" (Lara Zavala, "Las poéticas," 12; my translation).

9. Douglas Day provides a useful survey of the main levels of meaning construction in this book: the "chthonic," which includes topography, nature, the elements, but also man-made elements like the bars, the *cantinas*; the "human," meaning the characters; the "political"; the "magical," referring notably to the Cabbala symbols the Consul believes in; and the "religious" in the sense of man's struggle between heaven and hell (Day 327–50). Other classifications are of course possible, and Lowry himself in his letter to publisher Cape insists on such a plurality of simultaneously existing levels. Sherrill Grace speaks of "four basic narrative levels—story, fable, allegory, and myth" (*Voyage*, 37).

10. Lowry slightly fictionalized it by using the Nahuatl name "near the wood," in keeping with the pervasive forest symbolism echoing Dante's "selva oscura."

11. The Union Nacional Sinarquista was founded only in May 1939, but protofascist movements had been active before.

12. Maps, as any geographer knows, are also subject to discursive conventions of representation, political claims, and so forth.

13. The symbolic importance of landscape in this novel is obvious. Landscape features are so closely linked to the mindsets of the protagonists that Douglas W. Veitch explores the whole novel on the basis of an analysis of the landscape descriptions (Veitch 112–81).

14. For this and similar items, cf. Chris Ackerley and David Large, Malcolm Lowry Project; the website gives immensely helpful information about just about any textual passage. It complements Ackerley's *A Companion to "Under the Volcano,"* co-authored with Lawrence J. Clipper, and his later "'Plenty of Obscure Points': A Supplement to *A Companion to 'Under the Volcano.'*"

15. The significance of this passage was first pointed out to me by Professor Holger Helbig, at that time a student of mine. He and Barbara Gluch, who wrote excellent term papers on this novel, have helped me understand the function of the Mexican settings.

16. The allusion to Aeneas carrying his father Anchises is not to be missed.

*12. Post-Vietnam and Canadian Visitors*

1. That these passages are written in the future tense may, however, indicate that Rennie does not only have a past and a present but a future as well.

2. For the role of the tourist, see also Diana Brydon, "Caribbean Revolution."

3. It is close to Barbados; Grenada can be seen from there.

4. I owe this and other pieces of useful information concerning the political background of the novel to a term paper by my Erlangen student Katja Michalik.

5. Relations deteriorated further when President Reagan took office in 1981. Bishop's overthrow by a party rival, his murder by the military, and the US armed intervention to "establish order" in 1983 give Atwood's novel some kind of prophetic quality and highlight her ability as an observer of international politics from her Amnesty International perspective. It might be useful to compare Atwood's novel to others dealing with political unrest in the Caribbean. The political reality of a Caribbean island country, including the disastrous role of the CIA, is much more dominant and more explicitly demonstrated, for

instance, in US author Speer Morgan's *Brother Enemy*, which was published the same year as *Bodily Harm*. The fictionalized country there is Jamaica. Morgan uses British and American focalizing figures who are or get much more involved than Atwood's representative tourist ever will be. *Brother Enemy* has far more elements of a thriller and does not reach the literary quality of *Bodily Harm*. Cf. Michalik.

6. Many of these details reach Rennie only by hearsay and may thus be considered not entirely reliable, adding to the uncertainty she feels in the alien country.

7. When I asked Atwood at a Canadianists conference in Germany in 1992 why Rennie wasn't allowed to learn more specifics about the Third World country, for instance about the local gender roles, she replied that Rennie was "on vacation" and thus shared the blindnesses and preconceptions of tourist travelers as described in the stories of Susan Swan's *Unfit for Paradise*. She also emphasized that she had written not so much on local but on structural and therefore global forms of injustice, oppression, and human rights violations, taking much of her information from the goings-on in East Timor.

8. Atwood called the book an "anti-thriller." See Atwood, "An Interview with Margaret Atwood" by Betsy Draine, 379.

9. And to a certain extent, the voices are also British, if one remembers the nasty hotel official.

10. To my knowledge, the story was first published in an Austrian publication from 1986 by the German press Königshausen & Neumann, from which it is here quoted. It was reprinted in *Island* 50 (Autumn 1992): 40–43.

11. The characters reminisce about Edward VIII, who died that year.

12. This is a historical fact. The grave robbery was never cleared up and the skull never returned. Cf. Friedrich Katz 798.

13. It might be useful to read Hale's novel against the postrevolutionary, posttraumatic Guatemalan and Salvadoran fiction discussed by Rodríguez, notably in Chapter 4.

14. The Guatemalan civil war of 1960–96 resulted from the political situation described in Asturias's "¡Americanos Todos!" and continued the basic conflicts between landowners, rightist governments, military officers, and foreign interest-holders on the one side and leftist reformers or revolutionary groups and particularly the indigenous population on the other (cf. Chapter 1 n. 12 in this volume). Most of the approximately 200,000 victims belonged to the rural Maya population. The explicitness of Hale's description goes far beyond those in Asturias and may have been influenced by Rigoberta Menchú's autobiography. That the war atrocities in Guatemala even made it into the forensic thriller genre (cf. Kathy Reichs, *Grave Secrets*) doesn't make up for the shortage of other literary texts devoted to this chapter of Latin American and inter-American history.

15. Hale explains and defends her imaginary approach to historical and fictional characters, her "karmic appointments" ("Imagining," 67), her "elaborate fantasy of the inner lives of [. . .] dead people," and her panic about her "arrogance in entering into the intimate lives of real historical personages" (69) in her autobiographical essay "Imagining a Geometry of the Soul."

16. There are other anachronisms, such as the "coins" (186) Malintzín's mother is said to have received from the slave traders for selling her daughter.

# BIBLIOGRAPHY


*Primary Material*

Abish, Walter. *Alphabetical Africa*. New York: New Directions, 1974.

———. *Eclipse Fever*. New York: Knopf, 1993.

———. *How German Is It—Wie Deutsch Ist Es*. New York: New Directions, 1980.

———. "An Interview with Walter Abish on *Eclipse Fever*." By Maarten van Delden. *Annals of Scholarship* 10.3–4 (1993): 381–91.

Agustín, José. *Ciudades desiertas*. Barcelona: Grijalbo Mondadori Sa, 1986.

Alarcón, Daniel. "Second Lives." *20 under 40: Stories from the* New Yorker. Ed. Deborah Treisman. New York: Farrar, Straus & Giroux, 2010. 45–69.

Alexander, J. Park. *Mexico: Facts About the Republic of Mexico Gathered in a Recent Brief Visit, and Informally Set Down in Letters to His Family of Akron, O.* Akron: Beacon, 1890.

Armstrong, Jeannette C. "History Lesson." *Seventh Generation: Contemporary Native Writing*. Ed. Heather Hodgson. Penticton, BC: Theytus Books, 1989. 54–55.

Asturias, Miguel Ángel. *Week-end en Guatemala*. 1956. Repr., Buenos Aires: Editorial Losada, 1963.

Atwood, Margaret. *Bodily Harm*. 1982. London: Virago, 1983.

———. "An Interview with Margaret Atwood." By Betsy Draine. *Interviews with Contemporary Writers: Second Series, 1972–1982*. Ed. L.S. Dembo. Madison: University of Wisconsin Press, 1983. 366–81.

———. *Selected Poems 1965–1975*. Boston: Houghton Mifflin, 1987.

———. *Surfacing*. 1972. London: Virago, 1979.

———. "Using What You're Given: An Interview with Margaret Atwood." By Jo Brans. *Southwest Review* 68.4 (Autumn 1983): 301–15.

———, and Graeme Gibson, eds. *Desde el invierno: veintitrés cuentos canadienses*. Trans. Blanca Acosta and María Teresa Ortega. Havana, Cuba: Ediciones Unión; Toronto: McClelland Stewart, 1997.

Barlow, Joel. *The Works of Joel Barlow*. 2 vols. Ed. William K. Bottorff and Arthur L. Ford. Gainesville, FL: Scholars' Facsimiles and Reprints, 1970.

Beach, Rex Ellington. *Jungle Gold*. New York: Rinehart, 1935.

Beals, Carleton. *Mexican Maze*. Philadelphia: Lippincott, 1931.

———. *The Stones Awake*. Philadelphia: Lippincott, 1936.

Bell, Christine. *Saint*. Englewood, FL: Pineapple Press, 1985.

Berkeley, George. *The Works of George Berkeley, D. D.* 4 vols. Oxford: Clarendon Press, 1871.

Bierce, Ambrose. *The Letters of Ambrose Bierce*. Ed. Bertha Clark Pope. New York: Gordian P, 1967.

Bird, Robert Montgomery. *Calavar; or, The Knight of the Conquest: A Romance of Mexico*. Philadelphia: Carey, Lea & Blanchard, 1834.

———. *The Infidel; or, The Fall of Mexico*. Philadelphia: Carey, Lea & Blanchard, 1835.

Bishop, Elizabeth. *The Complete Poems, 1927–1979*. New York: Farrar, Straus & Giroux, 1983.

———. *Questions of Travel*. New York: Farrar, Straus & Giroux, 1965.

Borges, Jorge Luis. "El idioma analítico de John Wilkins." *La Nación*, Feb. 8, 1942.

Bradbury, Ray. *The Stories of Ray Bradbury*. New York: Alfred A. Knopf, 1980.

Carpentier, Alejo. *The Harp and the Shadow* (*El arpa y la sombra*, 1979). Trans. Thomas and Carol Christensen. San Francisco: Mercury House, 1990.

Castillo, Ana. "An Interview with Ana Castillo." By Bryce Milligan. *South Central Review* 16.1 (Spring 1999): 19–29.

———. *Massacre of the Dreamers: Essays on Xicanisma*. New York: Penguin, 1994.

———. *The Mixquiahuala Letters*. Binghamton, NY: Bilingual Press, 1986.

Cooper, James Fenimore. *Jack Tier; or, The Florida Reef*. 1848. *Cooper's Novels*. Darley Edition. New York: Townsend, 1860.

———. *The Letters and Journals of James Fenimore Cooper*. 6 vols. Ed. James F. Beard. Cambridge, MA: Harvard University Press, 1960–68.

———. *Mercedes of Castile, or, The Voyage to Cathay*. 1840. Cooper's Novels. Darley Edition. New York: Townsend, 1861.

———. *Notions of the Americans, Picked Up by a Travelling Bachelor*. 2 vols. New York: Ungar, 1963.

Crane, Stephen. *The Complete Short Stories and Sketches of Stephen Crane*. Ed. Thomas A. Gullason. Garden City, NY: Doubleday, 1963.

———. *Stephen Crane in the West and Mexico*. Ed. Joseph Katz. Kent, OH: Kent State University Press, 1970.

Curley, Daniel. *Mummy*. Boston: Houghton Mifflin, 1987.

Cushing, Caleb. Review of *Codice diplomatico Colombo-Americano, ossia Raccolta di Documenti originali e inediti, spettanti a Cristofero Colombo* [. . .]. *North American Review* 21 (1825): 398–429.

Davis, Richard Harding. *Soldiers of Fortune*. 1897. New York: Scribner's, 1927.

———. *Three Gringos in Venezuela and Central America*. 1896. New York: Harper, 1904.

Didion, Joan. *A Book of Common Prayer*. New York: Washington Square Press, 1977.

———. "Joan Didion, The Art of Fiction No. 71." Interview by Linda Kuehl. *Paris Review* 74 (Fall–Winter 1978). http://www.theparisreview.org./interviews/3439/the-art-of-fiction-no-71-joan-didion (11 pp).

———. "Joan Didion, The Art of Nonfiction No. 1." Interview by Hilton Als. *Paris Review* 176 (Spring 2006). http://www.theparisreview.org/interviews/5601/the-art-of-nonfiction-no-1-joan-didion (15 pp).

———. *Salvador*. New York: Vintage, 1983.

———. "A Visit with Joan Didion." By Sara Davidson. *New York Times Book Review*, Apr. 3, 1977. http://www.saradavidson.com/NytDidion.html (5 pp).

———. "Why I Write." *New York Times Book Review*, Dec. 5, 1976.

Dorfman, Ariel. *Heading South, Looking North: A Bilingual Journey*. New York: Penguin, 1999.

Dorris, Michael. *Morning Girl*. New York: Hyperion Book CH, 1992.

———, and Louise Erdrich. *The Crown of Columbus*. New York: HarperCollins, 1991.

Dos Passos, John. *1919*. 1932. Repr. as Pt. II of *U.S.A.* Modern Library Edition. New York: Random House, 1937.

———. *The 42nd Parallel*. 1930. Repr. as Pt. I of *U.S.A.* Modern Library Edition. New York: Random House, 1937.

———. *In All Countries*. London: Constable, 1934.

Everett, Edward. Review of D. Gregorio Funes, *Ensayo de la historia Civil del Paraguay, Buenos-Ayres, y Tucuman*. *North American Review* 12 (1821): 432–43.

Fernández Retamar, Roberto. *Caliban and Other Essays*. Trans. Edward Baker. Minneapolis: University of Minnesota Press, 1989.

Flandrau, Charles Macomb. *Viva Mexico!* New York: Appleton, 1908. Repr. ed., C. Harvey Gardiner. Urbana: University of Illinois Press, 1964.

Freneau, Philip. *The Poems of Philip Freneau: Poet of the American Revolution*. 2 vols. Ed. Fred L. Pattee. Princeton: University Library, 1902. Repr., Toronto: University of Toronto Libraries, 2011.

Fuentes, Carlos. *A Change of Skin* (*Cambio de piel*, 1967). Trans. Sam Hileman. New York: Farrar, Straus & Giroux, 1968.

———. *The Crystal Frontier* (*La frontera de cristal*, 1995). Trans. Alfred J. MacAdam. New York: Farrar, Straus & Giroux, 1997.

———. *The Old Gringo* (*Gringo viejo*, 1985). Trans. Margaret Sayers-Peden and the author. New York: Farrar, Straus & Giroux, pb. ed. 2007.

Gangemi, Kenneth. *The Volcanoes from Puebla*. London and Boston: Marion Boyers, 1979.

García Márquez, Gabriel. *The Autumn of the Patriarch* (*El otoño del patriarca*, 1975). Trans. Gregory Rabassa. New York: Harper & Row, 1976.

———. *One Hundred Years of Solitude* (*Cien años de soledad*, 1967). Trans. Gregory Rabassa. New York: Harper, 2006.

Gibson, Graeme. "Pancho Villa's Head." *Encounters and Explorations: Canadian Writers and European Critics*. Ed. Franz K. Stanzel and Waldemar Zacharasiewicz. Würzburg: Königshausen und Neumann, 1986. 20–28.

Gill, Tom. *Gentleman of the Jungle*. New York: Putnam, 1940.

Gonzales, Laurence. *El Vago*. New York: Atheneum, 1983.

Hagedorn, Hermann. *The Rough Riders: A Romance*. New York: Harper & Brothers, 1927.

Haggard, H. Rider. *Montezuma's Daughter*. 1893. Rockville, MD: Wildside Press, 2003.

Hale, Amanda. "Imagining a Geometry of the Soul." *Brno Studies in English* 36.2 (2010): 61–79.

———. *The Reddening Path*. Saskatoon: Thistledown Press, 2007.

Harrington, Alan. *The White Rainbow*. Boston: Little, Brown, 1981.

Hawthorne, Nathaniel. *The Scarlet Letter*. Norton Critical Edition. Ed. Seymour Gross et al. 3rd ed. New York: Norton, 1988.

Hazelton, Hugh, and Gary Geddes, eds. *Compañeros: An Anthology of Writings About Latin America*. Dunvegan, ON: Cormorant Books, 1990.

Hergesheimer, Joseph. *The Bright Shawl*. New York: Knopf, 1922.

Houston, Robert. *The Nation Thief*. New York: Pantheon, 1984.

Humboldt, Alexander von. *Ansichten der Kordilleren und Monumente der eingeborenen Völker Amerikas* (*Vues des Cordillères et Monumens des Peuples Indigènes de l'Amérique*, 1810). Ed. Oliver Lubrich and Otmar Ette. Trans. Claudia Kalscheuer. Frankfurt a. M.: Eichborn, 2004.

———. *Views of the Cordilleras and Monuments of the Indigenous Peoples of the Americas: A Critical Edition*. Ed. Vera M. Kutzinski and Ottmar Ette. Chicago: University of Chicago Press, 2013.

Hyde, Anthony. *A Private House*. Toronto: Penguin Canada, 2007.

Irving, Washington. *Journals and Notebooks, Vol. IV, 1826–1829*. Ed. Wayne R. Kime and Andrew B. Myers. *The Complete Works of Washington Irving*. Vol. 4. Boston: Twayne, 1984.

———. *The Life and Voyages of Christopher Columbus*. Ed. John H. McElroy. *The Complete Works of Washington Irving*. Vol. 11. Boston: Twayne, 1981.

Iverson, Marc. *Fire Storm*. New York: Crown, 1992.

Jefferson, Thomas. *Writings*. Ed. Merrill D. Peterson. New York: Viking Press, 1984.

Kerouac, Jack. *On the Road: Text and Criticism*. Ed. Scott Donaldson. New York: Viking, 1979.

Lawrence, D. H. *The Plumed Serpent*. 1926. Harmondsworth: Penguin, 1968.

Levertov, Denise. "Ways of Conquest." *The Freeing of the Dust*. New York: New Directions, 1975. 19.

Lewis, Oscar. *The Children of Sanchez: Autobiography of a Mexican Family*. New York: Vintage Books, 1961.

Lippard, George. *Legends of Mexico*. Philadelphia: T. B. Peterson, 1848.

London, Jack. *Best Short Stories of Jack London*. Garden City, NY: Sun Dial, 1945.

———. *Jack London Reports: War Correspondence, Sports Articles, and Miscellaneous Writings*. Ed. King Hendricks and Irving Shepard. Garden City, NY: Doubleday, 1970.

Lowry, Malcolm. *Under the Volcano*. 1947. London: Penguin, 1987.

Mann, Mary Peabody. *Juanita: A Romance of Real Life in Cuba Fifty Years Ago*. 1887. Ed. Patricia M. Ard. Charlottesville: University of Virginia Press, 2000.

Marlowe, Stephen (Milton S. Lesser). *The Memoirs of Christopher Columbus, with Stephen Marlowe*. 1987. New York: Ballantine Books, 1989.

Martí, José. *José Martí Reader: Writings on the Americas*. Intr. Ivan A. Schulman. North Melbourne: Ocean Press, 2006.

Mather, Cotton. *Magnalia Christi Americana: Books I and II*. Ed. Kenneth B. Murdock and Elizabeth W. Miller. Cambridge, MA: Belknap Press of Harvard University Press, 1977.

Melville, Herman. "Benito Cereno." 1855. *The Piazza Tales and Other Prose Pieces 1839–1860*. Ed. Harrison Hayford, Alma A. MacDougall, and G. Thomas Tanselle. *The Northwestern-Newberry Edition of the Writings of Herman Melville*. Vol. 9. Evanston and Chicago: Northwestern University Press and Newberry Library, 1987. 46–117.

———. *The Confidence-Man: His Masquerade*. 1857. Ed. Harrison Hayford, Hershel Parker, and G. Thomas Tanselle. *The Northwestern-Newberry Edition of the Writings of Herman Melville*. Vol. 10. Evanston and Chicago: Northwestern University Press and Newberry Library, 1987.

———. *Moby-Dick or The Whale*. 1851. Ed. Harrison Hayford, Hershel Parker, and G. Thomas Tanselle. *The Northwestern-Newberry Edition of the Writings of Herman Melville*. Vol. 6. Evanston and Chicago: Northwestern University Press and Newberry Library, 1988.

———. *Typee: A Peep at Polynesian Life*. 1846. Ed. Harrison Hayford, Hershel Parker, and G. Thomas Tanselle. *The Writings of Herman Melville: The Northwestern-Newberry Edition*. Vol. 1. Evanston and Chicago: Northwestern University Press and Newberry Library, 1968.

Menchú, Rigoberta. *I, Rigoberta Menchú: An Indian Woman in Guatemala*. 2nd ed. Trans. Ann Wright. London: Verso, 2010.

Miller, J. W. "Columbus. His Last Embarkment from the New World, A Captive." *The Legendary*. Ed. Nathaniel Parker Willis. Boston: S. G. Goodrich, 1828. 240–43.

Morgan, Speer. *Brother Enemy*. Boston: Little, Brown, 1981.

Morison, Samuel Eliot. *Admiral of the Ocean Sea: A Life of Christopher Columbus*. Boston: Little Brown & Co., 1942.

Morrison, Jessica (Jessica Raya). *The Buenos Aires Broken Hearts Club*. New York: 5 Spot, 2007.

New, William H. *Touching Ecuador*. Lantzville, BC: Oolichan Books, 2006.

Niggli, Josephina. *Mexican Village*. 1945. Albuquerque: University of New Mexico Press, 1994.

Noël, Francine. *La Conjuration des bâtards*. Montréal: Leméac, 1999.

Paley, Grace. *Later the Same Day*. New York: Viking Penguin, 1986.

Palmer, Frederick. *Central America and Its Problems; An Account of a Journey from the Rio Grande to Panama, with Introductory Chapters on Mexico and Her Relations to Her Neighbors*. New York: Moffat, Yard, 1910.

Paz, Octavio. *The Labyrinth of Solitude: Life and Thought in Mexico* (*El laberinto de la soledad*, 1950, enlarged ed. 1959). Trans. Lysander Kemp. New York: Grove Press, 1961.

Porter, Katherine Anne. *The Collected Essays and Occasional Writings of Katherine Anne Porter*. New York: Delacorte, 1970.

———. *The Collected Stories of Katherine Anne Porter*. New York: Harcourt, Brace & World, 1965.

Prescott, William H. *History of the Conquest of Mexico and History of the Conquest of Peru*. 1843, 1847. New York: Modern Library, n.d.

Reed, John. *Daughter of the Revolution and Other Stories*. Ed. Floyd Dell. New York: Vanguard, 1927.

———. *Insurgent Mexico*. New York: Appleton, 1914. Repr., preface by Renato Leduc. New York: International, 1969.

Reichs, Kathy. *Grave Secrets*. New York: Simon & Schuster, 2002.

Revard, Carter. "Report to the Nation: Claiming Europe." *Earth Power Coming: Short Fiction in Native American Literature*. Ed. Simon J. Ortiz. Tsaile, AZ: Navajo Community College Press, 1983. 166–181.

Rilke, Rainer Maria. *Duino Elegies. Bilingual Edition*. Trans. Edward Snow. New York: North Point Press, 2000.

Rodó, José Enrique. *Ariel*. 1900. Ed. Gordon Brotherston. Cambridge: Cambridge University Press, 1967.

Roosevelt, Theodore. *The Rough Riders: A History of the First United States Volunteer Cavalry*. New York: Scribner's, 1899.

Rumaker, Michael. "Gringos." 1966. *Gringos and Other Stories*. Rocky Mount: North Carolina Wesleyan College Press, 1991. 35–64.

Sarmiento, Domingo Faustino. *Facundo: Or, Civilization and Barbarism* (*Facundo*, 1845). Trans. Kathleen Ross. Berkeley: University of California Press, 2004.

Sigourney, Lydia H. "Columbus Before the University of Salamanca." *The Token*. Ed. Nathaniel Parker Willis. Boston: S. G. Goodrich, 1829. 99–101.

Silko, Leslie Marmon. *Ceremony*. New York: Viking Penguin, 1977.

Simmen, Edward, ed. *Gringos in Mexico: An Anthology*. Fort Worth: Texas Christian University Press, 1988.

Simms, William Gilmore. *The Damsel of Darien*. Philadelphia: Lea & Blanchard, 1839.

———. *Vasconcelos: A Romance of the New World*. New York: Redfield, 1853.

Snowden, Richard. *The Columbiad, or, A poem on the American war: in thirteen cantoes*. 1795. Repr., Farmington Hills, MI: Gale, Sabin Americana, 2012.

Steffens, Lincoln. *The Autobiography of Lincoln Steffens*. New York: Harcourt, Brace, 1931.

———. *The World of Lincoln Steffens*. Ed. Ella Winter and Herbert Shapiro. New York: Hill & Wang, 1962.

Stephens, John L. *Incidents of Travel in Central America, Chiapas and Yucatan*. 1841. 2 vols. New York: Dover, 1969.

Stevens, Wallace. *The Collected Poems*. New York: Vintage, 1982.

Stockton, Frank R. *The Adventures of Captain Horn*. 1895. *The Novels and Stories of Frank R. Stockton*. Vol. 9. New York: Scribner's, 1900.

———. *Mrs. Cliff's Yacht*. 1896. *The Novels and Stories of Frank R. Stockton*. Vol. 10. New York: Scribner's, 1900.

Stone, Robert. *A Flag for Sunrise*. New York: Knopf, 1981.

———. Interview by Robert Birnbaum. 2003. www.identitytheory.com/robert-stone/.

———. "An Interview with Robert Stone." By Kay Bonetti. *Missouri Review* 6.1 (1982): 91–115.

———. "Me and the Universe." *TriQuarterly* 65 (Winter 1986): 229–34.

———. "Robert Stone, The Art of Fiction No. 90." Interview by William C. Woods. *Paris Review* 98 (Winter 1985): 1–19. www.theparisreview.org/interviews/28455 the-art-of-fiction-no-90-robert-stone.

———. "Stroking the Sweet-Sour Depths: An Interview with Robert Stone." By Allan Vorda. *Face to Face: Interviews with Contemporary Novelists*. Houston: Rice University Press, 1993. 212–35.

———. "Two Interviews: Talks with Tim O'Brien and Robert Stone." By James Schroeder. *Modern Fiction Studies* 30.1 (1984): 135 [Stone: 151]–164.

———. "We Are Not Excused." *Paths of Resistance: The Art and Craft of the Political Novel*. Boston: Houghton Mifflin, 1989. 17–37.

Sukenick, Ronald. *The Death of the Novel and Other Stories*. New York: Dial Press, 1969.

Swan, Susan. *Unfit for Paradise*. Toronto: Christopher Dingle, 1991.

Szanto, George. *The Condesa of M*. Toronto: Cormorant Books, 2001.

———. *Second Sight*. Montreal: XYZ Publishing, 2004.

———. *The Underside of Stones*. 1990. Montréal: XYZ Publishing, 2004.

Taylor, Sheila Ortiz. *Faultline*. Tallahassee: Naiad Press, 1982.
Theroux, Paul. *The Mosquito Coast*. 1981. London: Penguin, 1982.
Titu Cusi Yupanqui. *An Inca Account of the Conquest of Peru*. Ed. and trans. Ralph Bauer. Boulder: University Press of Colorado, 2005.
Tourgée, Albion W. *Out of the Sunset Sea*. New York: Merrill & Baker, 1893.
Treisman, Deborah, ed. *20 under 40: Stories from the* New Yorker. New York: Farrar, Straus & Giroux, 2010.
Turner, John Kenneth. *Barbarous Mexico*. Chicago: C. H. Kern, 1911. Repr. ed., Sinclair Snow. Austin: University of Texas Press, 1969.
Twain, Mark (Samuel Langhorne Clemens). *A Connecticut Yankee in King Arthur's Court. The Works of Mark Twain*. Vol. 9. Ed. Bernard L. Stein. Berkeley: University of California Press, 1979.
———. *Pudd'nhead Wilson and Those Extraordinary Twins*. 1894. Harper & Brothers Edition. Vol. 5. New York: P. F. Collier & Son, n.d.
Updike, John. *Assorted Prose*. London: Deutsch, 1965.
———. *Brazil*. New York: Knopf, 1994.
———. *Self-Consciousness: Memoirs*. New York: Knopf, 1999.
Vargas Llosa, Mario. *The Storyteller* (*El Hablador*, 1987). Trans. Helen Lane. New York: Farrar, Straus & Giroux, 1989.
Vizenor, Gerald. *Fugitive Poses: Native American Indian Scenes of Absence and Presence*. Lincoln: University of Nebraska Press, 1998.
———. "Gerald Vizenor: The Trickster Heir of Columbus." Interview by Laura Coltelli. *Native American Literature Forum* 2–3 (1990–91): 101–15.
———. *The Heirs of Columbus*. Hanover, NH: Wesleyan University Press, 1991.
———. *Manifest Manners: Postindian Warriors of Survivance*. Hanover, NH: Wesleyan University Press, 1994.
———. "Reversal of Fortunes." *Shadow Distance: A Gerald Vizenor Reader*. Hanover, NH: Wesleyan University Press, 1994. 218–26.
Wallace, Lew. *The Fair God; or, The Last of the Tzins: A Tale of the Conquest of Mexico*. 1873. Boston: Houghton Mifflin, 1884.
Wetmore, Claude H. *In a Brazilian Jungle: Being a Story of Adventure. With an Insight into Brazilian Life and Industries*. Boston: W. A. Wilde, 1903.
Williams, Tennessee. *The Night of the Iguana*. 1961. New York: Dramatists Play Service, 1998.
Winterson, Jeanette. *Sexing the Cherry*. London: Vintage, 1990.
Wright, Rosalind. *Veracruz*. New York: Harper & Row, 1986.
Wylie, James. *The Sign of Dawn*. New York: Viking, 1981.

*Secondary Sources*

Achilles, Jochen. "Die Paradiesvorstellung von der Versöhnung des Menschen mit der Natur: Literaturgeschichtliche Betrachtungen zu einem Aspekt des amerikanischen Traumes." *Amerikastudien/American Studies* 35 (1990): 203–218.
Ackerley, Chris. "'Plenty of Obscure Points': A Supplement to *A Companion to 'Under the Volcano*.'" *Malcolm Lowry Review* 49, 50 (Fall 2001, Spring 2002).
———, and Lawrence J. Clipper. *A Companion to "Under the Volcano."* Vancouver: UBC Press, 1984.

———, and David Large. Malcolm Lowry Project: *Under the Volcano*. University of Otago, New Zealand. http://www.otago.ac.nz/english/lowry.

Adams, Rachel. *Continental Divides: Remapping the Cultures of North America*. Chicago and London: University of Chicago Press, 2009.

Adorno, Rolena. *The Polemics of Possession in Spanish American Narrative*. New Haven: Yale University Press, 2007.

———. "Washington Irving's Romantic Hispanism and Its Columbian Legacies." *Spain in America: The Origins of Hispanism in the United States*. Ed. Richard L. Kagan. Urbana and Chicago: University of Illinois Press, 2002. 49–105.

Aguilar, Alonso. *Pan-Americanism from Monroe to the Present: A View from the Other Side*. Trans. Asa Zatz. Rev. English ed. New York and London: Monthly Review Press, 1968.

Anderson, Benedict. *Imagined Communities: Reflections on the Origin and Spread of Nationalism*. London: Verso Editions, 1983.

Antweiler, Christoph. *Heimat Mensch: Was UNS ALLE verbindet*. Hamburg: Murmann, 2009.

———. *Inclusive Humanism: Anthropological Basics for a Realistic Cosmopolitanism*. Göttingen: V&R unipress, 2012.

Anzaldúa, Gloria. *Borderlands/La Frontera: The New Mestiza*. San Francisco: Aunt Lute Books, 1987.

Ard, Patricia M. Introduction. Mann, Mary Peabody. *Juanita: A Romance of Real Life in Cuba Fifty Years Ago*. 1887. Ed. Patricia M. Ard. Charlottesville: University of Virginia Press, 2000. xi–xxxviii.

Atwood, Margaret. *Survival: A Thematic Guide to Canadian Literature*. Toronto: Anansi, 1972.

Bak, Hans. "The Kaleidoscope of History: Michael Dorris and Louise Erdrich's *The Crown of Columbus* (with a coda on Gerald Vizenor's *The Heirs of Columbus*)." *Deferring a Dream: Literary Sub-Versions of the American Columbiad*. Ed. Gert Buelens and Ernst Rudin. Basel: Birkhauser, 1994. 99–119.

Bakhtin, Mikhail M. *The Dialogic Imagination: Four Essays*. Ed. Michael Holquist. Trans. Caryl Emerson and Michael Holquist. Austin: University of Texas Press, 1981.

Barry, Jackson G. "Narratology's Centrifugal Force: A Literary Perspective on the Extensions of Narrative Theory," *Poetics Today* 11 (1990): 295–307.

Bauer, Ralph. "Colonial Discourse and Early American Literary History: Ercilla, the Inca Garcilaso, and Joel Barlow's Conception of a New World Epic." *Early American Literature* 30.3 (1995): 203–32.

———. *The Cultural Geography of Colonial American Literatures: Empire, Travel, Modernity*. Cambridge: Cambridge University Press, 2003.

———. "The Hemispheric Genealogies of 'race': Creolization and the Cultural Geography of Colonial Difference across the Eighteenth-Century Americas." *Hemispheric American Studies*. Ed. Caroline F. Levander and Robert S. Levine. New Brunswick, NJ: Rutgers University Press, 2008. 36–56.

———. "Hemispheric Studies." *PMLA* 124 (2009): 234–50.

———. "Thomas Jefferson, the Hispanic Enlightenment, and the Birth of Hemispheric American Studies." *Dieciocho* 4 (Spring 2009): 49–82.

Bedini, Silvio A., ed. *The Christopher Columbus Encyclopedia*. 2 vols. New York: Simon & Schuster, 1992.

Beidler, Peter G. Review of *The Crown of Columbus*. *SAIL: Studies in American Indian Literatures* 3/4 (Winter 1991): 47–50.

Benítez-Rojo, Antonio. *The Repeating Island: The Caribbean and the Postmodern Perspective*. Trans. James E. Maraniss. Durham, NC: Duke University Press, 1992.

Bennett, Tony, Lawrence Grossberg, and Meaghan Morris, eds. *New Keywords: A Revised Vocabulary of Culture and Society*. London: Wiley-Blackwell, 2005.

Bercovitch, Sacvan. *The Rites of Assent: Transformations in the Symbolic Construction of America*. New York: Routledge, 1993.

Berger, Mark T. *Under Northern Eyes: Latin American Studies and US Hegemony in the Americas 1898–1990*. Bloomington: Indiana University Press, 1995.

Berger, Peter L., and Thomas Luckmann. *The Social Construction of Reality: A Treatise in the Sociology of Knowledge*. Garden City, NY: Anchor Books, 1966.

Bernecker, Walther L., ed. *1898: su significado para Centroamérica y el Caribe: ¿Cesura, Cambio, Continuidad?* Frankfurt a. M.: Vervuert; Madrid: Iberoamericana, 1998.

Beverley, John. *Latinamericanism after 9/11*. Durham, NC: Duke University Press, 2011.

———, and Marc Zimmerman. *Literature and Politics in the Central American Revolutions*. Austin: University of Texas Press, 1990.

Bhabha, Homi K. "DissemiNation: Time, narrative and the margins of the modern nation." *Nation and Narration*. Ed. H. K. Bhabha. 291–322. Rev. version in H. K. Bhabha, *The Location of Culture*. 139–170, 266–69.

———. *The Location of Culture*. London and New York: Routledge, 1994.

———, ed. *Nation and Narration*. London and New York: Routledge, 1990.

Biles, Robert E., ed. *Inter-American Relations: The Latin American Perspective*. Boulder and London: Lynne Rienner, 1988.

Binder, Wolfgang. "Romances of the War with Mexico: Variations of and Responses to Expansionist Discourse." Binder, ed., *Westward Expansion* 237–66.

———. "The Tropical Garden and the Mahanesque Resting-Place in the Caribbean: Remarks on the Early Incorporation of Puerto Rico by the United States of America." *An American Empire: Expansionist Cultures and Politics, 1881–1917*. Ed. Serge Ricard. Aix-en-Provence: Université de Provence, 1990. 85–104.

———, ed. *Westward Expansion in America* (1803–1860). Erlanger Studien 71. Erlangen: Palm und Enke, 1987.

Block, David. "Quincentennial Publishing: An Ocean of Print." *Latin American Research Review* 29.3 (1994): 101–28.

Borsò, Vittoria. "Images of the United States in Mexican Discourses of Identity and in Literary Writing: The *Contemporáneos*." *ZAA: Zeitschrift für Anglistik und Amerikanistik* 40 (1992): 346–55.

———. *Mexiko jenseits der Einsamkeit: Versuch einer interkulturellen Analyse. Kritischer Rückblick auf die Diskurse des Magischen Realismus*. Frankfurt a. M.: Vervuert, 1994.

Bourdieu, Pierre. "The Forms of Capital." *Handbook of Theory and Research for the Sociology of Education*. Ed. John G. Richardson. New York: Greenwood Press, 1986. 241–58.

Brading, David A. *The First America: The Spanish Monarchy, Creole Patriots, and the Liberal State, 1492–1867*. Cambridge: Cambridge University Press, 1991.

Braidotti, Rosi. *Nomadic Subjects: Embodiment and Sexual Difference in Contemporary Feminist Theory*. New York: Columbia University Press, 1994.

Breinig, Helmbrecht. "Alteritätsdiskurs und Literatur: Nordamerikanische Lateinamerikaromane der Gegenwart." *Zwischen den Kulturen? Die Sozialwissenschaften vor dem Problem des Kulturvergleichs*. Ed. Joachim Matthes. Göttingen: Otto Schwartz, 1992. 179–93.

———. "Hybrid Retrospections: Myth, Fiction, History and the Native American Historiographic Short Story." *Re-Visioning the Past: Historical Self-Reflexivity in American Short Fiction*. Ed. Bernd Engler and Oliver Scheiding. Trier: WVT, 1998. 313–41.

———. "Introduction: Culture, Economy, and Identity Locations—Representations of Difference and Transdifference." *Imaginary (Re-) Locations: Tradition, Modernity, and the Market in Contemporary Native American Literature and Culture*. Ed. Helmbrecht Breinig. Tübingen: Stauffenburg, 2003. 19–46.

———. *Irvings Kurzprosa: Kunst und Kunstproblematik im erzählerischen und essayistischen Werk*. Berne and Frankfurt\a.M.: Peter Lang, 1972.

———. "Native Survivance in the Americas: Resistance and Remembrance in Narratives by Asturias, Tapahonso, and Vizenor." Vizenor, ed., *Survivance* 39–59.

———. "'The sober page of history': Irvings kürzere historisch-biographische Schriften zwischen Faktographie und Dichtung." *Amerikastudien/American Studies* 20 (1975): 7–28.

———. "'Turn your mind on the ways of the inner country': Cooper and the Question of Westward Expansion." Binder, ed., *Westward Expansion* 47–64.

———, and Klaus Lösch. "Introduction: Difference and Transdifference." *Multiculturalism in Contemporary Societies: Perspectives on Difference and Transdifference*. Ed. Helmbrecht Breinig, Klaus Lösch, and Jürgen Gebhardt. Erlangen: Universitäts-Bibliothek, 2002. 11–36.

———, and Klaus Lösch. "Transdifference." *Journal for the Study of British Cultures* 13 (2006): 105–22.

Brickhouse, Anna. *Transamerican Literary Relations and the Nineteenth-Century Public Sphere*. Cambridge: Cambridge University Press, 2004.

Britton, John A. *Revolution and Ideology: Images of the Mexican Revolution in the United States*. Lexington: University Press of Kentucky, 1995.

Broege, Valerie. "Margaret Atwood's Americans and Canadians." *Essays on Canadian Writing* 22 (1981): 111–35.

Brotherston, Gordon. *Image of the New World: The American Continent Portrayed in Native Texts*. London: Thames & Hudson, 1979.

Brown, Russell M. "Atwood's Sacred Wells." *Essays on Canadian Writing* 17 (1980): 5–43.

Brushwood, John S. *Mexico in Its Novel: A Nation's Search for Identity*. Austin: Texas University Press, 1966.

Brydon, Diana. "Caribbean Revolution and Literary Convention." *Canadian Literature* 95 (Winter 1982): 181–85.

Buchenau, Barbara, and Annette Paatz, eds. *Do the Americas Have a Common Literary History?* Frankfurt and New York: Peter Lang, 2002.

Bull, Jeoffrey S. "'What about a problem that doesn't have a solution?' Stone's *A Flag for Sunrise*, DeLillo's *Mao II*, and the Politics of Political Fiction." *Critique: Studies in Contemporary Fiction* 40.3 (1999): 215–29.

Burgess, Benjamin V. "Elaboration Therapy in the Midewiwin and Gerald Vizenor's *The Heirs of Columbus*." *SAIL: Studies in American Indian Literatures* 18.1 (2006): 22–36.

Burke, Kenneth. *Counter-Statement*. Berkeley: University of California Press, 1931.

———. *The Philosophy of Literary Form: Studies in Symbolic Action*. 3rd ed. Berkeley: University of California Press, 1973.

Busch, Frieder. *Natur in Neuer Welt: Bericht und Dichtung der amerikanischen Kolonialzeit 1493–1776*. Munich: Fink, 1974.

Bushman, Claudia L. *America Discovers Columbus: How an Italian Explorer Became an American Hero*. Hanover and London: University Press of New England, 1992.

Butler, Judith. *Bodies That Matter: On the Discursive Limits of "Sex."* London: Routledge, 1993.

Byrd, Jodi A. *The Transit of Empire: Indigenous Critiques of Colonialism*. Minneapolis: University of Minnesota Press, 2011.

Calvo-Pascual, Mónica. *Chaos and Madness: The Politics of Fiction in Stephen Marlowe's Historical Narratives*. Amsterdam: Rodopi, 2011.

*Canadian Literature* 142/143 (Fall/Winter 1994). Spec. issue "Hispanic-Canadian Connections."

Canclini, Néstor García. *Hybrid Cultures: Strategies for Entering and Leaving Modernity*. Trans. Ch. L. Chiappari and S. L. López. Minneapolis and London: University of Minnesota Press, 1995.

Cañizares-Esguerra, Jorge. *Puritan Conquistadors: Iberianizing the Atlantic, 1550–1700*. Stanford: Stanford University Press, 2006.

Caramello, Charles. "On the Guideless Guidebooks of Postmodernism: Reading *The Volcanoes from Puebla* in Context." *Sun & Moon* 9–10 (1980): 59–99.

Cardwell, Guy. "Melville's Gray Story: Symbols and Meaning in 'Benito Cereno.'" *Bucknell Review* 8 (1959): 154–67.

Carr, David. *Time, Narrative, and History*. 2nd ed. Bloomington: Indiana University Press, 1991.

Carrington, Ildikó de Papp. "Another Symbolic Descent." *Essays on Canadian Writing* 26 (1983): 45–63.

Cassirer, Ernst. *Philosophie der symbolischen Formen. Zweiter Teil: Das mythische Denken*. 1924. Darmstadt: Wissenschaftliche Buchgesellschaft, 1973.

Chanady, Amaryll. "Magic Realism Revisited: The Deconstruction of Antinomies." *Canadian Review of Comparative Literature/Revue Canadienne de Littérature Comparée* 30.2 (June 2003): 428–44.

———, George Handley, and Patrick Imbert, eds. *Americas' Worlds and the World's Americas/Les mondes des Amériques et les Amériques du monde*. New York, Ottawa, and Toronto: LEGAS, 2006.

Chevigny, Bell Gale, and Gari Laguardia, eds. *Reinventing the Americas: Comparative Studies of Literature in the United States and Spanish America*. Cambridge: Cambridge University Press, 1986.

Christ, Tomás. *South of the Border—Al Norte del Río Grande: Grenzüberschreitungen und Fremdheitserfahrung in Texten von Cormac McCarthy, Genaro González und Carlos Fuentes*. Würzburg: Königshausen & Neumann, 1999.

Clifford, James. *The Predicament of Culture: Twentieth-Century Ethnography, Literature, and Art*. Cambridge, MA: Harvard University Press, 1988.

Coatsworth, John H., and Carlos Rico, eds. *Images of Mexico in the United States*. San Diego: Center for U.S.-Mexican Studies, University of California, San Diego, 1989.

Colley, Rae M. Carlton. "Class and Sexuality in a Mexican Landscape: Katherine Anne Porter's Marginalia on D. H. Lawrence." *Speaking the Other Self: American Women Writers*. Ed. Jeanne Campbell Reesman. Athens: University of Georgia Press, 1997. 39–53.

Collingwood, Robin George. *The Idea of History*. Oxford: Oxford University Press, 1946.

Cooper Alarcón, Daniel. *The Aztec Palimpsest: Mexico in the Modern Imagination*. Tucson: University of Arizona Press, 1997.

Couser, G. Thomas. *Altered Egos: Authority in American Autobiography*. New York: Oxford University Press, 1989.

Cowan, Bainard, and Jefferson Humphries, eds. *Poetics of the Americas: Race, Founding, and Textuality*. Baton Rouge and London: Louisiana State University Press, 1997.

Cowie, Lancelot. *El indio en la narrative contemporanea de México y Guatemala*. México, DF: Instituto Nacional Indigenista, 1976.

Cox, James H. *Red Land to the South: American Indian Writers and Indigenous Mexico*. Minneapolis: University of Minnesota Press, 2012.

Crenshaw, Kimberlé W. "Demarginalizing the Intersection of Race and Sex: A Black Feminist Critique of Antidiscrimination Doctrine, Feminist Theory and Antiracist Politics." *University of Chicago Legal Forum* (1989): 139–67.

Critchley, Simon. "Deconstruction and Pragmatism—Is Derrida a Private Ironist or a Public Liberal?" *Deconstruction and Pragmatism: Simon Critchley, Jacques Derrida, Ernesto Laclau and Richard Rorty*. Ed. Chantal Mouffe. London: Routledge, 1996. 19–40.

Crosby, Alfred W. *The Columbian Voyages, the Columbian Exchange, and Their Historians*. Washington, DC: American Historical Association, 1987.

Culler, Jonathan. *Structuralist Poetics: Structuralism, Linguistics and the Study of Literature*. Ithaca: Cornell University Press, 1975.

da Cunha, Euclides. *Rebellion in the Backlands (Os Sertões)*. Transl. and intr. Samuel Putnam. Chicago: University of Chicago Press, 1944.

Danto, Arthur C. *Analytical Philosophy of History*. Cambridge: Cambridge University Press, 1965.

Dawson, Graham. *Soldier Heroes. British Adventure, Empire and the Imagining of Masculinities*. London and New York: Routledge, 1994.

Day, Douglas. *Malcolm Lowry: A Biography*. New York: Oxford University Press, 1973.

Dean, Warren, ed. *Diplomatic Claims: Latin American Historians View the United States*. Ed. and trans. Warren Dean et al. Lanham, MD: University Press of America, 1985.

de Certeau, Michel. *The Practice of Everyday Life*. Berkeley: University of California Press, 1984.

DeGuzman, Maria. *Spain's Long Shadow: The Black Legend, Off-Whiteness, and Anglo-American Empire*. Minneapolis: University of Minnesota Press, 2005.

de la Campa, Román. *Latin Americanism*. Minneapolis: University of Minnesota Press, 1999.

Deleuze, Gilles, and Félix Guattari. *A Thousand Plateaus: Capitalism and Schizophrenia*. Trans. Brian Massumi. Minneapolis: University of Minnesota Press, 1987.

Delpar, Helen. *The Enormous Vogue of Things Mexican: Cultural Relations between the United States and Mexico, 1920–1935*. Tuscaloosa: University of Alabama Press, 1992.

Derrida, Jacques. *La bête et le souverain*. Vol. 2. Ed. Michel Lisse, Marie-Louise Mallet, and Genette Michaud. Paris: Galilée, 2010. English trans. *The Beast and the Sovereign*. Vol. 2. Trans. Geoffrey Bennington. Chicago: University of Chicago Press, 2011.

———. "Living On. Borderlines." Trans. James Hulbert. Harold Bloom, Paul de Man, Jacques Derrida, Geoffrey Hartman, and J. Hillis Miller. *Deconstruction and Criticism*. New York: Continuum, 1979. 75–176.

Desmond, Lawrence G., and Phyllis M. Messenger. *A Dream of Maya: Augustus and Alice Le Plongeon in Nineteenth-Century Yucatan*. Albuquerque: University of New Mexico Press, 1988.

Dobyns, Henry F. "Estimating Aboriginal American Population: An Appraisal of Techniques with a New Hemispheric Estimate." *Current Anthropology* 7 (1966): 395–416.

Drichel, Simone. "Regarding the Other: Postcolonial Violations and Ethical Resistance in Margaret Atwood's *Bodily Harm*." *Modern Fiction Studies* 54.1 (Spring 2008): 20–49.

Edmonds, Dale. "*Under the Volcano*: A Reading of the 'Immediate Level.'" Wood, ed., *Malcolm Lowry* 57–100.

Egan, Linda, and Mary K. Long, eds. *Mexico Reading the United States*. Nashville: Vanderbilt University Press, 2009.

Egan, Timothy. "A Battle Against Illegal Workers, with an Unlikely Driving Force." *New York Times*, May 30, 2005. http://www.nytimes.com/2005/05/30/national/30idaho.html.

Elias, Norbert. *The Civilizing Process: Sociogenetic and Psychogenetic Investigations*. 1939. Rev. ed. London: Blackwell, 2000.

Elwert, Georg. *Nationalismus und Ethnizität: Über die Bildung von Wir-Gruppen*. Ethnizität und Gesellschaft: Occasional Papers 22. Berlin: Das arabische Buch, 1989.

Epstein, Perle S. *The Private Labyrinth of Malcolm Lowry:* Under the Volcano *and the Cabbala*. New York: Holt, Rinehart & Winston, 1969.

Ernst, Christoph, Walter Sparn, and Hedwig Wagner, eds. *Kulturhermeneutik: Interdisziplinäre Beiträge zum Umgang mit kultureller Differenz*. Munich: Fink, 2008.

Fernández-Armesto, Felipe. *The Americas: A Hemispheric History*. New York: Modern Library, 2003.

Fifer, J. Valerie. *United States Perceptions of Latin America 1850–1930: A "New West" South of Capricorn?* Manchester: Manchester University Press, 1991.

Fish, Stanley E. *Self-Consuming Artifacts: The Experience of Seventeenth-Century Literature*. Berkeley: University of California Press, 1972.

Fitz, Caitlin A. *Our Sister Republics: The United States in an Age of American Revolutions.* New York: W. W. Norton/Liveright, 2016.

Fitz, Earl E. *Rediscovering the New World: Inter-American Literature in a Comparative Context.* Iowa City: University of Iowa Press, 1991.

Fluck, Winfried. *Das kulturelle Imaginäre: Eine Funktionsgeschichte des amerikanischen Romans 1790–1900.* Frankfurt\a.M.: Suhrkamp, 1997.

Fohrmann, Jürgen, and Harro Müller, eds. *Diskurstheorien und Literaturwissenschaft.* Frankfurt a. M.: Suhrkamp, 1988.

Ford, Arthur L. *Joel Barlow.* New York: Twayne, 1971.

Foster, E. M. *Aspects of the Novel.* London: Edward Arnold, 1927.

Foucault, Michel. *The Archaeology of Knowledge and The Discourse on Language (L'archéologie du savoir,* 1969, and *L'ordre du discours,* 1971). Trans. A. M. Sheridan Smith and Rupert Swyer. New York: Pantheon, 1972.

———. *The Order of Things: An Archaeology of the Human Sciences* (*Les mots et les choses,* 1966). New York: Vintage Books, 1994.

Frank, Manfred. 1988. "Zum Diskursbegriff bei Foucault." Fohrmann and Müller, eds., *Diskurstheorien* 25–44.

Fredrickson, Robert S. "Robert Stone's Decadent Leftists." *Papers on Language and Literature* 32.3 (1996): 315–34.

Freud, Sigmund. *Civilization and Its Discontents.* Trans. James Strachey. New York: Norton, 1961.

Freyre, Gilberto. *The Masters and the Slaves: A Study in the Development of Brazilian Civilization* (*Casa-Grande & senzala,* 1933). Trans. Samuel Putnam. Berkeley: University of California Press, 1987.

Friedl, Herwig. "Malcolm Lowry and the American Imagination." *Studien zur englischen und amerikanischen Prosa nach dem Ersten Weltkrieg.* Ed. Maria Diedrich and Christoph Schöneich. Darmstadt: Wissenschaftliche Buchgesellschaft, 1986. 186–99.

Frye, Northrop. *The Anatomy of Criticism.* Princeton: Princeton University Press, 1957.

Fussell, Edwin. *Frontier: American Literature and the American West.* Princeton: Princeton University Press, 1965.

Gabriel, Gottfried. *Fiktion und Wahrheit: Eine semantische Theorie der Literatur.* Stuttgart: Frommann Holzboog, 1975.

Gabriel, Markus. *Warum es die Welt nicht gibt.* Berlin: Ullstein, 2013.

Gadamer, Hans-Georg. *Truth and Method.* 2nd rev. ed. Trans. Joel Weinsheimer and D. G. Marshall. New York: Crossroad, 1989.

Galeano, Eduardo. *Open Veins of Latin America: Five Centuries of the Pillage of a Continent.* (*Las venas abiertas de America Latina,* 1971). Trans. Cedric Belfrage. New York: Monthly Review Press, 1998.

Gallie, W. B. *Philosophy and Historical Understanding.* London: Chatto & Windus, 1964.

Ganser, Alexandra. *Roads of Her Own: Gendered Space and Mobility in American Women's Road Narratives, 1970–2000.* Amsterdam and New York: Rodopi, 2009.

García Canclini, Néstor. *Hybrid Cultures: Strategies for Entering and Leaving Modernity.* Trans. Christopher L. Chiappari and Silvia L. López. Minneapolis: University of Minnesota Press, 1995.

Geertz, Clifford. *The Interpretation of Cultures: Selected Essays*. New York: Basic Books, 1973.

Geidel, Molly. *Peace Corps Fantasies: How Development Shaped the Global Sixties*. Minneapolis: University of Minnesota Press, 2015.

Gerbi, Antonello. *The Dispute of the New World: The History of a Polemic 1750–1900*. Trans. Jeremy Moyle. Pittsburgh: University of Pittsburgh Press, 1973.

Ghiban, Maria-Cristina. "'Shooting Arrows with My Heart'—An Exploration of Ana Castillo's Genre Jumping." *Label Me Latina/o* 2 (2012). Spec. issue "Latina Authors—Asserting Female Agency": 1–27. e-journal. http://labelmelatin.com/?p=226.

Gibson, Charles, ed. *The Black Legend: Anti-Spanish Attitudes in the Old World and the New*. New York: Random House, 1971.

Giddens, Anthony. *The Constitution of Society: Outline of the Theory of Structuration*. Cambridge, UK: Polity Press, 1984.

Givner, Joan. *Katherine Anne Porter: A Life*. New York: Simon & Schuster, 1982.

Goetsch, Paul. "Margaret Atwood: A Canadian Nationalist." *Margaret Atwood: Works and Impact*. Ed. Reingard M. Nischik. Rochester, NY: Camden House, 2000. 166–79.

Göhring, Heinz. "Lateinamerika—Vereinigte Staaten: Eine kontrastive Kulturanalyse." *Jahrbuch für Amerikastudien* 18 (1973): 83–107.

Goldie, Terry. *Fear and Temptation: The Image of the Indigene in Canadian, Australian and New Zealand Literatures*. Kingston: McGill-Queen's University Press, 1989.

Gonzales-Berry, Erlinda. "The [Subversive] *Mixquiahuala Letters*: I An Antidote for Self-Hate." *Chicana (W)Rites: On Word and Film*. Ed. Helena Maria Viramontes and María Herrera-Sobek. Berkeley, CA: Third Woman Press, 1995. 115–24.

Görling, Reinhold. *Heterotopia: Lektüren einer interkulturellen Literaturwissenschaft*. Munich: Fink, 1997.

Grace, Sherill E. *Violent Duality: A Study of Margaret Atwood*. Montréal: Véhicule Press, 1980.

———. *The Voyage That Never Ends: Malcolm Lowry's Fiction*. Vancouver: University of British Columbia Press, 1982.

Grassl, Anita. "Die Mexiko Darstellung in der neueren amerikanischen Romanliteratur und der Einfluss D. H. Lawrences." Unpubl. master's thesis, University of Erlangen, 1994.

Greeson, Jennifer Rae. *Our South: Geographic Fantasy and the Rise of National Literature*. Cambridge, MA, and London: Harvard University Press, 2010.

Gregory, Derek. *Geographical Imaginations*. Cambridge, MA: Blackwell, 1994.

Griffith, John. "*The Columbiad* and *Greenfield Hill*: History, Poetry, and Ideology in the Late Eighteenth Century." *Early American Literature* 10 (1975): 235–50.

Grimbert, Joan Tasker. "John Updike's *Brazil*: Tristan and Iseult in Black & White, White & Black." *Tristania* 23 (2004): 61–73.

Gruesz, Kirsten Silva. *Ambassadors of Culture: The Transamerican Origins of Latino Writing*. Princeton and Oxford: Princeton University Press, 2002.

———. "The Mercurial Space of 'Central' America: New Orleans, Honduras, and the Writing of the Banana Republic." Levander and Levine, eds. 140–65.

Gunn, Drewey Wayne. *Mexico in American and British Letters: A Bibliography of Fiction and Travel Books, Citing Original Editions*. Metuchen, NJ: Scarecrow, 1974.

Gutiérrez Girardot, Raffael. "Kritische Bemerkungen zu Heinz Göhring, 'Lateinamerika —Vereinigte Staaten: Eine kontrastive Kulturanalyse.'" *Jahrbuch für Amerikastudien* 18 (1973): 107–8.

Habermas, Jürgen. *Der philosophische Diskurs der Moderne: Zwölf Vorlesungen.* Frankfurt a. M.: Suhrkamp, 1985.

Hahner, June E., ed. *Women Through Women's Eyes: Latin American Women in Nineteenth-Century Travel Accounts.* Wilmington: Scholarly Resources, 1998.

Halfmann, Ulrich. "'A Faithful Representation of Our Experiences of Life': Zur Romantheorie von William Dean Howells." *Englische und amerikanische Literaturtheorie: Studien zu ihrer historischen Entwicklung.* Vol. 2. Ed. Rüdiger Ahrens and Erwin Wolff. Heidelberg: Winter 1979. 240–65.

Hall, Linda B., and Don M. Coerver. *Revolution on the Border: The United States and Mexico, 1910–1920.* Albuquerque: University of New Mexico Press, 1988.

Haraway, Donna. *The Companion Species Manifesto: Dogs, People, and Significant Otherness.* Chicago: Prickly Paradigm Press, 2003.

———. *When Species Meet.* Minneapolis: University of Minnesota Press, 2008.

Haring, Clarence H. *South America Looks at the United States.* New York: Macmillan, 1928.

Harrison, Barbara Grizzutti. "Joan Didion: Only Disconnect." *Off Center: Essays by Barbara Grizzutti Harrison.* 1980. http://www.writing.upenn.edu/~afilreis/103/didion-per-harrison.html.

Harrison, Brady. "'For a while they felt better': Negation in *A Flag for Sunrise.*" *European Journal of American Studies* 1, doc. 7 (2011). Web. http://ejas.revues.org/9396.

Hart, James D., and Phillip W. Leininger. *The Oxford Companion to American Literature.* 6th ed. New York: Oxford University Press, 1995.

Haselstein, Ulla. "Vom Urwald in die Wüste: Der Naturschutzpark als Metapher der Kulturkritik bei Freud und Baudrillard." *Amerikastudien/American Studies* 37 (1992): 393–414.

Hassan, Ihab. "Ecliptic Art." *Southern Review* 30.3 (1994): 627.

Hazlett, John D. "Literary Nationalism and Ambivalence in Washington Irving's *The Life and Voyages of Christopher Columbus.*" *American Literature* 55 (1983): 560–75.

Hedges, William L. *Washington Irving: An American Study, 1802–1832.* Baltimore: Johns Hopkins P., 1965.

Hegel, Georg Wilhelm Friedrich. *Lectures on the Philosophy of World History: Introduction* (*Vorlesungen über die Philosophie der Geschichte*, 1837/40). Trans. Hugh Barr Nisbet. Intr. Duncan Forbes. Cambridge: Cambridge University Press, 1981.

Heide, Markus. "Herman Melville's 'Benito Cereno,' Inter-American Relations, and Literary Pan-Americanism." *Amerikastudien/American Studies* 53 (2008): 37–56.

Heidegger, Martin. *Unterwegs zur Sprache.* Stuttgart: Klett-Cotta, 2007.

Hein, Christina. *Whiteness, the Gaze, and Transdifference in Contemporary Native American Fiction.* Heidelberg: Winter 2012.

Helsinger, Elizabeth K., Robin Lauterbach Sheets, and William Veeder, eds. *The Woman Question: Society and Literature in Britain and America, 1837–1883.* 3 vols. Manchester: Manchester University Press, 1983.

Herlinghaus, Hermann, and Utz Riese, eds. *Heterotopien der Identität: Literatur in interamerikanischen Kontaktzonen*. Heidelberg: Winter 1999.

———. *Sprünge im Spiegel: Postkoloniale Aporien der Moderne in beiden Amerikas*. Bonn: Bouvier, 1997.

Herman, David, Manfred Jahn, and Marie-Laure Ryan, eds. *Routledge Enyclopedia of Narrative Theory*. New York: Routledge, 2005.

Heydenreich, Titus, ed. *Columbus zwischen zwei Welten: Historische und literarische Wertungen aus fünf Jahrhunderten*. Vol. 2. Frankfurt a. M.: Vervuert, 1992.

Hoetink, H. *Slavery and Race Relations in the Americas: Comparative Notes of Their Nature and Nexus*. New York: Harper & Row, 1973.

Hofstede, Geert. "National Culture." Dimensions of National Cultures Project. http://geert-hofstede.com/national-culture.html.

Hollinger, David A. *Postethnic America: Beyond Multiculturalism*. 1995. Rev. ed. New York: Basic Books, 2000.

Hones, Sheila, and Julia Leyda. "Geographies of American Studies." *American Quarterly* 57 (2005): 1019–32.

Honneth, Axel. *Kritik der Macht: Reflexionsstufen einer kritischen Gesellschaftstheorie*. Frankfurt a. M.: Suhrkamp, 1985.

Horatschek, Annegreth. *Alterität und Stereotyp: Die Funktion des Fremden in den "International Novels" von E. M. Forster und D. H. Lawrence*. Tübingen: Gunter Narr, 1998.

Horl, Sabine. "Amerika als Identität: Utopisches Denken im hispanoamerikanischen Essay (1900–1935)." *Der Umgang mit dem Fremden: Beiträge zur Literatur aus und über Lateinamerika*. Ed. Titus Heydenreich. *Lateinamerika-Studien* 22. Munich: Fink, 1986. 17–61.

Howells, William Dean. *Criticism and Fiction*. 1891. Whitefish, MT: Kessinger Publishing, 2010.

Hoy, Helen. "A Second View." *SAIL: Studies in American Indian Literatures* 3.4 (Winter 1991): 50–55.

Huggins, Martha K. *Political Policing: The United States and Latin America*. Durham, NC: Duke University Press, 1998.

Hull, Gloria T., Patricia Bell Scott, and Barbara Smith, eds. *All the Women Are White, All the Blacks Are Men, But Some of Us Are Brave: Black Women's Studies*. Old Westbury, NY: Feminist Press, 1982.

Hutcheon, Linda. *A Poetics of Postmodernism: History, Theory, Fiction*. London: Routledge, 1988.

———. *The Politics of Postmodernism*. London: Routledge, 1989.

Huth, Hans. *Nature and the American: Three Centuries of Changing Attitudes*. 2nd ed. Lincoln: University of Nebraska Press, 1990.

Ickstadt, Heinz. "Plot, Komplott oder die Herrschaft des Zufalls: The Findung und Erfindung von Geschichte im postmodernen amerikanischen Roman." *Postmoderne —globale Differenz*. Ed. Robert Weimann and Hans Ulrich Gumbrecht. Frankfurt a. M.: Suhrkamp, 1991. 265–77.

Ingersoll, Earl G. *Margaret Atwood: Conversations*. Willowdale, ON: Firefly Books, 1990.

Irigaray, Luce. "Sexual Difference." *French Feminist Thought: A Reader*. Ed. Toril Moi. Oxford: Blackwell, 1987. 118–32.

Irmscher, Christoph. "Crossblood Columbus: Gerald Vizenor's Narrative 'Discoveries.'" *Amerikastudien/American Studies* 40 (1995): 83–98.

Iser, Wolfgang. "Representation: A Performative Act." *Prospecting: From Reader Response to Literary Anthropology*. Baltimore: Johns Hopkins University Press, 1989. 236–48.

Isernhagen, Hartwig. *Ästhetische Innovation und Kulturkritik: Das Frühwerk von John Dos Passos, 1916–1938*. Munich: Fink, 1983.

Jackson, Richard L. *Black Writers and Latin America: Cross-Cultural Affinities*. Washington, DC: Howard University Press, 1998.

Jacobson, Matthew Frye. "Where We Stand: US Empire at Street Level and in the Archive." *American Quarterly* 65 (2013): 265–90.

Jaksić, Iván. *The Hispanic World and American Intellectual Life, 1820–1880*. Basingstoke: Palgrave Macmillan, 2007.

Jameson, Fredric. "Modernism and Imperialism." *Nationalism, Colonialism, and Literature*. Ed. Terry Eagleton, Fredric Jameson, and Edward W. Said. Minneapolis: University of Minnesota Press, 1990. 43–66.

———. "On Cultural Studies." *Social Text* 34.1 (1993): 17–52.

Jones, Howard Mumford. *O Strange New World: American Culture—The Formative Years*. New York: Viking, 1964.

Jordan, David. M. *New World Regionalism: Literature in the Americas*. Toronto: University of Toronto Press, 1994.

Joseph, Gilbert M., Catherine C. Legrand, and Ricardo D. Salvatore, eds. *Close Encounters of Empire: Writing the Cultural History of U.S.-Latin American Relations*. Durham and London: Duke University Press, 1998.

Kaplan, Amy. *The Anarchy of Empire in the Making of U.S. Culture*. Cambridge, MA: Harvard University Press, 2002.

———. "Black and Blue on San Juan Hill." Kaplan and Pease, eds., *Cultures* 219–36.

———. "'Left Alone with America': The Absence of Empire in the Study of American Culture." Kaplan and Pease, eds., *Cultures* 3–21.

———, and Donald E. Pease, eds. *Cultures of United States Imperialism*. Durham, NC: Duke University Press, 1993.

Karcher, Carolyn L. *Shadow Over the Promised Land: Slavery, Race, and Violence in Melville's America*. Baton Rouge: Louisiana University Press, 1980.

Karl, Frederick R. *American Fictions 1940–1980*. New York: Harper & Row, 1983.

Karnes, Thomas L., ed. *The Latin American Policy of the United States*. Tucson: University of Arizona Press, 1972.

Katz, Friedrich. *The Life and Times of Pancho Villa*. Stanford: Stanford University Press, 1998.

Kenney, Alice P. "America Discovers Columbus: Biography as Epic, Drama, History." *Biography* 4 (1981): 45–65.

Kenworthy, Eldon. *America/Américas: Myth in the Making of U.S. Policy Toward Latin America*. University Park: Pennsylvania State University Press, 1995.

Kermode, Frank. *The Sense of an Ending: Studies in the Theory of Fiction*. London: Oxford University Press, 1966.

Khordoc, Catherine. "Looking Beyond the Elephant: The Mexican Connection in Francine Noël's *La Conjuration des bâtards*." Siemerling and Casteel, eds., *Canada* 231–45.

Kline, Marcia B. *Beyond the Land Itself: Views of Nature in Canada and the United States*. Cambridge, MA: Harvard University Press, 1970.

Knellessen, Olaf, Peter Passett, and Peter Schneider. Introduction. Knellessen, Passett, and Schneider, eds., *Übertragung* 7–17.

———, eds. *Übertragung und Übertretung*. Tübingen: edition diskord, 1998.

Kohl, Stephan. *Realismus: Theorie und Geschichte*. Munich: Fink, 1977.

Kolodny, Annette. *In Search of First Contact: The Vikings of Vinland, the Peoples of the Dawnland, and the Anglo-American Anxiety of Discovery*. Durham, NC: Duke University Press, 2012.

———. *The Lay of the Land: Metaphor as Experience and History in American Life and Letters*. Chapel Hill: University of North Carolina Press, 1975.

Krakau, Knud, ed. *Lateinamerika und Nordamerika: Gesellschaft, Politik und Wirtschaft im historischen Vergleich*. Frankfurt a. M. and New York: Campus, 1992.

Krauss, Clifford. *Inside Central America: Its People, Politics, and History*. New York: Touchstone, 1991.

Krell, David F. *Derrida and Our Animal Others: Derrida's Final Seminar, "The Beast and the Sovereign."* Bloomington and London: Indiana University Press, 2013.

Kristeva, Julia. "On the Women of China." Trans. E. Conroy Kennedy. *Signs* 1.1 (1975): 57–81.

———. *Powers of Horror: An Essay in Abjection*. Trans. Leon S. Roudiez. New York: Columbia University Press, 1982.

———. *Revolution in Poetic Language*. Trans. Margaret Waller. New York: Columbia University Press, 1984.

———. *Strangers to Ourselves*. Trans. Leon S. Roudiez. New York: Columbia University Press, 1994.

Krupat, Arnold. "'Stories in the Blood': *Ratio*- and *Natio*- in Gerald Vizenor's *The Heirs of Columbus*." *Loosening the Seams: Interpretations of Gerald Vizenor*. Ed. A. Robert Lee. Bowling Green: Bowling Green State U Popular P, 2000. 166–77.

Kutzinski, Vera M., and Ottmar Ette. "Inventories and Inventions: Alexander von Humboldt's Cuban Landscapes: An Introduction." Alexander von Humboldt. *Political Essay on the Island of Cuba*. Chicago and London: University of Chicago Press, 2011. vii–xxiii.

Kymlicka, Will. *Multicultural Citizenship: A Liberal Theory of Minority Rights*. Oxford: Oxford University Press, 1996.

Lang, Hans-Joachim. "Joel Barlows 'Dissertation on the Genius and Institutions of Manco Capac' als historisches Exemplum." *Exempla: Studien zur Bedeutung und Funktion exemplarischen Erzählens*. Ed. Bernd Engler and Kurt Müller. Berlin: Duncker & Humblot, 1995. 215–47.

———. "Kolumbus in der Literatur der Vereinigten Staaten von Amerika seit Melville: Genealogie und Verdrängung." Heydenreich, ed., *Columbus* 545–78.

Langley, Lester D. *America and the Americas: The United States in the Western Hemisphere*. Athens: University of Georgia Press, 1989.

———. *The United States and the Caribbean in the Twentieth Century*. 4th ed. Athens and London: University of Georgia Press, 1989.

———, and Thomas Schoonover. *The Banana Men: American Mercenaries and*

*Entrepreneurs in Central America, 1880–1930*. Lexington: University Press of Kentucky, 1995.

Lara Zavala, Hernán. "Las poéticas de *Bajo el volcán*." *Los Universitarios: Nueva época* (2009): 12–21. Web. http://www.revistas.unam.mx/index.php/uni/article/view/8920.

———. "Malcom Lowry." *Letras Libres* 31 (Jan. 2008). Web. http://www.letraslibres.com.

Larner, John P. "North American Hero? Christopher Columbus 1702–2002." *Proceedings of the American Philosophical Society* 137.1 (March 1993): 46–63.

Larsen, Neil. *Reading North by South: On Latin American Literature, Culture, and Politics*. Minneapolis: University of Minnesota Press, 1995.

Leahy, David. "Counter-Worlding *A/américanité*." Siemerling and Casteel, eds., *Canada* 62–84.

Leary, Lewis. *That Rascal Freneau: A Study in Literary Failure*. New Brunswick, NJ: Rutgers University Press 1941.

Leiken, Robert S., and Barry Rubin, eds. *The Central American Crisis Reader*. New York: Summit Books, 1987.

LeoGrande, William M. *Our Own Backyard: The United States in Central America, 1977–1992*. Chapel Hill and London: University of North Carolina Press, 1998.

Le Plongeon, Augustus. *Sacred Mysteries among the Mayas and the Quiches, 11,500 Years Ago: Their Relation to the Sacred Mysteries of Egypt, Greece, Chaldea and India. Free Masonry in Times Anterior to the Temple of Solomon*, 1886. London: Forgotten Books, 2012.

Levander, Caroline F., and Robert S. Levine, eds. *Hemispheric American Studies*. New Brunswick, NJ: Rutgers University Press, 2008.

Levin, David. *History as Romantic Art: Bancroft, Prescott, Motley, and Parkman*. Stanford: Stanford University Press, 1959.

Levinas, Emmanuel. *Totality and Infinity: An Essay on Exteriority*. Trans. Alphonso Lingis. The Hague: Martinus Nijhoff, 1979.

Lévi-Strauss, Claude. *Tristes Tropiques*. 1955. Trans. John Weightman and Doreen Weightman. New York: Penguin, 2012.

Lewis, James E., Jr. *The American Union and the Problem of Neighborhood: The United States and the Collapse of the Spanish Empire, 1783–1829*. Chapel Hill and London: University of North Carolina Press, 1998.

Liebmann Schaub, Uta. "Foucault's Oriental Subtext." *PMLA* 104 (1989): 306–16.

Limón, José E. *American Encounters: Greater Mexico, the United States, and the Erotics of Culture*. Boston: Beacon Press, 1998.

Lingis, Alphonso. *The Imperative*. Bloomington and Indianapolis: Indiana University Press, 1998.

Link, Jürgen. 1988. "Literaturanalyse als Interdiskursanalyse am Beispiel des Ursprungs literarischer Symbolik in der Kollektivsymbolik." Fohrmann and Müller, eds., *Diskurstheorien* 284–307.

Lösch, Klaus. "Das Fremde und seine Beschreibung." *Phänomene der Fremdheit—Fremdheit als Phänomen*. Ed. Simone Broders, Susanne Gruß, and Stephanie Waldow. Würzburg: Königshausen & Neumann, 2012.

Loschky, Helen. "The 'Columbiad' Tradition: Joel Barlow and Others." *Books at Brown* 21 (1967): 197–206.

Lotman, Yuri. *The Structure of the Artistic Text*. Trans. Gail Lenhoff and Ronald Vroon. Ann Arbor: University of Michigan, Department of Slavic Languages and Literatures, 1977.

Lowenthal, Abraham F., ed. *Exporting Democracy: The United States and Latin America*. 2 vols. Baltimore and London: Johns Hopkins University Press, 1991.

Lübken, Uwe. "'Americans All': The United States, the Nazi Menace, and the Construction of a Pan-American Identity." *Amerikastudien/American Studies* 48 (2003): 389–409.

Lubrich, Oliver, and Otmar Ette. Afterword. Alexander von Humboldt. *Ansichten der Kordilleren und Monumente der eingeborenen Völker Amerikas*. Trans. Claudia Kalscheuer. Frankfurt a. M.: Eichborn, 2004. 407–22.

Luce, Henry R. "The American Century." *Life* 10 (Feb. 17, 1941): 61.

Lucking, David. "In Pursuit of the Faceless Stranger: Depths and Surfaces in Margaret Atwood's *Bodily Harm*." *Studies in Canadian Literature/Études en Littérature Canadienne* 15.1 (1990): 76–93.

Luhmann, Niklas. *Soziologische Aufklärung: Aufsätze zur Theorie sozialer Systeme*. Vol. 1. Opladen: Westdeutscher Verlag, 1970.

Lukács, Georg. *The Historical Novel* (*Der historische Roman*, 1936/37). Trans. Hannah Mitchell and Stanley Mitchell. Lincoln: University of Nebraska Press, 1983.

Lyotard, Jean-François. *The Postmodern Condition: A Report on Knowledge*. Trans. Geoff Bennington and Brian Massumi. Minneapolis: University of Minnesota Press, 1984.

Mackay, James. "Ghosts in the Gaps: Diane Glancy's Paradoxes of Survivance." Vizenor, ed., *Survivance* 247–69.

Mackenthun, Gesa. *Fictions of the Black Atlantic in American Foundational Literature*. London: Routledge, 2004.

Madariaga, Salvador de. *Christopher Columbus: Being the Life of the Very Magnificent Lord Don Cristobal Colón*. New York: Macmillan, 1940.

Maligo, Pedro. *Land of Metaphorical Desires: The Representation of Amazonia in Brazilian Literature*. New York: Peter Lang, 1998.

Mann, Charles C. *1491: New Revelations of the Americas Before Columbus*. New York: Knopf, 2005.

———. *1493: Uncovering the New World Columbus Created*. New York: Knopf, 2013.

Martin, Terence. "American Literature Discovers Columbus." *Discovering Difference: Contemporary Essays in American Culture*. Ed. Christoph K. Lohmann. Bloomington and Indianapolis: Indiana University Press, 1993. 16–34.

Marx, Leo. *The Machine in the Garden: Technology and the Pastoral Ideal in America*. New York: Oxford University Press, 1964.

Mata, Óscar. *San Malcolm en las cantinas*. Mexico City: Universidad Autonoma Metropolitana, Direccion de Difusion Cultural, Departamento Editorial, 1988.

Maturo, Graciela. *La literatura hispanoamericana de la utopia al paraiso*. Buenos Aires: Fernando García Cambeiro, 1983.

Matzat, Wolfgang. *Lateinamerikanische Identitätsentwürfe: Essayistische Reflexion und narrative Inszenierung*. Tübingen: Gunter Narr, 1996.

May, Robert E. "Reconsidering Antebellum U.S. Women's History: Gender, Filibustering, and America's Quest for Empire." *American Quarterly* 57.4 (2005): 1155–88.

McCormack, Carol P. "Nature, Culture and Gender: A Critique." *Nature, Culture and Gender*. Ed. Carol P. McCormack and Marilyn Strathern. Cambridge: Cambridge University Press, 1980. 1–24.

McElroy, John Harmon. "The Integrity of Irving's *Columbus*." *American Literature* 50 (1978): 1–16.

McWilliams, John. "Poetry in the Early Republic." *Columbia Literary History of the United States*. Ed. Emory Elliott et al. New York: Columbia University Press, 1988, 156–67.

Merivale, Patricia. "Through Greene-land in Drag: Joan Didion's *A Book of Common Prayer*." *Pacific Coast Philology* 15 (1980): 45–52. Quoted from *The Critical Response to Joan Didion*. Ed. Sharon Felton. Westport, CT: Greenwood Press, 1994. 99–105.

Merk, Frederick. *Manifest Destiny and Mission in American History: A Reinterpretation*. New York: Knopf, 1963.

Merrill, John C. *Gringo: The American as Seen by Mexican Journalists*. Gainesville: University of Florida Press, 1963.

Meyer, Lorenzo. "Mexico: The Exception and the Rule." *Exporting Democracy: The United States and Latin America: Case Studies*. Ed. Abraham F. Lowenthal. Baltimore: Johns Hopkins University Press, 1991. 93–110.

Mignolo, Walter D. *The Idea of Latin America*. Hoboken, NJ: Wiley-Blackwell, 1991.

———. *Local Histories/Global Designs: Coloniality, Subaltern Knowledges, and Border Thinking*. Princeton: Princeton University Press, 2000.

Milich, Klaus. "Lektüre der fremden Zeichen: Walter Abishs Literarisierung der Wahrnehmung im intertextuellen Diskurs mit der postmodernen Anthropologie." *Amerikastudien/American Studies* 38 (1993): 181–202.

Miller, Perry. *Nature's Nation*. Cambridge, MA: Harvard University Press, 1967.

Minh-ha, Trinh T. *Woman, Native, Other: Writing Postcoloniality and Feminism*. Bloomington and Indianapolis: Indiana University Press, 1989.

Moreiras, Alberto. *The Exhaustion of Difference: The Politics of Latin American Cultural Studies*. Durham and London: Duke University Press, 2001.

———. "Global Fragments: A Second Latinamericanism." *The Cultures of Globalization*. Ed. Fredric Jameson and Masao Miyoshi. Durham, NC: Duke University Press, 1998. 81–102.

———. "Restitution and Appropriation in Latinamericanism." *Journal of Interdisciplinary Literary Studies* 7.1 (1995): 1–43.

Moussong, Lazlo. "Malcolm Lowry: El volcán no es como lo pintan." *Ruptures* 6 (Apr.–June 1994): 203–20.

Mukherjee, Arun P. "Whose Post-Colonialism and Whose Postmodernism?" *World Literature Written in English* 30.2 (1990): 1–9.

Murphy, Gretchen. *Hemispheric Imaginings: The Monroe Doctrine and Narratives of U.S. Empire*. Durham and London: Duke University Press, 2005.

———. *Shadowing the White Man's Burden: U. S. Imperialism and the Problem of the Color Line*. New York and London: New York University Press, 2010.

Oates, Joyce Carol. "A Taut Novel of Disorder." Review of Joan Didion, *A Book of Common Prayer*. *New York Times*, Apr. 3, 1977.

O'Brien, Thomas F. *Making the Americas: The United States and Latin America from the Age of Revolution to the Era of Globalization*. Albuquerque: University of New Mexico Press, 2007.

O'Gorman, Edmundo. *The Invention of America: An Inquiry into the Historical Nature of the New World and the Meaning of its History*. Bloomington: Indiana University Press, 1961.

Osborne, Richard. *Megawords: 200 Terms You Really Need to Know*. Thousand Oaks, CA: SAGE Publications, 2002.

Park, Stephen M. *The Pan American Imagination: Contested Visions of the Hemisphere in Twentieth-Century Literature*. Charlottesville and London: University of Virginia Press, 2014.

Parks, John G. "Unfit Survivors: The Failed and Lost Pilgrims in the Fiction of Robert Stone." *CEA Critic* 53.1 (1990): 52–57.

Patton, Marilyn. "Tourists and Terrorists: The Creation of *Bodily Harm*." *Papers on Language and Literature* 28.2 (1992): 150–73.

Paulk, Julia C. "Visions of Cuba: Mary Peabody Mann's *Juanita: A Romance of Real Life in Cuba Fifty Years Ago*." *Marquette University e-Publications@Marquette*, Oct. 1, 2009. http://epublications.marquette.edu/span_fac/13/.

Pease, Donald E. "New Perspectives on U.S. Culture and Imperialism." Kaplan and Pease, eds., *Cultures* 22–37.

Peckham, Morse. *Man's Rage for Chaos: Biology, Behavior, and the Arts*. New York: Schocken, 1980.

Pérez Firmat, Gustavo, ed. *Do the Americas Have a Common Literature?* Durham, NC: Duke University Press, 1990.

Perry, John. *Jack London: An American Myth*. Chicago: Nelson-Hall, 1981.

Peyser, Thomas. "How Global Is It: Walter Abish and the Fiction of Globalization." *Contemporary Literature* 40.2 (1999): 240–62.

Pike, Fredrick B. *The United States and Latin America: Myths and Stereotypes of Civilization and Nature*. Austin: University of Texas Press, 1992.

Pisarz-Ramírez, Gabriele. "Reinventing Mexico: Chicano/a Travelers and the Construction of Mexicanness." *ZAA: Zeitschrift für Anglistik und Amerikanistik* 47 (1999): 333–43.

Pizer, Donald. *Dos Passos'* U.S.A.*: A Critical Study*. Charlottesville: University of Virginia Press, 1988.

Poole, Deborah. "Landscape and the Imperial Subject: U.S. Images of the Andes, 1859–1930." Joseph, Legrand, and Salvatore, eds. 106–38.

Powell, Philip Wayne. *The Tree of Hate: Propaganda and Prejudices Affecting United States Relations with the Hispanic World*. New York: Stella Maris Books, 1971.

Pratt, Mary Louise. *Imperial Eyes: Travel Writing and Transculturation*. London: Routledge, 1992.

Preston, Thomas R. "Historiography as Art in Eighteenth-Century England." *Texas Studies in Literature and Language* 11 (1969): 1209–21.

Primeau, Ronald. *Romance of the Road: The Literature of the American Highway*. Bowling Green, Ohio: Bowling Green State University Popular Press, 1996.

Prosser, Jay. "Updike, Race, and the Postcolonial Project." *The Cambridge Companion to John Updike*. Ed. Stacey Olster. Cambridge: Cambridge University Press, 2006. 76–90.

Quijano, Aníbal, and Immanuel Wallerstein. "Americanity as a Concept, or the Americas in the Modern World-System." *International Social Science Journal* 134 (1992): 549–57.

Raab, Josef. "Mythologizing the Exotic: Brazil in Twentieth-Century U.S. American Literature and Film." *Transnational American Studies*. Ed. Udo Hebel. Heidelberg: Winter 2012. 401–22.

Rama, Carlos M. *La imagen de los Estados Unidos en la América Latina: De Simón Bolívar a Salvador Allende*. México, DF: SepSetentas, 1975.

Reckwitz, Andreas. "Kulturelle Differenzen aus praxeologischer Perspektive: Kulturelle Globalisierung jenseits von Modernisierungstheorie und Kulturessentialismus." *Kulturen vergleichen: Sozial- und kulturwissenschaftliche Grundlagen und Kontroversen*. Ed. Ilja Srubar, Joachim Renn, and Ulrich Wenzel. Wiesbaden: VS Verlag für Sozialwissenschaften, 2005. 92–111.

Reichenbächer, Helmut. "Von *The Robber Bridegroom* zu *Bodily Harm*. Eine Analyse unveröffentlichter Entwürfe Margaret Atwoods." *ZAA: Zeitschrift für Anglistik und Amerikanistik* 41 (1993): 54–65.

Reid, John T. *Spanish American Images of the United States 1790–1960*. Gainesville: University Press of Florida, 1977.

Ribeiro, Darcy. *The Americas and Civilization*. Trans. Linton Lomas Barrett and Marie McDavid Barrett. New York: Dutton, 1971.

Richardson, Robert. D., Jr. "The Enlightenment View of Myth and Joel Barlow's *Vision of Columbus*." *Early American Literature* 13 (1978): 34–44.

Ricoeur, Paul. *Temps et récit*. Vol. 1. Paris: Seuil, 1983.

Rignalda, Donald. *Fighting and Writing the Vietnam War*. Jackson: University Press of Mississippi, 1994.

Ristoff, Dilvo I. "When Earth Speaks of Heaven: The Future of Race and Faith in Updike's *Brazil*." *John Updike and Religion: The Sense of the Sacred and the Motions of Grace*. Ed. James Yerkes. Grand Rapids, MI: William B. Eerdmans, 1999. 64–79.

Rodríguez, Ana Patricia. *Dividing the Isthmus: Central American Transnational Histories, Literatures, and Cultures*. Austin: University of Texas Press, 2009.

Ronning, C. Neale, ed. *Intervention in Latin America*. New York: Knopf, 1970.

Rorty, Richard. "Texts and Lumps," *New Literary History* 17 (1985): 1–16.

Rose, Gillian. "On Being Ambivalent: Women and Feminisms in Geography." *New Words, New Worlds: Reconceptualising Social and Cultural Geography*. Ed. Chris Philo. Aberystwyth: Institute of British Geographers, 1991. 156–63.

Rowe, John Carlos. *Literary Culture and U.S. Imperialism: From the Revolution to World War II*. New York: Oxford University Press, 2000.

Ruprecht, Alvina, and Cecilia Taiana. *The Reordering of Culture: Latin America, The Caribbean and Canada in the Hood*. Ottawa: Carleton University Press, 1995.

Saenz, Rogelio. "Latinos and the Changing Face of Rural America." Paper delivered at Annual Conference of the German Association for American Studies, Erlangen, June 2, 2013.

Said, Edward W. *Covering Islam: How the Media and the Experts Determine How We See the Rest of the World*. Rev. ed. London: Vintage, 1997.

———. *Orientalism*. New York: Pantheon, 1978.

Saldaña-Portillo, María Josefina. *The Revolutionary Imagination in the Americas and the Age of Development*. Durham and London: Duke University Press, 2003.

Saldívar, José David. *The Dialectics of Our America: Genealogy, Cultural Critique, and Literary History*. Durham, NC: Duke University Press, 1991.

———. *Trans-Americanity: Subaltern Modernities, Global Coloniality, and the Cultures of Greater Mexico*. Durham and London: Duke University Press, 2012.

Sale, Kirkpatrick. *The Conquest of Paradise: Christopher Columbus and the Columbian Legacy*. New York: Knopf, 1990.

Samuels, Peggy, and Harold Samuels. *Teddy Roosevelt at San Juan: The Making of a President*. College Station: Texas A&M University Press, 1997.

Santí, Enrico M. "Latinamericanism and Restitution." *Latin American Literary Review* 40 (1992): 88–96.

Sarbin, Theodore R., ed. *Narrative Psychology: The Storied Nature of Human Conduct*. New York: Praeger, 1986.

Schiff, James A. *John Updike Revisited*. New York: Twayne, 1998.

Schöpp, Joseph C. *Ausbruch aus der Mimesis: Der amerikanische Roman im Zeichen der Postmoderne*. Munich: Fink, 1990.

Schoultz, Lars. *Beneath the United States: A History of U.S. Policy toward Latin America*. Cambridge, MA: Harvard University Press, 1998.

Schütz, Alfred. *The Phenomenology of the Social World* (*Der sinnhafte Aufbau der sozialen Welt*, 1932). Trans. George Walsh and Frederick Lehnert. Evanston, IL: Northwestern University Press, 1967.

Searle, John R. "The Logical Status of Fictional Discourse." *New Literary History* 6 (1975): 319–32.

Sharbach, Sarah E. *Stereotypes of Latin America, Press Images, and U.S. Foreign Policy, 1920–1933*. New York and London: Garland, 1993.

Shell, Kurt. "Die Herausforderung der amerikanischen Identität durch die Entwicklung von alternativen Kulturen." *Amerikastudien/American Studies* 36 (1991): 531–44.

Sheppard, R. Z. "Warning: The Rabbit Is Loose." *Time*, Feb. 14, 1994: 73.

Shields, David S. *Oracles of Empire: Poetry, Politics, and Commerce in British America, 1690–1750*. Chicago: University of Chicago Press, 1990.

Shukla, Sandhya, and Heidi Tinsman, eds. *Imagining Our Americas: Towards a Transnational Frame*. Durham and London: Duke University Press, 2007.

Shurbutt, T. Ray, ed. *United States-Latin American Relations, 1800–1850: The Formative Generations*. Tuscaloosa and London: University of Alabama Press, 1991.

Siebald, Manfred. "'Questions of Travel': Die Dekonstruktion des touristischen Blicks in der Reiselyrik Elizabeth Bishops." *Amerikastudien/American Studies* 41.4 (1996): 623–35.

Siemerling, Winfried, and Sarah Phillips Casteel. "Introduction: Canada and Its Americas." Siemerling and Casteel, eds., *Canada* 3–28.

———, eds. *Canada and Its Americas: Transnational Navigations*. Montreal: McGill-Queen's University Press, 2010.

Signer, David. "Übertragung und Übertretung als ethnologische Feldforschungsmethode." Knellessen, Passett, and Schneider, eds., *Übertragung* 87–104.

Simpson, Jeffrey. "Another PM, Another Latin American Dalliance." Toronto *Globe and Mail*, July 21, 2007: A 15.

Sinclair, Andrew. *Jack: A Biography of Jack London*. New York: Harper & Row, 1977.

Slotkin, Richard. *Regeneration Through Violence: The Mythology of the American Frontier 1600–1800*. Middletown, CT: Wesleyan University Press, 1973.

Smith, Henry Nash. *Virgin Land: The American West as Symbol and Myth*. Cambridge, MA: Harvard University Press, 1950.

Smorkaloff, Pamela Maria. "Shifting Borders, Free Trade, and Frontier Narratives: US, Canada, and Mexico." *American Literary History* 6.1 (1994): 88–102.

Soja, Edward. *Thirdspace: Journeys to Los Angles and Other Real-and-Imagined Places*. London: Blackwell, 1996.

Sommer, Doris. *Foundational Fictions: The National Romances of Latin America*. Berkeley: University of California Press, 1993.

Sparn, Walter. Einleitung. *Kulturhermeneutik: Interdisziplinäre Beiträge zum Umgang mit kultureller Differenz*. Ed. Christoph Ernst, Walter Sparn, and Hedwig Wagner. Munich: Fink, 2008. 11–22.

Spivak, Gayatri Chakravorty. "Poststructuralism, Marginality, Postcoloniality and Value." 1990. *Contemporary Postcolonial Theory: A Reader*. Ed. Padmini Mongia. London: Arnold, 1997. 198–222.

Stagl, Julius. "Die Beschreibung des Fremden in der Wissenschaft." *Der Wissenschaftler und das Irrationale*. Vol. 1. Ed. Hans Peter Duerr. Frankfurt a. M.: Syndikat, 1981. 273–95.

———. "Der Universalienstreit in der Ethnologie." *Erwägen, Wissen, Ethik/Deliberation, Knowledge, Ethics* 20.3 (2009): 387–89.

Stannard, David E. *American Holocaust: Columbus and the Conquest of the New World*. New York and Oxford: Oxford University Press, 1992.

Stephenson, Gregory. *Understanding Robert Stone*. Columbia: University of South Carolina Press, 2002.

Stilgoe, John R. "Fair Fields and Blasted Rock: American Land Classification Systems and Landscape Aesthetics." *American Studies* 22 (1981): 21–33.

Strandberg, Victor. "Passion and Delusion in *A Book of Common Prayer*." *Modern Fiction Studies* 27.2 (Summer 1981): 225–42.

Streeby, Shelley. *American Sensations: Class, Empire, and the Production of Popular Culture*. Berkeley, Los Angeles, and London: University of California Press, 2002.

———. *Radical Sensations: World Movements, Violence, and Visual Culture*. Durham and London: Duke University Press, 2013.

Sturgis, Cony. *The Spanish World in English Fiction: A Bibliography*. Boston: Faxon, 1927.

Summerhill, Stephen J., and John Alexander Williams. *Sinking Columbus: Contested History, Cultural Politics, and Mythmaking during the Quincentenary*. Gainesville: University Press of Florida, 2000.

Sundquist, Eric J. "'Benito Cereno' and New World Slavery." *Reconstructing American Literary History*. Ed. Sacvan Bercovitch. Cambridge, MA: Harvard University Press, 1986. 93–122.

Tichi, Cecelia. *New World, New Earth: Environmental Reform in American Literature from the Puritans through Whitman*. New Haven: Yale University Press, 1979.

Tiffin, Helen. "'Everyone is in Politics': Margaret Atwood's *Bodily Harm* and Blanche D'Alpuget's *Turtle Beach*. Part II: Voice and Form." *Australian/Canadian Literatures in English: A Comparative Perspective*. Ed. Russell McDougall and Gillian Whitlock. Melbourne: Methuen, 1987. 119–32.

Todorov, Tzvetan. *The Conquest of America: The Question of the Other*. Trans. Richard Howard. New York: Harper & Row, 1984.

Toliver, Harold. *Animate Illusions: Explorations of Narrative Structure*. Lincoln: University of Nebraska Press, 1974.

Topinka, Robert J., "Foucault, Borges, Heterotopia: Producing Knowledge in Other Spaces." *Foucault Studies* 9 (Sept. 2010): 54–70.

Torres, Hector A. "Story, Telling, Voice: Narrative Authority in Ana Castillo's *The Mixquiahuala Letters*." *Chicana (W)Rites: On Word and Film*. Ed. Helena Maria Viramontes and María Herrera-Sobek. Berkeley, CA: Third Woman Press, 1995. 125–45.

Trager, Oliver, ed. *Latin America: Our Volatile Neighbors*. An Editorials on File Book. New York: Facts on File, 1987.

Turk, Horst. "Alienität und Alterität als Schlüsselbegriffe einer Kultursemantik: Zum Fremdheitsbegriff der Übersetzungsforschung." *Kulturthema Fremdheit*. Ed. Alois Wierlacher. Munich: iudicium Verlag, 1993. 173–97.

Tusiani, Joseph. "Christopher Columbus and Joel Barlow." *Italian Americana* 3 (1976): 30–44.

Tylor, Edward B. *Primitive Culture: Researches into the Development of Mythology, Philosophy, Religion, Art, and Custom*. Vol. 1. London: J. Murray, 1871.

Uerlings, Herbert "Das Subjekt und die Anderen. Zur Analyse sexueller und kultureller Differenz." *Das Subjekt und die Anderen: Interkulturalität und Geschlechterdifferenz vom 18. Jahrhundert bis zur Gegenwart*. Ed. Herbert Uerlings, Karl Hölz, and Viktoria Schmidt-Linsenhoff. Berlin: Erich Schmidt Verlag, 2001. 19–53.

Unrue, Darlene Harbour. *Truth and Vision in Katherine Anne Porter's Fiction*. Athens: University of Georgia Press, 1985.

Urbanski, Edmund Stephen. *Hispanic America and Its Civilizations: Spanish Americans and Anglo-Americans*. Trans. F. K. Hendricks and B. Berler. Norman: University of Oklahoma Press, 1978.

Valkeakari, Tuire. "The Politics of Perception in Herman Melville's *Benito Cereno* and Charles Johnson's *Middle Passage*." *Studies in American Fiction* 33.2 (2005): 229–50.

Veitch, Douglas W. *Lawrence, Greene and Lowry: The Fictional Landscape of Mexico*. Waterloo, ON: Wilfrid Laurier University Press, 178.

Villanueva, Darío. *Theories of Literary Realism*. Trans. Mihai I. Spariosu and Santiago García-Castañón. Rev. ed. Albany: SUNY Press, 1997.

Vizenor, Gerald, ed. *Survivance: Narratives of Native Presence*. Lincoln: University of Nebraska Press, 2008.

Waldenfels, Bernhard. *Phenomenology of the Alien: Basic Concepts*. Trans. Alexander Kozin and Tanja Stähler. Evanston, IL: Northwestern University Press, 2011.

Walls, Laura Dassow. *The Passage to Cosmos: Alexander von Humboldt and the Shaping of America*. Chicago and London: Chicago University Press, 2009.

Walsh, Thomas F. *Katherine Anne Porter and Mexico: The Illusion of Eden*. Austin: University of Texas Press, 1992.

Wasserman, Renata R. Mautner. *Exotic Nations: Literature and Cultural Identity in the United States and Brazil, 1830–1930*. Ithaca and London: Cornell University Press, 1994.

*Webster's Third New International Dictionary of the English Language*. Springfield, MA: G. & C. Merriam, 1967.

Welz, Gisela. "Die soziale Organisation kultureller Differenz: Zur Kritik des

Ethnosbegriffs in der anglo-amerikanischen Kulturanthropologie." *Nationales Bewußtsein und kollektive Identität: Studien zur Entwicklung des kollektiven Bewußtseins in der Neuzeit* 2. Ed. Helmut Berding. Frankfurt a. M.: Suhrkamp, 1994. 66–81.

Wentzlaff-Eggebert, Harald. "José Eustasio Rivera: La Vorágine." *Der hispano-amerikanische Roman*. Vol. 1. Ed. Volker Roloff and Harald Wentzlaff-Eggebert. Darmstadt: Wissenschaftliche Buchgesellschaft, 1992. 119–31.

Wertheimer, Eric. *Imagined Empires: Incas, Aztecs, and the New World of American Literature, 1771–1876*. Cambridge: Cambridge University Press, 1999.

Wexler, Laura. *Tender Violence: Domestic Visions in an Age of U.S. Imperialism*. Durham: University of North Carolina Press, 2000.

Wey Gómez, Nicolás. *The Tropics of Empire: Why Columbus Sailed South*. Cambridge, MA, and London: MIT Press, 2008.

White, Hayden. *The Content of the Form: Narrative Discourse and Historical Representation*. Baltimore: Johns Hopkins University Press, 1987.

———. *Metahistory: The Historical Imagination in Nineteenth-Century Europe*. Baltimore: Johns Hopkins University Press, 1973.

———. *Tropics of Discourse: Essays in Cultural Criticism*. Baltimore: Johns Hopkins University Press, 1978.

Wikipedia. "History of Central America from 1700 to the Present." http://en.wikipedia.org/wiki/History_of_Central_America.

Wilgus, A. Curtis. *Latin America in Fiction: A Bibliography of Books in English for Adults*. Bibliographic Series 26. Washington: Pan American Union, 1941.

Williams, Raymond. *Keywords: A Vocabulary of Culture and Society*. Beckenham, Kent: Croom Helm, 1976.

———. *Problems in Materialism and Culture*. London: Verso, 1982.

Williams, Stanley T. *The Spanish Background of American Literature*. 2 vols. New Haven: Yale University Press, 1955.

Wilson, Christopher P. "Plotting the Border: John Reed, Pancho Villa, and Insurgent Mexico." Kaplan and Pease, eds., *Cultures* 340–61.

Wilson, Sharon R. "Camera Images in Margaret Atwood's Novels." *Margaret Atwood: Reflection and Reality*. Ed. Beatrice Mendez-Egle. Edinburg, TX: Pan American University, 1987.

Wood, Barry, ed. *Malcolm Lowry: The Writer and His Critics*. Ottawa: Tecumseh Press, 1980.

Wright, Terence. "*Under the Volcano*: The Static Art of Malcolm Lowry." *Ariel* 1.4 (Oct. 1970): 67–76.

Zamora, Lois Parkinson. *The Usable Past: The Imagination of History in Recent Fiction of the Americas*. Cambridge: Cambridge University Press, 1997.

Žižek, Slavoj. "Eastern Europe's Republics of Gilead." *New Left Review* 183 (Sept.–Oct. 1990): 50–62.

# INDEX